RETHINKING THE AMERICAN ENVIRONMENTAL MOVEMENT POST-1945

Rethinking the American Environmental Movement post-1945 turns a fresh interpretive lens on the past, drawing on a wide range of new histories of environmental activism to analyze the actions of those who created the movement and those who tried to thwart them.

Concentrating on the decades since World War II, environmental historian Ellen Griffith Spears explores environmentalism as a "field of movements" rooted in broader social justice activism. Noting major legislative accomplishments, strengths, and contributions, as well as the divisions within the ranks, the book reveals how new scientific developments, the nuclear threat, and pollution, as well as changes in urban living spurred activism among diverse populations. The book outlines the key precursors, events, participants, and strategies of the environmental movement, and contextualizes the story in the dramatic trajectory of U.S. history after World War II. The result is a synthesis of American environmental politics that one reader called both "ambitious in its scope and concise in its presentation."

This book provides a succinct overview of the American environmental movement and is the perfect introduction for students or scholars seeking to understand one of the largest social movements of the twentieth century up through the robust climate movement of today.

Ellen Griffith Spears is an associate professor in the interdisciplinary New College and the Department of American Studies at the University of Alabama. She is author of the award-winning *Baptized in PCBs: Race, Pollution, and Justice in an All-American Town* (2014).

AMERICAN SOCIAL AND POLITICAL MOVEMENTS OF THE TWENTIETH CENTURY

Series Editor: Heather Ann Thompson, University of Michigan

RETHINKING THE AMERICAN ENVIRONMENTAL MOVEMENT POST-1945

Ellen Griffith Spears

Routledge
Taylor & Francis Group

NEW YORK AND LONDON

First published 2020
by Routledge
52 Vanderbilt Avenue, New York, NY 10017

and by Routledge
2 Park Square, Milton Park, Abingdon, Oxon, OX14 4RN

Routledge is an imprint of the Taylor & Francis Group, an informa business

© 2020 Taylor & Francis

Library of Congress Cataloging-in-Publication Data
A catalog record for this title has been requested

ISBN: 978-0-415-52957-0 (hbk)
ISBN: 978-0-415-52958-7 (pbk)
ISBN: 978-0-203-08169-3 (ebk)

Typeset in Bembo
by Swales & Willis Ltd, Exeter, Devon, UK

CONTENTS

SERIES EDITOR'S INTRODUCTION

Welcome to the *American Social and Political Movements of the Twentieth Century* series at Routledge. This collection of works by top historians from around the nation and world introduces students to the myriad movements that came together in the United States during the twentieth century to expand democracy, to reshape the political economy, and to increase social justice.

Each book in this series explores a particular movement's origins, its central goals, its leading as well as grassroots fighters, its actions as well as ideas, and its most important accomplishments as well as missteps.

With this series of concise yet synthetic overviews and reassessments, students will not only gain a richer understanding of the many human rights and civil liberties that they take for granted today, but they will also newly appreciate how recent, how deeply contested, and thus how inherently fragile, are these elements of American citizenship.

Heather Ann Thompson
University of Michigan

ILLUSTRATIONS

ACKNOWLEDGMENTS

Warm thanks to series editor Heather Ann Thompson for the invitation to contribute to this valuable series. Appreciation is due to editor Kimberly Guinta, who guided me through the early stages of this project, and editors Margo Irvin and Eve Mayer, along with editorial assistants Daniel Finaldi, Theodore Meyer, and Zoë Forbes, who helped guide the project to completion. Research assistants Jamie Burke, Mary Heske, Susannah Robichaux, Sarah Asseff, Jaclyn Higgins, and Sumona Gupta provided much appreciated aid in various stages of the project. Beth Duncan prepared the index. At the University of Alabama, colleagues in New College the Department of American Studies, and a College of Arts and Sciences research grant provided valuable support. Publisher-in-Residence George F. Thompson offered keen insights. Pat Causey fielded endless interlibrary loan requests.

A committed team of eco-activist students shared their insights: Mallory Flowers, Caitlin McClusky, Mark Ortiz, Elyse Peters, and Heath Thompson. Special thanks to the Environmental Law Institute for granting permission to quote from their collection of oral histories conducted with environmental leaders. The Museum of African American History of Boston, Massachusetts, kindly provided the image of African American women hikers at Niagara Falls.

I am indebted also to Heather Elliott, Mark Fiege, Amy Hay, Adam Rome, and Jeffrey K. Stine for insights shared at conferences and via phone and email. Jennifer Meares provided brilliant editing advice. Chris Wells' comments on the entire manuscript proved extraordinarily helpful. *Rethinking the American Environmental Movement* draws on a robust literature of exemplary scholarship to suggest the contours of the contemporary reassessment of the field of movements that defines American environmentalism. Lapses in interpretation or fact are mine alone. A concise history of U.S. environmentalism is necessarily selective and can only hint at key themes a deeper inquiry might consider.

Thanks always to those nearest, for their love and support, especially Brian.

ABBREVIATIONS

AAA	Agricultural Adjustment Act
AAAS	American Association for the Advancement of Science
ACLU	American Civil Liberties Union
ACSH	American Council on Science and Health
AEC	Atomic Energy Commission
AFGE	American Federation of Government Employees
AFL-CIO	American Federation of Labor and Congress of Industrial Organizations
ALEC	American Legislative Exchange Council
ANWR	Arctic National Wildlife Refuge
ARCH	Architect's Renewal Committee in Harlem
ASPCA	American Society for the Prevention of Cruelty to Animals
ATSDR	Agency for Toxic Substances and Disease Registry (now combined with the National Center for Environmental Health, part of the U.S. Centers for Disease Control and Prevention)
BAN	Basel Action Network
BASF	Badische Anilin und Soda-Fabrik
BLM	Bureau of Land Management
BOR	Bureau of Reclamation
BP	British Petroleum
CASSE	Center for the Advancement of the Steady State Economy
CBI	confidential business information
CBTU	Coalition of Black Trade Unionists
CCC	Civilian Conservation Corps
CCL	Citizens' Climate Lobby
CCHW	Citizens' Clearinghouse on Hazardous Waste

CDC	U.S. Centers for Disease Control and Prevention
CEI	Committee for Environmental Information, Competitive Enterprise Institute
CEQ	Council on Environmental Quality
CERCLA	Comprehensive Environmental Response, Compensation, and Liability Act, also known as the Superfund Law
CFCs	Chlorofluorocarbons
CFDE	Center for the Defense of Free Enterprise
CHEJ	Center for Health, Environment, and Justice (CHEJ), successor to CCHW
CJN!	Climate Justice Now!
CMA	Chemical Manufacturers Association
CNI	Committee for Nuclear Information
CNVA	Committee for Non-Violent Action
COP	Conference of the Parties
CORE	Congress of Racial Equality
CRLA	California Rural Legal Assistance
CWA	Communication Workers of America
CWS	Chemical Warfare Service
CWWG	Chemical Weapons Working Group
DAPL	Dakota Access Pipeline
DLC	Democratic Leadership Council
DDT	dichloro-diphenyl-trichloroethane
ESA	Endangered Species Act
EDF	Environmental Defense Fund
EDGI	Environmental Data and Governance Initiative
EIS	Environmental Impact Statement (also EIA, Environmental Impact Assessment)
EPA	Environmental Protection Agency
EPCRA	Emergency Planning and Community Right-to-Know Act
EPN	Environmental Protection Network
EWG	Environmental Working Group
FDA	Food and Drug Administration
FEMA	Federal Emergency Management Agency
FAO	Food and Agriculture Organization
FOE	Friends of the Earth
FOIA	Freedom of Information Act
FOR	Fellowship of Reconciliation
FNCL	Friends National Committee on Legislation
FWPCA	Federal Water Pollution Control Act; Federal Water Pollution Control Authority
GAO	General Accounting Office (later Government Accountability Office)

GASP	Greater Birmingham Alliance to Stop Pollution
GATT	Global Agreement on Tariffs and Trade
GCC	Global Climate Coalition
GHGs	greenhouse gases
HHS	U.S. Department of Health and Human Services
HUD	U.S. Department of Housing and Urban Development
IARC	International Agency for Research on Cancer
IEN	Indigenous Environmental Network
IMF	International Monetary Fund
IPCC	Intergovernmental Panel on Climate Change
ITCPN	International Technical Conference for the Protection of Nature
IUCN	International Union for the Conservation of Nature and Natural Resources
IUPN	International Union for the Protection of Nature
LCHA	Love Canal Homeowners Association
LCV	League of Conservation Voters
LEAN	Louisiana Environmental Action Network
LEED	Leadership in Energy and Environmental Design
LVEJO	Little Village Environmental Justice Organization
MIA	Montgomery Improvement Association
MTR	mountain top removal
NAACP	National Association for the Advancement of Colored People
NACCE	North American Conference on Christianity and Ecology
NACRE	North American Conference on Religion and Ecology
NAFTA	North American Free Trade Agreement
NAPCA	National Air Pollution Control Administration
NCEH	National Center for Environmental Health
NCNW	National Council of Negro Women
NEJAC	National Environmental Justice Advisory Council
NEPA	National Environmental Policy Act
NGOs	nongovernmental organizations
NHANES	National Health and Nutrition Examination Survey
NIEHS	National Institute of Environmental Health Sciences
NIOSH	National Institute for Occupational Safety and Health
NPL	National Priorities List
NPRE	National Religious Partnership for the Environment
NRC	National Research Council
NRPEMS	National Park and Recreation Association Ethnic Minority Society
NWF	National Wildlife Federation
NRDC	Natural Resources Defense Council
OCAW	Oil, Chemical, and Atomic Workers International Union

OECD	Organization for Economic Co-operation and Development
OEJ	Office of Environmental Justice
OMB	Office of Management and Budget
OPEC	Organization of Petroleum Exporting Countries
OREPA	Oak Ridge Environmental Peace Alliance
OSHA	Occupational Safety and Health Act; Occupational Safety and Health Administration
PAC	political action committee
PAN	Pesticides Action Network
PCBs	polychlorinated biphenyls
PETA	People for the Ethical Treatment of Animals
POPs	persistent organic pollutants
PROTEST	People Reaching Out to Stop Shintech's Poisons
RAN	Rainforest Action Network
RCRA	Resource Conservation and Recovery Act
REACH	Regulation, Evaluation, and Authorisation of Chemicals (European Union protocol)
RECA	Radiation Exposure Compensation Act
SANE	Committee for a Sane Nuclear Policy
SARA	Superfund Amendments and Reauthorization Act
SCLC	Southern Christian Leadership Conference
SDI	Strategic Defense Initiative
SDS	Students for a Democratic Society
SEAC	Student Environmental Action Committee
SIPI	Scientists' Institute for Public Information
SLAPP	Strategic Lawsuit against Public Participation
SNCC	Student Nonviolent Coordinating Committee
SOC	Southern Organizing Committee for Social and Economic Justice
SRIC	Southwest Research and Information Center
STFU	Southern Tenant Farmers' Union
STP	Stop the Pollution
SWOP	Southwest Organizing Project
TAG	Technical Assistance Grant
TCE	trichloroethylene
TMI	Three Mile Island
TRI	Toxic Release Inventory
TSCA	Toxic Substances Control Act of 1976
TVA	Tennessee Valley Authority
TWS	The Wilderness Society
UAW	United Auto Workers
UCS	Union of Concerned Scientists
UEC	Urban Environment Conference

UFWOC	United Farm Workers Organizing Committee (later UFW)
UNCED	United Nations Conference on Environment and Development
UNESCO	United Nations Educational, Scientific, and Cultural Organization
UNEP	United Nations Environment Programme
UNFCCC	United Nations Framework Convention on Climate Change
UNSCCUR	United Nations Scientific Conference on the Conservation and Utilization of Resources
USDA	United States Department of Agriculture
USPHS	United States Public Health Service
WAND	Women's Action for New Directions (formerly Women's Action for Nuclear Disarmament)
WARF	Wisconsin Alumni Research Foundation
WHO	World Health Organization
WPA	Works Progress Administration
WRI	World Resources Institute
WRL	War Resisters League
ZPG	Zero Population Growth

INTRODUCTION

A Field of Movements

Within one remarkable week in April 2017 hundreds of thousands of people in Washington, D.C. and around the world marched for science and for the global climate, galvanized by a new U.S. administration poised to rescind nearly every protective measure environmentalists had won. The demands of the March for Science on Earth Day 2017 and the People's Climate Mobilization the following week went beyond fully funding the EPA and keeping the U.S. in the Paris Climate Accord. Environmentalists were girding for the fight of their lives. At precisely the moment that the U.S. environmental movement confronted its most significant human-ecological challenge—climate change—the movement faced the greatest assault on its political gains to date.

Marchers were facing down not just an offensive against climate protection but hostility toward many of the signature environmental achievements of the past half century. Those achievements included the passage of federal laws that brought marked improvements to the nation's ecosystems. Even as the economy has expanded, emissions that contribute to the most widespread air pollutants and acid rain have dropped steadily in most places in the U.S. since 1970 thanks to the Clean Air Act. A phasedown in leaded gasoline begun in 1975 has reduced airborne exposure to lead, a heavy metal particularly toxic to children. Iconic species have been plucked from the brink of extinction: the bald eagle, the grey wolf, and the brown pelican. Successive presidential administrations have expanded acreage of federal lands preserved in national parks, forests, and wilderness areas, wildlife refuges, bird sanctuaries, and marine sites. Public lands and private conservancies protect to some degree roughly one-third of the nation's terrain.[1]

Yet, a vigorous counter-movement and impending climate threats jeopardize the well-being of humans and the planet. Within weeks of taking office in 2017, administration officials announced plans to gut EPA protections for clean water, postpone tighter safeguards on vehicle emissions, sell off public lands, and issue leases for oil drilling in protected areas. Opponents of environmental regulation launched a frontal assault on science.

Facing these developments, activists highlighted persistent threats to environmental health and security. The U.S. has an outsized global climate footprint, with four percent of the world's population using 25 percent of the world's energy and generating 20 percent of the world's carbon emissions. The U.S. record is second to worst among the Organization for Economic Cooperation and Development (OECD) countries in draining underground water supplies—irreplaceable aquifers—for agricultural use. Almost one-half of federally protected lands allow extractive uses such as timber and mining.[2] Ever more extreme technologies for extracting fossil fuels, including hydraulic fracturing (known as "fracking"), now threaten decades of work to reduce groundwater pollution.

The Climate Justice Alliance, the Hip Hop Caucus, the National Association for the Advancement of Colored People (NAACP), Grassroots Global Justice, GreenLatinos, and the Indigenous Environmental Network joined the Center for Biological Diversity, the Sierra Club, the Natural Resources Defense Council, and more than 800 environmental groups and labor unions, voicing particular concern over inequalities in climate impact and unequal enforcement of environmental laws by race and class. Overall improvements in the quality of the water supply meant little to the people of Flint, Michigan, for example, who learned in early 2015 that lead from the contaminated water flowing from their faucets registered in their children's bodies, where it can be neurotoxic. Statistical reductions in air pollutants or particulate matter offer slight consolation to African Americans and Latinos in dense urban areas, who endure higher hospitalization rates due to preventable asthma attacks.[3] Marchers highlighted as well the Dakota Access Pipeline (DAPL) battle over Native American treaty rights and water protection. "Indigenous Rights = Climate Justice" was a frequent refrain.

Environmentalism Redefined

For a long time, American environmentalism was viewed as an extension of the conservation movement. In this view, the movement's founders were elite conservationists, influenced by mid-nineteenth century scientific developments and Transcendentalism, who in reaction against industrialization and urbanization, began the quest for wilderness protection during the Progressive Era. Nature preservationists, motivated by a spiritual reverence for untrammeled wilderness, and pragmatic conservationists, driven by a utilitarian faith in technological progress, dueled over how humans should steward nature. Both stood in uneasy alliance against the unchecked exploitation of nature's assets.

To conservationists and preservationists, the term *environment* meant *nonhuman* nature, the world outdoors, the wilderness. By contrast, environmental justice activist Dana Alston's 1990 reframing of the concept encompassed humans interacting with the places where we "live, work, and play," where we worship and go to school. Environmental historian William Cronon emphasized the point in a famous 1995 essay: equating *environment* with *wilderness* neglects the spaces people actually inhabit. Historian Carolyn Merchant likewise defined environment broadly to include "the natural and *human-created* surroundings that affect a living organism or a group of organisms' abilities to maintain themselves over time." Environment is not only the geophysical landscape but also the built environment in cities, where more than 80 percent of Americans now reside.[4]

However, the traditional conservation-preservation story still constrains our understanding of the environmental movement and its roots. As historian Chad Montrie has recently put it, "much of what we call the 'environmental movement' in America is hobbled by the story we tell about its origins."[5] The classic telling elided the diverse roots of environmental reform, ignored key constituencies, narrowed the scope of issues tackled, and failed to identify key participants, even within conservation circles. In the past few decades, activists and scholars have recast what we consider to be environmentalism—its constituencies and concerns, its places and eras, and its actions and impacts.

Emerging forcefully in the 1980s, environmental justice activists brought attention to class and racial inequalities, the unequal burden of pollution, and the lack of access to amenities in many communities of color and among the poor. Social justice environmentalism enlarged the scope of relevant concerns, encouraged a broader understanding of environmental activism, and prompted scholars to turn a fresh interpretive lens on the past.

Environmental Justice Defined

"Environmental justice embraces the principle that all people and communities are entitled to equal protection of our environmental laws. It means fair treatment, and it means all people—regardless of race, color or national origin—are involved when it comes to implementing and enforcing environmental laws, regulations and policies."

Sociologist Robert Bullard, Interview on the 20th Anniversary of President Clinton's Executive Order on Environmental Justice (2014)[6]

A Changing Narrative

This book presents several arguments—some of them perhaps surprising—that have emerged in the past two and a half decades as activists and scholars have insightfully reassessed the U.S. conservation and environmental movements. In these new histories of environmentalism, narratives of humans' technological triumphs over nature and apocalyptic accounts of ecological decline have given way to more nuanced accounts of often simultaneous advances and setbacks. Rachel Carson was not only a catalyst for, but embedded in, a movement she was helping to build. Earth Day 1970 was a "culmination" as well as the launch of something new.[7]

Highlighted in the new histories are the contested role of the national state in environmental protection, the postwar rise of conservative politics as an obstacle to environmental reform, and the centrality of science in both assessing environmental threats and designing protective measures. Chronicled are multiple ways in which the color lines drawn in U.S. society have hampered environmental reform movements; highlighted is activism by marginalized groups that has gone unnoticed or ignored. Greater attention is given to the global context of the movement.

The traditional narrative left out many constituencies—women, workers, indigenous populations, people of color, immigrants—and as a result left out the social justice roots of environmental reform. Movement historian Robert Gottlieb made clear in his 1993 volume *Forcing the Spring* that the roots of environmentalism were as diverse as Progressive Era women's drives for municipal sanitation, the labor movement's attention to safe working conditions, and public health reformers' attention to occupational medicine and public well-being.[8]

While conservationism and preservationism are important components of modern environmentalism, the contemporary movement has numerous precursors. Journalist Mark Dowie identified eight "mini-movements," all in existence prior to World War II: "resource conservation, wilderness preservation, public health reform, population control, ecology, energy conservation, anti-pollution regulation, and occupational health campaigns." These multiple elements remain, but the postwar period produced a new field of movements. Historian Christopher Sellers distinguishes post-World War II environmentalism from the conservation movement by its melding of ecological concerns about nonhuman nature and human bodies, its emphasis on participatory democracy, and its broad popular reach.[9]

Environmentalism is both a social movement and a collection of ethical values for deciding how people may live in ways that sustain their surroundings. Social movements involve people working in concert, in a collective, organized fashion, over a sustained period in an "effort to produce, prevent, or reverse social change," explain sociologists Jeff Goodwin and James M. Jasper. Contemporary social movement theorists have emphasized the importance of framing—how a movement articulates its mission—to the emergence and endurance of movements.[10] The term *environmentalism* was itself a reframing, braiding several strands of conservationist, public health, and consumer advocacy.

However, "'[e]nvironmentalism' is not—nor has it ever been—a universal or unified movement," write German environmental historian Christof Mauch and colleagues, "but should rather be understood as an umbrella term covering a spectrum of perceptions, values, and interests." Activist/scholar Phil

Brown has suggested that environmentalism can best be understood as a "field of movements. . . less as discrete organizational entities and more as communities that involve actors, organizations, and tactics not only from other social movements, but from science, academia, and government."[11]

The new histories also avoid conflating environmentalism with a narrowly circumscribed set of major environmental organizations, referred to as the "mainstream" groups or "the nationals." ("Mainstream" is a useful shorthand, widely deployed, but not fully satisfactory, as some groups expanded their work to include environmental justice and new groups proliferated.[12]) The nationals are an important part of the story, but only a part.

The major national environmental organizations and grassroots groups have pursued divergent strategies, which at times have hindered the achievement of common goals. The differing strategies parallel what historian Charles Payne, citing organizer Bob Moses, identifies as two traditions in the black freedom struggle: the mobilizing tradition and the organizing tradition. In the mobilizing model, leaders make decisions and define the course of actions; followers carry out their plans. By contrast, in the organizing tradition, organizers rely on affected constituencies to be involved in strategic decision-making, tactical planning, and implementing collective plans.[13] Both paradigms have run in parallel within the environmental movement.

Environmentalists diverge as well on perceived causes and solutions to environmental problems. Radical environmentalists consider environmental degradation to be a consequence of the capitalist embrace of private property and endless growth; in this view, only a fundamental restructuring will yield a society that is more equitable and protective of human and environmental health. Reform environmentalism, by contrast, seeks to ameliorate the consequences of unrestrained growth.

Increasing recognition exists that addressing inequality is fundamental to improving environmental health and well-being, including evaluating the extent to which "solutions" to environmental problems reinforce, sustain, or even produce inequality. This is true whether hazardous industrial byproducts and consumer waste from wealthy, white neighborhoods are displaced onto communities of color and low-income neighborhoods in the U.S. or the ecological burden of U.S. overconsumption is dumped onto third world landscapes and peoples.[14]

Useful here is literary scholar Rob Nixon's concept of "slow violence," which emphasizes that the effects of toxic contamination and other forms of environmental degradation develop slowly over time. Slow violence is less obvious than "personal violence," that is, direct physical assault, and often indirect. Like structural or institutional violence, slow violence is systemic, but differs, writes Nixon, in that it is "violence that occurs gradually and out of sight, a violence of delayed destruction that is dispersed across time and space, an attritional violence that is typically not viewed as violence at all."[15]

In evaluating the impact of environmental practices and policies, the new histories attend closely to the politics of place. Thousands of local, regional, and national organizations, from every region, and from across the political spectrum address issues from the hazardous waste dump next door to garbage lost in space. Fine-grained studies chronicle local grassroots movements. An emphasis on region and regionalism has long characterized the work of environmental historians, though the initial focus on New England, the Plains States, and the West has meant that only recently has the body of scholarship on environmental reform in the South become more robust.

Transformation after World War II

Defining environmental reform more broadly recalibrates the chronology of this expansive field of movements. The impulse for environmental reform follows the whole sweep of American history. The Progressive Era and the 1960s and 1970s remain important, but the period surrounding the nation's founding rises in significance. Long before Henry David Thoreau wrote *Walden*, urban dwellers sought to regulate stench and disease in Philadelphia as early as 1739. As settlers encroached, Native tribes battling for sovereignty fought to protect their fishing and hunting grounds. After the Civil War, Reconstruction Era public health reformers and African Americans claiming land are cast in a new light. New Deal agriculture and work programs take on added salience. The evolving conservationists of the immediate post-World War II period come into view.[16]

Scholars have offered multiple explanations for the explosive growth of the movement for environmental reform after World War II. Structural explanations highlight material changes on the landscape. In this view, postwar environmentalism surfaced as a result of rapid technological change, intensified industrial expansion, and population shifts, including extensive migrations to cities and suburbs. A rush of capitalist development brought unprecedented transformations of nature, with ever-greater impact on the Earth and its inhabitants. Changes in industrial production unleashed an exponential increase in pollution. The pace of change made environmental degradation recognizable and undeniable, spurring action.[17]

We now understand that the Earth has been altered so drastically by human activity that scientists have proposed designating a new geologic era called "the Anthropocene," a term coined by ecologist Eugene Stoermer in the 1980s. Dutch scientist Paul Crutzen, a Nobelist in chemistry for atmospheric ozone research, helped to spread the concept beginning in 2000. Crutzen and colleagues argue that observed changes in the ozone layer dating from beginning of the Industrial Revolution in the late-eighteenth century are so significant that they signal a new geophysical stage in the earth's history, "the Age of Humans."[18]

World War II marked a new stage of the Anthropocene. Historians John R. McNeill and Peter Engelke catalog the global consequences of "the great acceleration"—exponential increases in population, production, consumption, and pollution. Experiences of scarcity during the Depression and during wartime reinforced an imperative for economic growth. Wartime technologies as diverse as the atomic bomb, synthetic chemicals, and the bulldozer were repurposed for domestic use, reshaping the American landscape. The increased availability of cheap energy since World War II, McNeill and Engelke argue, brought "a crescendo of urbanization," dramatic changes in the earth's ecosystems, a precipitous loss in biodiversity, and the rapid deforestation of the global South.[19]

The postwar period marks the increased prominence of the U.S. as a dominant world power seeking to acquire and extend access to raw materials and markets. The global economic infrastructure established at the close of the war restructured global economies, increased the mobility of capital, and transformed production. This framework holds sway over everything from banking and finance to global food and agriculture policy, with profound effects on environments at home and abroad. After World War II, the West entered a long period of economic expansion and technological development as U.S. corporations gained wider access to global markets and resources, particularly oil. The aggressive expansion in the use of synthetic chemicals, fertilizers, and pesticides in manufacturing and industrial agriculture made work sites and neighborhoods more hazardous, provoking grassroots action.[20]

The advent of the Atomic Age brought new environmental threats: nuclear fallout and the potential for total war. The "new knowledge of nature" embodied in atomic weaponry led to re-envisaged relationships between humans, science, and nature.[21] The U.S. bombing of Hiroshima and Nagasaki disclosed the human capacity for total annihilation and set in motion the Cold War, with enormous environmental consequences. Highly militarized and state-subsidized patterns of energy use underwrote the oil and gas industry and defense research. At the same time, out of the atrocities of war arose an international human rights agenda that would foster social justice movements and exert rising influence over time.

Cultural shifts also motivate social movements. The postwar period saw the emergence of a culture of protest. Stimulated by the black freedom struggle and other social movements at home and abroad, a rising sense of efficacy developed, a belief that ordinary people could effect immense social change. The relative affluence of the postwar population, argued Samuel Hays, provided leisure and education that nurtured concern for wildlife, wilderness activities, and quality of life. Greater involvement by women in the public sphere widened the environmental agenda, bringing more attention, for example, to the effects of pollution on the intimate environment of the body. Political liberalism and counterculture radicalism enticed youth into activism.[22]

The Color Line

National Museum of African American History and Culture director Lonnie Bunch described in a 2017 essay *unacknowledged* environmental activism, noting that, like much of black history, this activism is "forgotten" or "hidden in plain sight." Recently, scholar Lisa Sun-Hee Park and colleagues have cast the untold stories of the environmental concerns of indigenous and marginalized groups as *omitted* environmentalism. Native Americans, African Americans, Latinos, and Asian and Pacific Islanders have long been engaged in environmental reform. These campaigns include not only land struggles by formerly enslaved people and by Native Americans, but also agricultural movements and the class-based mobilizations of populist agrarians. Chicano farmworker fights against poisonous pesticides are environmental battles, as are African American civil rights campaigns for equal access to recreational areas and to safe spaces in cities.[23]

Recovering this history acknowledges that people of color and the poor have shared the passion for wilderness and the natural world that motivates preservationists. In the early-twentieth century, for example, African American women and men hiked Niagara Falls and cycled in Yellowstone. George Washington Carver, as we know from historian Mark Hersey's 2011 study, explicitly cast his research and practice of agroecology in terms of conservation.[24]

The benefits of environmental citizenship are not and have not been distributed equally. People of color have fought to participate in the enjoyment of nature and the benefits to health those activities offered. "[T]he color line in any guise was inherently environmental," explains historian Mark Fiege. The spatial configuration of cities and towns, reservation boundaries, Jim Crow segregation on either side of the Mason-Dixon line, the contemporary policing of racialized spaces— all can be understood not only as battle lines in freedom struggles but also as unacknowledged elements of urban ecology, a denial of mobility, a constraint on access to space. "The criminalization of urban space," as scholar Yohuru Williams explains, increasingly has been recognized as a question of environmental justice.[25]

The environmental justice paradigm expands our understanding of what issues and concerns count as environmentalism. Native American groups lobby to redress exploitation of uranium miners. Organizations such as the Black Panthers and the Student Nonviolent Coordinating Committee (SNCC) identified environmental concerns not on the agenda of mainstream groups such as the need for rat eradication and demand for "community control" in urban areas. In their call for self-determination, black nationalists took up the slogan, "Free the Land."[26]

Social justice environmentalists have sought not just the inclusion of communities of color in the history and practice of conservationism, but a fundamental reorientation of the American environmental movement's concerns and aims. Calling for equal treatment of communities of color and for full participation by marginalized communities in environmental decision-making, environmental justice proponents emphasize questions of power and rights. Scholars have often described campaigns so rooted in broader social justice movements that they were not recognized as environmentalism. Excluded groups link their appreciation of nature and desire for healthy surroundings to a broader vision of social justice inseparable from full social and political rights.

Stimulated in part by this reorientation, new histories of environmentalism and, to a certain extent, the movement itself have begun confronting the more complex and difficult elements of the conservation movement's past. From its beginnings, conservationism echoed the nation's conflicts over race and inequality. Several prominent early conservationists were also eugenicists. White supremacy and nativism—hostility toward immigrants—were integral to the way many early conservationists understood their work. These ideas infused (and continue to infuse) debates about overpopulation, immigration, and resource policy.[27]

The early campaigns for wilderness preservation are now understood not only as preserving public lands and limiting habitat destruction but also as a race-making project, defining who could enjoy the full rights of citizenship. As historian Carolyn Finney and others have argued, the designation of national parks and wilderness areas often created "white spaces" by displacing native populations and excluding racial minorities.[28] Nevertheless, a strong, identifiable thread of social justice thought and action runs through U.S. movements for environmental reform. Individuals involved in environmental causes have often participated in actions to oppose racial injustice, eliminate poverty, and achieve gender equality. Such alliances have been essential to the success of the environmental movement.

Environmentalism and the State

Recent scholarship has focused on how the environmental movement has co-evolved with the administrative state. From its early manifestations, environmental reform has expanded the regulatory role of the state. As air and water pollution increased and spread across boundaries, people turned more and more to the federal government, particularly the executive branch, to manage land and water resources, predict the weather, or to protect against soil erosion, wildfires, and flooding. Advocates pressed for advances in environmental policy, defined as "the powers of government to exploit, transform, or control their natural surroundings." Those policies implemented at the federal level create what environmental historian Adam Rome has called "the environmental-management state." This shift also placed government ever more squarely as an arbiter, as often as not a non-neutral mediator, between competing interests.[29]

Throughout U.S. history, government has rarely been a neutral player when it comes to the environment. Historian Mark Fiege has argued, "the physical form and function of the American state embodied its fundamental purpose: the transformation of nature into wealth and power."[30] Governmental action often privileges capital. However, again and again, activists have mobilized to demand that the state restrict corporate prerogatives and intervene on behalf of protecting environmental quality and public health.

From the earliest stirrings of concern about polluted environments in colonial cities, urban sanitation was claimed as a matter of public rights. Progressive Era public health reformers raised "a new set of citizenship claims." In the face of pollution and environmental degradation, advocates have demanded the federal government guarantee the right to a healthy environment. But this right remains deeply contested. Neoliberal policies introduced in the 1970s sought a reduced role for the state and emphasized "strong private property rights, free markets, and free trade." With the ascendance of neoliberalism, deregulation overrules environmental protection.[31]

By working to ensure not just substantive but also procedural rights, environmentalists have helped democratize environmental decision-making, yielding greater public involvement and resulting in greater transparency from government and corporate actors. For example, the National Environmental Policy Act (NEPA), enacted in 1970, requires citizen involvement, published reports, and public hearings in major infrastructure projects with significant environmental impact.

Environmentalists have created a robust civil society sector that has co-evolved with the national state. Environmental organizations engage in policymaking and devising regulations, and demanding enforcement, challenging government but also becoming integral to the functioning of environmental policies. As successive administrations shift approaches, movement actors adjust in style and structure as well. As barriers to legislative and regulatory protection have been erected at the federal level, nongovernmental organizations (NGOs) have increasingly collaborated with corporate, state, and municipal actors on issues like climate change. Social movements challenge not only the government, Goodwin and Jasper argue, but also other "power holders" and "cultural beliefs and practices."[32] Independent of state efforts, nonprofit groups have, for example, directly acquired private lands to protect them or implemented international population control campaigns.

Conservation and Conservatism

A sharp rise in anti-environmentalism tracks the rise of conservatism in the United States. The move toward political conservatism in the U.S., Mark Fiege has argued, is at root an argument about the proper relationship of humans to the rest of nature. "Conservatism," notes Fiege, "gathered political power from the transformation of the American landscape and in reaction to the environmental, economic, social, and political crises generated by that transformation."[33] Conservationists likewise gained strength in response to these transformations but responded in very different ways. A debate over the appropriate role for a democratic government in regulating resources, production, and markets can be traced to America's founding, but in the hands of conservative strategists, these ideas became weapons wielded for political power.

For most of the twentieth century, conservationist and environmental policies garnered support across partisan lines. By 1994, however, bipartisanship had become the notable exception rather than the rule. Since then, environmental protection has consistently ranked among the most contentious of American political issues. Though anti-environmentalism is strongly associated with the Reagan era—often referred to as the Reagan counterrevolution—conservatives drew on a long history of opposition to conservation measures. Oil giants, timber corporations, and mining companies attacked Republican Theodore Roosevelt's and Democrat Franklin Delano Roosevelt (FDR)'s declarations of wilderness areas and public lands. The Sagebrush Rebellion of the 1980s and the "wise use" movement of the 1990s attempted to reverse pro-environment policies, particularly protections of public lands in the American West. An even broader "third war" on environmentalism swept in with full force after the 2016 elections. Present and former EPA employees, writing in June 2017, identified the assault on environmental protections as the "single greatest challenge ever faced by the EPA in its entire half-century of existence."[34]

The emergence of this opposition was not in itself surprising. "Movements evoke counter-mobilization," explain sociologist Mark Schneiberg and colleagues, "which can blunt challengers' efficacy, reverse gains, create or close off opportunities, and prompt challengers to shift venues or tactics."[35] But repeated conservative assaults require tactical parries and shifts, adjustments in strategy about which movement actors often disagreed.

A Transnational Movement

The new scholarship on environmentalism reveals a field of movements that is far more transnational than previously recognized. International geopolitical conditions, ideas about nature, and social movements have influenced U.S. environmentalism from its earliest inception. Europe industrialized early and developed conservation measures earlier than the U.S., fostering approaches that shaped the American conservation movement. Also, as historian Richard Grove has argued, colonial empires were a source of ecological ideas and practices that reshaped habits in colonizers' home territory. Even Henry David Thoreau, who deplored the railroad for its invasion of his New England landscape, historian Matt Klingle has noted, understood the trains bringing goods from around the globe made him "more like a citizen of the world." International trade—its production processes, distribution costs, and environmental impact—has become a key concern of environmental advocates, for it portends a 'race to the bottom' in environmental protection.[36]

Spanish environmental economist Joan Martínez-Alier described global social justice environmentalism as the *environmentalism of the poor*. Martínez-Alier spotlighted peasants living close to the land, "those who have a material interest in the environment as a source and a requirement for livelihood," though the term has taken on a broader use. In their 1998 assessment of the global movement, *Varieties of Environmentalism*, Ramachandra Guha and Martínez-Alier, while not romanticizing the environmentalism of the poor, speak of "implicit ecological awareness" among marginalized populations. "[I]n the many resource extraction and waste disposal conflicts in history and today," Martínez-Alier explains, "the poor are often on the side of the preservation of nature against business firms and the state."[37]

Environmentalism as a Science-based Movement

The March for Science in April 2017 took on special significance because the environmental movement is perhaps unique among major social movements in the degree to which activism has developed at the interface with scientific research. Darwin's theories of evolution served as midwife to the conservation movement; the science of ecology helped to reframe conservation and bring together distinct concerns, showing how ecosystems linked campaigns to preserve wild places with those to curb pollution and maintain urban health. (The environmental movement of the 1960s was often called *the ecology movement*.) Environmental historian Donald Worster defines ecology as "a study of the social relations of the natural world. . . the science of the *development* of communities," emphasizing interdependence and change over time.[38]

Environmentalists have frequently relied on science to determine the impact of advanced industrial societies on natural phenomena and human bodies. Like the state, however, science is not impartial. Science is not "a neutral tool of analysis," as environmental historian Linda Nash pointed out in a 2013 essay, "but a historical product already shot through with certain assumptions and perspectives, many of which served to further existing relations of power."[39]

Technical experts and expertise have at times played a disproportionate role in shaping the environmental reform agenda. Overreliance on experts can impede democratic participation in decision-making. Technocratic approaches to environmental reform, argues sociologist Robert J. Brulle, obscure the "social causes of ecological degradation."[40] Environmentalists and policymakers confront complicated disputes about the nature of knowledge and problems of risk, uncertainty, and conflicting information. All have been central to environmental reform, but often inaccessible to various publics. *Citizen science*, the direct involvement of lay people in conducting scientific studies, counters this trend that isolated the public from environmental research and decision-making.

Social justice environmentalism has focused greater attention on public health. As the ecology of disease has become better understood, activists have played a key role in democratizing environmental health research through right-to-know campaigns. *Popular epidemiology*—a community-based participatory approach to environmental health research—blends expert and lay knowledge to deepen the understandings gained from research.[41]

Opponents of environmental regulation have deployed competing "scientific" studies to undermine science. An entire industry of consultants has evolved to aid businesses in "manufacturing doubt" about claims that their products harm environmental or human health.[42] Nowhere has this politicization of science been more broadly evident than on the issue of climate change. The attacks on science and scientists have generated a new upsurge in science advocacy, as witnessed by the April 2017 marches and subsequent actions. At a time when science itself is fundamentally under threat, new histories highlight the extent to which scientific understanding—a shared knowledge of how nature works—undergirds democracy.

An Intersectional Movement

New histories recount how environmentalism has drawn strength and insights from intersections with other social movements. As originally conceived by black feminist and critical race studies scholar Kimberlé Crenshaw, intersectionality refers to multi-layered individual identities and experiences of oppression. Some contemporary activists have come to use the term to describe interconnected movements, such as anti-sweatshop campaigns that link labor activism and environmental health or the organic farming movement that links gender equity and food security. Scholars have sometimes called these "hybrid movements."[43]

For example, contrary to the impression that environmentalists have been mostly at odds with workers, working people and their organizations fought to eliminate industrial poisons, protect farmworkers from pesticides, and enact ecologically sound trade practices. Sharp differences between workers and environmentalists have received far more attention, but in fact, sectors of the labor movement have been strong proponents of environmental reform. From occupational health campaigns of the Progressive Era to United Auto Workers (UAW) President Walter Reuther's environmental initiatives, to the Coalition of Black Trade Unionists' support for communities fighting hazardous chemicals, and the Sierra Club/Steelworkers' Blue/Green Alliance, new histories of environmentalism demonstrate a durable, if fraught, history of collaboration between environmentalists and labor activists.[44]

Another example is the environmental movement's close and longstanding alliance with the peace movement. War and militarism—prominent causes of environmental degradation—served as impetus for the environmental movement, helping to shape the movement's goals, strategic focus, and its allies. War leaves a host of domestic environmental consequences, even in nations barely touched by physical combat. Nuclear testing, chemical and biological weapons, and conventional arms buildups pose direct hazards to people and the huge tracts of land they require become permanent *sacrifice zones*.[45] The consequences of exposure are written on the bodies of soldiers, war industry workers, and their families. Wartime technologies converted to domestic use bring new commercial opportunities and products, often with unseen consequences for human and environmental health.

The Cold War and the accompanying arms race, which dominated the first forty years of the postwar era, drained resources from programs promoting human well-being and environmental protection. Wartime exigencies and Cold War repression have also inhibited social movements, redirecting reform energies and muffling dissent. The decline in Cold War hostilities in the late 1980s led to breakthroughs in environmental diplomacy, though the period of U.S. unilateralism that followed constrained international cooperation to address global ecological concerns.[46]

While classic histories of U.S. environmentalism tended to emphasize the influence of religious *thought*, more recently the role of religion in animating environmental *activism* is receiving greater attention. Religious doctrine and church practices have both shaped justifications for resource exploitation and undergirded environmental protest. Prominent environmentalists trace their concern for nature to their faith and people of many faiths have enacted environmental stewardship as part of their mission.[47]

Scholars are beginning to illuminate a more complex portrait of American industry, chronicling both its engagement with and resistance to environmental reform. Many industries have been despoilers of nature and its inhabitants and many industry leaders have been the staunchest opponents of environmental regulation and environmentalists. Yet, from supporting anti-smoke campaigns in the late nineteenth century to reducing greenhouse gas emissions in the present, some business leaders have pursued environmentally protective measures, especially when the reforms have resulted in cost savings.[48]

The Climate Change Movement

The closing pages of this text focus on the contemporary climate change movement—the actors, organizations, tactics, and the results to date of their efforts. Climate warming has become the defining environmental concern of the early twenty-first century, affecting all life. No place—from the largest cities to remote wilderness areas to the deepest oceans—remains untouched. The climate change crisis encapsulates major characteristics of postwar environmentalism: the drastic transformation of the Earth conditioned by past energy and other policy choices; the increasingly global context in which U.S. players operate; the importance of protective policies by nation-states; and the potential for catastrophic harm due to inaction. The climate justice wing of the movement seeks to address inequalities and strives for an intersectional approach. Climate change demonstrates how thoroughly socio-cultural crisis is entwined with the biogeophysical conditions of the earth. Though a majority of Americans are concerned about climate change and want action, corporate resistance and the right-wing assault on science have blocked mitigation efforts. Key state actors are in turmoil. Unilateralist executive branch decisions—such as the 2017 announcement of plans to withdraw from the Paris Climate Accord—have isolated the U.S. from the world community. An unprecedented level of partisanship in Congress stymies reform. However, the political turbulence has energized rather than demoralized the movement.

In the decades since World War II, environmental advocates have wrought profound changes in the environmental quality of life for many people in the

United States. The fortunes of environmental activists have risen and fallen, often in conjunction with those of allied movements. Dedicated individuals and organizations have effectively used negotiation, mass protest, lobbying, litigation, boycotts, and nonviolent direct action to win new laws and measurable gains. One enduring result of the postwar environmental movement has been a fundamental shift in how many Americans envision their interconnections with the natural world.

Notes

1   U.S. EPA, *Air Trends: Air Quality National Summary*, 2019, cited in the American Lung Association's *State of the Air* 2018, www.lung.org/our-initiatives/healthy-air/sota/key-findings/ (accessed April 18, 2019). U.S.G.S. Press Release, Technical Announcement, "What's Protected, What's Not: New Protected Areas Database for United States' Land Now Available," April 21, 2009, 2.
2   Organization for Economic Cooperation and Development, *OECD Compendium of Agri-environmental Indicators*, OECD Publishing (2013) http://dx.doi.org/10.1787/9789264181151-en, 113; Giddens, *The Politics of Climate Change*, 87; U.S.G.S. Press Release, Technical Announcement, "What's Protected, What's Not: New Protected Areas Database for United States' Land Now Available," April 21, 2009, 2.
3   Mitman, *Breathing Space*, 134.
4   Alston, "The Summit," 14; William Cronon, "The Trouble with Wilderness," 69–90, in Cronon, *Uncommon Ground*; Merchant, *American Environmental History,* 1 (emphasis added); U.S. Census Bureau, "New Census Data Show Differences Between Urban and Rural Populations," Release no.: CB16-201, December 8, 2016.
5   Montrie, *The Myth of Silent Spring*, 158.
6   Robert Bullard, Interview by Mary Hoff, *Ensia*, June 12, 2014, https://ensia.com/interviews/robert-bullard-the-father-of-environmental-justice/ (accessed July 1, 2018).
7   Gottlieb, *Forcing the Spring*, 36.
8   Gottlieb, *Forcing the Spring*, 36.
9   Dowie, *Losing Ground*, 24; Sellers, *Crabgrass Crucible*, 7.
10 Goodwin and Jasper, "Editors' Introduction," *The Social Movements Reader*, 3; Taylor, "Rise of the Environmental Justice Paradigm"; Morris and Mueller, *Frontiers*, 135ff.
11 Mauch et al., "Introduction," in *Shades of Green*, 1; Brown, *Toxic Exposures*, 33.
12 Gottlieb, *Forcing the Spring*, 162.
13 Payne, *I've Got the Light of Freedom*, 3, citing Robert Moses, M. Kamii, S. Swap, and J. Howard, "The Algebra Project: Organizing in the Spirit of Ella," *Harvard Educational Review* 59 (November 1989): 423–43.
14 Sutter, "When Environmental Traditions Collide," 548.
15 Nixon, *Slow Violence*, 2.
16 Fiege, *Republic of Nature*; Smith, *African American Environmental Thought*; Maher, *Nature's New Deal*; Ekbladh, *The Great American Mission*.
17 McNeill and Engelke, *The Great Acceleration*, 136–38, 184–86.
18 McNeill and Engelke, *The Great Acceleration*, 1–2.
19 Steffen et al., "The Anthropocene," 617; McNeill and Engelke, *The Great Acceleration*, 112, 39.
20 Robertson, "Total War and the Total Environment," 339; Jundt, *Greening the Red, White, and Blue*.
21 Richard Rhodes, "Nuclear Options," *The New York Times Book Review*, May 15, 2005, 7–8.
22 Bullard and Wright, "Environmentalism and the Politics of Equity," 21; Hays, *Beauty, Health, and Permanence*, 269. On body and environment, see, for example: Nash,

Inescapable Ecologies; Langston, *Toxic Bodies*; Alaimo, *Bodily Natures*. Rome, "'Give Earth a Chance,'" 527.

23 Lonnie Bunch, "Black and Green: The Forgotten Commitment to Sustainability," 83–86, 86, in Kress and Stine, eds., *Living in the Anthropocene*; Ramachandra Guha and Joan Martínez-Alier in *Varieties of Environmentalism*, 76; "Tracing the Omitted: Environmentalism and the Uses of Race in Environmental History," Panel by Sara Fingal, Lisa Sun-Hee Park, Traci Voyles, and Stevie Raymond Ruiz, *American Society for Environmental History*, Riverside, California, March 16, 2018; Pulido, *Environmentalism and Economic Justice*; Wolcott, *Race, Riots, and Roller Coasters*; McCammack, *Landscapes of Hope*.

24 Mark Hersey, *'My Work is That of Conservation.'*

25 Fiege, *The Republic of Nature*, 320; Emmett, *Cultivating Environmental Justice*, 5; Williams, *Rethinking the Black Freedom Movement*, 115.

26 Alondra Nelson, "The Longue Durée of Black Lives Matter," *American Journal of Public Health* 106, no. 10 (2016): 1734–37; Rickford, "'We Can't Grow Food on All This Concrete,'" 957.

27 Gottlieb, *Forcing the Spring*, 24; Clapp and Dauvergne, *Paths to a Green World*, 246; Ben Zuckerman, "Nothing Racist About It," (Toronto, Canada) *Globe and Mail*, January 28, 2004.

28 Finney, *Black Faces, White Spaces*; Powell, *Vanishing America*; Stern, *Eugenic Nation*.

29 Ioris, *The Political Ecology of the State*; Wellock, *Preserving the Nation*, 15; Andrews, *Managing the Environment, Managing Ourselves*, ix; Rome, "What Really Matters in History?," 304; Nash, "Furthering the Environmental Turn," 134.

30 Fiege, *Republic of Nature*, 407.

31 Benjamin Franklin, "Letter to Mr. Franklin," *The Pennsylvania Gazette*, August 16, 1739; Sutter, "The World with Us," 105; Harvey, *A Brief History of Neoliberalism*, 2.

32 Goodwin and Jasper, "Editors' Introduction," *The Social Movements Reader*, 3.

33 Fiege, *Republic of Nature*, 423.

34 Sellers, "How Republicans Came to Embrace Anti-Environmentalism"; Sellers et al., *The EPA Under Siege*, 39.

35 Schneiberg et al. "Social Movements and Organizational Form," 656.

36 Richard Grove, *Green Imperialism*; Thoreau cited in Klingle, "Spaces of Consumption," 95; Sutter, "When Environmental Traditions Collide," 548.

37 Joan Martinez-Alier, *Environmentalism of the Poor*; Isabelle Anguelovski and Joan Martinez-Alier, "The 'Environmentalism of the Poor' Revisited: Territory and Place in Disconnected Glocal Struggles," *Ecological Economics* 102 (2014): 167–76, 167; Joan Martínez-Alier, "The Environmentalism of the Poor," *Geoforum* 54 (2014): 239–41, 240.

38 Worster, *Nature's Economy*, 204 (italics in the original).

39 Nash, "Furthering the Environmental Turn," 132.

40 Fischer, *Citizens, Experts, and the Environment*; Brulle, *Agency, Democracy, and Nature*, 273.

41 Brown and Mikkelson, *No Safe Place*, 4ff.

42 Oreskes and Conway, *Merchants of Doubt*.

43 Kimberlé Crenshaw, "Demarginalizing the Intersection of Race and Sex: A Black Feminist Critique of Antidiscrimination Doctrine, Feminist Theory, and Antiracist Politics," *University of Chicago Legal Forum*, 1989, 139–67; Michael T. Heaney and Fabio Rojas, "Hybrid Politics: Social Mobilization in a Multimovement Environment," *American Journal of Sociology* 119, no. 4 (January 2014): 1047–103, 1047.

44 Rector, "The Spirit of Black Lake"; Minchin, *Forging a Common Bond*.

45 McNeill and Unger, "The Big Picture," in *Environmental Histories of the Cold War*, 1–18, 11; Lerner, *Sacrifice Zones*.

46 Assunção, "Turning Its Back to the World?"

47 Mark Stoll, *Inherit the Holy Mountain*; Bron Taylor, *Dark Green Religion*; Bron Taylor, *Ecological Resistance Movements*; Evan Berry, *Devoted to Nature*.

48 Rosen, "Business Leadership in the Movement to Regulate Industrial Air Pollution."

1

ANTECEDENTS

A Wide Arc (prior to 1945)

The stench rising from the Dock Creek industrial district in Philadelphia had become so intolerable by 1739 that residents petitioned the colonial government—the Pennsylvania Assembly—to evict the leather tanneries and their waste pits from the city. The petitioners held that, in processing animal skins and disgorging offal into Dock Creek, nearby slaughterhouses not only spewed foul odors, but also lowered property values, impeded commerce, and exposed residents to disease. Benjamin Franklin's *Pennsylvania Gazette* claimed that freedom from these assaults on the senses and on public health was a matter of public rights. The commercial district and Dock Creek were part of the commons to be enjoyed by all, Franklin argued, and as such the people of Philadelphia were owed certain protections that the colonial government ought to enforce. Franklin blasted the tannery owners for fouling the creek, but they resisted any restriction on dumping.[1]

Better known for his roles as printer, journalist, and statesman, Franklin has been called "the first scientific American." A keen observer of nature, weather, and climate, and New World demography, Franklin was ecology-minded more than a century before the term came into use. For conserving wood and lessening indoor smoke, he devised the Franklin stove. He was even briefly a vegetarian. As founder of the American Philosophical Society, Franklin advocated making scientific knowledge widely available to the public.[2]

Dense populations compromised drinking water, as Franklin realized from witnessing the filth in London's streets. As early as 1768, the term conservation was being applied not only to forests but to sewers in England, where special courts saw to "the repairs of sea banks and sea walls; and the cleansing of rivers, public streams, ditches, and other conducts, whereby any waters are carried off." Covering the earth with pavement and impermeable surfaces affected the quality of water, Franklin noted, as a result "the water of wells must gradually grow worse, and in time be unfit for use." Lacking modern understanding of bacteriological or viral causes of disease—until the 1880s most ailments were attributed to miasma, a kind of fog or foul air—Franklin nevertheless made a connection between pollution and ill health. Having lost his four-year-old son to smallpox, understanding the connection between environment and disease was personal. Franklin thought Philadelphia's water problems so significant that he provided for future generations, granting in his will funds for the city to pipe in fresh drinking water.[3]

Environmental inequalities were stark. Street commissioners "ignore[d] the parts of the city inhabited by middling and poor people," historian Charles S. Olton noted. "[W]hatever temporary success Philadelphians of the Revolutionary era enjoyed in their efforts to make their city clean and pleasant and healthy," Olton continued, "depended intimately on . . . the willingness of the citizenry to make forceful and repeated demands for a better environment."[4]

Notwithstanding their persuasive and well-positioned advocate, the Dock Street petitioners lost their plea against the tannery owners. In the short term, the rights of entrepreneurs to conduct business in any place and manner they saw fit won out over residents' right to a commons free of industrial contamination. More than two decades later, Philadelphia's urban sanitation movement finally won limited water and sewer reform, having satisfied the assembly that regulating dumping was within its purview.[5]

In her analysis of the founders' vision of nature as shown through their gardens, historian Andrea Wulf writes that

> one of the greatest surprises was that the cradle of the environmental movement did not lie in the mid-nineteenth century with men like Henry David Thoreau or John Muir, but that it could be traced to the birth of the nation and the founding fathers.[6]

Elements of the anti-pollution campaign in the urbanizing colonial port of Philadelphia span the entire course of the environmental reform movement in the U.S.: the public's right to a clean environment; industry's resistance to regulation; contests over the appropriate role of government in protecting environments and public health; and the role of science in both the exploitation and the care of nature.

Natural Rights

As part of a rising class of tradesmen and merchants seeking health and order in the city, Franklin stands out as an early urbanist, "a self-conscious city-builder." His views about nature were shaped by the cities in which he lived: Boston, Philadelphia, London, Paris. He was thoroughly urban in his lifestyle and sensibilities. His younger counterpart in the Continental Congress from Virginia, was not. Although he also spent time in Paris, Jefferson was a dedicated agrarian, a proponent of the pastoral, who considered the rural garden or farm as the ideal mean between wilderness and civilization.[7] For Jefferson, the nation's independent freeholders, yeoman farmers cultivating individual plots of nature, formed the backbone of democracy.

Both Franklin and Jefferson were products of the Enlightenment, the seventeenth- and eighteenth-century revolution in science, philosophy, and political thought that put understanding nature at the center of its conceptions of government and political rights. In the Enlightenment view, democratic rights— freedom and equality—were "natural rights," derived neither from the divine nor from monarchs, but from nature. Reason, rather than divine law, provided a path to understanding nature. "The light of science," wrote Jefferson, led humankind to "the palpable truth." His generation of nation-builders, explains historian Mark Fiege, "would use their God-given, natural human capacities— reason and the senses—to discover, through experience, empirical observation, and scientific experiment, the natural laws of man and the physical matter of which he was made."[8]

Franklin, Jefferson, and their compatriots who founded the new republic sought to ground the nation they envisioned in natural law as they understood it. Their guiding political philosophy, as advocated by British philosopher John Locke among others, proposed a new contract between the rulers and the ruled. Cultivating land, improving it, Locke claimed, entitled men to property ownership, and the right to participate in governance. Because owning a plot of ground was a prerequisite for citizenship, nature formed the foundation of political rights. (French observer of early-nineteenth century America Alexis de Tocqueville noted that rural farmers would readily leave their crops to participate in town meetings on land policy.)[9]

As articulated in the Declaration of Independence, nature was a source of authority: the new nation would "assume among the powers of the earth, the separate and equal station to which the Laws of Nature and of Nature's God entitle them." Though his dependence on the slave system contradicted his ideals, for Jefferson, "men were born with an inherent right to their thoughts, their bodies, and the things their bodies produced—their property." Governments existed to protect those natural rights.[10]

Relying on natural law as the basis for democratic governance and a healthy society had its limits. Knowing nature is an ever-unfolding process. To consider nature the source of morality is to ignore what philosophers term the *naturalistic fallacy*, that is, all that exists in nature is not necessarily just or even good. Thinking so leads to a narrow *environmental determinism* that ignores the role of human agency, culture, and history. Natural law could be interpreted in ways that undergirded slavery, native dispossession, and European claims to superiority.

In the founders' view, natural rights did not inhere in all people. Those restricted from property ownership—women, enslaved persons, indentured servants, Native tribes—worked the land but lacked citizenship. The founders sought to limit the power of the working classes, which they viewed as uneducated rabble. Though he publicly opposed slavery, Franklin owned five slaves. His *Pennsylvania Gazette* advertised slave sales and printed fugitive slave notices. Franklin argued for humane treatment of Native peoples, but he also supported tribal dispossession to make way for white settlement.[11] Jefferson's Virginia and his Monticello were built upon slavery.

At the same time, theories of natural law grounded the nation on human freedom, laying the basis for the subsequent natural rights revolutions—among them movements against slavery, for Native land rights and sovereignty, and for women's suffrage. The health of social relationships to the land lay at the core of each of these nineteenth- and early-twentieth -century movements. These movements in turn nurtured precursors to postwar environmentalism: agrarian reform, urban public health activism, preservationism, and conservationism.[12] These antecedents of U.S. environmentalism encompass a wide arc.

Resistance to Slavery: A Claim about Nature

Slave resistance and abolitionism advanced the movement for natural rights in the nineteenth century, spurring the launch of other social movements, including American conservationism. Nineteenth-century abolitionism had at heart a claim about nature. Slavery violated the natural rights of human beings, abolitionists declared. By virtue of natural law, African slaves' humanity entitled them to full political rights. In addition, properly caring for the land required full political and civil rights for all. "Anti-slavery advocates argued that only when the land was worked by free and equal citizens would agriculture thrive," notes political scientist Kimberly Smith.[13]

The anti-slavery movement bequeathed philosophies and methods of organizing to subsequent movements. Abolitionism directly influenced the Transcendentalists and was thereby critical to both the spiritual and practical foundations of conservationism. The legacies of the anti-slavery movement, historian Manisha Sinha has noted, include upholding the right of ordinary citizens to make claims about human rights, to define the nature of democracy, and to debate the ideal structures of governance, including cooperatives and various forms of socialism. The right to speak freely and to vote undergirded other rights, including the right to move freely in public spaces. Abolitionists sent petitions to government, maintained a network of newspapers, utilized the public lecture circuit, and published and distributed narratives of life under slavery and broadsides condemning the institution. The Free Produce Society and the American Free Produce Association, founded by abolitionists in Philadelphia in the late 1820s, and advanced especially by Quaker women, launched boycotts of slave-grown products, especially cotton, coffee, and sugar. Slaves practiced civil disobedience through daily acts of individual resistance as well as broader, covertly organized slowdowns and sickouts. *Marronage*, escaping to dense swamps for temporary or more permanent refuge, relied on nature as a place of sanctuary.[14]

A Question of Sovereignty

For Native peoples, preserving nature was a question of land rights and tribal sovereignty. Indians had nurtured the very abundance that made the land so rich and attractive to the Europeans. Tribes' use of fire—burning edge regions of forests to attract small game—for example, cultivated biodiversity. Nonetheless, the first wave of Europeans pictured North America as a "howling wilderness," hostile and threatening, to be subdued. As settlements spread, colonizers envisaged an empty territory—with vast, inexhaustible natural wealth—to be occupied and subjugated. Among the justifications for *manifest destiny*, the belief that white Europeans had not only the divine right but a duty to conquer and supplant the Native population, was the notion that tribes failed to cultivate the land to its fullest.[15]

Ecological imperialism, environmental historian Alfred Crosby termed colonizers' transport of flora and fauna that disrupted native ecologies; the transfer of disease pathogens devastated native populations throughout the Americas. The term highlighted the environmental consequences of the European quest for new sources of wealth and solutions to internal natural resource shortages through domination of other lands and peoples. In fact, colonialism drove the development of conservationism, argued historian Richard Grove, as the encounter between colonizers and distant lands and peoples revealed the need to protect resources, an endeavor usually informed by indigenous practices. First, colonial mercantilism and then a capitalist transformation to a commodity-based economy so dramatically altered human relationships to the land as to constitute what environmental historian Carolyn Merchant and others have termed *ecological revolutions*.[16]

The imposition of new land regimes based in private property ownership met with opposition—through both armed defiance and diplomatic means. The central dispute concerned Native rights to sovereignty—the right and power to control land and resources sufficient for human survival. Native populations viewed tribal lands as held in common by the tribe: Shawnee chief Tecumseh queried in a speech to Governor William Henry Harrison likely given in 1810, "Why not sell the air, the clouds, and the great sea, as well as the earth? Did not the Great Spirit make them all for the use of his children?"[17]

Tribal negotiators disputed land seizures. Seneca leader and orator Sagoyewatha, nicknamed Red Jacket because he had served as courier for the red-coated British soldiers, addressed white audiences more than one hundred times in the late eighteenth and early nineteenth centuries, including delivering "well-publicized anti-development lectures" to missionaries and land speculators. In a 1794 speech, Sagoyewatha said, "You white people have increased very fast on this island, which was given to us Indians by the Great Spirit. We are now become a small people. You are cutting off our lands piece by piece." Access to the commons was necessary for survival. "[F]rom Cayuga to Buffalo Creek we wish to reserve on account of the fisheries," Sagoyewatha continued, "that our women and children may have use of them."[18]

Cherokee women also petitioned against land cession and removal. An 1818 letter addressed to their "Beloved Children" (establishing the writers' authority as mothers of the negotiators) cast their "rights of the soil" in terms of "common rights":

> We have heard with painful feelings that the bounds of the land we now possess are to be drawn into very narrow limits. The land was given to us by the Great Spirit above as our common right, to raise our children upon, & to make support for our rising generations. We therefore humbly petition our beloved children, the head men & warriors, to hold out to the last in support of our common rights, as the Cherokee nation have been the first settlers of this land; we therefore claim the right of the soil.[19]

Some who were displaced took legal action to protect their land rights. After President Andrew Jackson defied a U.S. Supreme Court ruling and expelled many Cherokees and Creeks from Georgia and Alabama in the late 1830s Trail of Tears, one intrepid Creek grandmother challenged the seizure of her land in northeast Alabama. Sally Ladiga, widow of a former Chief, pursued her fight all the way to the U.S. Supreme Court. Ladiga won her case in 1844, but having been driven to Oklahoma, neither she nor her heirs were able to reclaim the land.[20]

The assault on native sovereignty continued with the Dawes Act, signed by President Grover Cleveland in 1887. Under the paternalistic guise of reducing poverty and promoting assimilation, the Dawes or General Allotment Act separated collectively held tribal lands into individually owned plots. Reviled by tribes, the Dawes Act severed communal ties and displaced many Indian landowners. Tribe members resisted, but were often swindled by white settlers, land speculators, mining companies, and timber interests. The Indian Land Tenure Foundation (formed in 2002 to combat the continued decline in Indian land ownership) estimates that allotment ultimately deprived Native peoples of ninety million acres.[21]

Reimagining Nature

Transcendentalism emerged as a school of humanistic religious thought within Unitarianism in the 1830s. Captured in the Romantic naturalism of writers such as Henry David Thoreau and his mentor, Ralph Waldo Emerson, Transcendentalism was not only a literary phenomenon or spiritual practice, but also a social movement. Called "the first American youth movement, the nation's first counterculture" by literary scholar Lawrence Buell, Transcendentalism embraced a tenet of abolitionism: the belief that society is capable of deliberate transformation. Black abolitionist and historian William Cooper Nell, co-founder of Boston's African American pre-Civil War intellectual society, the Adelphic Union, interacted with Emerson and other white anti-slavery advocates, embracing Transcendentalism and its vision of the divine in "natural phenomena, the high mountains, the boundless ocean, and the 'countless tribes of plants.'" Centered in and around Boston and Concord, Massachusetts, the Transcendental movement was regional, though its influence reached across the Appalachians to the western territories. Proponents engaged in pamphleteering, public speaking, and a rich outpouring of books and poetry. Transcendental Clubs formed; some flirted with utopianism in short-lived rural communes at Brook Farm and Fruitlands.[22]

Thoreau would be read and emulated by 1960s environmentalists, but his mentor and patron Ralph Waldo Emerson's views on nature were more influential in their time. The leading Transcendentalist spokesperson and orator, Emerson, published in 1836 his essay *Nature*, which historian Nell Irvin Painter identifies as "the transcendentalists' manifesto." In *Nature*, Emerson celebrated nature as a source of spiritual values. His views on nature preservation were contradictory, however. Emerson's 1844 essay, "Wealth," celebrated capitalism and the men who transformed natural resources, the "sap and juices of the planet," into commercial products. He was wary of the destruction of nature wrought by industrialism and technology but lauded the advent of coal, which powered the second industrial revolution: "Every basket is power and civilization."[23]

Transcendentalists argued for directly engaging nature to understand life and to comprehend the divine. "The earth I tread on is not a dead inert mass," wrote Thoreau, "It is a body—has a spirit—is organic—and fluid to the influence of its spirit—and to whatever particle of that spirit is in me."[24] Thoreau's *Walden: or, Life in the Woods*, an engaging account of nearly two years spent in a small cabin in the woods near Concord, Massachusetts in the mid-1840s, would inspire generations of wilderness advocates and future back-to-the-landers.

Transcendentalists believed in the power of direct observation of and participation in the natural world to liberate the human spirit and animate democracy. Celebrated for his lyrical writing, Thoreau was also a scientific naturalist who carefully observed life around Walden Pond. Thoreau combined a reverence for nature, opposition to slavery, and commitment to civil disobedience to right social wrongs. An early internationalist, he refused to pay taxes in protest of the U.S.'s expansionist war with Mexico and was briefly jailed in 1846 as a result. He assisted escaped slaves traveling the Underground Railroad through Concord to Canada. Emerson also spoke out against slavery, especially after the passage of the Fugitive Slave Law in 1850. However, as Nell Irvin Painter has observed, and as was true of the majority of his white contemporaries, "Emerson's disapproval of slavery in no way reflected racial egalitarianism."[25]

Often linked aesthetically to the Transcendentalists, painters Thomas Cole, Frederick Edwin Church, Albert Bierstadt, and other members of the mid-century Hudson River School movement venerated wilderness landscapes as inspiring awe and dread. The idealization of rural areas appealed to well-to-do urbanites seeking an escape from crowded, dirty, and heterogeneous cities. Later, these sensibilities found a wider audience as horticulturalist Liberty Hyde Bailey gave voice and national exposure to the "country life movement" in *Country Life* magazine, first published in 1901.[26]

The Piggery Wars and Swill Milk: Urban Public Health Reform

Concentrations of people in urban centers brought a set of ecological problems not faced in the countryside. Urban dwellers rose from five percent of the nation's population in 1790 to 13 percent in 1850.[27] As population density increased, mud ridden streets, roaming livestock, open sewers, and haphazard disposal of household garbage and dead animals threatened public health. Draughts of smoke from coal-burning factories and debris from overcrowding assaulted the senses. In coastal cities, steamy summers brought mosquitoes, fleas, and flies carrying infectious diseases from port to house.

Nineteenth-century urban betterment campaigns such as New York City's hog wars helped establish public health as a motivation for environmental reform and illustrate the class and racial conflicts confronting early urban reform movements. For much of the first half of the nineteenth century, hogs, a dietary staple, presented a noxious environmental health problem for cities. As historian Catherine McNeur has described, proposals to limit the commons in New York City by prohibiting individuals from allowing pigs to roam freely rooting for garbage elicited class antagonism. As early as the mid-1810s, middle-class white reformers had pressured the city's Common Council to rid the streets of roaming hogs, citing offensive smells, noise, and risk to public health. Opponents cited the subsistence needs of the poor. On such grounds, Adam Marshall, an African American chimney sweep, led a successful campaign to block a restrictive 1818 hog ordinance. Working-class Irish and African Americans resisted the hog regulations with petitions and riots; even as late as 1841, city agents had not effectively banished roving swine. A campaign to rout commercial hog operations culminated in the 1859 Piggery War, an all-out assault on New York City hog pens and the corruption that kept them in operation. That year, in a victory that demonstrated the increased influence of public health inspectors, police removed nine thousand hogs from New York City piggeries and destroyed three thousand pens.[28]

The campaign to eliminate dangerously unhealthy milk from impoverished New Yorkers' tables provides another early example of urban environmental public health activism. Industrialized mass production of dairy operations in urban areas led to the distribution of milk that was "unfit to sustain life [and] highly conducive to disease." The "swill milk," so called because the cows were fed on leavings from hops and other grains after distilleries brewed beer and whiskey, was often so unrecognizable as milk that dairy owners adulterated their product with "magnesia, chalk, and plaster of paris to give it a rich, creamy texture and appearance."[29]

Beginning in the 1830s, journalists, clergy, and temperance leaders advocated swill milk reform. Newspaperman Frank Leslie campaigned against swill milk in *Frank Leslie's Illustrated Newspaper* and found an unlikely ally in Robert M. Hartley, of the New York Temperance Society, who opposed the association with distilleries. Broadsides and petitions linked adulterated milk to high rates of infant mortality. Change came slowly, largely because swill milk distributors were well-connected in municipal government. Led by middle-class advocates, the campaign lacked support from affluent and influential citizens, who could afford unadulterated milk from rural dairies. However, the campaign eventually led to a (weakly enforced) law regulating the sale of swill milk in 1862. Such mid-nineteenth-century environmental public health campaigns enlarged the regulatory role of municipal government. However indispensable to modern sanitation, regulating agricultural land uses in rapidly urbanizing areas narrowed the urban commons as a resource for the poor.[30]

Reconstruction and Public Health Reform

The social upheaval of the Civil War disrupted relationships to the land, restricted food sources, and increased the burden of disease, leading to a strong push for what was then termed sanitary reform. The war "produced the largest biological crisis of the nineteenth century," medical historian Jim Downs has noted. More soldiers died or were injured due to illness than from warfare. Medical crises associated with large numbers of people dislocated by the war affected civilian populations as well. Neither civilian nor military leaders were prepared for the health emergency. Voluntary efforts by physicians and female reformers led to the establishment of the U.S. Sanitary Commission and spurred public health reform.[31]

Freedpeople were hardest hit by dislocation and their hardships persisted long after armed conflict ceased. In the wake of the Civil War, freedpeople engaged in campaigns for environmental health, including petitioning the Freedmen's Bureau. The formerly enslaved faced mass displacement, lack of adequate shelter and food, and weakened resistance to contagious diseases such as smallpox, cholera, and yellow fever. As Downs argues, "by requesting federal medical intervention, freedpeople expanded the notion of political rights" to include measures to improve public health.[32]

Black women led public health reform efforts on behalf of the formerly enslaved. After escaping from a lascivious slave master in North Carolina, Harriet

Jacobs had joined northern free black women in anti-slavery work. After the war, she engaged in public health advocacy, arranging a benefit for the Freedman's Hospital in Alexandria, Virginia. In Richmond, Virginia, Dr. Rebecca Crumpler, the "only known black female medical doctor employed by the [Freedman's] Bureau," was among those who first "recognized that the most fatal threat to freed people's health was the lack of shelter, clothing, and nutrition." Written for a female popular audience, her 1883 book, *Medical Discourses*, was "a sophisticated analysis of disease causation," noted Downs. To Crumpler, overcoming illness required not only medical treatment but also improved living conditions and preventative measures.[33]

Freedom opened possibilities for uniting families, for mobility, and for owning land. African American intellectuals and reformers saw in land the potential for independence, an opportunity to achieve physical, social, and spiritual well-being. "The grand old earth," Frederick Douglass declared in 1873, "has no prejudices against race, color, or previous condition of servitude, but flings open her ample breast to all who will come to her for succor and relief." Douglass argued that agriculture could serve as a "refuge for the oppressed." The short-lived, but revolutionary experiment of Reconstruction briefly augured a promise of the rights of citizenship, including land ownership for the formerly enslaved. The sharecropping system proved a poor substitute for the promise of land redistribution. Despite the demise of Reconstruction in 1877 and the rise of Jim Crow laws, black southerners acquired considerable land, totaling fifteen million acres by 1910, land area twice the size of Maryland.[34]

The black towns movement campaigned for self-governing safe spaces where African Americans could farm, work, and live in relative peace and prosperity. African Americans established black towns and agricultural communities across the South and in the Plains states. Nicodemus, Kansas, was among the first in 1877. A mass exodus of roughly six thousand "Exodusters" left the South for Kansas in 1879, and more followed. Founded in 1903 by freed slaves who had been held by Creek Indians at the time of the Trail of Tears, Boley, Oklahoma was one of more than fifty black towns in Oklahoma. Some black communities such as Rosewood, Florida, were targets of racial violence. Many black towns did not survive. Freedpersons' hold on land was often tenuous, circumscribed by lack of capital, threats of racial violence, and marginal soil. (After 1910, black land ownership declined throughout the twentieth century.)[35]

Growing Interest in Natural Science

Nineteenth-century Americans' campaigns for the protection of nature were spurred by revolutionary scientific discoveries. Popular interest in the natural world was piqued by the writings of German botanist Alexander von Humboldt, who traveled nearly every continent in search of flora that would explain how nature worked. Invited to America, Humboldt spent a week in the nation's capital in 1804 with President Jefferson, where the two men discussed their mutual interests in the natural world. Jefferson had just launched the exploratory expedition, led by Meriwether Lewis and William Clark, to map and lay claim to western lands. Several decades later, Humboldt's first volume of *Cosmos* was published in 1845, describing nature as a "living whole." Several thousand copies were distributed in the U.S., indicating wide interest in natural history. According to Humboldt biographer Andrea Wulf, Humboldt was "the first to understand climate as a system of complex correlations between the atmosphere, oceans and land masses."[36]

Charles Darwin's new scientific naturalism reinforced the natural rights revolution in human thought. Darwin's re-conception of species' origins, outlined in 1859, laid a basis for understanding nature as a historical process. Darwin described how patterns of reproduction and adaptation ensured species' long-term survival. Evolutionary biology upheld monogenesis, explaining in scientific terms the common origins of humans and the wide variation in human bodies. The implication of Darwin's work—that all humans evolved from a common ancestor—reinforced the principle of human equality and therefore, universal human rights.[37]

At the same time, as environmental historian Donald Worster has pointed out, Darwin reinforced the notion of an evolutionary scale, suggesting that the indigenous populations he encountered in South America were less developed than Europeans. In so doing, Darwin provided "a new rationale for Anglo–American imperial expansion over the earth's surface," Worster continued, that helped fuel an "environmental philosophy of domination," and the belief that the "ideal of civilization almost always depended vitally on the vigorous conquest of nature by science and technology."[38]

Conservationism Emerges

Influenced by Transcendentalism and by Darwin's work, polymath George Perkins Marsh was a New England farmer, lawyer, and noted linguist (reportedly literate in twenty languages). As congressman from Vermont (1843–1849), Marsh helped to found the Smithsonian Institution to provide government support for the study of natural science. His 1864 treatise, *Man and Nature: Physical Geography as Modified by Human Action*, stated in plain terms the basic rationale for conservation, protesting "man's ignorant disregard for the laws of nature" and posing an ecological argument against the deleterious effects of industrialism. In Marsh's words, "Man has too long forgotten that the earth was given to him for usufruct alone, not for consumption, still less for profligate waste." Writing in terms freshly relevant today, Marsh identified humans as the primary cause of ecological disruption. "[M]an is everywhere a disturbing agent," he wrote. "Wherever he plants his foot, the harmonies of nature are turned to discords." Especially concerned with deforestation, Marsh argued that extensive timber harvesting meant not simply the depletion of resources needed for building, cooking, and heating, but ecological damage: soil erosion, watershed destruction, and loss of habitat for game. Writing *Man and Nature* during his stint as U.S. ambassador to Italy during the American Civil War, Marsh, an anti-slavery New Englander, observed that

> [t]he cost of one year's warfare, if judiciously expended, would secure, to almost every country that man has exhausted, an amelioration of climate, a renovated fertility of soil, and a general physical improvement, which might almost be characterized as a new creation.[39]

Foreshadowing twentieth-century developments in ecology, Marsh described a world that was organically interrelated, one in which human interference in nature portended potential havoc for complex earth systems. Marsh believed in the human potential to reverse the damage inflicted by industrialism through government intervention, scientific research, and popular education. He helped persuade the American Association for the Advancement of Science (AAAS) in 1873 to urge Congress to establish a forestry commission.[40]

Campaigns for the Protection of Nature

Land riddled with tree stumps, once considered a sign of progress, was by the mid-nineteenth century raising alarms. "Man's warfare on the trees is terrible," New England poet Lydia Hunter Sigourney wrote in 1844. By the 1870s, deforestation had become symbolic of America's dwindling resources. The Arbor Day movement was a patriotic push to reforest America. Inspired in part by Marsh's writings, massive tree-planting campaigns popularized conservation. After the first major tree-planting event in Nebraska in 1872, Arbor Day parades and civic celebrations were held in nearly every state, involving tens of thousands of schoolchildren by the end of the century. In Ohio, a particularly deforested state, the 1882 Arbor Day event in Cincinnati reportedly attracted fifty thousand citizens.[41]

The American Society for the Prevention of Cruelty to Animals (ASPCA), founded by American diplomat Henry Bergh in 1866, couched its work in a belief in animals' capacities for language, feeling, and communication. The ASPCA traced its roots to eighteenth- and early- nineteenth-century British political reformer Jeremy Bentham, who regarded animals as sentient beings worthy of humane care. Darwin's ideas about humans' shared ancestry with animals also inspired animal protection. The ASPCA enjoyed no less an advocate in 1869 than novelist and abolitionist Harriet Beecher Stowe.[42]

As awareness increased of declines of fauna, especially birds, more ecologically-oriented conservation groups emerged. Spurred by the work of ornithologist and painter John James Audubon, local and state Audubon Societies formed beginning in the late 1880s, aiming to protect numerous bird species from extinction.

With many of its members women, the Society decried the use of plumage on women's hats and organized a boycott of feathered millinery. Bird advocates found allies in the Boone and Crockett Club, an elite men's hunting club founded by Theodore Roosevelt, George Bird Grinnell, and others in 1887. Prompted by "the dawning realization that hunters needed to conserve animals to keep killing them," the club both promoted "manly sport" and advocated for wildlife protection.[43]

Together, bird enthusiasts and Boone and Crockett members convinced Iowa Republican representative John F. Lacey to sponsor the first federal law protecting game. The Lacey Act of 1900 made it illegal to transport protected birds across state lines. Revealing class biases, conservationists campaigned to protect elite sport but restrict subsistence hunting. Audubon Society members in Pennsylvania protested the killing of birds by Italian immigrants, supporting the regulation of "alien hunters"; in the South and West, complaints were lodged against the hunting practices of African Americans, Japanese immigrants, Mexican Americans, and Native Americans. In 1918, the Migratory Bird Treaty Act made it "unlawful to pursue, hunt, take, capture, kill, possess, sell, purchase, barter, import, export, or transport any migratory bird."[44]

Anti-corporate Populist Agrarianism

Radical agrarian movements arose in working landscapes to protest the rapid industrialization of agriculture that followed the introduction of the steam-powered tractor in the mid-1800s and a gasoline-powered version in 1892. Organizations such as The Grange and the Farmers' Alliance resisted the impact of the emerging corporate order on agricultural production, distribution, and sales. The fencing of former range lands by the enclosure movement and the concentration of ownership into large, mono-cropped landholdings left small farmers hard-pressed. The Grange (also known as the Patrons of Husbandry), which first peaked in the mid-1870s, was part of a larger anti-corporate populist movement driven by "declining commodity prices and struggles against rail carriers, banks, and other big businesses." Both alliances focused on "cooperation, improvement of the physical conditions of farm life, and education," as environmental historian Jack Temple Kirby has described.[45]

More successful than the Grange, the Farmers' Alliance, founded in 1877, boasted one million members at its peak in 1890. A Colored Farmers' Alliance was organized in southern states and sometimes supported Farmers' Alliance candidates. Based in the Midwest, the Plains states, and the South, these groups favored regional over national markets and established cooperatives to market their crops. Involving a high proportion of immigrants and aimed at organizing farmers, the Grange re-emerged in the 1910s and 1920s to demand legislation enabling cooperatives, establishing marketing federations, and breaking monopolies. Though many farming cooperatives endured, the campaign to require banks to expand credit to farmers failed and the Grangers increasingly turned to emerging scientific agriculture, introducing imported or synthetic fertilizers and herbicides to boost yields and sustain farms.[46]

Land degradation was a product of social inequality, nineteenth-century reformer and anti-monopolist newspaperman Henry George argued. George's *Progress and Poverty* focused on "the persistence of poverty amidst advancing wealth." Published in 1879, the book quickly sold three million copies. Though not explicitly a conservationist, George was concerned about "the destructive character of our agriculture, which is year by year decreasing the productiveness of our soil." In George's view, "Land monopolisation and speculation had set in and cut off the poor man's access to nature's storehouse." Though George's opposition to Chinese immigration would undermine his standing as a broad-minded reformer, his ideas on collective land ownership spawned several utopian experiments. [47]

In some locales, farmers clashed with industrial capitalists over land policy, resource use, and pollution. One such dispute, a lawsuit filed by the state of Georgia in 1904, yielded the first air pollution case to reach the U.S. Supreme Court. At Ducktown, Tennessee, near the borders of Georgia and North Carolina, pollutants from copper mining and smelting poisoned the soil for agricultural use. As historian Duncan Maysilles has described, when smelters increased output around 1890, nearby farm families breathed harmful smoke and their crops were ruined. The result: a desert larger than Manhattan in a region that benefitted from sixty inches of rainfall each year. Beginning in 1896, rural residents of the surrounding area filed more than 200 lawsuits to end open heap roasting, a particularly polluting method of copper smelting, alleging the "wholesale destruction of forests, orchards, and crops." The U.S. Supreme Court enjoined the smelting operation in a 1907 decision, though litigation continued for decades.[48]

Transforming Urban Landscapes

Urban reformers linked the structure of cities and the presence of nature within them to public health. The landscape architect, Frederick Law Olmsted, sought to beautify urban places by creating idealized pastoral landscapes within cities. Olmsted advised the city of New York on creating Central Park, constructed an "emerald necklace" of parks in Boston, and planned a string of parks in the Druid Hills suburb of Atlanta. Influenced by Emerson and Marsh, Olmsted linked nature and health in his designs for public landscapes. In a plea to protect Yosemite's natural beauty, Olmsted argued that "a public park would enable the 'reinvigoration' of the health, intelligence, well-being, and happiness of 'the great body of the people.'"[49]

The urban population in the U.S. nearly tripled between 1860 and 1890, prompting hazards for residents and distress among city elites. The City Beautiful movement, an urban beautification drive introduced at the Columbian Exposition in Chicago in 1893, appealed to middle- and upper-class reformers who sought to eliminate the sense of disorder brought on by rapid growth, economic depression, rioting, and strikes of the late 1880s and early 1890s. At their peak in 1905, City Beautiful reformers counted nearly 2,500 local improvement societies in cities large and small across the country. Often led by women, these groups had by 1920 been crowded out by the advent of the professional urban planner (most were men) and by lack of funds.[50]

Perhaps more influential than the City Beautiful movement was the Garden Cities movement promoted by British urban planner Ebenezer Howard. His 1902 book, *Garden Cities of Tomorrow* (first published in 1898 as *Tomorrow: A Peaceful Path to Real Reform*), "stressed the creation of balanced urban communities within balanced regions." Adopted by architects and urban planners in the U.S. in the 1920s, the Garden Cities movement promised to combine a "field for enterprise" and the "flow of capital" with the best of town and country: "freedom," the "beauty of nature," and "social opportunity," with "no smoke" and "no slums."[51]

With the advent of suburbs in the late-nineteenth century, middle- and upper-class people left the city, leaving the industrial pollution, the poor, and immigrant populations behind. Beginning around 1915, sociologists Robert Park and Ernest Burgess at the University of Chicago used an "ecological model" to study demographic patterns. In what became known as "the Chicago School," Park, Burgess, and their adherents saw cities as organisms. Burgess's Concentric Zone schema posited that new immigrant groups followed patterns of "invasion" and "succession," similar to those of biotic communities. Urban ecology connected the physical attributes of the city with the moral character of its residents. As environmental historian Carl Zimring has noted, this "urban ecology model [fit] squarely in the existing tradition of social Darwinism."[52]

Theodore Roosevelt: Conservation and Empire

Conservationists' push to establish federal lands profited directly from the support of President Theodore Roosevelt, "a Darwinian naturalist." An avid hunter and amateur taxidermist from childhood, Roosevelt defined his personal and political identity during encounters in the wild in the American West. The impact of Theodore Roosevelt's presidency on the conservation movement and on federal land preservation was profound.[53]

Beginning with Pelican Island in Florida in 1903, Roosevelt established fifty-one National Bird Reservations in seventeen states and territories, stretching from Puerto Rico to Alaska. Roosevelt often acted unilaterally under the 1906 Antiquities Act, which empowered the president to designate national monuments by executive order. In total, notes journalist Elizabeth Kolbert, he set aside "some two hundred and thirty million acres—an area larger than Texas."[54]

In 1908, Roosevelt convened nine Supreme Court justices, governors from thirty-four states, and representatives of sixty-eight national associations for a Governors' Conference on Conservation. The goal: "to consider the weightiest problem now before the Nation," he told the conference attendees, "the fact that the natural resources of our country are in danger of exhaustion if we permit the old wasteful methods of exploiting them longer to continue." Roosevelt called for "wise utilization" of resources to "preserve soil, forests, water power as a heritage for the children and the children's children" and created a National Conservation Commission to carry out the work. Subsequently, four out of five states took up the cause, creating conservation commissions.[55]

Not satisfied with domestic achievements, the conservationist president convened a North American Conservation Conference before leaving office in 1909.[56] But his goal of a truly international conservation conference would not be realized for another forty years.

The Progressive Era, writes historian Neil Maher, "linked natural resource policy to contestation over the expanding power of the federal state." The expansion of federal executive authority to protect wildlife, set aside public lands, and regulate hunting rights generated brisk opposition. The National Public Domain League attacked not only Theodore Roosevelt's declarations of public land but also the very idea of conservation. Opposition could be merciless, even deadly. In 1905, the American Ornithologists' Union assigned a game warden to protect bird life in the Everglades from plume hunters who would, if left unchecked, slaughter native birds into extinction. The warden, Guy Bradley, was murdered and left adrift in his patrol boat after he attempted to rout a particularly notorious plume hunting gang operating from the bird sanctuary. (Outraged, members of the National Audubon Society formally incorporated a few weeks later.)[57]

Theodore Roosevelt's role in American conservationism cannot be separated from his Rough Riders vision of American power abroad. "Conservation," writes Australian historian Ian Tyrrell, "became inseparable from geopolitical competition in an imperial world." The takeover of the Philippines, Cuba, and Pacific Islands represented a grab for resources and an expansion of an American empire. "Conservation was fundamental to this settler vision," writes Tyrell, "since it involved the idea of white intruders justifying their demographic takeover and their rule over indigenous peoples by putting down a deeper stake in the land than pioneers had accomplished—by husbanding it." Race pervaded conservation policies on issues ranging "from irrigation and waterways to human health and agriculture." In Roosevelt's geopolitical vision, demonstrating superior conservation of resources—building better dams and bridges, leading the way in scientific forestry and agriculture—would assist the U.S. in rivaling Britain in consolidating Anglo-Saxon hegemony around the globe.[58]

The Hetch Hetchy Fight

Often cast as the origin of U.S. conservationism, the battle for wilderness pro-tection in the Hetch Hetchy Valley in California was waged over urban needs: to supply the growing population of San Francisco with water. In 1906, an earthquake shook the city, which lacked sufficient water supplies to fight the extensive fires that ensued. Leaders of the scorched city gained momentum for their proposal to dam the Hetch Hetchy Valley, at the gateway to the Yosemite National Park in the Sierras. The controversy that ensued pitted resource con-servationist Gifford Pinchot against nature preservationist John Muir. Pinchot, a trained forester, supported building the dam. Son of wealthy Episcopalian New England merchants and a proponent of the Progressive Era "gospel of effi-ciency," Pinchot, then chief of the U.S. Forest Service, favored the "wise use" of resources for the benefit of commerce and industry. Pinchot's 1910 book, *The Fight for Conservation*, outlined his utilitarian view. "Conservation," to Pinchot meant "the greatest good to the greatest number for the longest time." In the book, Pinchot argued his case to presidents and the public in terms of national interest, writing that "conservation of natural resources is the basis, and the only permanent basis, of national success."[59]

Scottish-American John Muir was the product of a stern Midwestern Protestant upbringing whose commitment to preserving wild places invoked transcendent spirituality. Muir was profoundly influenced by Thoreau's adage: "In wildness is the preservation of the world." The intellectual strands of pres-ervationism took organizational form in Muir's Sierra Club, founded in 1892. Before Hetch Hetchy, the club had waged a largely successful fight to keep loggers, miners, and sheep ranchers from whittling acreage from the recently expanded million-acre Yosemite National Park. While Muir and Pinchot became bitter opponents over building the dam near Yosemite, both men opposed the ravages of *laissez faire* capitalism. "For whose benefit shall they [natural resources] be conserved," wrote Pinchot, "for the benefit of the many, or for the use and profit of the few?"[60]

The Hetch Hetchy debate drew the federal government more deeply into water rights issues in the West, concerns that had formerly been the purview of state or local policy. The dispute took on national significance because it affected federal lands, and therefore the dam required Congressional approval. Progressive Era women made Hetch Hetchy a mass campaign. Lydia Adams-Williams' 1909 essay, "A Million Women for Conservation," documented the wide interest in the protection of nature among women in four major national organizations: the District of Columbia Federation of Women's Clubs (5,000), the General Federation of Women's Clubs (800,000), the Daughters of the American Revolution (58,000), and the Women's National Rivers and Harbors Congress (12,000). The upper- and middle-class white women who comprised these groups wrote letters and petitioned Congress, largely in opposition to the dam.[61] In 1913, Congress approved damming the Hetch Hetchy Valley in Yosemite. John Muir died a year later.

In 1916, as if in consolation to Muir, Congress passed the Organic Act, establishing a national park system. The act marked "the federalization of the conservationist impulse," notes Alexandra Stern.[62] Soon thereafter, the National Parks Association (later the National Parks and Conservation Association) formed, aiming to reorient the newly created federal agency from an almost exclusive focus on generating tourism toward preserving wilderness.

Nature Study and Conservation Reform

While conservation was dominated by elites, the movement had grassroots adherents. Contact with rural nature was deemed a curative for urban dwellers, including the children of the working poor. As early as the 1870s, the Fresh Air Fund supported summer trips for urban youth to the countryside. The American Nature Study Society held its first national meeting in Chicago in 1908. The nature study movement, argues environmental historian Kevin Armitage, made nature appreciation a mass phenomenon. The effort was also a political project, cultivating not only nature but patriotism. Uniquely American resources were held out as sources of national wealth and pride. The nature study movement was loosely organized, with no national center and only one major periodical, *Nature-Study Review*. Nature study programs nevertheless reached tens of thousands of young people through schools and clubs like the Boy Scouts, Girl Scouts, Woodcraft Indians, and the Campfire Girls. These organizations were not policy-oriented but they introduced generations of young people to conservation.[63]

Nature study advocates projected their educational campaigns as a modernizing influence, introducing school children to science through nature, and at the same time, a response to the deleterious effects of industrialization and urbanization, a romantic anti-modern return to a past that was slipping away, explains Armitage. Offering a nostalgic view of bygone days in the out-of-doors, the message of these youth programs was likewise complicated by attitudes towards Native Americans. Scouting organizations and naturalists cast native populations as primitive preservers of Mother Earth. Scouting troops and other nature groups offered young whites the opportunity to experience nature by "playing Indian," thereby appropriating elements of Native culture as they learned about conservation. Nature study took organizational form in 1930 in the Research and Education Unit of the National Park Service.[64]

Nature study was often taught by women. Biologist, artist, and educator Anna Botsford Comstock published her *Handbook of Nature Study* in 1911. The book influenced one Maria Carson, who used it to teach her children, among them daughter Rachel, the joys of the natural world.[65]

Progressive Era Women Advocate Reform

"[I]n the great national crisis which now confronts us—the necessity for economizing and preserving our fast-disappearing resources for ourselves and our children—woman is found the willing and ready partner to carry on the work," wrote Lydia Adams-Williams, a member of the Women's National Press Association and chair of the waterways committee of the General Federation of Women's Clubs, in 1908. As urban centers grew and patterns of industrial production and consumption shifted, so did roles for women. The women's suffrage movement was in its sixth decade. Meanwhile, conservation activism provided an avenue for middle- and upper-class women to break into the public sphere. Though a "cult of domesticity" had relegated middle-class women to the home, "new women" argued that the care of neighborhoods and cities was a logical extension of their work in the private sphere. For example, the newsletter of the New York Ladies' Health Protective Association, published in 1894, advocated "municipal housekeeping," a gender-coded frame that created space for women in the public sphere. Their achievements were significant; the Brooklyn branch "could boast in 1901 of getting the city to stop dumping garbage into the ocean (where it would wash up on and befoul the beach) and instead to incinerate household wastes."[66]

Progressive Era women led important conservation causes. Mrs. Lovell White, a leader in the General Federation of Women's Clubs in California worked in 1900 to save the Calaveras Grove of sequoias; Mrs. Philip N. Moore, president of the General Federation from 1908–1910, was a leader in the National Conservation Congress. The Florida Federation of Women's Clubs was among the first to propose the designation of a national preserve in the Everglades. Women formed more than one-third of Audubon members in 1905 and more than one-half by 1915. Formed to build upon winning suffrage, the League of Women Voters has worked diligently, often behind the scenes, on nature protection, water policy, and other environmental issues since the 1920s.[67]

Not all women accepted "municipal housekeeping," nor the "cult of domesticity," as the framework for their activism. As historian Maureen Flanagan has argued, while their male counterparts promoted the "city profitable," middle-class white Chicago clubwomen proposed the "city livable" through work on "lakefront development, urban cleanliness, air pollution, and housing." Moreover, the suffrage movement defied the very notion of separate spheres. Literary figures such as Mary Austin challenged the "glorification of the home," argues feminist scholar Stacy Alaimo; women's involvement in conservation campaigns evidenced "feminist and class struggles for increased social power."[68]

Conservation activism was linked with the suffrage movement, both its empowering aspects and its less noble ones, revealing a racist undercurrent. Proponents argued that women's votes were needed to render dirty and polluted urban areas clean. Municipal cleanup operations were associated with whites' desires for "racial order." Even as they sought greater social power for themselves, many white, female conservation activists, writes Alaimo, couched their appeals in terms of "racial purity, class privilege, and retrogressive notions of womanhood" and espoused anti-immigrant views.[69]

Even as Jim Crow deepened, African American women mounted conservation and urban improvement activities of their own, examples of unacknowledged or forgotten environmental public health activism. The National Association of Colored Women, formed in 1896, exhorted dairies to provide pasteurized milk for infants, for example. Lugenia Burns Hope, who attended the Chicago Art Institute and settled in Atlanta after her marriage to John Hope, the first African American president of Atlanta Baptist College (now Morehouse College), launched the Neighborhood Union in Atlanta. This racial uplift organization formed in the wake of the Atlanta Race Riot of 1906. Amid its "politics of respectability" approach to intraracial work, the group sought sanitation and other improvements for neighborhoods around the college's campus on the west side of Atlanta.[70]

African American Thought and Conservation Activism

In *Negro Problems of Philadelphia* (1899), W.E.B. DuBois detailed the occupational segregation that characterized the city's workforce, which left African American citizens in hazardous work and the cleaning professions. Inequality and the spatial hierarchy of segregation, he showed, were both source and result of environmental degradation. Forced to cluster in urban areas to be near employment in private homes, hotels, and large stores, he explained, "Negroes as a class dwell in the most unhealthful parts of the city." Black urban dwellers faced not only a lack of social advancement, but also higher death rates than whites. Racial violence and lynchings, from the Wilmington, North Carolina, race riots in 1898 to the Tulsa, Oklahoma, attacks in 1921, circumscribed physical spaces open to African Americans. Violent restriction of social space was evident in a host of "sundown towns," cities and towns that implemented ordinances or unwritten policies forcing African Americans out of town by dusk.[71]

Race discrimination and disfranchisement obstructed African American influence on the conservation movement, which had limited impact in the South, where most black people lived. Moreover, black environmental thought after the Civil War, explains historian Kimberly Smith, "diverges from progressive environmentalism in its focus on how social structures— laws, rights, and social and economic systems—mediate a group's relationship to the natural world."[72]

Nevertheless, some African Americans were conservationists. As environmental historian Mark Hersey has shown, African American scientist George Washington Carver put conservation at the center of his work on agroecology and sustainable farming in Alabama's Black Belt. In 1896, having received his

PHOTO 1.1   Elite conservationists' associations of wilderness with cultivating white
racial vigor took little account of relationships between persons of
color or ethnic immigrants in enjoying nature. Although their interest
in natural landscapes was long ignored, African Americans participated
in activities traditionally classed as conservation, taking part in hiking
and neighborhood beautification efforts. This group, many of them
women, are hiking at Niagara Falls. Photo by Hamilton Sutton Smith,
c. 1905, courtesy of the Museum of African American History, Boston,
Massachusetts.

master's degree in agricultural science with training in ecology from the Iowa
Agricultural College (now Iowa State University), Carver took up what would
become a lifelong post at Tuskegee Institute. Hired by Tuskegee President Booker
T. Washington, Carver trained students in "a practical ecological approach to

the problems of the region's African American farmers," knowledge they disseminated across the South. Carver worked with and on behalf of farmers and farm workers, many of whom could ill afford fertilizers and were threatened by the growth of industrial agriculture. Employing principles of ecology, he taught farmers how to build up the soil using nature's processes, by collecting mast from nearby woods, muck from swamps, and manure from livestock to enrich their fields. In stating, "My Work is That of Conservation," Carver explicitly claimed the term. (He connected with other conservationists through his position on the editorial board of the *Nature-Study Review*.) At a time when many African Americans were leaving rural areas and migrating to cities, Carver sought to instill among his students and African Americans in general a continuing connection to and respect for the land.[73]

Black and whites alike should be concerned about conditions of black life in the segregated South, Booker T. Washington told the Negro Organization Society of Virginia at a meeting in Norfolk in 1914. "Wherever the Negro is segregated," said Washington,

> it usually means that he will have poor streets, poor lighting, poor sidewalks, poor sewerage, and poor sanitary conditions generally. These conditions are reflected in many ways in the life of the race to its disadvantage and to the disadvantage of the white race.

Soon thereafter, Washington launched Negro Health Week, which later deployed local agents who urged residents to develop subsistence gardens, raise small livestock, and organize neighborhood clean-ups.[74]

Settlement Houses Anchor Urban Reform

The urban health concerns of the poor were central for a network of social welfare organizations with an alternative vision for social development. The most famous of the "Settlement Houses," as they were called, was Jane Addams' Hull House on the southside of Chicago. Established in 1889, Hull House was a gathering place for reformers, most of them women, who addressed urban sanitation, occupational health and safety, consumer protection, and conservation. Led by women, settlement houses gave these remarkable reformers a measure of independence from Victorian era restrictions that women faced in the family, university, church, and labor union. Liberty from gender strictures made Hull House "one of the most politically effective groups of women reformers in U.S. history," historian Kathryn Kish Sklar has argued. The settlement house model provided structures of support for women reformers and their families. When socialist organizer Florence Kelley left a failing marriage and arrived at Hull House at Christmastime 1891 with children aged six, five, and four, Jane Addams helped her establish a supportive living arrangement and schooling for her young family. So situated, Kelley earned a law degree at Northwestern in 1894. Hull House, and later the Henry Street Settlement in New York City, provided a home base for the Kelley who, as head of the National Consumers League, was a leading organizer against sweatshops, and for the eight-hour day, a pure food and drug law, and measures against child labor.[75]

Based in the neighborhoods where a largely immigrant workforce did the tough, dirty jobs associated with the stockyards, settlement house workers "recognized the structural causes of poverty," noted Nell Irvin Painter. Addams organized with immigrant women garbage patrols that routinely monitored waste practices. Addams' allies included author Upton Sinclair, who frequently took his meals at Hull House. Sinclair's 1906 novel *The Jungle* vividly portrayed the filthy conditions in the stockyards and meat packinghouses and helped to spur the passage of the Pure Food and Drug Act by Congress. Settlement worker Lillian Wald, of the Henry Street Settlement, historian Elizabeth Blum has noted, explicitly linked "child conservation," with the "conservation of material wealth, mines, and forests, hogs, and lobsters." Hull House remained open long after Addams died in 1935. Black settlement houses formed in Chicago and other cities. Margaret Murray Washington, wife of Booker T. Washington, established a rural settlement house in Macon County, Alabama, near Tuskegee.[76]

Centered at Hull House were not only Addams and Kelley, but also physician Alice Hamilton, a pioneering industrial toxicologist. Hamilton embodied the strong connections between women's suffrage, the settlement movement, labor rights, and public health reform. Born in 1869, Dr. Hamilton lived to see "her most important institutional legacy," the Occupational Safety and Health Act, passed one hundred years later, in 1970. Hamilton's work in occupational health and safety grew out of more than two decades in Chicago, where she visited the stockyards and meatpacking houses and called to account the industrial meat industry. A bacteriologist and later federal investigator of industrial workplace conditions for the U.S. Department of Labor, Hamilton took her crusade right to the factory floor. Her investigations led Hamilton to focus on the impact of chemical poisons and heavy metals on workers' bodies. She became the leading researcher on lead poisoning. Appointed assistant professor of Industrial Medicine at Harvard Medical School in 1919, Hamilton was the first woman elected to the Harvard Faculty. Even after moving to Cambridge, she kept a room at Hull House. Hamilton's books, *Industrial Poisons in the United States* in 1925 and *Industrial Toxicology* in 1934, became handbooks for the emerging field of industrial hygiene and toxicology. She and a small handful of toxicologists unsuccessfully opposed the addition of tetraethyl lead to gasoline in 1925; the U.S. would not begin to phase out leaded gas until the mid-1970s. Hamilton became president of the National Consumers' League in 1944, bridging industrial hygiene and worker health with the expanding consumer movement.[77]

Occupational health gained additional attention as a result of radium exposure among factory workers at the U.S. Radium plant in Essex County, New Jersey, who painted radium on the dials of watches. Between 1917 and 1926, roughly four thousand "Radium Girls" employed at various plants contracted radiation sickness. Women were favored for the detail work of painting the tiny numerals on watch dials. Though male chemists and plant managers understood the danger of exposure and took protective measures themselves, the female dial painters were instructed to lick their paintbrushes to form a sharp point. Some of the women painted their fingernails and lips with the luminous paint for fun. At least fifty of the watch dial painters had died prematurely by 1927. The Consumers' League of New Jersey and its national organization, still headed by Florence Kelley, advocated on behalf of the female workers, sharing information with doctors and assisting with court cases.[78]

Ecology: An Emerging Discipline

The emergence of ecology as a mode of scientific inquiry informed the conservation movement and its urban counterparts. German zoologist Ernst Haeckel coined the term "ecology" in 1866, naming the field for the Greek word, "oikos," meaning home. Haeckel envisioned ecology as "the study of the organic and inorganic conditions on which life depends." Haeckel chose for nature the metaphor of household: "the place each organism takes in the household of nature, in the economy of all nature."[79]

The first person to apply the term ecology in the U.S. context was Ellen Swallow Richards. As the first female professor at the Massachusetts Institute of Technology, Richards taught sanitary chemistry and consulted on air and water quality with the Massachusetts State Board of Health. A nutritional and industrial chemist, Richards applied modern science to the traditionally women's purview of home economics. A generation older than the Hull House reformers, Richards nevertheless collaborated with them. Prolific as a writer and indefatigable in traveling to speak to audiences about sanitation and health, she co-authored *Air, Water, and Food from a Sanitary Standpoint* (1900), which enjoyed multiple reprintings. "Preeminently a successful organizer," she was president of the American Home Economics Association, co-founded the American Association of University Women, established a forerunner of school lunch programs, and promoted women's access to scientific study.[80]

Women's participation in the conservation movement declined for a time after 1910. Carolyn Merchant has suggested that among the reasons was the increasing reliance on academically trained professionals, particularly in ecology, agroscience, mining, city planning, medicine, and forestry. An explosion in the commercial exploitation of science gave scientists extraordinary power as society's experts. This process not only sidelined women, who were generally denied access to institutions of higher education, but also curbed democratic participation in decision-making.[81]

Conservationism and White Racial Advancement

As Roosevelt's imperial vision indicated, by the end of the nineteenth century, early conservationists often justified protecting the landscape with a perceived need to enhance white racial vitality, while denigrating nonwhite peoples and restricting immigration, historian Miles A. Powell has noted. Espousing the perspective of settler colonialism frequently deployed to justify Native dispossession, George Perkins Marsh wrote in 1864, "[T]he task of the pioneer settler is to become coworker with nature in the reconstruction of the damaged fabric which the negligence or wantonness of former lodgers [Native inhabitants] has rendered untenantable." Revealing the class and anti-immigrant biases of early conservation advocates, Marsh also decried the "'improvident habits of the backwoodsman' and the 'slovenly husbandry of the border settler.'" He opposed Irish Catholic immigration claiming concerns about population growth.[82]

Much of early conservation activism romanticized the American frontier. After the U.S. Census Bureau declared in 1890 that the nation was settled from coast to coast and therefore that the frontier was "closed," the influential historian Frederick Jackson Turner predicted a profound transformation in American life. Turner believed that the encounter with wilderness along the frontier was uniquely formative of an American character. He described the nation as drawing its strength as a democracy from being a frontier nation of small farmers taming the wild, directly connected to the land, as in the Jeffersonian ideal. Turner's "frontier thesis" was riddled with weaknesses. His theory was ahistorical and ethnocentric, peering only from East to West and never considering the vantage point of Native populations from the other side of the frontier line. Turner's thesis exemplified *environmental determinism*, the assumption that physical surroundings, not culture, shaped the individual and society. Like conservationists, Turner idealized wilderness.[83]

By the Progressive Era, writes Powell, "the wilderness—now seen partly as a font of national and racial rejuvenation—held no place for indigenous peoples." In *My First Summer in the Sierras*, Muir wrote disparagingly of the native populations in the region, environmental historian Carolyn Merchant has pointed out. Muir described the Mono Indians living near Yosemite Valley in terms that make the reader recoil: "A strangely dirty and irregular life these dark-eyed, half-happy savages lead in this clean wilderness." Sierra Club co-founders and other conservationists linked eugenicist beliefs in biological difference and genetic capacity, selective breeding and species endangerment, and anti-immigrant fervor. In preserving nature, these wilderness advocates were preserving their notion of race. Wilderness was a place for cultivating white racial vigor. Conservation organizations' priorities included evicting Native populations from national parks and suppressing immigration from non-Anglo-Saxon countries.[84]

Virulent racism within conservation circles revealed itself most baldly in an incident at the Bronx Zoo in 1906, prompting strong reaction from the city's African American clergymen. In September, the New York Zoological Society installed a Congolese man, Ota Benga (called a "pygmy" or "Bushman" in the parlance of the time) in a display with the orangutans. Ota Benga was among a group of Africans that explorer Samuel Phillips Verner had brought to the U.S. for display at the 1904 St. Louis Exposition. Attired in white trousers and a khaki coat but without shoes, Ota Benga was confined in an iron cage in the Monkey House at the zoo, taunted by children and harassed by zoo visitors. The Colored Baptist Ministers' Conference called for "an indignation meeting" to protest the "'the degrading exhibition' of a human being in a cage disporting himself with apes" and demanded the exhibit's immediate dismantling.[85]

The exhibit, soon dubbed "the Scandal at the Zoo," opened under the administration of the first director and chief curator of the New York Zoological Society, William Temple Hornaday. Known through his work with the American Bison Society, Hornaday had played a key role in preserving these endangered creatures. He was a prolific writer and author of *Our Vanishing Wild Life: Its Extermination and Protection* (1913). A social Darwinist, Hornaday appealed to the Society's members to "take up their share of the white man's burden" and "preserve the wild life of our country." The Secretary of the New York Zoological Society, who had approved the exhibit, was conservationist Madison Grant. Grant later wrote *The Passing of the Great Race: The Racial Basis of European History* (1916), the eugenicist text in which he pronounced Aryan descendants to have a unique "inherent capacity for development and growth." Together with paleontologist and president of the American Museum of Natural History Henry Fairfield Osborn, Sr., Grant founded the American Eugenics Society.[86]

Mount Olivet Baptist Church pastor Dr. Matthew W. Gilbert called the exhibit an "outrage" and joined with other African American ministers to gain Ota Benga's release. "We are frank enough to say we do not like this exhibition of one of our race with the monkeys," said James H. Gordon, superintendent of the Howard Orphan Asylum, in Brooklyn, a member of the group. "Our race, we think, is depressed enough without exhibiting one of us with the apes," said Gordon. "We think we are worthy of being considered human beings, with souls." Within two weeks, the ministers' protests forced Hornaday and Grant to relent. With the aid of an attorney, the group managed to free Ota Benga and arrange a place for him to live.[87]

Other conservationists shared the racial views of Hornaday and Grant. Ernst Haeckel, coiner of the term "ecology," was an early eugenicist, arguing in 1868 for death for the "unfit." Paleontologist Henry Fairfield Osborn, Sr., an early member of the Boone and Crockett Club, co-founder of the Save the Redwoods

League in 1918, and president of the American Museum of Natural History for twenty-five years, wrote an admiring foreword to Grant's eugenicist tract. The stance of these early conservationists thus established a lasting barrier to collaboration with persons of color and members of ethnic and immigrant groups who shared conservation concerns. Manifestations of this view would continue to reappear, especially in discussions of population control.[88]

The New Deal Era

As memorialized in fiction in John Steinbeck's *The Grapes of Wrath* (1939), environmental refugees fled the Midwest during the 1930s on a massive scale. Nearly 300,000 Dust Bowl migrants left hardscrabble Midwestern plots for California and other parts west between 1935 and 1939. The migration represented a disruption of lives, farming, and commerce that could not be ignored on the national level. The Dust Bowl became the archetypal image of failed agricultural practices, a crisis in anthropogenic change. A 1936 report from a committee appointed by President Franklin Roosevelt, "The Future of the Great Plains," acknowledged that "the Dust Bowl was a wholly manmade disaster."[89] Disasters, whether caused by humans or by nature, New Deal technocrats believed, could be overcome through human ingenuity and technology.

Whereas Progressivism strove to reign in corporate abuses, the New Deal aimed to unleash corporate development. The 1929 Wall Street crash seemed to suggest that the U.S. economic system was failing. New Dealers sought to demonstrate the strength of liberal capitalism in the face of fascism and communism. Showcasing technocratic and scientific management, big infrastructure ventures and major public works projects would harness nature and demonstrate the superiority of the American system. FDR was also the major backer of the big dam projects of the thirties, an idea for development that became U.S. policy around the globe in the postwar period.[90] New Deal policies also spurred the formation of new nature protection organizations in the 1930s.

Franklin Delano Roosevelt's leadership was crucial to the federal lands designations made in the 1930s. Though a member of the New York elite, FDR frequently identified himself as an upstate tree farmer. He modeled sustainable forestry on the 1,200-acre estate his family owned at Hyde Park. Like his cousin, Theodore, he brought to the presidency a deep personal commitment to conservation. Roosevelt's New Deal brought a new set of state actors into the arenas of conservation, agricultural reform, and environmental public health. In addition to the ongoing work of the Department of the Interior and the Department of Agriculture, the Roosevelt administration established several new agencies with conservation duties: U.S. Fish and Wildlife (the former U.S. Biological Survey), the Farm Security Administration, and the Tennessee Valley Authority (TVA).[91]

Perhaps Roosevelt's most important conservation-related appointment was Harold Ickes, who served as Secretary of the Interior throughout FDR's presidency. A blunt Chicago lawyer who had counseled immigrants at Hull House, Ickes's appointment was considered a win for progressives and for conservation. Ickes also directed the Public Works Administration, which put unemployed people to work on large-scale public works projects. During his time at Interior from 1933 to 1946, Ickes pushed through multiple initiatives, including new federal lands and wild-life refuges. Under Roosevelt's direction, Ickes sought to establish a Department of Conservation, or at least to shift oversight of the national forests out of the Department of Agriculture, where timber interests had a great deal of influence, but he was unsuccessful in doing so.[92]

Many New Deal programs had their roots in Jeffersonian agrarianism, even as they further prepared the way for large-scale industrial agriculture that little resembled Jefferson's self-sufficient yeoman farm. In fact, New Deal programs such as the Agricultural Adjustment Act (AAA), passed by Congress in 1933, marginalized the poor, for the benefits accrued to farm owners, not their tenants. Powerful landowners accepted AAA subsidies that withdrew land from plant-ing to reduce surpluses and lift prices and drove tenants off the farms. Black and white tenant farmers and sharecroppers in Arkansas formed the Southern Tenant Farmers' Union (STFU) in 1934. Under the leadership of H.L. Mitchell, over the next three years the group signed up more than thirty thousand members and staged militant protests of New Deal agricultural policies.[93]

The clash between New Deal soil conservationists and the Navajo (Diné) people of the Four Corners area in the Southwest, chronicled by historian Marsha Weisiger, demonstrated another failure of technocratic modernizers. The encroachment of large-scale sheep ranches owned by Euro-Americans barred Diné herders from moving their animals between summer and winter grazing grounds, resulting in overgrazing in Navaho country. Diné crowded the Senate Committee on Indian Affairs hearings in 1931 to protest the plans for a massive cull of sheep and goats to combat the effects of drought, climate, and severe overgrazing. Despite promises not to reduce herds, the stock reduction program carried out in 1934 slaughtered 7,500 goats and 3,400 sheep, which "were shot *en masse* and left to rot," food for vultures and buzzards. It was only the first round in intended cuts of 400,000 animals. The slaughter, which took place under Ickes's leadership at Interior, left families destitute. The Diné used the sheep primarily for wool, but they kept goats for food. "New Deal conservationists," writes Weisiger, "lost sight of the fact that a truly sustainable relationship with the natural world requires an ethical relationship with the land, with those who people it, and with the cultures that give them meaning." Ickes did assist in creat-ing in 1939 a special grazing district that gave Navajos effective control over land areas they claimed, preventing a complete takeover by white ranchers.[94] But the damage had been done.

Combatting the effects of the Dust Bowl both lifted the status and enlarged the purview of the relatively new field of ecological science. As awareness of "land abuse" increased in the 1920s, ecologists were needed to advise on national agricultural policy. After studying the agricultural crisis, ecologists shifted their focus from simply maintaining the biological community to recognizing the need for adapting agriculture to climate. This shift also required acknowledging the impact of human actions.[95]

The Dust Bowl compounded the consequences of economic loss that followed the 1929 crash. Up to one-fourth of the nation's jobseekers were unemployed. A nationwide crisis of homelessness developed. Between 1933 and 1942, young working-class men in search of jobs joined Roosevelt's Civilian Conservation Corps (CCC), which served a triad of purposes: putting people to work, boosting the economy, and implementing environmental controls. The CCC laborers would do "simple work," Roosevelt told Congress, "not interfering with normal employment and confining itself to forestry, the prevention of soil erosion, flood control and similar projects."[96]

All told, the Corps employed three million men nationwide in conservation, road-building, and construction projects. Many of the projects involved building or enhancing recreational sites, for, beginning in the 1920s, increased leisure time and the automobile encouraged urban dwellers to go camping. Local people were not always pleased with the program, which brought men from other parts of the country, displacing local labor. Native American and African American men also served in the CCC, largely in segregated camps. Though few in number and often remote, these camps met resistance from local whites. Nevertheless, with projects in congressional districts across the nation, the program built broad bipartisan support for conservation measures, and enhanced the power of the national state in managing nature. New Deal initiatives helped to lay the groundwork for postwar environmentalism by associating conservation with public health, broadening understanding of ecological balance, and making conservation a key element of improving the economy.[97]

Outdoor work was designed to mold men's character as well as their bodies, argues historian Bryant Simon, shaping an enduring image of robust manhood cultivated by work in nature. The CCC reinforced the connection between conservation, "manhood, whiteness, and nationalism," explains historian Neil Maher. Manual labor in nature prepared a generation for fighting wars, strengthening their bodies and stirring up patriotism. "By continuing this man-building program, the Nation will continue to strengthen national defense," noted CCC director James McEntee in 1940, and indeed, 90 percent of the CCC workers served in World War II.[98]

At the same time, the CCC also helped to democratize conservationism, Maher has argued. The camp lodges and dams built by CCC workers and the stream restoration projects they carried out were visible in local communities and introduced people to conservation ideas and practices. "The result was a more broad-based movement," notes Maher, one "that mirrored, and to a certain extent helped to produce, the grassroots character of post–World War II environmentalism."[99]

New Conservation Groups

As people flocked to cities, conservation efforts expanded. The country's population had become majority urban by 1920, though regional differences persisted, with the South remaining majority rural until 1960. The rapid rise in the early 1920s of the Izaak Walton League, with its publication *Outdoor America*, evidenced concern about wildlife protection among hunters and fishers, especially in the upper Midwest. Formed in January 1922 and named for the English conservationist and author of *The Compleat Angler*, the League grew to a massive 100,000 members in just three years. Described by historian John Opie as "nostalgic for lost youth, nature worship, and outdoor masculinity," the League also secured some early policy successes. Working in alliance with groups such as the National Institute of Park Executives and the American Society of Landscape Architects, the League persuaded the U.S. Forest Service not to construct new roads in the Superior National Forest in upper Minnesota. The group succeeded in establishing a wildlife refuge in the Upper Mississippi after Secretary of Commerce Herbert Hoover, a League board member, helped gain President Calvin Coolidge's approval. During the economic decline of the 1930s, the League's membership dropped to twenty thousand, though its work for water quality and rural wildlife habitat continued.[100]

Key conservation organizations formed during the social upheaval of the Depression Era include The Wilderness Society and the National Wildlife Federation. The two remain among the largest and most influential wilderness-focused organizations today. At the helm of the Wilderness Society was Robert Marshall, who had been a staffer at the Interior Department and a key adviser to Harold Ickes. Bob Marshall shared John Muir's passion for wilderness. A supporter of the American Civil Liberties Union, social equality, and the labor movement, Marshall "combined traditional frontier romanticism with a brand of radical politics not usually associated with the preservationist movement," writes historian Paul Sutter. (At the same time, during his 1930s tenure at the Bureau of Indian Affairs at Interior, Marshall established roadless areas on sixteen reservations, without consulting the tribes.) At the 1934 convention of the American Forestry Association in Knoxville, Tennessee, during a field trip to a nearby CCC camp, Marshall, Harvey Broome, Bernard and Miriam Frank, and Appalachian Trail proponent Benton MacKaye, discussed the need for protecting wilderness areas from the onslaught of the automobile. The group persuaded professional forester Aldo Leopold, former National Park Service advocate Robert Sterling Yard, and other conservationists to join them in forming The Wilderness Society.[101]

The Society was a reaction to several trends in the 1920s and 1930s, notes historian Brian Allen Drake: "the rise of the automobile, the growing popularity of auto-centered recreation and a consumerist approach to nature, and the explosion of road building in U.S. Forest Service lands." Paradoxically, for the founders of the Wilderness Society, notes environmental historian William Cronon, "the commitment of the National Park Service to automobile-based tourism made it an adversary of the very places it was legally supposed to protect."[102]

The National Wildlife Federation, also founded in 1935, chose political cartoonist Jay "Ding" Darling to lead the group. Darling, a Hoover Republican, served as Chief of the Biological Survey (forerunner of the Fish and Wildlife Service) in the Interior Department under Ickes. Darling urged Roosevelt to sponsor the first National Wildlife Conference in 1936, and pushed legislative initiatives to protect wildlife, including the Federal Aid in Wildlife Restoration Act, passed in 1937. Later a winner of two Pulitzer prizes, Darling sketched sequences such as "What a Few More Seasons Will Do to the Ducks," depicting a flourishing flock slaughtered to near extinction by hunters. As an organization of hunters partly funded by large manufacturers of ammunition, the National Wilflife Federation (NWF) faced internal conflicts between its base and members who supported wildlife protection.[103]

The Audubon Society and the Sierra Club, the conservation organizations founded a generation earlier, endured, though Audubon came under fire from conservation advocate Rosalie Edge in the 1930s for its members' wanton slaughter of birds. A wealthy socialite and suffragist, Edge lobbied Ickes about conservation causes—from establishing the Olympic National Park to designating a hawk preserve in Pennsylvania. She did so through her largely one-woman Emergency Conservation Committee, later labeled "the most militant nature advocacy organization of its time." Edge transformed the Audubon Society, wrote sociologist Robert Brulle, "from a gun-company-controlled hunting organization to an advocate for the protection of wildlife as beings with their own purposes and ends other than to serve human needs." Dubbed by *The New Yorker* in 1948 as "the only honest, unselfish, indomitable hellcat in the history of conservation," she sought to "break open the tunnel vision imposed by a man centered view of the universe." Called by her biographer "the activist who saved nature from the conservationists," Edge reconciled with the Audubon Society in 1962, just weeks before she died.[104]

Race, Occupational Hazards, and Human Health

World War I had hastened the transformation of the natural world into resources for imperial conquest. The blockade that followed the German declaration of war in Europe cut off access to the key ingredients for chemical manufacturing, spurring significant growth in the American chemical industry. With that growth came workplace hazards often unseen until they were manifested in the bodies of workers. War simultaneously subsidized the growth of the chemical industry and diverted attention from chemicals' deleterious effects.[105]

The connections between occupational hazards and human health became more widely recognized during the New Deal Era. In the late 1920s, the Union Carbide and Carbon Company recruited miners to dig a tunnel through the mountains at Gauley Bridge, West Virginia. Water pumped through the Hawks' Nest Tunnel would power a hydroelectric dam on the New River. The men were digging through a geological formation of pure silica. Most of the miners contracted silicosis, a life-threatening lung condition. As a result, more than 750 miners, most of them African Americans, died. Federal authorities investigated the Hawks' Nest disaster and relatives sued for compensation.[106]

Damage done to workers who labored in nature found its way into the public consciousness through artistic expression, including poetry and song. Blues guitarist Josh White's 1936 lament, "Silicosis is Killing Me," put the link between occupational exposure and deadly disease in popular form on radio:

> I was there diggin' that tunnel for just six bits a day;
> I was diggin' that tunnel for just six bits a day;
> Didn't know I was diggin' my own grave,
> Silicosis was eatin' my lungs away.[107]

Against the backdrop of a sustained Depression and rising inequality, the religious Social Gospel movement spread, reaching a broader swath within American churches than it had at its inception in the mid-1870s. The Social Gospel-oriented Federal Council of Churches of Christ in America included thirty Protestant denominations, including the African Methodist Episcopal and the Christian (Colored) Methodist Episcopal churches. Some Social Gospel religious observances venerating nature reached across the racial divide, to create parallel if not unified activities. In the 1930s and 1940s, prompted by concern over soil conservation, the Federal Council encouraged Rural Life Sundays, also called Nature Sundays. Alongside Race Relations Sundays and Labor Sundays, these religious observances included sermons focused on nature and respect for creation.[108]

The pre-World War II Field of Movements

At the beginning of a century that would be unmatched in the intensity of environmental change and the extent to which it is caused by humans, a wide-ranging group of reformers emerged.[109] Robust conservation, occupational and public health, and agrarian activism characterized the decades between the Civil War and World War II. Conservation organizations reflected advocacy not only among elites, but also rising ecological awareness among a loosely affiliated middle-class nature study movement, CCC workers, and organizing among farmers, field workers, and industrial laborers.

As the U.S. entered World War II, an eclectic array of forces had carved out arenas in which to work for the public's right to a clean environment, whether or not they framed it as such. The aggregation of interests that reflected what would now be listed among environmental concerns was far more multi-faceted—and had been more effectual—than has been acknowledged. The organized, sustained efforts of multiple conservation and public health constituencies could mark several achievements. Nearly every state had laws and municipal ordinances regulating smoke and stream pollution. Campaigns sought to preserve and improve not only wilderness areas, but also urban and working rural landscapes. Agitation by women was critical to persuading municipalities, states, and the federal government to act. In concert with organized labor, public health reformers worked to reduce occupational disease and implement public health regulations of food and drugs that were precautionary in tone, while preserving industry prerogatives to pollute. Executive branch decisions preserved vast lands, especially in the West. Militating against reform, however, was conservation leaders' adherence to white supremacy and population eugenics, which discouraged interracial and cross-class alliances.[110]

The Depression followed by rationing during World War II only increased concern that the nation's ecological abundance had given way to resource scarcity. Two essays by Interior Secretary Ickes, who also served as Petroleum Administrator (the Oil Czar) during the war—"We're Running Out of Oil" (1943) and "War and Our Vanishing Resources" (1945)—helped to set the stage for the postwar preoccupation with controlling access to raw materials, particularly oil, at home and abroad.[111] Many of the same impulses that had generated prewar environmental reform persisted, even intensified, after the war, but some of the anxieties that drove postwar environmentalism were entirely new.

Notes

1 A. Michal McMahon, "'Small Matters': Benjamin Franklin, Philadelphia, and the 'Progress of Cities,'" *The Pennsylvania Magazine of History and Biography*, 116, no. 2 (April 1992): 157–82, 168; Benjamin Franklin, "Letter to Mr. Franklin," *The Pennsylvania Gazette*, August 23–30, 1739, cited in McMahon, "Small Matters," 169.
2 Chaplin, *The First Scientific American*, 7, 74.
3 William Blackstone, Wilfrid R. Prest, David Lemmings, Simon Stern, Thomas P. Gallanis, and Ruth Paley, *Commentaries on the Laws of England*, The Oxford edition of Blackstone, First edition. ed. (Oxford; New York: Oxford University Press, 2016, orig. publ. 1774); McMahon, "'Small Matters,'" 163, 180–81; "The Last Will and Testament of Benjamin Franklin," The Constitution Society, www.constitution.org/primary sources/lastwill.html (accessed February 18, 2017).
4 Charles S. Olton, "Philadelphia's First Environmental Crisis," *The Pennsylvania Magazine of History and Biography, The Historical Society of Pennsylvania* 98, no. 1 (January 1974): 90–100, 97, 100.
5 McMahon, "'Small Matters,'" 167, 175–76.
6 Wulf, *Founding Gardeners*, 10–11.
7 Leo Marx, *The Machine in the Garden*, 72.
8 Fiege, *The Republic of Nature*, 70; Wulf, *Founding Gardeners*, 161–62; Thomas Jefferson to Roger Weightman, June 24, 1826, Library of Congress Digital Collections, www.

loc.gov/exhibits/jefferson/214.html (accessed August 19, 2017); Fiege, *The Republic of Nature*, 60.

9 Fiege, *The Republic of Nature*, 72–74; Doris Kearns Goodwin, *A Team of Rivals* (New York: Simon and Schuster, 2005), 60–61, citing Alexis de Tocqueville, *Democracy in America*, trans. Harvey Claflin Mansfield and Delba Winthrop (Chicago: University of Chicago Press, 2000, orig. pub. 1835), 232.

10 U.S., The Declaration of Independence, 1776; Fiege, *The Republic of Nature*, 59–60.

11 Benjamin Franklin, "Remarks Concerning the Savages of North America," before January 7, 1784, Founders Online, https://founders.archives.gov/documents/Franklin/01-41-02-0280 (accessed August 12, 2017); Chaplin, *The First Scientific American*, 182.

12 Smith, *African American Environmental Thought*, 66; Valenčius, *The Health of the Country*. See also, Mart A. Stewart, "If John Muir Had Been an Agrarian."

13 Fiege, *The Republic of Nature*, 89; Finseth, *Shades of Green*, 39; Smith, *African American Environmental Thought*, 39.

14 Ira Berlin, "The Slave's Cause: A History of Abolition," *The New York Times Book Review*, February 26, 2016; Sinha, *The Slave's Cause*, 228, 178–79, 382.

15 Newman, *Love Canal*, 26; Cronon, *Changes in the Land*, 51; Tyrrell, *Crisis of the Wasteful Nation*, 16.

16 Crosby, *Ecological Imperialism*; Grove, *Green Imperialism*; Merchant, "The Theoretical Structure of Ecological Revolutions," 265.

17 Tecumseh Transcription from Vine Deloria, Jr. and Arthur Junaluska (Speakers), as reproduced in *Great American Indian Speeches*, Vol. 1 (Phonographic Disc) (New York: Caedmon, 1976).

18 Newman, *Love Canal*, 29, citing Granville Ganter, ed., *The Collected Speeches of Sagoyewatha, or Red Jacket* (Syracuse: Syracuse University Press, 2006), xxi, 140–42; William L. Stone, *The Life and Times of Red Jacket or Sa go ye wa ta: Being the Sequel to the History of the Six Nations* (New York and London: Wiley and Putnam, 1841), 134, 133.

19 Petition by Cherokee Women as reproduced in Kilcup, *Fallen Forests*, 35.

20 *Ladiga v. Roland*, 43 U.S. 581 (1844).

21 White, *The Republic for Which It Stands*, 606; "Land Tenure History," Indian Land Tenure Foundation, https://iltf.org/land-issues/history/ (accessed July 20, 2017).

22 Buell, "Introduction," *The American Transcendentalists*, xiii, xxi, xii; Sinha, *The Slave's Cause*, 489; Peter Wirzbibki, "Black Transcendentalism: William Cooper Nell, the Adelphi Union, and the Black Abolitionist Intellectual Tradition," *The Journal of the Civil War Era* 8, no. 2 (June 2018), 269–90, 282–83, citing William C. Nell, "Colored Ministers," *North Star*, April 7, 1848.

23 Painter, *The History of White People*, 153; Ekbladh, *The Great American Mission*, 16; Emerson, *Nature*; Ralph Waldo Emerson, "Wealth," *The Prose Works of Ralph Waldo Emerson*, Vol. II, Rev. ed. (Boston: Fields, Osgood, and Co., 1870), 365, 362.

24 Thoreau's *Journals*, as reprinted in McKibben and Gore, eds., *The American Earth*, 8.

25 Thorson, *Walden's Shore*; Kent Curtis, "The Virtue of Thoreau: Biography, Geography, and History in Walden Woods," *Environmental History* 15 (January 2010): 31–53, 33; Walls, *Henry David Thoreau*, xix; Painter, *The History of White People*, 186.

26 Zimring, *Clean and White*, 30; Sellers, *Crabgrass Crucible*, 18.

27 Campbell Gibson, *Population of the 100 Largest Cities and Other Urban Places in the United States: 1790 to 1990*, Population Division, U.S. Bureau of the Census, Washington, D.C., June 1998. Population Division Working Paper No. 2.

28 McNeur, *Taming Manhattan*, 32–41, 160–74.

29 McNeur, *Taming Manhattan*, 134, 150–60; Michael Egan, "Organizing Environmental Protest: Swill Milk and Social Activism in Nineteenth-Century New York City," 39–63, in Crane and Egan, *Natural Protest*, 41.

30 Egan, "Organizing Environmental Protest," 39–63; McNeur, *Taming Manhattan*, 173, 3.

31 Downs, *Sick from Freedom*, 4, 28–30.

32 Downs, *Sick from Freedom*, 9.

33 Downs, *Sick from Freedom*, 90, 118–19, citing Rebecca Crumpler, *A Book of Medical Discourses* (Boston: Cashman, Keating, 1883), 4.

34 Address Delivered by Hon. Frederick Douglass at the Third Annual Fair of the Tennessee Colored Agricultural and Mechanical Association on Thursday, September 18, 1873, at Nashville, Tennessee (Washington, D.C., 1873), 9–10; Frederick Douglass, *Narrative of the Life of Frederick Douglass an American Slave*, Chapter XI, (Boston: Anti-Slavery Office, 1845), Project Gutenberg version; Smith, *African American Environmental Thought*, 51; Eric Foner, *A Short History of Reconstruction, 1863–1877*. 1st ed. (New York: Harper & Row, 1990); Edward Pennick, Heather Gray, and Miessha Thomas, "Preserving African American Rural Property: An Assessment of Intergenerational Values Toward Land," 153–73, 154, in Jordan et al., *Land and Power*.

35 Painter, *Exodusters*.

36 Wulf, *The Invention of Nature*, 117–19, 294, 290–91.

37 Darwin, *The Origin of Species*; Finseth, *Shades of Green*, 40.

38 Finseth, *Shades of Green*, 42; Worster, *Nature's Economy*, 172, 173.

39 Marsh and Lowenthal, *Man and Nature*, 11, 36, 381.

40 Lowenthal, *George Perkins Marsh*, 303.

41 Lydia Hunter Sigourney, "Fallen Forests," *Scenes in my Native Land* (Boston: James Munroe and Company, 1845), reprinted in Kilcup, *Fallen Forests*, 86; Leigh Eric Schmidt, "From Arbor Day to the Environmental Sabbath," 303.

42 Susan Pearson, "Speaking Bodies, Speaking Minds: Animals, Language, History" *History and Theory*, no. 52 (December 2013): 91–108; Harriet Beecher Stowe, "The Rights of Dumb Animals," *Our Dumb Animals* 1, no. 9 (1869), 69.

43 Wellock, *Preserving the Nation*, 47; Brian Roberts, review of Jones, *Epiphany in the Wilderness*, in *Environmental History* 23, no. 2 (April 2018): 417–18, 417.

44 Brinkley, *Wilderness Warrior*, 364–65; Warren, *The Hunter's Game*, 25–28; Taylor, *The Rise of the Conservation Movement*, 214–15; Linton Weeks, "Hats Off to Women Who Saved the Birds," *NPR History Dept*, July 15, 2015.

45 Kirby, *Rural Worlds Lost*, 18.

46 Schneiberg et al., "Social Movements and Organizational Form," 638; Smith, *African American Environmental Thought*, 76.

47 George, *Progress and Poverty*, 12; Henry George, *The Complete Works of Henry George* (Garden City; New York: Doubleday, Page, and Co., 1911), 234; Henry George Jr., *The Life of Henry George* (New York: Doubleday and McClure Company, 1900), 32. White, *The Republic for Which It Stands*, 381.

48 Maysilles, *Ducktown Smoke*, 6–8; *Georgia v. Tennessee Copper Company*, 206 U.S. 230 (1907), 236. The mine site, which closed in 1987, remains so hazardous to groundwater that it requires environmental remediation in perpetuity.

49 Taylor, *The Environment and the People*, 236; Fiege, *The Republic of Nature*, 427, citing Frederick Law Olmsted, *Yosemite and the Mariposa Grove: A Preliminary Report, 1865* (Yosemite National Park, Calif.: Yosemite Association, 1993), 1–28, 13, 18.

50 Taylor, *The Environment and the People*, 201–02.

51 Gottlieb, *Forcing the Spring*, 112; Howard, *Garden Cities of To-Morrow*, plate after page 16.

52 Zimring, *Clean and White*, 149.

53 Brinkley, *Wilderness Warrior*, 498, 22; Tyrrell, *Crisis of the Wasteful Nation*, 232.

54 Brinkley, *Wilderness Warrior*, 17; Elizabeth Kolbert, "Obama the Conservationist," *The New Yorker*, September 12, 2016.

55 Brulle, *Agency, Democracy, and Nature*, 153, citing Blanchard Proceedings of a Conference of Governors in the White House, May 13–15, 1908 (Washington, D.C.:

Government Printing Office, 1909), 3, 10–11; Lowenthal, *George Perkins Marsh, Prophet of Conservation*, 305; Tyrrell, *Crisis of the Wasteful Nation*, 8.

56 Brinkley, *Wilderness Warrior*, 790.

57 Maher, *Nature's New Deal*, 4; Brinkley, *Wilderness Warrior*, 499; Davis, *The Gulf*, 208.

58 Tyrrell, *Crisis of the Wasteful Nation*, 16.

59 Hays, *Conservation and the Gospel of Efficiency*; Pinchot, *The Fight for Conservation*, 48, 4.

60 Turner and McKibben, *David Brower*, 15; Armitage, *The Nature Study Movement*, 30–31; Char Miller, "The Greening of Gifford Pinchot," *Environmental History* 16, no. 3 (1992), 7; Pinchot, *The Fight for Conservation*, 109.

61 Lydia Adams-Williams, "A Million Women for Conservation," *Conservation: Forests, Waters, Soils and Minerals, The American Forestry Association* 15, no. 6 (June 1909): 346–47.

62 Stern, *Eugenic Nation*, 163.

63 Kiechle, *Smell Detectives*, x; Armitage, *The Nature Study Movement*.

64 Armitage, *The Nature Study Movement*, 43, 65, 81–85; Powell, *Vanishing America*, 136; Stern, *Eugenic Nation*, 163.

65 Armitage, *The Nature Study Movement*, 209; Lear, *Witness to Nature*, 14.

66 Lydia Adams-Williams, "Conservation—Woman's Work," *Forestry and Irrigation* 14, no. 6 (June 1908): 350–51, 351; Rome, "'Political Hermaphrodites,'" 444; Zimring, *Clean and White*, 59.

67 Merchant, *Earthcare*, 119; Paul S. Sutter, Foreword, Davis, *An Everglades Providence*, xv; Merchant, *Earthcare*, 136; Hay, "Dispelling the 'Bitter Fog,'" 175; Terriane K. Schulte, "Citizen Experts: The League of Women Voters and Environmental Conservation," *Frontiers: A Journal of Women Studies* 30, no. 3 (2009): 1–29.

68 Maureen A. Flanagan, "The City Profitable, the City Livable: Environmental Policy Gender, and Power in Chicago in the 1910s," *Journal of Urban History* 22, no. 2: 163–90, 168; Alaimo, *Undomesticated Ground*, 64, 98.

69 Zimring, *Clean and White*, 83; Alaimo, *Undomesticated Ground*, 67.

70 Dianne D. Glave, "Rural African American Women, Gardening, and Progressive Reform in the South," 37–50 in Glave and Stoll, *To Love the Wind and the Rain*, 42; David Fort Godshalk, *Veiled Visions: The 1906 Atlanta Race Riot and the Reshaping of American Race Relations* (Chapel Hill: University of North Carolina Press, 2005), 210.

71 W.E.B. DuBois, and Isabel Eaton, *The Philadelphia Negro: A Social Study*. Publications of the University of Pennsylvania Series in Political Economy and Public Law (Philadelphia: Published for the University, 1899), 296, 98, 148; Zimring, *Clean and White*, 112ff.; Loewen, *Sundown Towns*.

72 Smith, *African American Environmental Thought*, 73–74, 95.

73 Sutter, "Foreword," Mark Hersey, "*My Work Is That of Conservation*," xi; Mark Hersey, "*My Work Is That of Conservation*," 107–09, 147, 34.

74 Carl Zimring, *Clean and White*, 105, citing Booker T. Washington, "An Address before the Negro Organization Society of Virginia, Norfolk, Va., November 12, 1914." In *Booker T. Washington Papers*, vol. 13, 1914–15, edited by Louis R. Harlan, Raymond W. Smock, Susan Valenza, and Sadie M. Harlan, 169 (Urbana: University of Illinois Press, 1984); "Negro Health Service Work is Begun Here," *Anniston Star*, December 4, 1930; "Colored People Make Plans for Raising Own Food," *Anniston Star*, March 16, 1932.

75 Kathryn Kish Sklar, "Hull House in the 1890s: A Community of Women Reformers," *Journal of Women in Culture and Society* 10, no. 4 (1985): 658–77, 660.

76 Painter, *The History of White People*, 242; Sinclair, *The Jungle*; Blum, *Love Canal Revisited*, 125; Taylor, *The Environment and the People*, 175–77.

77 Mark Stoll, *Inherit the Holy Mountain*, 194; "Woman in Harvard Post; Dr. Alice Hamilton First of Her Sex Elected to the Faculty," *The New York Times*, March

12, 1919; Gottlieb, *Forcing the Spring*, 83–88; Markowitz and Rosner, *Deceit and Denial*, 138.

78 Clark, *Radium Girls*, 205–06.

79 Merchant, *American Environmental History*, 177–78.

80 H.P. Talbot, *Technology Review* 13, (1911) 365–73; Ellen H. Richards and Alpheus G. Woodman, *Air, Water, and Food from a Sanitary Standpoint* (New York: J. Wiley, 1900); Clarke, *Ellen Swallow*.

81 Merchant, *Earthcare*, 132; Fischer, *Citizens, Experts and the Environment*, 6.

82 Powell, *Vanishing America*, 46–47; Marsh, *Man and Nature*, 35; Jacoby, "Class and Environmental History," 326, referencing Marsh, *Man and Nature*, 233, 257; Powell, *Vanishing America*, 40.

83 Frederick Jackson Turner, "The Significance of the Frontier in American History," American Historical Association, 1893; Giles Gunn, "American Studies as Cultural Criticism," *The Yale Review* 72 (Winter 1983): 296; White, "American Environmental History," 297; Cronon, "Revisiting the Vanishing Frontier," 166n33, 170.

84 Powell, *Vanishing America*, 6; Merchant, "Shades of Darkness," 382, citing Muir, *My First Summer in the Sierra*, 205, 218; Stern, *Eugenic Nation*, 143–48.

85 "Bushman Shares a Cage with Bronx Park Apes; Many Are Not Pleased," *The New York Times*, September 9, 1906; "The Mayor Won't Help to Free Caged Pygmy," *The New York Times*, September 12, 1906; "Legal Fight for Pygmy," *The New York Times*, September 13, 1906; "Negro Ministers Act to Free the Pygmy," *The New York Times*, September 11, 1906.

86 William T. Hornaday, *Wildlife Conservation in Theory and Practice* (New Haven: Yale University Press, 1914), v; Smith, *African American Environmental Thought*, 109; Madison Grant, *The Passing of the Great Race: The Racial Basis of European History* (New York: Charles Scribner, 1916), 85; Tyrrell, *Crisis of a Wasteful Nation*, 182.

87 "Man and Monkey Show Disapproved by Clergy," *The New York Times*, September 10, 1906; "Negro Ministers Act to Free the Pygmy," *The New York Times*, September 11, 1906; "Colored Orphan Home Gets the Pygmy," *The New York Times*, September 29, 1906. Ten years later, Benga committed suicide in Lynchburg, Virginia. "Ota Benga, Pygmy, Tired of America: The Strange Little African Finally Ended Life at Lynchburg, Va.," *The New York Times*, July 16, 1916. See also, Powell, *Vanishing America*, 115–18.

88 Ray, *The Ecological Other*, 52; Powell, *Vanishing America*, 12.

89 Worster, *Nature's Economy*, 223, 230.

90 Ekbladh, *The Great American Mission*, 48, 38–39.

91 Brinkley, *Rightful Heritage*, 45, 80.

92 Maher, *Nature's New Deal*, 181–83.

93 Jason Manthorne, "The View from the Cotton: Reconsidering the Southern Tenant Farmers' Union," *Agricultural History*, Winter (2010): 20–45, 28.

94 Weisiger, *Dreaming of Sheep*, 159, 175, 11, 188.

95 Worster, *Nature's Economy*, 219, 236.

96 Roosevelt's message to Congress cited in Maher, *Nature's New Deal*, 20.

97 Sutter, *Driven Wild*, 48; Maher, *Nature's New Deal*, 116, 106, 110, 4, 13, 10–11.

98 Simon, "New Men in Body and Soul," 80–102; Maher, *Nature's New Deal*, 109, 213.

99 Maher, *Nature's New Deal*, 11.

100 Izaak Walton, *The Compleat Angler* (London, Printed by T. Maxey for R. Marriot, 1653; 1907); John Opie, *Nature's Nation*, 419; Dawn Merritt, "90 Years of Conservation Success: From the Jazz Age to World War II," Publications, Izaak Walton League of America, www.iwla.org/publications/outdoor-america/article/outdoor-america-2012-issue-2/90-years-of-conservation-success-from-the-jazz-age-to-world-war-ii (accessed March 4, 2017).

101 Sutter, *Driven Wild*, 236, 227–34; Fox, *The American Conservation Movement*, 351; Sutter, *Driven Wild*, 3, 5; Mark Stoll, *Inherit the Holy Mountain*, 268.

102 Drake, *Loving Nature*, 143; William Cronon, "Foreword," Sutter, *Driven Wild*, xi.

103 McKibben, *American Earth*, 224.

104 Furmansky, *Rosalie Edge: Hawk of Mercy*, 1; Brulle, *Agency, Democracy, Nature*, 224; Willard Van Name, *The New Yorker*, April 17, 1948, 46; Fox, *The American Conservation Movement*, 181; Furmansky, *Rosalie Edge: Hawk of Mercy*, 250.

105 Russell, *War and Nature*.

106 Cherniak, *The Hawk's Nest Incident*; Gottlieb, *Forcing the Spring*, 308–13.

107 Josh White (Pinewood Tom), "Silicosis is Killing Me," *Conqueror*, 1936.

108 Mark Stoll, *Inherit the Holy Mountain*, 168; Schmidt, "From Arbor Day to the Environmental Sabbath," 312ff.

109 McNeill, *Something New under the Sun*, xxii.

110 Aaron Mair, "A Deeper Shade of Green," *Sierra Club*, March 9, 2017, https://sierra club.org/change/2017/03/deeper-shade-green (accessed May 18, 2018).

111 Barber, *A House in the Sun*, 76.

2

THE GREAT ACCELERATION
AND THE POSTWAR RISE OF
ENVIRONMENTALISM (1945–1962)

Until recently, environmental activism in the 1940s and 1950s has been over-shadowed by the explosion of protest that followed. However, the immediate postwar period saw campaigns on a range of environmental concerns: nuclear fallout, population growth, air and water pollution, land use, and toxic chemicals. Drives for wilderness protection were waged alongside efforts to respond to urban renewal's massive demolition of inner cities and to mitigate the impact of ground-grabbing suburban development. New technologies arising out of war research provided benefits but also threatened the environment and human health. Intense economic pressure put new technologies in place before their impact on the landscape and on human bodies was well understood. During the 1950s, the prewar "mini-movements" were melded into environmentalism. Postwar activists were more focused on public health, more scientifically grounded, and more intertwined with other social movements than were their predecessors.[1]

Global geopolitics and international exchanges among conservation advocates profoundly shaped the postwar emergence of environmentalism, as historian Thomas Robertson has argued. When the newly formed United Nations held its Monetary and Financial Conference in July 1944 at Bretton Woods, New Hampshire, Allied leaders established financial institutions that would shape and constrain national economies and their ecological footprints for the coming century. The International Monetary Fund (IMF) would now regulate exchange rates and capital flows between nations. The International Bank for Reconstruction and Development, also known as "the World Bank," would set the terms for investment in reconstruction and underwrite loans to war-damaged countries and developing nations. The liberal utilitarian view with its emphasis on growth outlined by British economist John Maynard Keynes, who attended the conference, claimed the attention of President Franklin Roosevelt and other leaders at Bretton Woods.[2]

Spurred by revulsion against Nazi ideology and wartime atrocities, postwar powers also signed the U.N. Declaration on Human Rights in Paris in December 1948. The declaration was broader than the U.S. Constitution's Bill of Rights, articulating not only political and civil freedoms but also economic and social rights. While not explicitly referencing "environmental rights," Article 25 of the Declaration implied them: "Everyone has the right to a standard of living adequate for the health and well-being of himself and of his family, including food, clothing, housing and medical care and necessary social services."[3] The human rights framework would increasingly influence the rhetoric, policy aims, and standards of conduct urged by social justice movements, including environmentalism.

Americans had long been aware of pollution and other forms of environmental degradation, which they had been addressing through a wide array of reform efforts. But after World War II, rapid industrialization and changes in production and consumption worsened some longstanding harms. Some problems—fallout from atomic testing, for example—were altogether new. The Cold War both propelled the race for economic supremacy and constrained the response to industrialization's worst effects. However, recognition grew that assaults on the landscape were escalating and affecting human health. Important, too, was a growing sense of efficacy, a belief that environmental crises must and could be addressed.[4]

The rate and scale of environmental change in the postwar period—the Great Acceleration—was unparalleled. War had concentrated the wealth of large corporations, which had received the largest share of wartime procurement contracts, leading to expansion of markets and "exponential growth in corporate power." The era saw a dramatic rise in the use of fossil fuels. A brief dalliance with solar-generated electricity quickly faded as oil and other fossil fuel companies crowded out alternatives and dominated national energy policy. The availability of cheap energy would transform "mining, fishing, urban design, and tourism"—with environmental consequences. Inexpensive fuel made timber harvesting and other mechanized forms of agriculture vastly more efficient and immeasurably more damaging to the land. Petroleum fueled the bulldozers that levelled forests to make way for suburbs and razed whole neighborhoods in major cities. Cheap oil powered the automobiles now needed to transport people from bedroom communities to jobs, pumping a substantial increase in lead and other pollutants into the air.[5] The dismantling of an enviable rail network to make way for the personal automobile marked a societal choice with environmental consequences that were only dimly anticipated.

A multitude of new products were made from oil byproducts. As chemists unlocked the structures and uses of hydrocarbons, "synthetic chemical production (by weight) expanded 350-fold between 1940 and 1982." The synthetics revolution transformed the contents of manufactured goods from nylon stockings and upholstery fabrics to pharmaceuticals, fertilizers, and pesticides. Chemical exposures during production cost dearly to worker health. Increased production added to the dramatic increase in non-decomposable waste.[6]

Atomic weaponry was the most potent symbol of the extent of human dominance over the earth and the danger human activity posed to public health and the environment. The bomb "transformed not only military strategy and international relations," writes historian Paul Boyer, "but the fundamental ground of culture and consciousness." Nuclear weapons were "embodiments of a new knowledge of nature," historian Richard Rhodes has argued, transforming how people understood atomic structures of life. The weapons U.S. bombers dropped on Hiroshima and Nagasaki in early August 1945 killed more than 100,000 Japanese citizens instantly. Vivid accounts, photographs, and newsreels of the carnage testified that through nuclear war, on a scale previously unimagined, humans possessed the capacity to annihilate life on earth. That realization inaugurated a new culture of fear.[7]

The subsequent drive for nuclear superiority launched an arms race and fueled the Cold War between the West and the Soviet Union. The escalating imperative to counter Soviet power around the world led to a scramble for resources and competition for spheres of influence, especially in the face of rising anticolonialism in Africa and Asia. With decolonization in the Third World, Western investors found new resources and new markets to exploit, with both predictable and unanticipated environmental consequences. Decolonization stimulated deindustrialization in developed countries, increased the use of extractive technologies in developing nations, and accelerated the shift of wastes from developed countries to developing ones. The Cold War threatened environments in multiple ways: the domestic use of chemical toxics devised for wartime; military secrecy that shrouded an expanded arsenal of chemical, biological, and radiological weaponry; and agroeconomic intervention in developing nations. The export of chemical-intensive agriculture, dubbed the "Green Revolution," was part of the propaganda mission to attract countries into the U.S. orbit. Hybrid seeds and new farming practices produced higher crop yields but disrupted local ecologies, limited biodiversity, and unsettled farming economies and ways of life.[8]

Multiple industrial and chemical disasters in the U.S. and overseas in the late 1940s and early 1950s highlighted the ecological costs and public health impact of unregulated industrial development. In Donora, Pennsylvania, in 1948, pollution from the local steel mill trapped in the Monongahela River valley by adverse weather conditions killed twenty people and hospitalized thousands more with respiratory distress. Even more deadly was Britain's "London Fog" of 1952. During an extreme cold snap an unusual weather pattern confined smoke from overworking household coal furnaces at street level over a five-day period, making visibility difficult and impairing breathing. Deaths from asphyxiation were estimated at roughly twelve thousand.[9]

Disasters made headlines; the unspectacular, routine course of manufacturing and chemical production also resulted in pollution on an epic scale. In the U.S., women protesting with mops and brooms in St. Louis and Pittsburgh in the 1930s had succeeded in gaining passage of stronger municipal ordinances regulating coal smoke. After the London crisis, more cities followed suit, upgrading laws and enforcement.[10]

Knowledge of deleterious conditions grew. Among practitioners in fish, wildlife, and game management fields, scientists studying ecology, and the general public, awareness of the dangers of nuclear fallout, food contamination, and pollution from manufacturing increased. Congress took modest steps to protect water quality, register pesticides, and limit food additives, but in many areas, conditions continued to deteriorate.

The nuclear threat, especially, generated tremendous opposition and fostered alliances among conservationists and the peace movement. Some activists, like evolutionary biologist Barry Commoner, advocated a scientifically informed public as the most effective antidote to the nuclear specter. Others challenged the military and civilian uses of atomic science through nonviolent direct action. A rising black freedom struggle showed that nonviolent protest could bring about change.

The Cold War and McCarthyism constrained protest. Antipathy to communism became a rationale to justify repression of dissent. Named for Wisconsin Senator Joseph McCarthy, McCarthyism attacked as treasonous various communist and socialist thinkers, labor leaders, artists, entertainers, and their allies. Despite the suppression of protest, activism continued; new organizations emerged to protect wilderness and human health.

In sum, as historian Robertson has noted, the ascendant American empire "created new imperatives to manage resources, new sciences with which to do so, new forms of environmental crisis, new anti-modern doubts, and ultimately new policy frameworks."[11] A new environmentalism would emerge to match.

The Rise of Environmentalism

Surveying the origins of the postwar environmental movement, historian Samuel Hays ascribed the growing interest in environmental protection to the newfound affluence of a rising middle class. For Hays, the search for "the good life" yielded not only a desire for more material goods, but also "new human values about what people want in their lives." Affluence brought a new sensibility, an appreciation for open space, outdoor recreation, clean air, and clean water. As people had more occasion to enjoy natural settings—and more time to work for nature preservation—environmental attitudes began to shift. In this context, the very values that shaped Americans' notions of the good life—individualism, personal choice, private land ownership, more and better material goods—presented a conflict to the values required by an environmentally sensitive way of living.[12]

Attributing the rise of environmentalism solely to postwar affluence, however, downplays the fact that, as biologist Barry Commoner argued at the time, the technological revolution and production processes introduced new hazards. Those hazards "provoked stern reaction from a much broader base," as Commoner biographer Michael Egan has noted. Moreover, as historian Thomas Jundt has suggested, Hays's 'quality of life' argument ignored postwar environmentalism's origins as "a broadside against the growing power of corporate capitalism." Crediting the affluent consuming public for the upsurge in environmental activism also discounts the concerns of the non-affluent, what has come to be termed the 'environmentalism of the poor.'[13]

Conservation and World Peace

In the aftermath of the war, the drive for peace helped set the conditions for renewed conservation efforts. Franklin Roosevelt had sought to ensure that conservation was a priority for the new U.N. in its bid for peace. "Conservation is the basis of permanent peace," he had written in 1944, in advance of the Dumbarton Oaks consultations that led to the formation of the United Nations.[14]

World War II had been, in part, what historians have identified as a "resource war," with nations fighting to retain or obtain natural resources for national defense and civilian use. War also depleted resources—food and animals, metals and timber. After the war, with Gifford Pinchot prompting President Truman and Harold Ickes urging his successor at Interior, Truman was convinced to recommend that the U.N. place conservation on its agenda. "The real or exaggerated fear of resource shortages and declining standards of living has in the past involved nations in warfare," wrote Truman in his call for an international conservation conference. He became convinced, as FDR had been, of the importance of resource availability for military defense and economic power. Truman's Point Four program, announced in 1949, advocated "TVA-style" modernization programs around the world as a vital strategy to extend U.S. influence amid the Cold War. In effect, the U.S. aimed to globalize the New Deal.[15]

"A Fight for Democracy"

Two 1948 international bestsellers linked American national security with warnings about the ecological crisis that would result from policies that encouraged unlimited growth. Fairfield Osborn Jr.'s *Our Plundered Planet* and William Vogt's *Road to Survival* expanded the scope and scale of conservation concerns to a global level.[16] The books placed the need for conservation before the general public. Both books sold millions of copies in the U.S. and were translated into multiple languages.

A veteran of World War I and former Wall Street banker, Fairfield Osborn, Jr. had begun articulating "a new view of humans, technology, and nature" during World War II while head of the New York Zoological Society. "[T]he tide of the earth's population is rising, the reservoir of the earth's living resources is falling," wrote Osborn, "there is only one solution: Man must recognize the necessity of cooperating with nature. He must temper his demands and use and conserve the natural living resources of this earth in a manner that alone can provide for the continuation of his civilization." Osborn raised concerns about "modern chemical agriculture," including the use of dichloro-diphenyl-trichloroethane (DDT). To Osborn, finding solutions to ecological problems required democratic participation. In a statement that was a challenge both to the postwar corporate order and to the Soviets, Osborn wrote, "The conservation drive is at the core of the fight for democracy."[17]

A transitional figure between conservationism and environmentalism, Osborn worked with Aldo Leopold and William Vogt to launch the Conservation Foundation in 1948 with grants from the Rockefeller Brothers Fund to support scientific research and conservation education. With Osborn as its first president, the new foundation aimed to be a scholarly clearinghouse addressing issues such as population control, chemical pollution, and other ecological concerns not yet on the agendas of the Sierra Club and The Wilderness Society. Osborn took to the airwaves, speaking about "Man and His Environment" on shows such as CBS's "People's Platform" and NBC's "Living in 1950." Conservation exhibits he arranged to have mounted at the Bronx Zoo attracted more than 500,000 visitors a year. Osborn's *The Limits of the Earth*, published in 1953, highlighted potential dangers for the U.S. of failing to understand the consequences of rising population and failing to provide sufficient support for agriculture in the developing world. Osborn also helped to found Resources for the Future in 1952, a business-oriented think tank focused on ensuring U.S. access to global resources amid increasingly contentious international relations.[18]

In *Road to Survival*, the best-selling conservation book until *Silent Spring*, ornithologist William Vogt wrote about "human ecology," highlighting similar themes, especially the population pressures on the planet. The increasing use of land for agriculture to feed the world's growing population was reaching biotic limits, argued Vogt, eroding landscapes, depleting soils, destroying forests, and reducing water supplies. The solution, for Vogt, was radically limiting population growth through birth control and tempering capitalism. "One of the most ruinous limiting factors is the capitalistic system," wrote Vogt, portending a shift leftward in the environmental movement. "Free enterprise—divorced from biophysical understanding and social responsibility. . .must bear a large share of the responsibilities for devastated forests, vanishing wildlife, crippled ranges, a gullied continent, and roaring flood crests." Because he had targeted capitalism, Vogt felt the sting of McCarthyism in the early 1950s; he lost his seat on the Conservation Foundation advisory council and *Road to Survival* was temporarily dropped from the foundation's reading list.[19]

The influence of Osborn and Vogt helped to create a mass movement for population control in the 1950s. By then, overpopulation had become a concern of conservation groups, including the Sierra Club and the Wilderness Society. Vogt directed Planned Parenthood from 1951 to 1961 and returned to the Conservation Foundation as executive secretary in 1964. Vogt's invocation of the nineteenth-century population control advocate Thomas Malthus revealed an ugly ethnocentrism beneath the 1950s preoccupation with stemming population growth in what would come to be known as the "Third World." In *Road to Survival*, Vogt advocated sterilization programs targeting "the physically and psychologically marginal" and disparaged "the unchecked spawning of India, China and other countries."[20]

Population growth would remain a motivating concern for many environmentalists and a source of conflict. Fears of overpopulation infused Cold War ideology as well. "Policymakers also feared that overpopulation engendered poverty, which invited communism," explains environmental historian Miles Powell.[21] However, population control advocates who targeted developing countries often neglected the fact that technological development, relative affluence, and rising levels of consumption in developed countries had disproportionate impact on the planet's capacity to support life.

International Influences

The transatlantic network of conservation advocates grew in the postwar period. The International Union for the Protection of Nature (IUPN) was founded in 1948 in France and established its headquarters in Switzerland. Initially focused on preserving declining populations of megafauna in newly independent African and Asian countries, the organization was renamed International Union for the Conservation of Nature and Natural Resources (IUCN) as its concerns broadened.

As a result of Truman's call for a global conservation conference, not one, but two U.N. convenings were held in 1949. The gatherings reflected growing global interest in the subject, as well as a shift in conservationism that was underway, as historian Thomas Jundt has noted. Both conferences took place at Lake Success on Long Island, where the United Nations was temporarily located. The larger of the two meetings, the United Nations Scientific Conference on the Conservation and Utilization of Resources (UNSCCUR), focused on traditional conservation themes of resource conservation and management. The International Technical Conference on the Protection of Nature (ITCPN), sponsored by the United Nations Educational, Scientific, and Cultural Organization (UNESCO), offered a more direct critique of corporate and commercial approaches to resource development. Though some delegates attended both events, the conferences revealed a divide within international conservationism over how to best balance the needs and goals of developing nations with those of developed nations, particularly in terms of food policy and agricultural development.[22]

As the first global conservation conference, UNSCCUR convened 530 delegates from 49 countries, bringing government representatives and prominent conservationists into conversation. Cold War hostilities were already evident; the Soviet Union did not attend. The U.S. delegation included the U.S. Forest Service, the U.S. Army Corps of Engineers, the Bureau of Reclamation, and academics and engineers from the fields of oil, gas, and mining. Significantly, the Congress of Industrial Organizations and the textile workers' union attended as well, representing organized labor's progressive wing. Fairfield Osborn, Jr. attended on behalf of the New York Zoological Society and the Conservation Foundation. After the formal meetings, UNSCCUR attendees visited the Tennessee Valley Authority dams in Chattanooga and Knoxville, Tennessee, and Muscle Shoals, Alabama, where U.S. officials showcased corporate and government collaborations on forestry, agriculture, fisheries, waterfowl conservation, and malaria control. UNSCCUR conferees heard several proponents of organic agriculture, but on the whole, the program followed the U.S. government delegates in promoting fertilizers and pesticides to extract greater yields.[23]

By contrast to UNSCCUR, presenters at the concurrent ITCPN conference argued for agricultural policies suited to local conditions, improved organic techniques that promoted essential microorganisms and retained better soil. Revisiting these events offers a reminder that postwar environmentalism arose in part, wrote Jundt, "as a critique against the growing power of corporate capitalism at home and in the new liberal international order in Western Europe, in the wake of decolonization."[24]

The ITCPN roster listed leaders of twenty U.S. nature preservation organizations including Howard Zahniser and O.J. Murie of The Wilderness Society and Robert Cushman Murphy, leader of the Nature Conservancy of Long Island. "Conservation is a way of life, but it is not the traditional American way," said Ollie Fink of Friends of the Land. Aldo Leopold's *A Sand County Almanac*, published just before the conference, with its new "land ethic," offered an alternative approach for the conservation movement—an ecocentric argument for protecting the land as part of a community. With an emphasis on environmental education and the development of "an ecological conscience," the ITCPN conference provided the beginnings of a vision for a new environmentalism.[25]

Global Resource Development Strategy

In a 1949 opinion piece in *The Saturday Evening Post*, William Vogt expressed concern that "destructive exploitation" might accompany the Point Four global development program proposed by President Truman. Vogt predicted that by promoting fertilizer and pesticide intensive agricultural practices abroad, the U.S. would "be known not as beneficent collaborators but as technological Vandals."[26]

Exporting agricultural products and practices formed one aspect of the Point Four program. U.S. officials also worried that shortages of raw materials would retard national economic growth and limit preparedness for future wars. In response, in 1951, President Truman established the Materials Policy Commission to assess and analyze the nation's access to minerals, heavy metals, and petroleum. Nicknamed the Paley Commission, after its head, William S. Paley, chair of the Columbia Broadcasting System (CBS) and a founding director of Resources for the Future, the group undertook "a global resource review" of raw materials for suppliers of the U.S. military. The commission's report, *Resources for Freedom*, indicated that the United States was rapidly depleting its reserves. Ultimately, however, national security interests prevailed in shaping resource policy. Commission members rejected the conservationist approach in favor of a Keynesian equation of progress with growth.[27]

The availability of sufficient energy resources to power the new American ascendancy loomed large in the postwar era. The rich petroleum stocks of the U.S., mostly from the Gulf of Mexico, helped the Allies to win World War II, but the war left oil reserves depleted. The first postwar heating oil shortage occurred in the winter of 1947–48, putting the nation on notice about resource limitations. The U.S. would become a net importer of oil for the ensuing decades. "[T]he global dimensions of the crisis," were beginning to come clear, as architectural historian Daniel Barber has argued, "as it was on global terms that an oil network would develop."[28]

Threats of resource scarcity prompted a brief "golden age for solar energy investment" during the late 40s and early 50s, Barber noted. Promoted by Julius Krug, Truman's Secretary of the Interior, solar energy was high on the agenda at UNSCCUR. Architects and planners in the U.S. and around the world designed living spaces that could run on solar power. The "World Solar Energy Project," a World Symposium on Applied Solar Energy, was held in Phoenix, Arizona, in early November 1955. The Eisenhower administration, however, backed away from investing in solar, preferring fossil fuel-based development, giving only modest support to the small-scale solar projects supported by non-governmental organizations.[29]

Conservationism in Transition

Best known through his classic collection of essays, *A Sand County Almanac*, published posthumously in 1949, Aldo Leopold trained at the Yale Forest School (now the Yale School of Forestry). After graduating in 1909, Leopold took a position managing game in Arizona and New Mexico for the U.S. Forest Service under Gifford Pinchot. Leopold's changing views over the ensuing decades reflect conservationism in transition. Leopold highlighted the need for an ethical relationship with the land that many New Deal development projects lacked.

Leopold's deep experience of the wild led to his transformation from a conservationist game manager in the mold of Pinchot to an ecologist who approached the natural world more holistically. He described his personal moment of awakening in a now famous passage in *A Sand County Almanac*, "Thinking Like a Mountain." After an encounter in which he shot a female wolf during the forestry department's overzealous campaign to eliminate predators, the young forester witnessed "a fierce green fire" dying in her eyes. Moved by this experience, Leopold convinced the Forest Service to alter its approach to predator-prey management, not killing all predators but preserving some in wilderness locales.[30]

Leopold moved to Madison, Wisconsin, in 1924 and became a professor of Game Management at the University of Wisconsin, where he trained a generation of students. He distilled his experience in the field in the 1933 textbook *Game Management*. Leopold's eighty-acre retreat in the sand counties of central Wisconsin served as laboratory and inspiration for his ideas about ecology. Leopold lamented that despite having created modern technology, people had not mastered "the oldest task in human history: to live on a piece of land without spoiling it."[31]

Leopold's perspective on the goals of conservation changed from ensuring an abundance of game for hunters to maintaining the health of the land, using methods that he attempted to put in practice on the Wisconsin prairie. Leopold was concerned that the wildlife preservationists' focus on "spectacular scenic resources" took them away from attending to overall "land health." Central to Leopold's ethic is the holistic ecological claim that "A thing is right when it tends to preserve the integrity, stability, and beauty of the biotic community. It is wrong when it tends otherwise." The greater good of the ecosystem took priority for Leopold, shifting attention from, perhaps even sacrificing, its individual parts. Published posthumously in 1949, a year after Vogt's and Osborn's impassioned books, *A Sand County Almanac* was slow to gain traction. In time though, Leopold's articulation of "The Land Ethic" inspired a new wave of wilderness advocates and became an iconic text. As a guide to action, however, Leopold's ecocentric maxim posed conundrums. It was not always possible to know which choice best preserved the integrity and stability of the land; ecologists and wildlife protectionists differed on this score.[32]

One conservation organization that bridged the transition from conservation to environmentalism is all but unknown today. Friends of the Land, founded in Washington, D.C., in 1940, promoted ecologically-sound agriculture. Leopold was a charter member. The group's mission: "to reconcile the ways of Man to Nature and make this a green and permanent land." The group popularized the principles of ecology through publications, educational forums, speaking tours, conservation camps, and training for elementary and secondary school teachers. Friends of the Land, wrote historian Randal Beeman, "foreshadow[ed] the grassroots strain of the early environmental movement." An outgrowth of the New Deal response to the Dust Bowl, that harked back to the "grangers," Friends of the Land was an "international 'clearinghouse' for conservation information," linking human health to soil health. Prominent individuals—including writers

John Dos Passos and E.B. White, former Harding administration Secretary of Agriculture Henry C. Wallace, President Eisenhower's younger brother Milton Eisenhower, and Rachel Carson—penned articles for the group's *Land Quarterly*. Nonetheless, Friends of the Land struggled financially and organizationally and by 1960 folded what remained of its dwindling membership into the Izaak Walton League.[33]

Ecology: Science and Activism

Perhaps more than any other social movement in the United States, environmental activism has developed in concert with scientific inquiry. Scientists were instrumental in creating the bomb and chemical pesticides, but scientists also identified, publicized, and sought means to repair environmental problems. The complex role of scientific research in shaping postwar environmentalism can be explored through the scientists who pursued pathbreaking work in botany, evolutionary biology, physics, and ecology. By spelling out the connections between landscapes and health, the science of ecology strengthened the basis for linking the conservation movement with concerns about pollution and public health.

The 1950s were a time of dramatic change in the field of ecology—the study of the interrelationships between living beings (biotic) and their geophysical (abiotic) surroundings. While humans had long been practicing ecosystem management, the study of the interactions of coexisting organisms was still young.

The Ecological Society of America had formed in 1915 and gained stature during the New Deal. A committee of the Ecological Society of America, the Committee for the Preservation of the Natural Conditions, first established in 1917, had long pushed for the professional group to take a more activist role, to directly pursue conservation projects. In 1946, the society's activist wing became the Ecologists' Union. That group changed its name to The Nature Conservancy and incorporated as a non-profit in 1951. The group began acquiring parcels of land to set aside, often in collaboration with various levels of government. The Conservancy also pursued "conservation easements," arrangements under which landowners retained ownership but granted to the Conservancy the right to manage the land using conservation principles.[34]

In the 1950s, the science of ecology underwent a paradigm shift, as plant biologist Michael G. Barbour has argued. Until that time, most ecologists adopted the view held by botanist Frederic Clements that communities of interacting species in particular terrains underwent a cyclical process of decline and recovery, tending toward a climax state. In this view, individual species were integrated in an association or community, which Clements likened to an organism, with a life cycle. If damaged or destroyed, the ecological community would restore itself in a process called "succession," and reach a foreseeable steady state of equilibrium.[35]

Other ecologists, including Henry Allen Gleason, by contrast, had long suggested that relationships between individual species were complex and did not resemble an organism. In Gleason's view, ecological change occurred much more unpredictably, more randomly. Determining a baseline, a "real nature" to restore, was difficult, if not impossible. Therefore, "restoration" and "recovery" were not the most appropriate metaphors for safeguarding ecologies.[36]

Empirical observations offered evidence for both views but by the end of the 1950s most ecologists favored the probabilistic view, otherwise known as the continuum concept. Gleason anticipated the views of contemporary ecologists, including adherents of complexity theory, who put much more emphasis than had Clements on probability and constant change. Transitions in the study of ecology, Barbour suggests, both mirrored and animated changes in American culture. In both, predictability and order were supplanted by "impermanence and uncertainty." Then, as now, science was not insulated from politics. Clements' view was rejected in part because, as historian Sharon Kingsland explains, it invoked the idea that human qualities were fundamentally determined by genetic differences, by climate and ecology, a notion associated with ethnocentric and totalitarian views.[37]

In 1953, brothers Eugene Odum and Howard T. Odum published *Fundamentals of Ecology*, the first widely used textbook in the field. *Fundamentals of Ecology* elaborated the concept of an ecosystem—the interaction of co-existing organisms—and highlighted the necessity of considering the role of humans within ecosystems. "Ecosystem ecology," writes Kingsland, "sought to move beyond general conceptions of ecological processes by adding exact measurements, experiments, and tests of hypotheses."[38] For his pathbreaking research in the field, Eugene Odum is often called 'the father of modern ecosystem ecology.' The field of ecology was shaped by the "deep anxieties and high hopes," of the Cold War era, argues Kingsland, "[t]he perception of ecology as a science with a new mission reflected the changing priorities of American science in the atomic age." Not surprisingly, then, funding for ecological research in the 1950s came from the successor to the Manhattan Project—the Atomic Energy Commission (AEC)—and the newly created National Science Foundation. Congress had passed the Atomic Energy Act in 1946, creating the AEC to manage the development of both military and civilian uses of nuclear weapons. The enterprise attracted a new generation of scientists, working in labs and in the field. Eugene Odum's University of Georgia Savannah River Ecology Laboratory received national security funding to study the baseline ecology at the newly constructed nuclear weapons site in Aiken, South Carolina. The AEC hired the Odums to examine the after-effects of nuclear fallout at Eniwetok Atoll in the South Pacific.[39]

Ecologists and geographers gathered in 1955, at a symposium at Princeton organized by geographer Carl O. Sauer and sponsored by the National Science Foundation. Attendees at "Man's Role in Changing the Face of the Earth" reflected on the work and writings of the mid-nineteenth-century author of *Man and Nature*, George Perkins Marsh. The conference considered two major themes: the long-term consequences of anthropogenic alteration of the earth and the rejection of environmental determinism. Although the symposium generated new enthusiasm for the study of ecology, attendees "envisaged no role for a concerned public."[40]

The Wilderness Movement Grows: Echo Park and Beyond

True to its roots in the work of John Muir, the Sierra Club's national leadership launched several campaigns to preserve wild places from hydroelectric and other development projects. One campaign, the Echo Park fight, which saved Dinosaur National Monument from western dam-building fever, gave the conservation movement a new sense of its power. In fact, environmental historian Hal Rothman called Echo Park "the galvanizing issue that paved the way for the modern environmental movement."[41] At stake was not just the fate of one national monument in a remote, little-visited corner of the American West. The Echo Park battle was about drawing a line—a rejoinder to Hetch Hetchy— against dam development in the national parks.

Sierra Club director David Brower, who was hired in 1952 as the seven thousand-member organization's first paid staffer, and Wilderness Society leader Howard Zahniser led the Echo Park campaign to success. Brower and Zahniser were part of a new generation of conservation leaders, less bound to elite circles, more directly political, and more assertive in challenging policymakers. They combined energetic organizing of supporters with an aggressive lobbying campaign, using scientific data to support their proposals. A transitional figure between conservationism and environmentalism, Brower became a new archetype of the wilderness advocate, a towering presence in the postwar movement. He led the Sierra Club for seventeen years, until he and the club parted ways in 1969. Like Brower, Howard Zahniser, who had replaced Robert Sterling Yard as leader of the Wilderness Society, was known as a fighter, following in Wilderness Society co-founder Bob Marshall's footsteps.[42]

In 1950, the Department of the Interior approved a proposal by the U.S. Bureau of Reclamation for a system of dams on the Green and Colorado rivers, which converged in Utah near the Colorado border. The western states had experienced growth due to war-related government contracts and the region's political leaders sought additional investment. Hydroelectricity from the dams along the Colorado would serve not only the growing cities in the Southwest, but also military installations in the western states, including atomic sites in Nevada and Utah.[43]

However, the Bureau of Reclamation, which managed water and power resources in the western states and was often at odds with preservationists, would become the major obstacle in the Echo Park fight. The 1950s were a high point in the agency's history. The Bureau was "the builder of great American technological monuments that testified to mid-century concepts of the national will," noted Hal Rothman, "as the power to transform landscapes passed from private industry to the federal government."[44]

The Echo Park Dam was part of the Colorado River Storage Project, a string of dams that required approval—and funding—from Congress. A dam at Echo Park would have flooded the nearly 200,000-acre terrain surrounding Dinosaur National Monument, near ancient petroglyphs and the fossilized remains of dinosaurs. The conservationists who sought to save Dinosaur moved away from classic preservationist themes proffered during the Hetch Hetchy debate—scenic beauty and spiritual renewal—and turned to ecological arguments to oppose dam construction. Testifying before Congress, Brower used scientific data to illustrate that the Bureau's calculations of evaporation rates from the reservoir were faulty.[45]

Invoking the loss at Hetch Hetchy, conservationists made Echo Park a national fight over the sanctity of the national parks. They circulated pamphlets and a film about the destruction of natural and human history that would result. The publisher Alfred Knopf personally opposed the dam, and quickly brought out a book of essays about Echo Park, edited by writer Wallace Stegner, with photographs of the stunning terrain. A copy of *This is Dinosaur: The Echo Park Country and Its Magic Rivers* was sent to every member of Congress.[46]

The sheer number of organizations involved in the Echo Park fight demonstrates the breadth of American conservation activism in the mid-1950s. The coalition included an impressive seventy-eight national conservation organizations and 236 state-based groups in opposition to the dam. The emergence of nonprofit advocacy organizations was still a new phenomenon. Existing limitations on lobbying by nonprofits receiving tax deductible contributions were reinforced by a 1954 court decision, so conservation leaders met in New York to form the Council of Conservationists. The new group received *non-deductible* donations and could register as a lobby group, publish pamphlets, purchase print and radio ads, and advocate for or against legislation.[47]

The Audubon Society, the Izaak Walton League, the National Parks Association, and numerous hunting and fishing clubs all opposed the Echo Park Dam project. Rosalie Edge's Emergency Conservation Committee got involved. Dam opponents forged alliances with legislators and wielded considerable clout in Congress. They rejected the entire Colorado River Storage Project until the Echo Park Dam was removed from the plan. With letters to Congress running eighty to one against construction, opponents succeeded in scuttling plans for the Echo Park Dam. The final version of the Act included the following: "It is the intention of Congress that no dam or reservoir constructed under the authorization of this Act shall be within any national park or monument."[48]

In negotiating with legislators to save Dinosaur National Monument, however, representatives of organizations pledged that they would not oppose dams in the Bureau's master plan that were being built outside of national parks. Brower later expressed profound regret about the tradeoff. "All our victories are temporary; all our defeats are permanent," Brower is quoted as saying after the construction of the Glen Canyon Dam. In succeeding decades, the Glen Canyon Dam and other massive hydrologic projects reduced the once powerful Colorado River to a trickle as it nears the sea.[49]

Popular artists and cultural figures played important roles in the campaign to preserve wilderness areas, especially in the American West. Photographers and writers documented majestic locales they hoped to spare. Photographer Ansel Adams had offered his talents in service of the 1938 campaign to establish Kings Canyon National Park in California. Eliot Porter took photos of the area that was to be flooded by the building of the Glen Canyon Dam, published in a book called *The Place No One Knew*.[50]

State-based conservationists, many of them women, had impact beyond their numbers in similar campaigns to preserve iconic locales during this period. Born in 1890, Marjory Stoneman Douglas worked for women's suffrage and the preservation of the Everglades and is harbinger of intersections between emerging environmentalism and the women's movement. Douglas's book, *The Everglades: River of Grass*, appeared in 1947, simultaneously with the postwar dedication of the Everglades as the nation's largest new national park by President Truman. Douglas continued her long campaign—she was president of Friends of the Everglades until age one hundred—to save the Florida swamplands from destruction. Along with Marjorie Harris Carr and Florida Defenders of the Environment, founded in 1969, she opposed the Cross-Florida Barge Canal. The Canal was officially decommissioned in 1990.[51]

Even before World War II, an expanding tourist industry placed additional ecological pressure on the nation's parks. With wartime restrictions on gasoline and rubber lifted, and with newfound access to automobiles, middle-class Americans were taking to the woods in record numbers. The immediate postwar era saw a marked increase in hunting and fishing; eight million hunting licenses were issued in 1945, an increase of one million over prewar totals.[52]

National parks, though paid for by tax dollars, were not accessible to everyone. Recreational spaces for African Americans were circumscribed by law in the Jim Crow South and by custom almost everywhere else in the U.S. As leisure travel burgeoned in the postwar era, as historian Carolyn Finney has described in *Black Faces, White Spaces*, "a racialized outdoor leisure identity" was forced upon black vacationers. Middle-class African Americans preferred auto travel, in part to avoid the Jim Crow rail cars. Helping them on their way was the Negro Motorist Green Book, named for its author and publisher, Victor Hugo Green. Published from 1936 to 1966 (with a hiatus during World War II), the guide provided information about safe and welcoming places for African Americans to stay, eat, and visit. With the assistance of the Green Book, African American travelers made their way to black resorts such as Idlewild, Michigan, or Port Monmouth, New Jersey.[53]

At the same time, African Americans called for desegregating the American landscape, from public accommodations in crowded urban areas to national and state parks. Violent beatings and molestation by whites at public swimming pools and recreation areas prevented African Americans from enjoying leisure in nature. "Among the most coveted urban spaces were those that encouraged young men and women to put aside their daily cares, flirt, and play," explained historian Victoria Wolcott. "This potential for romance, and [whites'] association of African Americas with dirt and disorder, led to whites' insistence that recreational spaces be racially homogenous."[54]

A violent race riot had erupted in Chicago in 1919 when a white bather threw a rock at a young black swimmer whose raft had drifted into the designated white section of the Lake Michigan beach, drowning the boy. NAACP special counsel Thurgood Marshall successfully pursued a 1941 case based on the civil rights laws in Illinois to grant access to a public beach bathhouse to African Americans, but even after the court's decision, the manager of the beach concession met black beachgoers with violence, preventing access. In Miami, Florida, white officials blocked the use of federal funds for recreational amenities for black residents. Pressure for beach access opened Virginia Key, an island beach between the city and Key Biscayne, to African Americans, by 1945. Struggles by African Americans to enjoy public recreational spaces not only challenged segregation but were also a form of unacknowledged environmental activism.[55]

The Bureau of Colored Works had been established by the National Recreation Association in 1919 to provide recreational services to African Americans. Extending that work, the National Park and Recreation Association Ethnic Minority Society (NRPEMS) emerged out of a meeting of the Black Caucus of the Congress for Recreation and Parks at the group's 1969 meeting in Chicago. Formally founded in 1971, NRPEMS goals included desegregating the nation's parks and "productively representing the recreation, park and related leisure service interests and rights of minorities while participating in the overall efforts of the park and recreation profession." The group participated in a National Forum on Blacks and the Park, Recreation, and Conservation Movement at Howard University in 1986 and continues its work to the present.[56]

Atomic Activism

"The age of ecology opened on the New Mexican Desert," wrote historian Donald Worster, "near the town of Alamogordo, on July 16, 1945, with a dazzling fireball of light and a swelling mushroom cloud of radioactive gases."[57] Of the events that impelled postwar environmental activism, none was more cataclysmic than the atomic bomb. Horror over the devastation of Hiroshima and Nagasaki was compounded by alarm about nuclear fallout. As peace advocates became better informed of the dangers posed by atmospheric radiation, they targeted nuclear proliferation and atmospheric testing on ecological grounds.

The disarmament campaign of the 1950s may not have been perceived as "environmental" but it helped to launch environmentalism in several ways: (1) framing issues to focus on the ecological and public health impact of nuclear fallout, nuclear weapons testing, and atomic energy plants; (2) utilizing tactics such as nonviolent direct action protest that environmentalists in Greenpeace, for example, would later replicate; and (3) supplying personnel, connecting scientists and lay activists, many of whom went on to join and form environmental groups. The movement against nuclear armaments also linked rising environmental consciousness—at least within some circles—to anti-colonialism and racial justice.

Harnessing the atom had contributed to the notion that humans were "masters of the universe," Fairfield Osborn, Jr. had noted. That sense of control over nature dissipated over the course of the 1950s, with the ominous recognition that radiation had the capacity to alter nature itself in unseen and unpredictable ways. News coverage of nuclear fallout increased public understanding about ecological relationships. The fear of total annihilation was compounded by the knowledge that, even without nuclear war, fallout from atomic testing permeated human bodies, food, and soil. The bomb, writes Thomas Jundt, "not only forced humans to ponder other ways that they might be destroying the planet; it also provided a means for environmental thinkers to frame the issue in a way that would gain greater attention for their cause."[58]

By 1956, nuclear fallout from atomic tests had met with enough public concern that Democrat Adlai Stevenson highlighted the issue in stump speeches during his unsuccessful presidential bid. Religious leaders, including those of large Protestant denominations, condemned the bomb. With nuclear weapons central to his administration's national security policy, however, Eisenhower responded unequivocally that H-bomb testing "does not imperil the health of humanity."[59]

Again, scientists played a key role in transforming the nuclear threat into an environmental cause. Washington University in St. Louis biologist Barry Commoner began researching the ecological and health impact of nuclear fallout in the mid-1950s. A 1957 petition to the United Nations organized by scientist and Nobel winner Linus Pauling (drafted in Commoner's Washington University office) garnered signatures from more than eleven thousand scientists worldwide seeking a halt to nuclear weapons testing. When humanitarian, physician, theologian, and Nobel Peace Prize winner Albert Schweitzer called for an end to nuclear testing, he noted levels of radioactivity in the Columbia River near the Hanford, Washington, nuclear weapons production facility as one justification. Schweitzer's "Declaration of Conscience" was broadcast from Oslo, Norway, in April 1957. The Declaration helped to inspire the formation of the Committee for a Sane Nuclear Policy, or SANE. Civil rights leader Coretta Scott King was among the group's co-founders.[60]

The year 1957 was a pivotal year for the movement against nuclear testing. That year, in a full-page ad in *The New York Times*, entitled "We Are Facing a Danger Unlike Any Danger That Has Ever Existed," SANE warned that testing nuclear bombs could "contaminate the air that belongs to all peoples, devitalize the land, or tamper with the genetic integrity of man himself." The SANE ad evidenced the turn toward ecological arguments for disarmament. It also joined peace and civil rights movement leaders in presenting those arguments to the public. The four dozen public figures and celebrities signing the ad included Rev. Martin Luther King and Dorothy Height, leader of the National Council of Negro Women (NCNW). Within a year, SANE boasted 130 chapters and an estimated membership of 25,000.[61]

Black Americans had been among the first to denounce Truman's decision to drop the bomb. In the African American-owned newspaper the *Chicago Defender*, W.E.B. DuBois decried the bomb as "a marriage between science and destruction. We have always thought of science as the emancipator. We now see it as the enslaver of mankind." Poet Langston Hughes had written in the *Defender* in 1945, "The atom bomb has terrified the heart of man." Hughes articulated the widespread belief that racism factored into Truman's decision to use the bomb on the Japanese. "So they wait until the war is over in Europe to try them out on colored folks," Hughes wrote.[62]

Expressing opposition that was internationalist in character, African Americans in many walks of life came to see "colonialism, racism, and the bomb as links in the same chain," explains historian Vincent Intondi. NAACP Director Walter White and actor and activist Paul Robeson, among others, expressed internationalist concerns that were also ecological. They opposed the bomb in part because of the impact on workers in what was then called the Belgian Congo, where uranium for nuclear weapons was extracted.[63]

Representatives of twenty-nine African and Asian nations, many of them newly independent, gathered in Bandung, Indonesia, in 1955 to articulate their stance as non-aligned nations in the Cold War and express opposition to the bomb. In June 1962, Ghanaian president Kwame Nkrumah convened "The World Without the Bomb" conference, which several eminent African Americans attended. African and African American opposition to nuclear weapons was also aroused by French plans to test a nuclear weapon in the Sahara Desert. Africans viewed the planned test in the Sahara as a new form of colonialism, and made an ecological argument as well as an economic one, fearing that the planned tests would also devastate the cacao industry in Ghana.[64]

In the 1950s, U.S. activists were reading Richard Gregg's *The Power of Nonviolence* (1934). The Committee for Non-Violent Action (CNVA), a Quaker-initiated effort to unite groups and individuals who advocated nonviolent direct-action protests, originated as Action Against Nuclear Weapons. The CNVA joined the British Direct Action Committee in the Sahara Project to oppose the French tests. One of the principal figures in the Sahara Project was American civil rights leader Bayard Rustin, a close advisor to Rev. Martin Luther King, best known for coordinating the 1963 March on Washington. Rustin had trained in nonviolence while working for the Fellowship of Reconciliation (FOR) and was the person most responsible for nonviolence training early in the Montgomery Bus Boycott. Rustin's upbringing in the Quaker faith converged with Gandhi's radical notion of using nonviolence to confront entrenched and overwhelming power. Named executive secretary of the War Resisters League (WRL) in 1953 and a leading member of CNVA, Rustin traveled to Ghana to oppose French nuclear testing.[65]

King articulated the widespread anxiety of the Atomic Age in 1959 at the War Resisters League's thirty-sixth annual dinner. "Not only in the South, but throughout the nation and the world, we live in an age of conflicts, an age of biological weapons, chemical warfare, atomic fallout and nuclear bombs," said Rev. King, "Every man, woman, and child lives, not knowing if they shall see tomorrow's sunrise," King continued, underscoring the environmental and public health impact of atomic weaponry. "What will be the ultimate value of having established social justice in a context where all people, Negro and White, are merely free to face destruction by strontium 90 or atomic war?"[66]

Citizen Science

In 1952, the U.S. detonated in the South Pacific the hydrogen bomb, a thermonuclear giant six hundred times more powerful than the bomb dropped on Hiroshima. Afterward, levels of strontium 90, a radioactive isotope chemically similar to calcium, increased around the globe. Lodging in teeth and bones, strontium 90 can cause cancer. A 1958 U.S. Public Health Service survey found that St. Louis, Missouri, led the nation in levels of strontium 90.[67] Working with other scientists and with Quaker activists, Barry Commoner founded the Greater St. Louis Citizens' Committee for Nuclear Information (CNI) to research and disseminate information about the health impact of nuclear testing.

For Commoner, the fields of movement were all connected—labor, peace, environment, and civil rights. As a student, at Columbia and then Harvard in the late 1930s, Commoner had encountered the American Left, supported labor union activism, and protested lynchings. Among his Navy duties during World War II was supervising the construction of a DDT sprayer (for beachhead landings) that killed flies, but also fish. As a Navy congressional liaison after the war, he was assigned to work with atomic scientists from Los Alamos as they debated the ethics and future of atomic energy with members of Congress.[68] These experiences led to lifelong commitments to democratizing science and to environmental advocacy.

Commoner helped popularize the understanding that, in his words, "The greatest single cause of environmental contamination of this planet is radioactivity from test explosions of nuclear weapons in the atmosphere." For Commoner, fallout was an illustration of the "destructive impact of technology."[69]

An innovative study that Commoner helped launch in the late 1950s brought into American homes awareness of the radiation threat. The Baby Tooth Survey, as the study was dubbed, documented the presence of strontium 90 in children's teeth. Sponsored by the Committee for Nuclear Information and directed by internist and CNI co-founder Dr. Louise Zibold Reiss, the Baby Tooth Survey received support from the Consumers Union, the American Cancer Society, and the U.S. Public Health Service. The Leukemia Guild of Missouri and Illinois also supported the program.[70]

An early example of "citizen science," the Baby Tooth Survey was brilliantly conceived to educate Americans by involving the public in scientific research. The study also helped to reframe the nuclear issue, linking concerns about war and peace to public health and environmental impact. The success of the Baby Tooth Survey in bringing public attention to fallout was due in part to its focus on maternal and child health. Though the study focused on St. Louis, children and their parents mailed in baby teeth from all over the country. Children received a button reading, "I gave my tooth to science." Volunteers from CNI and the Women's Auxiliary of the St. Louis Dental Society catalogued a total of 320,000 teeth. Reiss, who volunteered full-time for the first three years of the survey, published initial findings in 1961 in *Science*: a marked increase in the levels of strontium 90 in children born after the hydrogen bomb was tested in 1952.[71]

The Baby Tooth Survey demonstrated basic ecological lessons: that bodies are permeable, and that uptake of radioactive material by bodily systems could be harmful, particularly to the young. The portion of the study that analyzed fetal exposure documented that fetuses absorbed radiation, which could yield birth defects as well as cancer.[72]

Knowledge that radiation threatened reproduction mobilized women in particular, who became a key constituency in this growing, ecologically conscious movement. Linking the campaign against nuclear weapons to the threat radiation posed to maternal and child health circumvented McCarthyist attacks that cast critics of American nuclear testing as conspirators in a communist-inspired plot to weaken national security. The Baby Tooth Study is credited with pushing President Kennedy to sign the Partial Test Ban Treaty in 1963.[73]

In May of 1958, Commoner published "The Fallout Problem" in *Science*, in which he called on scientists not only to dispassionately interpret how a specific policy might disturb natural processes, but also to take a moral stand. The article critiqued capitalist production. The nuclear industry, Commoner argued, was attempting to shift concern about environmental contaminants to the postproduction risk of exposure rather than limiting chances of exposure by changing the production process itself. Commoner had a gift for succinct, if oversimplified, formulations of ecological concepts. "Everything is connected to everything else," was his first law of ecology. A botanist of considerable note, Commoner helped to launch a science information movement, co-founding the Scientists' Institute for Public Information (SIPI) in 1963. University-based research institutes such as Commoner's Center for the Biology of Natural Systems, which moved to Queens College in New York in 1981, became nodes of activism.[74]

Commoner would remain an important figure in U.S. environmental and social justice circles for more than half a century. *Time* featured him on its cover in 1970, and again in 1980, when, at age sixty-three, he became a Citizens Party candidate for President. His books *Science and Survival* (1966) and *The Closing Circle* (1971), highlighted the crucial role of science-based inquiry and information. CNI provided information through its newsletter *Nuclear Information*. Committee members shared their findings on radio and television, via periodicals, such as the *National Observer*, and through other organizations such as the Audubon newsletter. Over time, the organization broadened its environmental agenda. *Nuclear Information* became *Scientist and Citizen* in 1964, and CNI changed its name to Center for Environmental Information (CEI) in 1967. The bulletin turned its attention to water pollution in the Mississippi River; its magazine took the name *Environment* in 1969.[75]

Nonviolent Direct Action

As new constituencies sought to counter the worst and most obvious effects of the postwar technological revolution, activists turned increasingly to tactics and forms of organization novel to the conservation cause. They drew on longstanding traditions from the abolitionist movement and on Gandhian philosophy—adding civil disobedience to moral persuasion.[76]

In 1958, Albert Bigelow, a wealthy, white retired navy officer, captained the yacht *The Golden Rule* as it sailed into the Eniwetok Atoll nuclear test zone in the South Pacific. *The Golden Rule*, named for the popular maxim, had a mission, called "Thoreauesque" by the *Boston Herald*: to block scheduled nuclear tests at Eniwetok by positioning the craft near the test site. A Quaker, Bigelow had become a pacifist in the mid-1950s after he and his wife hosted two women from Hiroshima who were in the U.S. for reconstructive surgery. He co-founded the CNVA. In piloting *The Golden Rule* into the nuclear test zone, Bigelow and his crew were practicing one of the most intense forms of nonviolent direct action: nonviolent intervention. Crew members accepted greater personal risk than usually accompanied other forms of nonviolence, protests—marches, parades, vigils—and noncooperation—strikes, economic or election boycotts.[77]

While unsuccessful in two attempts to block the South Pacific tests—*Golden Rule* crew members were arrested by the Coast Guard and sentenced to sixty days in a Honolulu jail—their boldness captured public attention. In so doing, they achieved one of the main goals of nonviolent direct action: creating a spectacular display that aroused sympathy—or at the least notice—of onlookers and opponents alike. "In varying proportions," writes historian Frank Zelko, CNVA activists "blended Quaker pacifism, the Marxist critique of capitalism, anarchism's suspicion of centralized power, an emerging countercultural sensibility, and *Satyagraha* [nonviolence] into a forceful critique of Cold War militarism and a striking set of protest strategies."[78]

As with Bayard Rustin's work, the *Golden Rule* journey illustrates how the movements for disarmament, civil rights, and environmentalism were intertwined.

In 1961, Bigelow signed on with fellow Harvard grad and crew member Jim Peck to be among the first wave of Freedom Riders demanding desegregation of bus and rail terminals throughout the South. When Freedom Riders on the first bus sponsored by the Congress of Racial Equality (CORE) were assaulted by whites at a bus station in Rock Hill, South Carolina, the then fifty-five-year-old Bigelow interposed himself between the assailants and SNCC activist John Lewis, taking blows until a policeman intervened.[79]

Anti-nuclear activists were concerned not only about atomic weaponry, but also about nuclear energy policies developing in the shadow of the Cold War. As bomb development continued, advocates from industry and in Congress made a forceful push for a civilian nuclear energy program. Congress protected the civilian atomic energy industry from full accountability via the 1957 Price-Anderson Act, limiting the liability from a nuclear accident to $560 million.[80] The provision seemed to confirm the staggering magnitude of the potential hazards of nuclear power.

Opposition to nuclear weapons testing led to the signing in 1963 of the partial Nuclear Test Ban Treaty. The treaty was an extraordinary achievement at a crucial moment in the Cold War, not long after the Cuban Missile crisis. "A shaft of light cut into the darkness," President Kennedy called the agreement with the Soviet Union, Great Britain, and other nations that banned nuclear testing in the atmosphere, underwater, and in outer space. The treaty did not halt production, nor did it ban underground testing of nuclear weapons. The move also yielded another technological and environmental threat—a resurgence of chemical and biological weaponry. Spending on these toxic weapons tripled during the Kennedy administration.[81]

New Understandings of the Ecology of Disease

The radiation threat and its connection to cancer were not the only technological developments prompting greater attention to the ecology of disease. Many of the concerns of the late 1940s, "population growth, patterns of agricultural production, and urban decay," as historian Daniel Barber has noted, are now considered environmental issues. Debate about these issues, wrote Barber, "extended prewar conservationist doctrine to more technologically informed analyses of human health, and the health of human surroundings."[82]

Increased industrialization of agriculture in the postwar period escalated the use of pesticides, fertilizers, and growth hormones. The rapid commercialization of synthetic pesticides and other industrial chemicals, including plastics, elevated public concern over hazardous substances in food. Consumer groups and the National Cancer Institute campaigned throughout the 1950s to strengthen oversight of the nation's food and drug supply; they lobbied to limit cancer-causing additives, including pesticides, in the American diet. Led in Congress by James Delaney of Queens, New York, the campaign yielded the amendment in 1958 of the Food, Drugs, and Cosmetic Act Congress had passed two decades earlier. Though the law weakened thresholds for some chemical additives, the Delaney Clause set a zero-tolerance standard for potentially cancer-causing ingredients in food.[83]

The Movement to the Suburbs

"[S]uburbia," argues environmental historian Adam Rome, was "the most rapidly changing environment in the nation" in the postwar years. The rise of environmentalism can be traced to the suburbs, especially to suburban, middle-class white women, Rome contends. "Because the suburbs were domestic places— and women traditionally were caretakers of the domestic," Rome argues, "threats to environmental quality in suburbia were threats to 'the women's sphere.'"[84]

The move to the suburbs was undergirded by an ecological claim: people would be healthier, children freer to roam in the out-of-doors if removed from city soot and industrial squalor. The real estate industry promoted suburban housing developments as the antidote to urban slums. The construction of suburbs was not a new phenomenon, having begun in the nineteenth century, but the postwar period saw unprecedented growth and booms in housing construction in urban as well as suburban centers. The GI bill underwrote home loans for many returning soldiers; the push for home ownership extended housing into vast suburbs. In a January 1958 essay in *Fortune*, William H. Whyte popularized the term "sprawl" to describe the growing suburban landscape. Wider availability of automobiles and a growing network of roads gave access to suburban locations. As Samuel Hays wrote, "after World War II [white] blue-collar workers were able to escape the industrial community as a place of residence."[85]

Suburban developments touted as healthful were not always as pristine as advertised. Racial discrimination was widespread. As environmental public health historian Christopher Sellers has noted, Long Island residents from predominately African American Ronek Park subdivision protested "at a 1952 hearing by a congressional house committee in nearby Bay Shore" against well contamination resulting from closely spaced septic tanks on small suburban lots.[86]

The great migrations of African Americans from the Jim Crow South to American cities north and west reshaped American cities. Begun in the post-Civil War era and picking up during World War I, the largest migration occurred during the second World War. Federal housing policy supported segregation, facilitating whites' departure from cities. As Carl Zimring underscores in *Clean and White: A History of Environmental Racism in the United States*, the occupational and residential segregation that African Americans faced in northern cities left new residents with greater exposure to toxic industries and hazardous wastes.[87]

Urban Ecologies

The flip side of suburban development was the re-engineering of cities in the 1950s. Developers and their critics were busy remaking the urban landscapes through massive urban renewal projects. Cultural historian Francesca Russello Ammon notes the dynamic destruction of cities that resulted. Earth-moving equipment that had been used to dig trenches and buttress armaments during World War II was repurposed for civilian use.[88] An environmental health argument—the need to eliminate unhealthy tenements—moved the bulldozers forward. But the consequences could also be destructive to health.

The National Urban League's neighborhood block club movement was initiated in the late 1910s and flourished with New Deal support in the 1930s, but it had its most successful run between 1945 and 1954 in northern cities, such as Pittsburgh and Chicago. The Chicago Urban League's Block Beautiful contest, co-sponsored by the *Chicago Defender* beginning in the 1940s, exemplified conservation efforts in urban African American neighborhoods. Under the motto "We Fight Blight," block clubs targeted fire hazards and disease-carrying rats and conducted neighborhood cleanup and beautification projects. The annual winner of "Mrs. Block Beautiful," explains environmental historian Sylvia Hood Washington, "was the embodiment of the mature African American women who tried to salvage and transform the brutal environmental conditions that most African Americans found themselves trapped in because of racist housing policies." By 1952, ninety-seven Chicago blocks had clubs. Most were organized by female volunteers. Individual clubs met in neighborhood councils; committees focused on "Health and Sanitation," "Foods and Nutrition," and "Street Alleys and Garbage Collection." The National Association of Colored Women operated a similar campaign. Funded by Sears, Roebuck, and Company, the Community Project Contest awarded prizes to the chapter with the best neighborhood improvement efforts.[89]

Struggles over segregated space that highlighted injustices offer some of the clearest examples of unacknowledged environmentalism. When the Montgomery Improvement Association (MIA) campaigned to desegregate the bus system and open jobs to black citizens in Alabama's capital city, five of the organization's eight primary demands presaged environmental justice themes. Laid out in a flyer entitled "Negroes' Most Urgent Needs," the MIA's concerns included "Negro Representation on the Parks and Recreation Board," "Sub-division for housing," "Congested areas, with inadequate or no fireplugs," "Lack of sewage disposals makes it necessary to resort to out-door privies, which is a health hazard," and, "Narrow streets, lack of curbing, unpaved streets in some sections."[90] All are urban matters that would today be regarded as environmental concerns.

DDT Activism: "A Real Health Movement"

Long before Rachel Carson published her landmark book about DDT, residents of Claxton, Georgia, protested the chemical's effects on their lives. DDT had proved an efficacious means of killing insects, including fleas, lice, and mosquitoes, and thereby limiting transmission of diseases such as typhus and malaria. Military crews sprayed the chemical widely on soldiers and on battle terrain during World War II. Even before manufacturers released DDT for domestic commercial use in August 1945, the U.S. Army began an aggressive spraying campaign in malaria-prone southern states. As public health historian Elena Conis has documented, two sisters, Dottie Colson and Mamie Ella Plyler, began raising questions almost immediately about the damaging effects of an unidentified chemical on their children, farm animals, including dairy cows, and helpful insects, such as bees. The families lived near a defense installation in middle Georgia, Camp Stewart, where they began to suspect that DDT was being sprayed. ("Chemical fallout"—Carson later called it—continued to be sprayed on crops and fields after the war.) When children drank milk from cows doused with DDT, the women complained, "their mouths and throats 'burned, hurt, and swelled.'"[91]

A Georgia health department official did little to address the families' plight but collected from other states "harrowing stories of insecticide poisonings that he kept in his files: the woman who died within hours after eating blackberries bordering a recently sprayed cotton field; the deaths of pilots who flew cotton-dusters; the tenant farmer found collapsed in a sprayed tobacco field," and more. Unable to obtain answers from the Army or health officials and unable to halt the spraying, Colson queried the National Health Council in New York City in 1949 for "advice about how to start a 'real health movement' in her hometown." The following year, Plyler wrote to Georgia Governor Herman Talmadge summarizing the situation and requesting assistance. Plyler and Colson formally petitioned the Georgia Department of Public Health, "to restrict 'the uses of, and methods of applying, insecticides in residential areas,' on the grounds that the chemicals caused 'distressing symptoms, acute suffering and even death in humans and other warm blooded farm animals and fowl.'" Firsthand reports from people like Colson and Plyler informed Rachel Carson's work.[92]

The environmental and public health impact of DDT was talked about, written about, and lobbied about in the late 1940s. Scientists discussed chemical poisoning at international conferences. DDT's deadliness to beneficial insects and bees was understood. Mainstream periodicals including *Harper's*, the *Atlantic Monthly*, and *The New Yorker* ran articles about the dangers of DDT as early as 1945. Carson herself had tried that year to interest *Reader's Digest*, a magazine read at the time by millions, many of them women, in publishing a story about DDT, but the magazine declined. In 1947, Congress passed modest reforms regulating the sale, distribution, and application of what were then known as "economic poisons," including DDT, but did not prevent their use. Widespread spraying continued—on crops, homes, even swimming pools.[93]

Though they lived on the perceived periphery in the rural South, people like Colson and Plyler found themselves at the center of global processes that reshaped human relationships with nature. These women were among those who melded opposition to pesticides and public health advocacy, generating a new movement. As military installations in America brought unregulated wartime technologies to agricultural landscapes, grassroots rural activism grew. As an ingenious array of synthetic chemicals moved from battlefields and workplaces into the middle-class home, women became an important constituency. Socially defined as caregivers, women were often the first to notice the effects of chemicals on infants and children. Colson and Plyler actively sought to form a "real health movement" that would stem the indiscriminate application of harmful chemicals in rural Georgia, near their homes and farms. These citizens, and others like them, would be caught up in the postwar institutions that worshipped the economics of growth. In the industrial workplace, in urban neighborhoods, and sprawling suburbs, Americans confronted a technological revolution that yielded unprecedented ecological disturbance.

The environment-focused legislative achievements of the immediate postwar period were modest, though not insignificant. The Federal Water Pollution Control Act of 1948 and the Air Pollution Control Act of 1955 provided funds for research and cleanup, but left taxpayers, not industry, responsible for financing cleanup. The Federal Insecticide, Fungicide, and Rodenticide Act of 1947 set standards for and required registering and labeling chemicals used in agriculture. "To critics, however," wrote Thomas Jundt, "those standards appeared to be aimed more at legitimizing and defending an emerging chemical industry than at protecting consumers and the environment."[94]

The late 1950s saw a new round of activism regarding DDT. Massive airborne spraying of DDT in the spring of 1957 to fight gypsy moths that were devouring leaf matter and denuding trees on Long Island caused the deaths of birds and fish. Thirteen wealthy residents filed suit to block the U.S. Department of Agriculture (USDA) from continuing to spray. Robert Cushman Murphy, former chief curator of ornithology at the American Museum of Natural History, a mentor and friend to William Vogt, and head of the Long Island chapter of the Nature Conservancy, was among the petitioners. This was no ordinary group of Nassau and Sussex County suburbanites stirred up by DDT spraying. Their work reflected long experience in the conservation movement, as well as international influences on U.S. actors. Robert Cushman Murphy had long traveled internationally as part of his work at the American Museum of Natural History and had represented the Museum at the 1949 ICTPN conference at Lake Success right nearby. Among the plaintiffs who joined Murphy was Archibald Roosevelt, son of former President Theodore Roosevelt.[95]

While her husband traveled, activist Grace Murphy organized, forming in 1956 Women United for Long Island, later Conservationists, United, for Long Island. Mary "Polly" Richards, whose organic garden was sprayed repeatedly by state and federal control planes using DDT mixed in fuel oil, and Marjorie Spock, sister of the famed pediatrician Benjamin Spock, also organized and raised funds for the suit. Ultimately, the suit failed and the U.S. Supreme Court refused to hear an appeal. However, the Long Island DDT lawsuit was among the incidents that motivated Rachel Carson to write *Silent Spring*.[96]

Rachel Carson

Carson's long association with conservation organizations gives evidence that she was deeply involved in the movement she was helping to launch. Her mother was a devotee of the Nature Study movement, so Carson's childhood in rural Pennsylvania pointed her toward exploring nature. A marine biologist who was already an influential writer in the early 1950s, Carson was a much sought-after speaker. She won the National Book Award for her 1951 book *The Sea Around Us*, which stayed on the *New York Times* best-seller list for eighty-six weeks. She maintained ties with women's groups and conservation organizations. She had been elected to the board of the Audubon Society in 1948 and had been a member of the Wilderness Society since 1950. She urged friends to write to the president as part of the campaign against the Echo Park Dam.[97]

Aware of Commoner's work, Carson regarded the St. Louis Committee for Nuclear Information, with its commitment to science and use of volunteer researchers, as a model for research. Carson built upon the broad popularity of the Ban the Bomb campaign and made vivid use of the atomic threat to frame the hazards of chemicals in *Silent Spring*. She called DDT "a new kind of fallout" and compared the chemical to radiation as "the sinister and little-recognized partners of radiation in changing the very nature of the world."[98]

PHOTO 2.1 American marine biologist and conservationist Rachel Carson (1907–64), shown here at work at her home near Silver Spring, Maryland, in August 1962, was deeply involved in the movement she is often credited with launching. Photo by Alfred Eisenstaedt, The *LIFE* Picture Collection, Getty Images.

Silent Spring was greeted in 1962 by a public predisposed to hear her message. In addition to anxiety over nuclear fallout, readers of *Life* and other popular magazines had learned of other ecological disasters, including the 1959 herbicide poisoning of cranberries that made them unfit for Thanksgiving tables. As *Silent Spring* appeared, news of birth defects caused by the drug thalidomide administered to pregnant women was unfolding in the national press.[99]

Like many conservationists, Carson had worked in government, as a biologist for the Fish and Wildlife Service. She also castigated government for failing to regulate chemical pesticides. Carson communicated extensively with other scientists in reporting on the impact of DDT. Like Commoner, Carson was a public scientist, an advocate as well as a writer. She testified twice before Congress about the hazards of pesticides in June 1963, first before a subcommittee of the Committee on Government Operations and then again before the U.S. Senate Committee on Commerce.[100]

Most importantly, Carson pushed a rethinking of conservation principles. She brought together scientific understanding of DDT's impact on avian and other wildlife species with her research into human exposures to DDT. *Silent Spring* told the story of pesticides destroying wildlife and impact on human health in a skillful accessible style. Overuse of pesticides was pushing some species to extinction, she explained. She popularized ecological understandings that chemicals bioaccumulated at different trophic levels. That is, as species moved up the food chain, chemical concentrations multiplied, compounding potential negative effects. She also chronicled widespread opposition to wholesale spraying, in the Northeast against the gypsy moth, and in the South, against the USDA's ill-conceived campaign to eradicate the fire ant.[101]

Despite *Silent Spring*, manufacture of DDT for commercial use ramped up in the U.S. Municipalities struggling with mosquito problems sprayed everywhere, including residential neighborhoods. Scientists soon recognized two big problems with DDT: the chemical killed or injured non-targeted species and failed to kill mosquitos that developed resistance. Once birds had ingested worms and insects containing the chemical, they exhibited characteristic tremors and convulsions and then died. Anti-DDT activism arose in other locales, including Hanover, New Hampshire, where Dartmouth is located, in 1962. In Wisconsin, hearings held by WARF (the Wisconsin Alumni Research Foundation) in 1966, further documented Carson's claims.[102]

Carson raised major themes that continue to concern contemporary environmentalists, including feminist and other historians of science, questioning whether humans "could or should master nature." Carson linked ecosystem ecology with the impact of pesticides on the human health. She explored the ecology of the body, the permeability of the skin, noting the routes of exposure to chemicals. She saw the overuse of pesticides as indicative of the limits of technological progress. She raised questions about the postwar culture of science and the role of experts in determining safe levels of chemical exposure. Moreover, she cast environmental ethics in terms of "rights." Experts had relevant knowledge to contribute, of course, but she felt regular citizens had a "right to know" about the chemicals they were unwittingly ingesting. She anticipated a major theme that would emerge more forcefully in the 1990s, with environmentalists' emphasis on precautionary approaches to chemical regulation.[103]

Carson's revelations about DDT brought attention to the lack of regulation from which the chemical industry benefited. In response, the industry launched a vicious and well-funded attack on Carson's claims. The Monsanto Chemical Company parodied her work in an op ed sent to news outlets nationwide. Entitled "The Desolate Year" and imitating the introduction to *Silent Spring*, the essay envisioned a world without pesticides. Carson had not, in fact, advocated a total ban on chemical pesticides. The assault took a gendered tone, questioning Carson's scientific credentials and accusing her of being "an emotional feminist alarmist." At the same time, in a sly suggestion about her sexual orientation, a former Secretary of Agriculture is reported to have wondered "Why a spinster with no children was so concerned about genetics?"[104] The controversy generated by these attacks may well have gained her readers.

Carson's book crystallized the recognition that humans were fundamentally altering the environment. "The history of life on earth has been a history of interactions between living things and their surroundings," wrote Carson, putting the classic definition of ecology in easy-to-grasp terms. However, now, she pointed out, a qualitative change had taken place. "Only within the moment of time represented by the present century has one species—man—acquired significant power to alter the nature of his world," she wrote. "During the past quarter century this power has not only increased to one of disturbing magnitude but it has changed in character."[105]

Though Carson has been often portrayed as a gentle nature writer—a role she may even have cultivated to reach a wider audience—her message about human health was strong and pointed. The alacrity with which her message took hold suggests the importance it held in reframing conservation and catalyzing a broader social movement. Carson melded previously distinct concerns—wildlife protection and human health—into a coherent framework that helped to bring disparate constituencies together. Carson's work and the activism inspired by *Silent Spring* led to increased government regulation of toxic chemicals in the United States. U.S. Environmental Protection Agency (EPA) administrator William Ruckelshaus issued a ban on DDT in 1972.

The two decades following World War II, then, were not as quiet on the environmental front as people once believed. Conservationism, long linked with nation and patrimony, was reframed as a fight for democracy. For some, conservation was necessary to American supremacy in the Cold War, not incompatible with a doctrine of growth. Others began calling never-ending growth into question as they witnessed the effects of accelerating capitalism on ecological landscapes and on human lives.[106] Local activists and national conservation coalitions achieved gains, not only in the Northeast and West, but also in rural Georgia and the Florida swamps. Arguments for conserving became more ecologically oriented; traditional organizations began attracting a grassroots base. Organizations formed in the period between the 1880s and World War II—The Audubon Society, the Sierra Club, the Izaak Walton League, the Wilderness Society, and the National Wildlife Federation—persisted; most gained strength. However, these groups would have to evolve quickly. The postwar momentum for racial equality, labor rights, women's liberation, and against the expanding conflict in southeast Asia was transforming social activism. To attract new adherents and remain relevant in the upsurge of the 1960s, significant shifts in focus, tactics, and composition would be required.

Notes

1 On the importance of the immediate postwar period, see Robertson, "This is the American Earth," and Jundt, *Greening the Red, White, and Blue*. Dowie, *Losing Ground*, 24; Sellers, *Crabgrass Crucible*, 7.

2 Robertson, "Total War and the Total Environment," 336, 339, 347.

3 United Nations, General Assembly, *Universal Declaration on Human Rights*, A/RES/3/217 A, December 10, 1948, available from un-documents.net/a3r217a.htm.

4 Bullard and Wright, "Environmentalism and the Politics of Equity," 21.

5 Jundt, *Greening the Red, White, and Blue*, 28, 31; Barber, *A House in the Sun*, 7; McNeill and Engelke, *The Great Acceleration*, 39.

6 McNeill, *Something New under the Sun*, 28.

7 Boyer, *By the Bomb's Early Light*, xxi. Casualty estimates vary widely, www.atomicarchive.com/Docs/MED/med_chp10.shtml (accessed May 31, 2017). Richard Rhodes, "Nuclear Options," *New York Times Book Review*, May 15, 2005, 7–8; John Hersey, *Hiroshima*.

8 McNeill, *Something New under the Sun*, 221–26; Jundt, "Dueling Visions," 46; Russell, *War and Nature*; Russell, "Evolutionary History," 214.

9 Davis, *When Smoke Ran Like Water*, 5–9; McNeill and Engelke, *The Great Acceleration*, 22.

10 Jundt, "Dueling Visions," 55; McNeill and Engelke, *The Great Acceleration*, 118.

11 Robertson, "'This Is the American Earth,'" 564.

12 Hays, *A History of Environmental Politics since 1945*, 22.

13 Egan, *Barry Commoner*, 3; Jundt, *Greening the Red, White, and Blue*, 2; Martinez-Alier, *The Environmentalism of the Poor*.

14 Memo from FDR to Secretary of State Cordell Hull, 1944, in Brinkley, *Rightful Heritage*, 561, citing Edgar B. Nixon, ed., Franklin D. Roosevelt and Conservation, 1911–1945, vol. 2 (New York: Franklin D. Roosevelt Library, 1957), 599; Jundt, "Dueling Visions," 44.

15 Klare, *Resource Wars*; Jundt, "Dueling Visions," 44, 45, 47; Ekbladh, *The Great American Mission*, 9.

16 Robertson, "'This is the American Earth,'" 572; Mann, *The Wizard and the Prophet*, 86–87.

17 Robertson, "'This is the American Earth,'" 564; Osborn, *Our Plundered Planet*, 201; Jundt, "Dueling Visions," 59; "Conservation Unit Set Up to Warn U.S.," *The New York Times*, April 6, 1948, 2.

18 Jundt, *Greening the Red, White, and Blue*, 25, 26, 34; Osborn, *Limits of the Earth*.
19 Vogt, *Road to Survival*, 276, 28ff., 34, 133; Mann, *The Wizard and the Prophet*, 393.
20 McCormick, *Reclaiming Paradise*, 70; Vogt, *Road to Survival*, 282–83, 77.
21 Powell, *Vanishing America*, 183.
22 Jundt, "Dueling Visions," 44, 56.
23 McCormick, *Reclaiming Paradise*, 36–37; UNSCCUR, *Proceedings*, n.p.; Jundt, "Dueling Visions," 53–54.
24 UNESCO, *Proceedings and Papers ITCPN*, 214–19; Jundt, "Dueling Visions," 45.
25 UNESCO, *Proceedings and Papers ITCPN*, 3–6; Jundt, "Dueling Visions," 64, citing Ollie E. Fink, "Let's Teach Water Conservation" *Proceedings and Papers ITCPN*, 214–19, 215; Leopold, "The Land Ethic," *A Sand County Almanac*, 237–63.
26 William Vogt, "Let's Examine Our Santa Claus Complex," *Saturday Evening Post*, July 23, 1949, cited in Robertson, "Total War and the Total Environment," 355–56.
27 *Resources for Freedom*, Volume I, Foundations for Growth and Security, A Report to the President by The President's Materials Policy Commission, June 1952, https://babel.hathitrust.org/cgi/pt?id=mdp.39015028172412 (accessed May 31, 2017); Robertson, "Total War and the Total Environment," 336, 339, 356.
28 Barber, *A House in the Sun*, 77–78, 76.
29 Barber, *A House in the Sun*, 156, 158, 165, 188, 166.
30 Leopold, *A Sand County Almanac*, 137–41, 138.
31 Leopold and Brooks, *Game Management*; Brinkley, *Rightful Heritage*, 415, citing Leopold's 1938 essay, "Engineering and Conservation."
32 Gottlieb, *Forcing the Spring*, 69–70; Leopold, *A Sand County Almanac*, 262; Gottlieb, *Forcing the Spring*, 212–13.
33 Beeman, "Friends of the Land," 5, 14, 4, 9, 11, 13.
34 "Our History," The Nature Conservancy, www.nature.org/en-us/about-us/who-we-are/our-history/ (accessed January 19, 2019).
35 Barbour, "Ecological Fragmentation in the 1950s," 233–55, in Cronon, ed., *Uncommon Ground*.
36 Barbour, "Ecological Fragmentation."
37 Barbour, "Ecological Fragmentation," 238–39, 249. William Cronon provides a succinct summary of this debate in *Changes in the Land*, 10–11; Kingsland, *The Evolution of American Ecology*, 162–63.
38 Kingsland, *The Evolution of American Ecology*, 179; Odum and Odum, *Fundamentals of Ecology*.
39 Kingsland, *The Evolution of American Ecology*, 183, 180; Robertson, "'This is the American Earth,'" 574.
40 Lowenthal, *George Perkins Marsh*, 409; Kingsland, *The Evolution of American Ecology*, 155–56; Lowenthal, *George Perkins Marsh*, 412.
41 Rothman, *Saving the Planet*, 99.
42 Dowie, *Losing Ground*, 30; Fox, *The American Conservation Movement*, 279, 281–89.
43 Rothman, *Saving the Planet*, 86; Harvey, *A Symbol of Wilderness*, 266.
44 Rothman, *Saving the Planet*, 98.
45 Rothman, *Saving the Planet*, 106.
46 Stegner, *This Is Dinosaur*; Fox, *The American Conservation Movement*, 285.
47 Rothman, *Saving the Planet*, 103; Harvey, *A Symbol of Wilderness*, 260.
48 Colorado River Storage Act, 43 U.S.C. § 620 et seq.; Public Law 485, 84th Cong. 2d Sess. §3.
49 Harvey, *A Symbol of Wilderness*; Stewart Brand, "California Dreaming; Ill-Informed Ingrates," *New Scientist* (April 3, 1980): 45.
50 Rothman, *Saving the Planet*, 87.
51 Davis, *An Everglades Providence*, 392; MacDonald, *Marjorie Harris Carr*, 192.
52 Brinkley, *Rightful Heritage*, 582.

53 Young, "'The Struggle to Desegregate National Park Campgrounds'"; Finney, *Black Faces, White Spaces*, 79; Herb Boyd, "Victor H. Green and His Indispensable 'Green Book,'" *The New York Amsterdam News*, April 14–20, 2016, 30; McCammack, *Landscapes of Hope*, 60ff.

54 Wolcott, *Race, Riots, and Roller Coasters*, 2.

55 McCammack, *Landscapes of Hope*, 32; Wolcott, *Race, Riots, and Roller Coasters*, 25–26, 39–40, 163–64.

56 Hurley J. Coleman, Jr., "Ethnic Minority Society Recognizes 25 Years of Cultural Diversity," *Parks & Recreation* 31, no. 6 (June 1996): 14; National Recreation and Park Ethnic Minority Society, Inc., *The Colors of Recreation* (Philadelphia: Quantum Leap Publisher, 1996), xv–xvi; National Recreation and Park Ethnic Minority Society, Inc. website, http://nrpems.org/ (accessed October 28, 2018); Kuzmiak, "The American Environmental Movement," 274.

57 Worster, *Nature's Economy*, 342.

58 Jundt, "Dueling Visions," 59; Jundt, *Greening the Red, White, and Blue*, 34.

59 Jundt, *Greening the Red, White, and Blue*, 16; Laurence S. Wittner, "Blacklisting Schweitzer," *Bulletin of the Atomic Scientist*, May/June 1995, 55–61, 56; Egan, *Barry Commoner*, 53.

60 Egan, *Barry Commoner*, 54–55, 38; Kinchy, "African Americans in the Atomic Age," 313.

61 "We Are Facing a Danger Unlike Any Danger That Has Ever Existed," Committee for a Sane Nuclear Policy (SANE), *The New York Times*, November 15, 1957; Intondi, *African Americans Against the Bomb*, 59; Daniel Geary, "'Becoming International Again': C. Wright Mills and the Emergence of a Global New Left, 1956–1962," *Journal of American History* 95, no. 3 (December 2008): 710–36, 722.

62 Intondi, *African Americans Against the Bomb*, 1; Kinchy, "African Americans in the Atomic Age," 297; Langston Hughes, *Chicago Defender*, August 14, 1945, cited in Arnold Rampersad, *The Life of Langston Hughes*. 2nd ed., vol. 2. (Oxford; New York: Oxford University Press, 2002), 103; Intondi, *African Americans Against the Bomb*, 15, citing Langston Hughes, "Here to Yonder: Simple and the Atomic Bomb," *Chicago Defender*, August 18, 1945, 14.

63 Intondi, *African Americans Against the Bomb*, 12; Kinchy, "African Americans in the Atomic Age," 295.

64 Intondi, *African Americans Against the Bomb*, 4, 46–47, 51.

65 Gregg, *The Power of Nonviolence*; Intondi, *African Americans Against the Bomb*, 52–55.

66 Intondi, *African Americans Against the Bomb*, 64.

67 Bryce Nelson, "Scientist and Citizen: St. Louis Group Broadens Educational Role," *Science* 157, no. 3791 (August 25, 1967): 903–07; J.E. Campbell, G.K. Murthy, A.S. Goldin, H.B. Robinson, F.J. Weber, C.P. Straub, and K.H. Lewis, "The Occurrence of Strontium-90, Iodine-131, and Other Radionuclides in Milk—May 1957, through April 1958," *American Journal of Public Health* 49, no. 2 (February 1959): 225–35, 233.

68 Egan, *Barry Commoner*, 19, 21, 29.

69 Egan, *Barry Commoner*, 47, citing Barry Commoner, "Fallout and Water Pollution—Parallel Cases," *Scientist and Citizen* 6 (December 1964): 2–7, 2; McCormick, *Reclaiming Paradise*, 70.

70 Louise Zibold Reiss, "Strontium-90 Absorption by Deciduous Teeth," *Science* 134, no. 3491 (1961): 1669–73, 1673.

71 Reiss, "Strontium-90 Absorption," 1669, 1671, Table 2.

72 Reiss, "Strontium-90 Absorption," 1672.

73 Dennis Hevesi, "Dr. Louise Reiss, Who Helped Ban Atomic Testing, Dies at 90," *The New York Times*, January 19, 2011.

74 Barry Commoner, "The Fallout Problem," *Science* 127, no. 3305 (May 2, 1958): 1023–26, 1025; Egan, *Barry Commoner*, 90; Commoner, *The Closing Circle*, 33; Egan, *Barry Commoner*, 93.

75 Egan, *Barry Commoner*, 63; Bryce Nelson, "Scientist and Citizen: St. Louis Group Broadens Educational Role," *Science*, New Series 157, no. 3791 (August 25, 1967): 903–07, 903; Egan, *Barry Commoner*, 88.

76 Manisha Sinha, "Did Abolitionists Cause the Civil War?," 108, in Andrew Delbanco, John Stauffer, Manisha Sinha, Darryl Pinckney, and Wilfred M. McClay, *The Abolitionist Imagination* (Cambridge: Harvard University Press, 2012).

77 Zelko, *Make it a Green Peace!*, 14–15; Sharp, *The Politics of Nonviolent Action*, 158.

78 Bigelow, *The Voyage of the Golden Rule*; Zelko, *Make it a Green Peace!*, 16, 20.

79 Ray Arsenault, *Freedom Riders: 1961 and the Struggle for Racial Justice* (Oxford; New York: Oxford University Press, 2006), 122, 145–46.

80 42 U.S. Code § 2210: Indemnification and limitation of liability. Congress has raised the liability limit several times.

81 John F. Kennedy, "Speech to the Nation on the 1963 Nuclear Test Ban Treaty," July 26, 1963; Harris and Paxman, *A Higher Form of Killing*, 206.

82 Barber, *A House in the Sun*, 92.

83 Langston, *Toxic Bodies*, 62, 71, 82–83.

84 Rome, "Give Earth a Chance," 538; Rome, *The Genius of Earth Day*, 34.

85 William H. Whyte, "Urban Sprawl," *Fortune*, September 1957; Hays and Hays, *Beauty, Health, and Permanence*, 23.

86 Sellers, *Crabgrass Crucible*, 114.

87 Zimring, *Clean and White*.

88 Ammon, *Bulldozer*, 6.

89 Sylvia Hood Washington, "Mrs. Block Beautiful," in Jordan et al., *Land and Power*, 134, 144–47; Blum, *Love Canal Revisited*, 133–39.

90 "Negroes' Most Urgent Needs" by the Montgomery Improvement Association, Inez Jessie Baskin Papers, Alabama Department of Archives and History, Montgomery, Alabama, as displayed at the Birmingham Civil Rights Institute.

91 Letter from Mrs. B.C. Plyler to R.H. Fetz, April 27, 1951, Folder: T-47: Toxicology–Economic Poisons–Insecticides–Mrs. Plyler & Colson, Box 3, Record Group 26, Subgroup 4, Series 21, Georgia Archives, cited in Elena Conis, "DDT Disbelievers: Health and the New Economic Poisons in Georgia after World War II," *Southern Spaces*, October 28 2016, https://southernspaces.org/2016/ddt-disbelievers-health-and-new-economic-poisons-georgia-after-world-war-ii#footnote1_i5cjg95 (accessed February 28, 2017).

92 Conis, "DDT Disbelievers"; Letter from Mrs. H.J. Colson to The National Health Council, January 31, 1949, Folder: T-47: Toxicology–Economic Poisons–Insecticides–Mrs. Plyler & Colson, Box 3, Record Group 26, Subgroup 4, Series 21, Georgia Archives, cited in Conis, "DDT Disbelievers"; Letter from Mrs. B.C. Plyler to Hon. Herman Talmadge, August 17, 1950, Folder: Plyler and Colson; Petition submitted to the Georgia Department of Public Health, October 24, 1950, Folder T-47: Toxicology – Economic Poisons – Insecticides – Mrs. Plyler & Colson, all in Box 3, Record Group 26, Subgroup 4, Series 21, Georgia Archives, cited in Elena Conis, "DDT Disbelievers"; Carson, *Silent Spring*, 27, 159.

93 Associated Press, "DDT Kills Bees, Other Insects Helpful to Man," *Augusta Chronicle*, August 28, 1945, 1; McCormick, *Reclaiming Paradise*, 214n54; The Federal Insecticide, Fungicide, and Rodenticide Act, 7 U.S.C. Ch. 6. §136.

94 Jundt, "Dueling Visions," 68.

95 Sellers, *Crabgrass Crucible*, 103; UNESCO, *Proceedings and Papers ITCPN*; Lear, *Rachel Carson: Witness for Nature*, 319.

96 Sellers, *Crabgrass Crucible*, 99; Lear, *Rachel Carson: Witness for Nature*, 306, 319; *Murphy v, Butler*, 362 U.S. 929 (1960); Sellers, *Crabgrass Crucible*, 135.

97 Lear, *Rachel Carson: Witness for Nature*, 258.

98 Lear, "Introduction," Carson, *Silent Spring*, xi; Lear, *Rachel Carson: Witness for Nature*, 182, 180; Egan, *Barry Commoner*, 87; Carson, *Silent Spring*, 39, 6.

99 "Mercy, Ma! No Cranberries?" *Life*, November 23, 1959, 29ff.; John Mulliken, "A Woman Doctor Who Would Not Be Hurried," *Life*, August 19, 1962, 28ff.; Lear, *Rachel Carson: Witness to Nature*, 359, 411.

100 Carson, *Silent Spring*, 39.

101 Carson, *Silent Spring*, 158–61, 161–69.

102 Wurster, *DDT Wars*, 1–25.

103 Langston, *Toxic Bodies*, 85; Lear, *Rachel Carson: Witness to Nature*, 429; Sarah L. Thomas, "A Call to Action: Silent Spring, Public Disclosure, and the Rise of Modern Environmentalism," 185–203, 186–87, in Crane and Egan, *Natural Protest*; Carson, *Silent Spring*, 278.

104 Lear, *Rachel Carson: Witness to Nature*, 429–31.

105 Carson, *Silent Spring*, 5–6.

106 Robertson, "Total War and the Total Environment," 354–55.

3

EXPANDING THE FIELD OF MOVEMENTS ·

(1963–1980)

If a movement is to be judged by its policy victories, by far the most successful era for environmentalism extended from the passage of the Wilderness Act of 1964 to the enactment of the Superfund law in 1980. Among developments that contributed to a remarkable number of policy successes was a string of pollution disasters that awakened the media. The most visible and spectacular toxic incidents were broadcast via television into American homes. Pop culture made ecology fashionable. The public flocked to decades-old wilderness protection groups like the Sierra Club and The Wilderness Society, and new direct-action organizations, such as Greenpeace, formed. Nonprofits dedicated to melding environmental science and litigation, including the Environmental Defense Fund and the Natural Resources Defense Council, began to wield muscle in court. Environmentalists rallied to enact policy changes, partnering with labor unions, public health professionals, and the consumer movement. Ecology activism intersected with other social movements that were centered on identity, power, and inequality—movements for women's liberation, racial justice, and an end to the Vietnam War. Struggles over the environmental conditions in cities and the farmworkers' campaign against pesticides operated alongside wilderness advocacy. Spurred by protests, teach-ins, and community pressure, legislators began to act.

In the early 1960s, politicians generally accepted the notion, which had roots in the Progressive Era, that government had a role in curbing industrial pollution. Reform liberalism envisioned an even broader role for government not only in protecting traditional liberalism's commitments to private property, individual rights, and the rule of law, but also in underwriting equal opportunity and a better quality of life. A majority in Congress voted to expand upon basic New Deal era economic security programs.[1] The emerging discourse staked a new citizenship claim for Americans: the right to a clean and healthy environment.

Environmental protection legislation so abounded that the era has been tagged, now somewhat wistfully, as "the Golden Age" of environmental policy reform. However, the work was not easy and the outcome never assured.

The 1960s were both a period of optimism and a time of uncertainty and fear. A wave of assassinations shook the nation to its core—President John F. Kennedy (November 22, 1963) Malcolm X (February 21, 1965), Rev. Martin Luther King, Jr. (April 4, 1968), and Bobby Kennedy (June 6, 1968). The Cold War and lingering McCarthyism hung over every policy dispute. U.S. involvement in Vietnam deepened, provoking intense national debate. By the 1970s, even as environmentalists scored some of their biggest legislative victories and real improvements in air and water quality, economic transformation and conservative realignment began to undercut their ambitious agenda.

The Wilderness Act of 1964

Nature advocates' first major legislative victory in the 1960s was the passage of the Wilderness Act of 1964. The legislative push to maintain wilderness zones on public lands had begun in earnest almost a decade earlier, spurred by the conservation movement's success in defeating Echo Park Dam and the desire to forestall further attempts at land grabs in national parks. Interest in outdoor recreation had soared since World War II, but the upsurge in road-building to accommodate burgeoning tourism threatened the very wildlands that people wanted to visit. Extractive uses of public lands—mining, logging, grazing—had also expanded significantly.

In 1956, at the urging of the Wilderness Society, Minnesota Senator Hubert Humphrey introduced a bill that the Society's executive secretary Howard Zahniser had helped to craft. Characterized by Muir biographer Stephen Fox as "one of the least known and most influential conservationists since World War II," Zahniser, despite ill health, spent the next eight years crisscrossing the country, mobilizing allies, and lobbying to pass the measure. Under his leadership the Wilderness Society had grown from a "small and select" five hundred members in 1945, to 3,500 in 1949, and 25,000 in 1964. The campaign for wilderness zones rallied many of the same organizations and individuals who had helped protect Dinosaur National Monument. The General Federation of Women's Clubs, the American Planning and Civic Association, and organized labor, in the form of the America Federation of Labor-Congress of Industrial Organizations (AFL-CIO), joined The Wilderness Society, the Sierra Club, the Nature Conservancy, and the National Wildlife Federation in pressing for the bill. Financial support from the Robert Marshall Wilderness Trust, left by Marshall at his untimely death in 1939, undergirded the long campaign for the Act's passage.[2]

The proposed measure was bold, aiming to maintain roadless areas to prevent any further incursion of motorized vehicles upon designated public lands. Opponents included manufacturers of off-road vehicles and motorboats as well as timber, mining, and grazing interests, who were accustomed not only to motorized access but also to significant income from low-cost leases of public land. The National Park Service and the Forest Service at first objected to the proposal as limiting their discretion to manage public lands. Still smarting from the Echo Park Dam fight, Colorado Democratic congressman Wayne Aspinall opposed the bill and succeeded in ensuring congressional oversight vis-à-vis the executive branch over designating future wilderness lands. Cast by opponents of the legislation as anti-modern and anti-growth, Zahniser told a Sierra Club audience in San Francisco in 1961, "We are not fighting progress, we are making it." Zahniser died of a heart attack a week after testifying for the Act before Congress. Advocates overcame significant opposition in part by linking "patriotism, spirituality, outdoor recreation, and a respect for nature."[3]

Passed with significant majorities in both houses, the law established the National Wilderness Preservation System, designating more than nine million acres of public lands as roadless, thereby protected from motorized vehicles and chain saws. Importantly, the law made provisions for creating additional wilderness areas. Pragmatic compromises permitted grazing and recreational tours, as well as mineral exploration for a limited period. As defined by the Act, "A wilderness, in contrast with those areas where man and his works dominate the landscape, is hereby recognized as an area where the earth and its community of life are untrammeled by man, where man himself is a visitor who does not remain." For novelist Wallace Stegner, whose 1960 "Wilderness Letter" is credited with helping to build support for the Act, protecting wilderness was "a means of reassuring ourselves of our sanity as creatures, a part of the geography of hope." Though implementation was beset with challenges, prolonged advocacy would bring a more than tenfold expansion of areas designated as wilderness over the next fifty years.[4]

Fighting Pesticides

The suburban scientists and birders who had lost their challenge to DDT spraying on Long Island in the 1950s renewed their efforts in the mid-1960s, backed by Carson's research and a shift in public opinion. Representing the group in a 1966 lawsuit was an aggressive young personal injury attorney, Victor Yannacone, a Long Island resident who adopted the motto "Sue the Bastards." Victor, his wife Carol, and the Brookhaven Town Natural Resources Committee, sought an injunction against DDT spraying by the Suffolk County Mosquito Control Commission. Yannacone made use of a legal tool that had worked for civil rights lawyers: the class action lawsuit. The suit yielded a temporary injunction on spraying that remained in place long enough for residents to persuade the local Mosquito Commission to stop using DDT. Awakened to the prospect that connecting science and the law might prove a fruitful method of winning conservation victories, the Long Island group incorporated the Environmental

Defense Fund in 1967. The name, echoing that of the NAACP Legal Defense Fund, acknowledged the influence of the civil rights movement.[5]

Few groups were more harshly affected by DDT and other pesticides than farmworkers, many of whom were recruited from Mexico to plant, pick, and process fruits and vegetables for American tables. Temporary status and racial oppression restricted farmworkers' avenues for protest. Nevertheless, in 1962, Cesar Chavez and Dolores Huerta launched the National Farm Workers Association, which in 1966 became the United Farm Workers Organizing Committee (UFWOC, later the UFW). Initially, organizing efforts focused in the San Joaquin Valley in California, where, given the Mediterranean climate and long growing season, farmworkers had nurtured a rich agricultural region. The struggle for a contract and against pesticides linked workers' rights, Chicano/Latino identity, and environmental health in an intersectional campaign. Chavez and Huerta are now viewed as major figures in the movement for environmental justice, though the term had not been coined when they began organizing against pesticide exposures in the field.

The pesticide poisoning problem was severe. In 1967, the California Department of Public Health reported that between 1954 and 1967, "agriculturally related pesticide injuries [had] continuously accounted for over 60 percent of all reported injuries." Growers posted little to no information about the chemicals deployed in the fields. "As long as the present policy of secrecy is maintained," reported the farmworker newsletter *El Malcriado* in 1969, "the government agencies will remain servants of the oil, chemical, and agribusiness industries, profits will take precedence over public safety, and America's food supply will be subject to increasing contamination and poisoning."[6]

The focus on pesticide exposure was key to the union's success. "We will not tolerate the systematic poisoning of our people," wrote Chavez in a letter to growers in 1969. Chavez's appeal to growers was explicitly environmental. "What could have been the harm of such a private and frank discussion of how best we could promote good health, safety, a balanced ecology, and a clean environment in the production of table grapes?" Chavez and Huerta pursued legal and administrative challenges to pesticide use as well as a consumer boycott of table grapes. These measures proved crucial in shifting the unequal power dynamic between the growers and marginalized workers to win union contracts.[7]

Farmworkers received "only minimal assistance from established environmental organizations," social scientist Laura Pulido has noted. The San Francisco Bay Area Chapter of the Sierra Club, for example, focused its opposition to DDT on ending spraying inside Yosemite National Park. Pulido attributes the lack of support to the environmental movement's historical focus on wilderness protection and the conservative politics of the Valley region. UFWOC leaders did find a few allies among national groups, including the Environmental Defense Fund (EDF), which was already opposing DDT spraying on Long Island. UFWOC's

PHOTO 3.1 Congressional hearings in 1969 revealed an epidemic of pesticide exposure among farmworkers, *El Malcriado: The Voice of the Farm Worker*, November 16–30, 1969. Photo by Walter P. Reuther Library, Archives of Labor and Urban Affairs, Wayne State University.

campaign also received support from Barry Commoner at the Scientists' Institute for Public Information, from Tony Mazzocchi of the Oil, Chemical, and Atomic Workers Union (OCAW), and from Ralph Nader's Agribusiness Accountability Project, directed by Texas populist Jim Hightower.[8]

Working with California Rural Legal Assistance (CRLA) and the EDF, the UFW first petitioned the Food and Drug Administation (FDA) for a ban on DDT under the Delaney Clause of the Food and Drug Act that prohibited cancer-causing additives to food. Bowing to pressure from agribusiness, the FDA refused.[9]

The UFW won a pathbreaking contract with Delano, California, table grape growers in July 1970. The contract included a significant health and safety provision, prohibiting altogether growers' use of certain chemicals, including DDT, aldrin, dieldrin, endrin, and parathion. The contract endorsed co-management regarding chemicals, establishing a Health and Safety Committee of workers to participate in making rules for the handling of pesticides in the fields. The contract also gave the worker the right to refuse to work if "to do so would immediately endanger his health or safety." The struggle shifted to enforcing the contract provisions in the fields. (The 1970 Occupational Safety and Health Act, which offered some protection to industrial workers, exempted farmworkers, who were subject to much less protective EPA rules. The EPA finally banned DDT in 1972.) The alliance between the EDF and the UFW—which EDF attorney Charles Wuster later termed a "marriage of convenience"—did not endure.[10]

1960s Counterculture Embraces Ecology

Creating and sustaining an oppositional culture—one that positions itself as an alternative to the status quo—is crucial to movement-building. In the 1960s, pop culture popularized environmental concerns and shaped individuals' identities as environmentalists. Activist folk-singer Malvina Reynolds' "Fallout," released in 1962, became an anthem for the test ban treaty movement. Taking aim at pollution, satirical singer/songwriter Tom Lehrer urged tourists to enjoy American cities in 1965, but just "Don't drink the water and don't breathe the air!" Spirit lead vocalist Jay Ferguson's song "Fresh Garbage," from the group's 1968 debut album, declared, "The world's a can for your fresh garbage." Folky blues artist Richie Havens, who had recorded a song about the urban pollution crisis, was the opening act at Woodstock, the iconic counterculture event in August 1969. "Smothered cities choke and yell with fumes and gas," he sang. The destruction of nature—replacing the Hawaiian paradise with a parking lot—was the subject of Joni Mitchell's iconic refrain in "Big Yellow Taxi." Mitchell also urged listeners to "Put away that DDT." Marvin Gaye's "Mercy Me (The Ecology)," which came out in 1971, linked multiple environmental causes. As pop music historian James E. Perone has noted, Gaye targeted "radiation underground and in the atmosphere, urban overcrowding, poisoned oceans, and the dying birds, fish, and other animals that are impacted by humans' abuse of the environment."[11]

At the heart of the counterculture that emerged in the 1960s was a critique of technocratic society. Theodore Roszak's *The Making of a Counter Culture: Reflections on the Technocratic Society and Its Youthful Opposition* appeared prescient on the subject, coming out two weeks after Woodstock. Roszak spoke about and to youth "radically disaffiliated" from mainstream culture, who sought "to discover new types of community, new family patterns, new sexual mores, new kinds of livelihood, new esthetic forms, new personal identities on the far side of power politics, the bourgeois home, and the consumer society." Neo-Marxist philosopher Herbert Marcuse's 1964 book, *One-Dimensional Man*, explicitly linked technology with the destruction of nature and, ultimately, of human well-being.[12]

By 1970, major news outlets were hiring reporters to cover the ecology beat; investigative journalists were exposing hazardous industry practices. Environmental organizations themselves published newsletters, specialized periodicals, and topical reports. Entrepreneurial writer Stewart Brand's *The Whole Earth Catalog*, published annually between 1968 and 1972, was avidly read by counterculture eco-activists. The large format book featured "Access to Tools" for saving the planet. "Google in paperback," Apple founder Steve Jobs later called the *Catalog*. Welcoming technological solutions to the environmental crisis, Brand once said, "[T]echnology is liberating if you make it so." For Brand, individual consumers and entrepreneurial innovation, not government, were key to reducing human impact on the planet. As historian Ted Steinberg put it, "The future would rest on a change in lifestyle, not on regulation or protest." Despite championing simple living, the *Catalog* was chockful of consumer goods, an early manifestation of "green consumption."[13] Green consumerism could be two-edged: consumers could help steer the marketplace by boycotting ecologically harmful products and buying eco-friendly ones, but they were still participating in a wasteful consumption-driven economy.

Ecology-minded activists also gravitated to European economist Ernst Friedrich Schumacher's *Small is Beautiful: Economics as If People Mattered*, first published in 1973. Schumacher helped to shape what became known as the "appropriate technology" movement, advocating simple and inexpensive or "intermediate" technologies that could lighten the burden of work, especially for the poor in developing nations. While acknowledging that individuals could do much to save the planet, Schumacher, who had helped design the British social security system, argued for a broad political transformation—a decentralized form of socialism, perhaps including nationalization of larger industries. Conservation was necessary, he argued, given that humans "had broken into nature's larder and now [are] emptying it out at a breathtaking speed." Schumacher made several speaking tours of America. In 1977, he attracted an audience of five thousand in Ann Arbor, Michigan, and met with President Carter.[14]

Ralph Nader, the foremost figure in the fight for safer consumer goods during this period, published in 1965 his best-known work, *Unsafe at Any Speed*, exposing the dangers automobiles pose to people and the environment. Nader attributed 55 to 60 percent of air pollution to the auto industry. Because industry was by far the main source of pollution, Nader's organizations, including the Public Interest Research Group and Public Citizen, demanded corporate accountability.[15] Volunteering as one of "Nader's Raiders" was a plum position for environmentalist law students.

The American Left influenced the environmental movement directly and indirectly. However, amid memories of McCarthyism, the overriding anticommunism of the Cold War, repression within the Soviet Union, and strategy differences, the major environmental organizations distanced themselves from outward relationships with the communist and socialist left, where the labor, public health, and consumer movements had traditionally found support in America. As journalist Mark Dowie later put it, "critics of capitalism. . .have never been welcome in leadership circles" in the mainstream environmental movement.[16]

Nevertheless, social ecologist Murray Bookchin, a member of the Communist Party USA in the 1930s and the Socialist Workers Party in the 1940s, developed a following as an anarchist ecologist after publishing *Our Synthetic Environment* under the pen name of Lewis Herber in 1962. A proponent of radical ecology, a philosophy he labeled "communalism," Bookchin called for "new patterns of production, reproduction, and consciousness," including governance by citizens' assemblies. Bookchin later founded the School of Social Ecology in Vermont. "To radical leftists such as Bookchin, Marcuse, and Commoner," writes historian Michael Egan, the peace and environmental movements were "part of a larger critique of capitalist modes of production and power, and the unequal distribution of wealth and welfare."[17]

Many participants in the New Left, including the young activists of Students for a Democratic Society (SDS), shared ecology concerns but were ambivalent toward mainstream environmentalism. Critical of the movement's failure to articulate a more thoroughgoing indictment of capitalist production and consumption, the New Left also opposed government power at a time when conservationists and other environmental advocates were turning to the state for greater regulatory control, if not the recognition of "environmental rights."[18]

Theologies for the Earth

Religion remained an enduring source of many environmentalists' dedication to protecting the planet and its inhabitants. "Blessed be the nation that keeps its waters clean," wrote songwriter and social justice advocate Pete Seeger in a poem to his daughter while camping on an island in Maine in 1964. Eastern religion offered an alternative spiritual source of reverence for nature. Buddhism found an increasing number of adherents in the United States, especially among counterculture activists. Nature poet and activist Gary Snyder, for example, was profoundly influenced by Buddhism.[19]

As early as the mid-1950s, Lutheran theologian Joseph Sittler, Jr. had called for "A Theology for Earth." Sittler, who lectured widely, condemned the practice of using nature "as a godless warehouse or to rape as a tyrant." Instead, he argued for a Christian theology that placed humans alongside nature, in partnership. Historian of science Lynn White's provocative speech to a snowbound gathering of the American Association of Arts and Sciences in Washington, D.C., in 1967 spurred discussion of religion and ecology. Environmentalist Christians were profoundly shaken by his talk, "The Historical Roots of our Ecologic Crisis," published that year in the journal *Science*. White charged that the Judeo-Christian tradition encouraged anthropocentrism and justified humans' exploitation of nature. Beginning with the call in Genesis for human dominion over the Earth, biblical injunctions contributed to environmental degradation, White argued. "Christianity bears a huge burden of guilt," wrote White, "We shall continue to have a worsening ecologic crisis until we reject the Christian axiom that nature has no reason for existence save to serve man." The requisite response, White argued, was religious social action to reverse environmental damage. Theologians and other scholars critiqued White's interpretation of scripture and identified a long tradition of Judeo-Christian worldviews sympathetic to environmental protection. In the wake of White's critique, thousands of local study and action groups in many denominations began working for ecological protection.[20]

Responses to Urban Ecological Problems

In the nation's cities, activists took on environmental concerns like highways and housing, pollution and parks. New York City master developer Robert Moses's plan to bulldoze a cross-town expressway through Lower Manhattan propelled *Architectural Forum* journalist Jane Jacobs and her neighbors into action. Jacobs' book *The Death and Life of Great American Cities* (1961) critiqued the modernist urban renewal programs of the 1950s for sapping cultural vitality and "organized complexity" from city life. Jacobs proposed that cities draw strength and security from the social interaction encouraged by stoops and sidewalks in neighborhoods rich in shops, markets, and low-rise dwellings. She put her ideas to work, leading successful movements to save Greenwich Village from demolition and to block construction of the expressway.[21]

Urbanist Lewis Mumford, whom Indian historian Ramachandra Guha has called "the forgotten environmentalist," likewise critiqued city planners' strategies for urban development. In a fifty-year career, spanning the 1920s through the 1960s, Mumford chronicled the history of cities. A proponent of regional planning, Mumford helped organize the Face of the Earth Conference in 1955. Guha and Spanish economist Joan Martínez-Alier credit Mumford with "some of the earliest and finest thinking on bioregionalism, anti-nuclearism, biodiversity, alternate energy paths, ecological urban planning, and appropriate technology." Mumford "focused simultaneously on cultural diversity and relations of power *within* human society, refusing to divorce individual attitudes to nature from their social, cultural and historical contexts."[22]

Activists found urban environmental inequalities deeply connected to political marginalization. The sanitation workers' strike Dr. King was in Memphis to support in 1968 emphasized human rights and dignity for the men and women whose dirty jobs linked them directly to maintaining a clean urban environment.[23] The Memphis march focused on racial justice and labor rights but also targeted previously unacknowledged environmental inequalities.

In Harlem, black urbanites defined their campaigns not as environmentalism but as demands for "community control." "Black power urbanism," explained historian Brian D. Goldstein, countered top-down plans for urban renewal projects with community-based design. Formed in 1964, the Architects'

Renewal Committee in Harlem (ARCH) engaged in "advocacy planning," establishing "the first community design center—a new vehicle for citizen participation that would soon proliferate across all major American cities." ARCH also joined East Harlem residents in protesting a proposed sewage plant on the Hudson River in 1968. Kenneth Simmons, an African American architect from San Francisco who worked with ARCH, wrote in 1967, "We must. . .control our land; control our geographic community."[24]

In October 1968, in Washington, D.C., Urban League Director Sterling Tucker spoke on "Nature and the Ghetto Dweller" in a symposium on "Man and Nature in the City" initiated by Secretary of the Interior Stewart Udall and sponsored by the Interior Department's Bureau of Sport Fisheries and Wildlife. (Udall's 1963 book, *The Quiet Crisis*, had directly addressed urban decay as well as the need for conservation of natural resources.) Not only were there fewer city parks in black neighborhoods, said Tucker, they were "esthetically and functionally inadequate." "Rotting garbage can be found on almost any ghetto block," Tucker continued. "[T]here is a great challenge for all of us to find a way to bring these beauties [of nature] and these new aspects of life closer to the environment and the realities of the youngsters in the city, the children of the ghetto."[25]

Black revolutionary organizations such as the Black Panthers, founded in 1966, also worked on issues that today would be considered environmental. Violent confrontations between the Black Panthers and the police have overshadowed the organization's legacy. However, through their "Serve the People" breakfast programs and free medical clinics in long disfranchised communities, the Panthers furthered a new ecology of public health in urban black neighborhoods. The Panthers spearheaded rat eradication programs, held screenings for lead paint poisoning, and demanded city officials clean up neglected neighborhoods. The Party's attention to "social health" and fighting racial discrimination, writes sociologist Alondra Nelson, "underscored that extramedical factors, and not just biological ones, contributed to the disparate illness burden on poor Black communities."[26]

Black agrarianism underwent a resurgence in the 1960s and 1970s as revolutionary nationalists linked local demands for community control to broader struggles for self-determination and control of land. As historian Russell Rickford explains, "Liberation was worthless, these thinkers argued, unless it delivered meaningful black sovereignty—a goal that required control of the critical social space, natural resources, and means of production that land embodied."[27]

Rural Advocacy

Civil rights workers in the rural South also engaged with environmental concerns. Student Nonviolent Coordinating Committee organizer Doris Derby's work with the Child Development Group of Mississippi, forerunner to national Head Start, included conducting nature study classes with African American children. Fannie Lou Hamer, the voting rights trailblazer who led the Mississippi Freedom Democratic Party delegation to the 1964 Democratic

National Convention, in 1969 launched the Freedom Farm Corporation, an interracial cooperative farming venture, and the Sunflower County Pig Bank, which distributed pregnant hogs for raising and let households "butcher [their] dividends." With support from Dorothy Height and the National Council of Negro Women, these initiatives sought food security and economic self-sufficiency for Mississippi Delta communities.[28]

African American activists were often first to join forces with other people of color facing environmental threats. For example, in 1966, comedian and civil rights activist Dick Gregory was jailed in Washington state for participating in a "fish-in" held by the Nisqually Indians and other tribes to protest restrictions on Native fishing rights. Inspired by civil rights sit-ins and organized by the Survival of the American Indian Society, these protests at Frank's Landing in Puget Sound sought to prevent overfishing by commercial fisheries and to restore native treaty rights to fish in the region's bays and streams. At issue were the tribes' ecological heritage and livelihoods, as well as treaty rights and tribal sovereignty. Dr. King telegraphed his support. The Southern Christian Leadership Conference (SCLC) endorsed the effort; the NAACP Legal Defense Fund and the American Civil Liberties Union (ACLU) provided legal assistance.[29]

One of the most important cases in American Indian law, the treaty battle continued for more than a decade. In 1974, a court decision, *U.S. v. Washington*, known as the *Boldt* decision (after the trial court judge George Hugo Boldt), upheld the tribes' rights to an equitable portion of the catch and co-management of the fish stocks in the Puget Sound watershed and nearby offshore waters. "The decision established a major precedent for tribes using treaty rights to protect habitat from harmful development," notes geographer Zoltán Grossman. (The tribes' rights were reaffirmed in June 2018 when the U.S. Supreme Court let stand a lower court ruling requiring the State of Washington to remove barriers to salmon spawning.)[30]

A National Environmental Policy

Following a path pursued successfully by civil rights advocates, environmentalists turned increasingly to the federal government as guarantor of rights. Working with allies in Congress, environmentalists erected a new framework of environmental law in less than a generation, much of it during the Nixon administration. A series of telegenic disasters proved instrumental in eliciting change.

In January 1969, just days after President Richard M. Nixon took office, a blowout at a Union Oil rig spewed oil into California's Santa Barbara estuary. Six months later, in Cleveland, Ohio, the Cuyahoga River, which flowed past the city before dumping its contents into Lake Erie, caught fire. Oil slicks and industrial wastes from innumerable factories and refineries upstream had left the water so polluted that fires had become a frequent occurrence. This particular fire brought the City's mayor to the scene and with him the national press. Cleveland's mayor in 1969 was Carl Stokes, the first African American elected to head a large U.S. city. Not just Cleveland, but the nation faced "a crisis in the urban environment," said Stokes, "a crisis of immense proportions." With the burning river as his backdrop, Stokes linked racial progress and anti-pollution measures.[31]

Public outcry over the Santa Barbara oil spill and the Cuyahoga fire pressured Congress to act, passing the National Environmental Policy Act, which President Nixon signed on January 1, 1970. NEPA did not create the EPA, as some assume; that was accomplished by executive order approved by Congress later that year. The law did establish the Council on Environmental Quality (CEQ) to advise the President. NEPA also gave citizens valuable tools for addressing environmental problems, mandating public participation in the permitting process. Any proposal for a large development would require an environmental impact statement (EIS) on the likely ecological impact as well as alternative proposals—say, fewer units, fewer trees destroyed, or substitute drainage plans. Developers and the permitting agencies were not *required* to choose the alternative with the least impact, but the new procedures gave environmental advocates a forum for raising objections and additional time for mobilizing opposition to particularly devastating projects. Considered one of the nation's most effective environmental laws, NEPA has been "emulated in various degrees by almost half the states and by an estimated 80 or more countries abroad."[32]

Drawing on advocates' framing of environmental protection as a right of citizenship, the Senate bill sponsor Henry "Scoop" Jackson (D. – Wash.) had proposed that NEPA declare that "each person has a fundamental and inalienable right to a healthful environment." The idea was not new. In the closing pages of *Silent Spring*, for example, Carson had considered the public's right to know about chemicals in their environments a question of constitutional rights. EDF attorney Victor Yannacone argued in 1969 for a "constitutional guarantee of 'the right to a salubrious environment.'" Other advocates, including environmental philosopher William T. Blackstone and Supreme Court Justice William O. Douglas, would go on to cast a claim to environmental citizenship in terms of rights. In 1972, Massachusetts voters ratified Article 97 of the state constitution, which granted the right to a clean environment and protected conservation easements acquired by the state. "The right to a good environment is coming to be regarded as one of the fundamental inalienable rights," French-born American bacteriologist and Pulitzer Prize-winning author René Dubos would argue in 1977. Ultimately, however, Jackson's rights-oriented language was dropped in the final version of NEPA. Instead, Congress underscored individual responsibilities not collective obligations: "The Congress recognizes that each person should enjoy a healthful environment and that each person has a responsibility to contribute to the preservation and enhancement of the environment."[33]

Earth Day 1970

On a sunny April day in 1970 in central Manhattan, where ordinarily would have been thickly congested Wednesday afternoon traffic in central Manhattan, a small group spread a yellow and white quilt on the asphalt and enjoyed their lunch on Fifth Avenue at 57th Street. The group sat among a throng of 100,000, imagining for a moment the city thoroughfare without cars. In Alabama, the Greater Birmingham Alliance to Stop Pollution (later known simply as GASP) held a weeklong series of "Right to Live" events targeting air pollution from the local steel industry and the heavy use of coal in the city. In San Diego, California, and Topeka, Kansas, kids made their way to school on "horseback, bicycles, roller skates and skateboards" to make a point about vehicular air pollution. Speaking to a crowd in Fairmount Park in Philadelphia, Maine Senator Edmund Muskie underscored the enormity of the pollution problem by calling for "an environmental revolution." Nationwide, an estimated twenty million people participated that first Earth Day.[34]

Though often cast as the launch date for the modern environmental movement, Earth Day was as much a manifestation of the momentum of environmentalism in the 1960s as it was a harbinger of something new. For the previous year, Ecology Action, an umbrella organization for more than one hundred independent groups, had been holding teach-ins—a strategy borrowed from the anti-war movement. Former JFK advisor Fred Dutton had first suggested a national teach-in to Wisconsin Senator Gaylord Nelson. Nelson had played a prominent role in hearings on DDT and had been deeply moved by a flyover of the disaster area created by the Santa Barbara oil spill. Spurred by a sense that legislators needed to hear mass demands for environmental protection before they would act, he initiated Earth Day in part to pressure his Congressional colleagues. In a speech at Indiana University, Nelson predicted challenging work ahead, telling students, "We could stop our involvement in Laos [in the war in Southeast Asia] in 30 days, and we should, but the battle to restore man to his proper place in the environment will take a commitment beyond anything we have done before."[35]

Nelson asked Republican senator Pete McCloskey to co-chair Earth Day and hired former Stanford University student body president Denis Hayes, who left graduate school at Harvard's Kennedy School of Government to direct the teach-ins. As lead organizer for Environmental Teach-In, Inc., Hayes set up an office in Washington and hired a staff. Nelson found federal funding ($125,000) and support from conservationist Laurance Rockefeller ($18,000). The AFL-CIO contributed $1,000 and the UAW donated $2,000 and in-kind support, printing the teach-in newsletter, *Environmental Action: April 22*.[36] The organizers planned a mass mobilization on the National Mall modeled on earlier civil rights and anti-war marches on the capitol.

The range and variety of the events surrounding Earth Day exceeded organizers' expectations. Initially conceived as encouraging college campus-based teach-ins, Earth Day drew a surprising number of middle and high school teachers. The Earth Day national office was inundated with mail from teachers who were looking for a good way to get sixth through twelfth graders interested in science, Denis Hayes said later. The staff also heard from twenty-five- to thirty-five-year-old mothers; the environment "tugged at their souls," said Hayes.

Three months before the march, organizing committees had already formed at 350 campuses and in three hundred high schools. The "genius" of Earth Day, as environmental historian Adam Rome has observed, was in linking "the power of the Establishment with the energy of the grassroots."[37]

Some longstanding conservation groups were skeptical of Earth Day. "I didn't realize the extent to which [Earth Day] would catalyze a lasting change in public opinion," former Sierra Club executive director Michael McCloskey told historian Thomas Jundt in 2003. What was more, said McCloskey, "Industrial lobbies were just thunderstruck."[38]

The environment "may well be the gut issue that can unify a polarized nation," wrote *TIME* magazine in February 1970, expressing a common hope of the time. Denis Hayes countered suggestions that "the march on pollution [would] co-opt people from other pressing social concerns," such as poverty, civil rights, and the Vietnam War. Environmental problems posed a systemic challenge to those who were concerned only with profit, Hayes argued. "Ecology is concerned with the total system—not just the way it disposes of its garbage," said Hayes. At Washington's Earth Day rally, Hayes challenged the Vietnam War and the use of the chemical defoliant Agent Orange as an "ecological catastrophe"—to strong applause. "But even if that war were over tomorrow," he continued, "we would still be killing this planet. We are systematically destroying our land, our streams, and our seas. We foul our air, deaden our senses, and pollute our bodies, and it's getting worse."[39]

Other speakers at the Washington monument, including D.C.-based African American minister the Reverend Channing Phillips, emphasized interconnections between environmentalism and other causes. Rev. Phillips, a major figure in the Coalition of Conscience, a King-inspired alliance of ministers and civic leaders, declared that "[R]acial injustice, war, urban blight, and environmental rape have a common denominator in our exploitative economic system." Chicago Seven defendant Rennie Davis also targeted capitalism as the source of environmental ills. Iconoclastic journalist I.F. Stone warned the crowd, "The pollution issue is real enough, but it cannot be solved in isolation."[40] Progressive cultural icon Pete Seeger performed.

In L'Enfant Square, at a tiny rally for government workers, civil rights leader and then assistant secretary at the Department of Health, Education, and Welfare James Farmer spoke: "The garbage. The trash. The carbon monoxide. The junk. Who suffers most from it if not the poor, and so the poor, especially the ghettoized poor, the black and the brown and the red, stand to benefit first from any successes in cleaning up the environment."[41] His was an explicit articulation of environmental justice themes.

"Black Ecology"

Though environmental organizations inherited much from the black freedom struggle—rhetoric, organizational models, class action lawsuits, march tactics, an understanding of the importance of federal protections—Earth Day organizers missed an opportunity to build a sustained alliance between the civil rights and environmental movements. Whites' insensitivity to structural racism within the environmental movement proved to be a major barrier. While a student at Howard University in Washington, D.C., Lonnie Bunch attended the second annual Earth Day event at the Washington Monument, close to where he now directs the Smithsonian National Museum of African American History and Culture. A young white woman approached Bunch and his three friends, asking, "What are you black guys doing here? This isn't a civil rights demonstration."[42]

African American environmentalism took diverse forms. "The emergence of the concept of ecology in American life is potentially of momentous relevance to the ultimate liberation of black people," wrote *The Black Scholar* publisher Nathan Hare in April 1970. Hare posited a distinct "black ecology": black urban and white suburban environmental problems had different causes and required different solutions. From Hare's perspective, "the solutions set forth for the 'ecological crisis' are reformist and evasive of the social and political revolution which black environmental correction demands."[43]

"There was no singular or monolithic African American response to environmentalism or the first Earth Day," notes scholar and editor of the journal *Environmental Justice* Sylvia Hood Washington. Some black freedom struggle activists viewed environmental concerns as a distraction from more pressing and serious human rights issues. There was "a belief at this time," explains Washington, "that the nation's inordinate attention to the environmental movement and the First Earth Day was, in fact, a manifestation of its desire to escape from the discourse of civil rights—a discourse that had increasingly focused on full participation in the political economy for African Americans." National Urban League president Whitney Young, Jr. is usually quoted in this context for commenting in 1970, "The war on pollution is one that should be waged after the war on poverty is won." But the same year, Young wrote an Earth Week column in the African American-owned Cleveland, Ohio *Call and Post* insisting, "The choice isn't between the physical environment and the human. Both go hand in hand, and the widespread concern with pollution must be joined by a similar concern for wiping out the pollutants of racism and poverty."[44]

African American mayor Richard Hatcher of Gary, Indiana spoke at a rally of fifty thousand in Michigan in 1970. Hatcher had successfully built a coalition in Gary that linked "efforts to control rats and cockroaches in African-American neighborhoods" with campaigns to control industrial air and water pollution. But, as noted in *TIME* magazine, Hatcher feared that "the nation's concern with the environment has done what George Wallace was unable to do: distract the nation from the human problems of Black and Brown America." Because racial and political boundaries restricted efforts to address urban environmental problems, these statements were widely interpreted at the time (and since) as rejections of environmental reform, rather than as a challenge to broaden the ecology agenda by more fully embracing the movements against poverty and inequality. Whitney Young, Hatcher, and Stokes each emphasized the interconnections between urban ecological decline, poverty, and racial injustice. "African Americans did believe that they had a stake in an environmental movement," Sylvia Hood Washington wrote in 2009, "and ironically today's current environmental goal of sustainable communities mirrors their original vision of a more inclusive and realistic environmental agenda." Indeed, Detroit Mayor Coleman Young demonstrated that vision by initiating in the early 1970s a "Farm-A-Lot" program, providing seeds and technical advice for residents who gardened lots in the city's abandoned—by white flight—downtown.[45]

Native Americans and the Ecology Movement

At a pre-Earth Day teach-in at Northwestern University in January 1970, twenty-five Native Americans in ceremonial dress seized the podium and, in a militant statement of Native rights to a clean environment, demanded the University "stop aiding financially companies which have been polluting us to death and begin assisting Indian survival against the forces of pollution." Instead of embracing the action as a lesson in solidarity for teach-in attendees, Earth Day organizers published a terse article in their newsletter, headlined simply "Interrupted."[46]

At the same time, popular culture romanticized "the ecological Indian." The iconic image of "Iron Eyes" Cody featured a photo of the "Crying Indian" (who was in fact an Italian–American actor) shedding a single tear (actually glycerin) at the sight of the despoiled, litter-strewn landscape. During Earth Day 1971, the ubiquitous image appeared on posters and billboards advertising the corporate-sponsored Keep America Beautiful campaign. The ad was controversial not only because it traded on Native stereotypes. The image was accompanied by the tag-line, "People Start Pollution; People Can Stop It," implying that pollution was simply a problem of litter, and solely a question of individual responsibility, rather than a crisis created by industrial manufacturing, packaging, and dumping.[47]

The cultural misappropriation of Native American environmentalism resurfaced in a widely circulated speech credited to Chief Seattle, the Suquamish chief who negotiated the transfer of Puget Sound with representatives of the U.S. Commissioner of Indian Affairs in the mid-1850s. In fact, the speech most often marketed as Chief Seattle's 1854 address had been recrafted by scriptwriter Ted Perry in 1970 for use in an environmental film produced by the Southern Baptist Convention.[48]

A Fertile Time in Court

"You can't just play in the woods," Georgia trial attorney Ogden Doremus repeatedly admonished environmental activists during his long career litigating environmental issues.[49] Getting new laws passed was not enough; vigilance was necessary to ensure they were enforced. Initially, however, gaining access to the courts was itself a barrier.

In a landmark case decided in 1965, a group of New York residents sought to block construction of a massive hydroelectric plant that Consolidated Edison, the power company that served New York City, planned to build on the Hudson River. The Scenic Hudson Preservation Conference sued the Federal Power Commission, which had issued a permit for the facility, arguing that the huge pump station would damage Storm King Mountain, a renowned scenic area just north of the city. The *Scenic Hudson* case set two important legal precedents. First, the appeals court ruled that federal agency actions were subject to judicial review. Second, plaintiffs did not have to show they had been injured *economically* in order to seek redress. That is, the potential impairment of recreational and aesthetic interests sufficed to give the *Scenic Hudson* plaintiffs "standing," the legal term for having the right to sue.[50]

On the West Coast, the Sierra Club, which spun off its Legal Defense Fund in 1971 (the group changed its name to Earthjustice in 1997), also laid groundwork for liberalizing standing rules and increasing access to courts. The case involved a Walt Disney theme park planned for the heart of picturesque Mineral King Valley, California, a favorite locale for hikers. The Sierra Club found a high-level ally in Supreme Court Justice William O. Douglas. An avid preservationist and sportsman, Douglas had been appointed in 1939 by FDR and served until 1975. His memoir, *Of Men and Mountains*, celebrated a lifelong engagement with nature. An activist as well as a jurist, Douglas had led two hikes to publicize the need for wilderness protection, one in 1954, to preserve the 185-mile old C&O Canal route just outside Washington, D.C., the other in 1958, to preserve Pacific Coast Beach in Washington state. Douglas strongly supported Rachel Carson and served on the national board of the Sierra Club from 1960 to 1962. In his dissent in *Mineral King*, Douglas favored assigning "standing" to litigants "in the name of inanimate objects about to be despoiled, defaced, or invaded by roads and bull-dozers and where injury is the subject of public outrage." In support of his view, Douglas cited legal philosopher Christopher D. Stone's famous 1972 law review essay, "Should the Trees Have Standing?," which argued for recognizing the legal rights of natural objects. Though the U.S. Supreme Court ultimately ruled against the Sierra Club, the proposed theme park was never built.[51]

David Sive, who played an instrumental role in the *Scenic Hudson* fight, is often called "the father of environmental law." In 1970, he co-founded the Natural Resources Defense Council (NRDC) with colleagues and a group of Yale Law School students that included James Gustave "Gus" Speth. Like EDF, NRDC was modeled on the NAACP Legal Defense Fund. Whereas EDF began as a group of scientists who engaged with the law, NRDC was an environmental law firm that collaborated with scientists. By the end of its first decade, NRDC had grown to a staff of nearly one hundred, mostly attorneys. The litigation groups were winning in court. "The 1970s were the most fertile time," Gus

Speth explained in 2012. "We won almost all the cases that we brought. . . .The courts were with us. The media were with us," Speth continued, "It's not that way today."[52]

The Environmental Protection Agency, 1970

The momentum generated by Earth Day 1970 spurred President Nixon to create and Congress within two months to approve the EPA. Nixon was no champion of the environment, but he was practical and calculating, aware of the movement sweeping the country, and looking to defeat pro-environment Democratic challengers in upcoming elections. As a discrete federal agency dedicated to environmental protection, the EPA both signaled the importance of protecting the environment and institutionalized a heightened federal commitment to doing so. The EPA opened its doors on December 1, 1970. Earth Day organizers and participants were rightfully pleased with the pace of their success.

With a budget of $1.4 billion and a staff of six thousand, the agency represented a sizeable commitment of federal resources. The EPA would have responsibility for administering the Federal Water Pollution Control Act, conducting "studies on the effects of insecticides, herbicides, fungicides, and pesticides upon the fish and wildlife resources of the United States," monitoring radiation exposures, and establishing a coordinated program of pollution control, including standard-setting, monitoring, and enforcement.[53] Held to account by mainstream groups, grassroots activism, and extensive media attention, the agency set out to address the fragmentation of federal responsibilities for environmental oversight, to coordinate with states and municipalities, and to define the responsibilities of private industry.

The limitations of the EPA soon became apparent, however. The new agency fell short of the cabinet level Department of Environmental Quality many activists had sought. Despite the consolidation, distinct responsibilities remained spread across the federal bureaucracy, in the departments of the Interior, Agriculture, Labor, and Health, Education and Welfare (now Health and Human Services (HHS)). Further, the division of laws by medium—air, water, solid waste—led to fragmentation even within the agency. And, despite significant startup funding, never was the EPA funded at a level commensurate with its responsibilities.

Environmental advocates helped to shape the EPA, at times nudging and cajoling, and when necessary, filing suit. Of particular importance in the new environmental laws were provisions that allowed citizens to sue to require the EPA to enforce the law and its own regulations. "Within a few years, environmentalists had filed an avalanche of lawsuits which delayed or halted federal projects ranging from canals to oil pipelines to atomic power projects, on the basis that the required Environmental Impact Statement was either flawed or nonexistent," explained one analyst in the mid-1970s. By 1975, the Army Corps of Engineers, whose dam and highway construction projects were often the target of such lawsuits, complained that litigation had "been responsible for modifications, delays, or halts in 350 of its projects."[54]

A Rising Movement Wins Legislative Gains

For about fifteen years after passage of the Wilderness Act in 1964, the environmental movement achieved major legislative goals in quick succession with bipartisan support in Congress. The federal government began moving into arenas of environmental policy traditionally handled at the municipal or state level, such as waste disposal, with passage of the Solid Waste Disposal Act (1965). In October 1970, Nixon signed Sen. Nelson's National Environmental Education Act, mandating and funding environmental education in public schools. Anti-smog protests in multiple cities, a concern long advanced by the League of Women Voters among others, led to the Clean Air Act (1970), authorizing comprehensive federal air quality standards, and requiring significantly improved vehicle emissions controls. The Clean Water Act (1972) gave the EPA authority "to restore and maintain" the nation's waters, including regulating discharges. The Endangered Species Act (1973) protected designated wildlife species and their habitats. Though many had precursors, the new laws were much stronger. The Republican president, Richard Nixon, promptly signed these measures into law.[55]

Another round of legislative achievements came in 1976. The Toxic Substances Control Act (TSCA) gave the EPA authority to regulate toxic chemicals, and the Resource Conservation and Recovery Act (RCRA) required the EPA to set standards within four years for hazardous waste treatment, storage, and disposal at the more than fifty thousand hazardous waste dumps in the U.S.[56]

The vast body of legislation and implementing regulations, and the massive number of people whose duty it was to devise and enforce them, created what historian Adam Rome has termed "the environmental-management state." At the same time, "seeing beyond the state" made visible a robust array of nongovernmental environmental organizations and individuals who helped to fashion the new laws, to shape the implementing regulations, and to press continually for enforcement.[57]

A New Movement Infrastructure

Most longstanding conservation groups had experienced dramatic growth in the period *before* Earth Day. "In 1969–70, annual membership in the five major U.S. environmental organizations was growing at 16–18 percent; membership in the

Sierra Club alone had tripled since 1966," noted Stephen Fox. After Earth Day, the movement's lobbying efforts increased and grew more sophisticated. The number of registered environmental lobbyists grew from two in 1969 to eighty-eight in 1985.[58] With the transformation came inevitable growing pains.

The shift from protest strategies of the 1960s to a significant commitment to legislative action and litigation required a different sort of infrastructure for the movement. To gain the ability to take on long-term projects, including litigation that could last a decade or more, and the capacity to build expertise, necessitated institutionalization. Staff grew in numbers as well as in skill at fundraising. Institutionalization brought a level of stability.

The shift in emphasis toward strategies for legislative victory often meant toning down the rhetoric and moderating protest. Environmental journalist Mark Dowie called the tenor of 1970s environmentalism as one of "polite revolution," suggesting that the leaders of mainstream environmental groups engaged in a "politics of respectability" that softened the critique of polluters and made some environmental organizations too amenable to compromise.[59]

The requirements for becoming federally-recognized nonprofit or charitable organizations also reshaped grassroots environmental groups. Many groups had initially operated by consensus, shared leadership, and collaborative decision-making, but IRS guidelines for establishing nonprofit status meant formalizing board structures and by-laws and restricting the percentage of time devoted to lobbying.

Establishing strong fundraising mechanisms helped to ensure that financial uncertainties did not forestall or interrupt environmental campaigns. Conservation measures had historically relied on the backing of elites, who remained a critical source of high dollar gifts. The Conservation Fund, founded in 1948, and the World Wildlife Fund, founded in 1961, financed wilderness and wildlife protection efforts. The Trust for Public Lands, established in 1972, negotiated conservation easements and land acquisition in public-private partnerships. The Ford Foundation provided significant funding to the litigation groups, including EDF, NRDC, and the Sierra Club LDF. Increasingly, organizations sought out celebrity endorsers and funders to extend their influence. John Denver, for example, established the Windstar Foundation in 1976 and actor Robert Redford became a significant donor and board member at NRDC.[60]

The constituent base also shifted. To support the growth in infrastructure of the late 1970s, national organizations launched direct mail campaigns and door-to-door canvass operations, bringing substantial increases in membership. However, in moving to direct mail recruitment, organizations were *mobilizing* rather than *organizing* new members in ways that directly involved constituents in shaping and advancing campaigns. The direct mail campaigns tended to channel an organization's work toward "expedient" or popular causes not because they were the most urgent and important, but because they promised the strongest returns. Rarely did urban infrastructure improvements elicit as much sympathy as baby pandas or polar bears. Door-to-door canvass operations lent the appearance of grassroots organizing but were often outsourced to contractors and sometimes even resulted in a negative cash flow. Concentrated in densely popu-lated, sympathetic, urban neighborhoods, canvasses neglect rural areas and poor neighborhoods, places deemed less likely to be either ideologically or financially supportive. Members recruited via these methods often lacked deep commitment to the cause. The individual who wrote an occasional check or signed a petition was not necessarily an activist.[61]

As they grew, several national groups broke with more radical leaders, which tended to further isolate them from the grassroots. The divide sharpened between cautious national groups—who sought institutional legitimacy and the backing of powerful elites—and their more radical constituencies and staff members. A dis-pute within the Sierra Club provides a case in point. When it had been revealed in 1958 that Pacific Gas and Electric (PG&E) planned to build the nation's first commercial nuclear reactor to produce electricity at Bodega Bay, north of San Francisco, Brower and other Sierra Club staffers wanted to aggressively oppose the plant. They sought to move beyond the club's traditional appeals to scenic beauty and wilderness preservation, to a sharper critique of the nuclear industry, its anti-democratic tactics for pushing projects, and the potential radiation hazards of nuclear power plants, especially if located on the San Andreas fault. Whereas Sierra Club staffers wanted to directly challenge industry executives and scientists and their industry supporters in government and academe, the board insisted on quiet negotiations, at one point expressly forbidding testimony criticizing government officials. Ultimately, the Bodega Association, a more radical group formed by an ex–Sierra Club staffer, led the coalition that defeated the reactor by holding mass demonstrations and using creative tactics that included balloon releases to demonstrate where wind patterns could deposit fallout from an acci-dent at the plant.[62]

In *Encounters with the Archdruid* (1971), writer John McPhee called Sierra Club leader David Brower "unshakably the most powerful voice in the conservation movement." The differences between the Sierra Club board and their tough, charismatic director were multiple and longstanding. Brower had attempted to desegregate the club in 1959, but the board had voted down a resolution against excluding minorities. Brower weathered the Bodega Bay fight, only to have disa-greements burst forth again in the 1960s over how best to challenge PG&E's plan to site a nuclear plant further south at Diablo Canyon. After the series of run-ins over strategy, Brower's leadership style, and the temporary loss of the club's non-profit status, Brower and the Sierra Club parted ways in 1969.[63] (Ironically, the club began to expand its issue areas of concern *after* Brower's departure.)

Undeterred, Brower immediately launched Friends of the Earth (FOE), with a base in San Francisco and partners in England, Sweden, and France, thereby joining an increasingly international movement. FOE was willing to take on the nuclear power industry and the oil industry when other groups were not. Brower also helped launch the League of Conservation Voters in 1970 to track voting records of members of Congress, to lobby on Capitol Hill, and to help elect pro-environment candidates.[64]

Institutionalizing board structures, designing fundraising mechanisms, creating membership policies and professionalizing staff had conflicting effects. On the one hand, professionalization established environmentalists' credentials, easing the way for lobbying efforts and facilitating communications by environmental advocates with congressional representatives and EPA staff. On the other hand, the focus on Washington, D.C., shifted attention away from grassroots constituencies and concerns, weakening the capacity to identify emerging environmental threats and the power to respond to them.[65]

Greenpeace Emerges

The trajectory of Greenpeace was unique among environmental organizations. The group formed in 1971 among a group of U.S. expats, Quakers, and peace activists in Vancouver, some of whom had moved to Canada to protect their sons from being sent to fight in Vietnam, in a war they found unconscionable. The group's tactics diverged sharply from those groups who focused on lobbying Washington. "More than any other organization," writes Greenpeace historian Frank Zelko, "Greenpeace pioneered both direct action ecological activism and international environmentalism." Quaker faith, holistic ecology, nonviolence, and the counterculture were key influences on Greenpeace's founders. "Ecological evangelists," journalist Rex Weyler calls them. Greenpeace was transnational from its outset, and for many years, the group was anchored in Europe. However, the U.S. branch has been quite strong and has exerted influence on the organization's many chapters around the world. Influenced by Gandhian nonviolence, Greenpeace adopted the approach that the CNVA had employed in the late 1950s against nuclear testing in the Pacific. The three categories of nonviolent resistance, as outlined by political scientist and nonviolence proponent Gene Sharp, include: (1) nonviolent protest and persuasion; (2) noncooperation, including strikes, economic boycotts, and the refusal to take part in elections; and (3) nonviolent intervention or civil disobedience, "sit-ins, nonviolent obstruction, nonviolent invasion, and setting up a parallel government." Greenpeace campaigns tended toward nonviolent intervention and civil disobedience and risked severe repression.[66]

The group's actions were dramatic, even spectacular, and caught the attention of the press. For its first campaign, Greenpeace mounted a sea-based effort to block U.S. tests at the Aleutian island of Amchitka, Alaska, scheduled for October 1971. The Atomic Energy Commission's postponement of the test and winter weather blocked the group's journey to the test site, but the activists were welcomed warmly as they took their anti-nuclear campaign to tribal communities and Alaskan coastal towns along their route back to Vancouver. The Greenpeace activists applied the same direct-action approach to subsequent campaigns, maneuvering their small craft between huge whales and the harpoons of giant whaling ships or physically positioning their bodies on ice floes between seal hunters and seal pups. Only much later, with the formation of Greenpeace Action in 1988, did Greenpeace engage in significant lobbying campaigns.[67]

Cold War Militarization: Native American Tribes Resist

As was the case with African Americans, the priorities of Native American environmentalists differed somewhat from the mainstream groups. Whereas anti-nuclear groups organized against the production and deployment of atomic weapons by challenging the siting of nuclear power plants and waste storage facilities, Native American groups took the lead on fighting the effects of nuclear technologies at their source, targeting the mining and processing of uranium.

War can exact a profound toll on human health and the geophysical environment, even in places untouched by physical combat. "The Cold War left its imprint on the biosphere on every continent and in every ocean," historians John McNeill and Peter Engelke have noted. Though *détente* moderated U.S.-Soviet relations somewhat during the middle 1970s, the prolonged militarization brought on by the Cold War continued to manifest on U.S. landscapes in the manufacture and storage of chemical, biological, and radiological weapons and waste.[68]

Native activists regarded uranium mining not only as an environmental assault but a form of colonization that used native environmental knowledge to undermine tribal sovereignty and economic well-being. During World War II, the Manhattan Project's secret requisitions for uranium for the atomic bomb sent prospectors to Indian lands, where roughly 60 percent of U.S. uranium reserves were located. After the war, rising Cold War enmity between the U.S. and the Soviet Union fueled a nuclear arms race and increased demand for the radioactive element. The result, argues historian Ward Churchill, was "the radioactive colonization of Native North America."[69] Like colonization, uranium mining aroused resistance.

In the Black Hills region in the upper Midwest, for example, the Black Hills Alliance formed in 1979. Lakota Sioux and other Black Hills residents, including local environmental activists and non-Indian ranchers, fought further uranium mining in the area. In the Southwest on the Laguna and Navajo (Diné) reservations, where the most extensive mining of "yellow dirt," or *leetso* took place, hundreds of Native American men found jobs in the relatively well-paying uranium mines and mills. Uranium mining resulted in radioactive contamination of Native lands and had severe environmental health consequences for mine and mill workers and their families. Estimates of radiation levels taken inside a Shiprock, New Mexico, mine in 1959, for example, measured "ninety-to-a-hundred times the maximum permissible for worker safety." Breathing in the radon and radioactive byproducts that accumulated in underground mines caused lung cancer. Deaths among Navajo miners disrupted families, leaving widows and children without support. Radiation poisoning came not only from mining, but also from radiation-contaminated soil used to construct hogans, or dwellings, where miners' families lived. Uranium mining operations violated sacred lands, obstructed livestock grazing, and contaminated water supplies. A July 1979 dam break at Church Rock, near Gallup, New Mexico, in a mill pond where United Nuclear had been storing mine waste sent 93 million gallons of radioactive water into Rio Puerco, leaving the river water unusable for drinking, livestock, or agriculture for more than a decade. The water contaminated sheep, ruining the market for wool and meat on which many Navajo depended. The Rio Puerco radioactive release was greater than the more widely reported near meltdown of the Three Mile Island reactor in March of that year. Activists noted that problems with the dam were known to United Nuclear months before it broke.[70]

Navajo widows began organizing in the 1960s, talking with each other about their husbands' experiences with lung cancer and launching a campaign to determine the cause. The Southwest Research and Information Center (SRIC) formed in Albuquerque in 1971 to provide information "on the effects of energy development and resource exploitation on the people and their cultures, lands, water, and air of New Mexico and the Southwest."[71]

Native American activists also made a focal point of the Kerr-McGee mine at Shiprock, organizing on behalf of miners, their families, and the surrounding community. Birth defects, including cleft palate and Down Syndrome, the latter previously unknown in the population, appeared among Diné infants. In 1968, Congress failed to extend workers' compensation to uranium miners. By 1980, ninety-five of 150 Navajo uranium miners at Shiprock suffered from "serious respiratory ailments and cancers"; thirty-eight had died. A lawsuit seeking compensation for the injured miners against the Atomic Energy Commission and Kerr-McGee was unsuccessful. The Uranium Mill Tailings Radiation Control Act (1978) authorized funding through the Department of Energy to clean up the remnants of uranium and thorium at twenty-two abandoned sites. But cleanup was slow and only took place after the Navajo Environmental Protection Committee convinced tribal leaders to commit their own resources to the effort.[72] The survivors' campaign would take decades to yield compensation for the injured workers and their families.

"Ecological Agrarianism"

During the 1960s and early 1970s, thousands of ecology-minded activists participated in a *back-to-the-land* movement, attempting to live the adage that a healthy future required reducing the population's footprint on the planet. Organic farming had a long history in the U.S. J.I. Rodale promoted composting on a large scale, having first published *Pay Dirt: Farming & Gardening with*

Composts in 1945. Rodale's periodical *Organic Farming and Gardening* boasted 100,000 readers in 1948, 500,000 by 1970.[73]

Demonstrating their mistrust of government and opposition to industrial farming as well as urban living, many would-be farmers trekked to Vermont to visit Old Left radicals Helen and Scott Nearing for inspiration and practical advice on leading "the good life" and practicing organic agriculture. Meanwhile, the health foods movement enjoyed another revival. Frances "Frankie" Moore Lappé's *Diet for a Small Planet* (1971) documented the outsized ecological footprint of a meat-based diet and urged vegetarianism for environmental well-being as well as human health.[74]

Many back-to-the-landers found inspiration in Wendell Berry, whose return to farm life in Kentucky formed the basis of his poetry, fiction, and non-fiction writings. Through "a culture of stewardship," Berry sought "to forge a politically effective union of small farmers and environmentalists," writes his biographer political scientist Kimberly Smith. Berry re-envisioned American agrarianism, suggesting that farmers are essential to not just the political but the ecological health of the nation. Smith contrasts Berry's "ecological agrarianism" with Jefferson's "American democratic agrarianism." Ecological agrarianism is no simple anti-modern reversion to a mythical uncomplicated past, Smith argues. Nor was Berry's approach anti-technological. His was a search for a genuinely new understanding of "how industrialization has affected the countryside." Berry sought to prompt a reconsideration of the values of "individual independence, the sanctity of property rights, and the meaning of economic freedom."[75]

Labor and Environmental Reform

Unions often took on environmental health concerns of workers. Textile workers' unions fought for health coverage and compensation for their members who contracted brown lung; the reform movement within the United Mine Workers, Miners for Democracy, pushed hard for recognition and medical treatment miners disabled by black lung disease.[76]

Labor unions and environmental groups had often worked together. One of the clearest examples of labor-environment cooperation was the broad coalition formed during the 1970s to pass comprehensive chemical policy legislation. Until then, anti-pollution laws focused primarily on protecting the "sinks" where noxious wastes were being dumped—air, water, and land—rather than on regulating the manufacture and use of hazardous substances themselves. During the 1970s, an alliance of environmental groups, consumer advocates, and labor union leaders, including the AFL-CIO and, most significantly, the Oil, Chemical, and Atomic Workers Union, worked with allies in Congress to pass the Toxic Substances Control Act (TSCA, pronounced tŏs-că).

With leadership from the union's legislative director Tony Mazzocchi, OCAW rallied other unions to push for federal regulation of toxic chemicals.

Union leaders expressed special concern for protecting workers health, when as John J. Sheehan, legislative director for the United Steelworkers of America, put it, "Our primary method of identifying hazardous substances is counting the bodies that they leave behind." The coalition favored pre-market scrutiny, that is, testing and regulating chemicals *before* they were manufactured and sold. Opposition was formidable. The chemical industry lobby did "everything it could to sabotage the legislation," said Senate sponsor John V. Tunney.[77] The bill passed in 1976. It marked a significant achievement for the labor-environment-consumer coalition, although provisions for pre-market evaluation were weak.

The TSCA coalition was one of several manifestations of the labor-environment-civil rights alliance in the mid-1970s. In November 1972, the Conservation Foundation, under the leadership of progressive Sydney Howe, sponsored a Conference on Environmental Quality and Social Justice in Woodstock, Illinois, to promote dialogue among social justice-oriented activists and mainstream environmentalists. But the Conservation Foundation replaced Howe in 1973 with a more traditional conservationist, and the effort was not sustained.[78]

The UAW, under the leadership of Walter Reuther, had made pollution in auto plants an issue in collective bargaining as early as 1970. The UAW convened a "National Action Conference" on "Working for Environmental and Economic Justice and Jobs" at the union's training center at Black Lake, Michigan, in May 1976. Rank-and-file workers and labor leaders understood that "reducing industrial pollution served the material interests of working-class people," explains historian Josiah Rector. The collaboration among social movements, Rector has pointed out, marked an explicit linkage of environment and justice. Attendees at the Black Lake conference numbered 350, including labor representatives from the UAW, the Communication Workers of America (CWA), the Steelworkers, and the A. Philip Randolph Institute, which had been established in 1965 by black labor leader Randolph and Bayard Rustin. The Audubon Society and the National Wildlife Federation also supported the effort, which brought together "labor, industry, native Americans, southern mountaineers, blacks, Chicanos, welfare rights activists, League of Women Voters leaders and many more."[79]

Unemployment in Detroit at the height of the energy crisis in 1975 was 23.6 percent. As carmakers blamed new environmental regulations for the loss of auto industry jobs, the UAW reluctantly supported delaying emissions limits on new vehicles. The labor-civil rights coalition—joined by environmental and women's groups—worked to pass full employment legislation, which proponents hoped would be a barrier to the use of such "environmental blackmail" by industry. The legislation—the Humphrey-Hawkins bill of 1978—was "more symbolic than substantive," notes Rector. Nevertheless, Rector concludes, "[t]he history of such alliances confounds characterizations of environmentalism as 'post-economic'—opposed to the interest of workers, primarily localist and defensive, and unconcerned with redistribution."[80]

Following the Black Lake meeting, the Urban Environment Conference (UEC) continued to convene coalition partners. But with organized labor, civil right forces, and environmental advocates all under pressure from the Reagan administration, the UEC, which was dependent in part on federal grants, lasted only until 1984. The UEC's last major event was a conference in New Orleans in November 1983 on "Taking Back Our Health: An Institute on Surviving the Toxics Threat to Minority Communities." The UEC gathering brought together more than two hundred labor leaders, anti-toxics activists, and minority health professionals; more than half of attendees were people of color, including Navajo, Sioux, Mohawk, and Cherokee activists fighting the consequences of uranium mining in their communities.[81]

Deindustrialization Dims Coalition Prospects

Even as labor and environmental organizations pushed for stronger environmental regulation at the federal level, structural economic changes were underway that would hamper coalition efforts and impede further environmental reform. The implementation of neoliberal economic policies around 1970 yielded deindustrialization—structural disinvestment from manufacturing—as U.S. multinationals found cheaper labor overseas and began closing factories in the U.S. By then, the U.S. had already become the world's first postindustrial power, with service sector jobs outstripping manufacturing.[82] Plant closures left behind not only unemployed workers but also degraded landscapes, with few provisions for cleanup. Disinvestment weakened unions, depleting membership and their ability to fight for environmental measures that protected labor.

The year 1970 represents a turning point in the "explosion of wage inequality in the United States," notes economist Thomas Piketty. As incomes and wealth diverged, Piketty explains, oil and chemical industrialists and other financial interests gained outsized influence over policy by underwriting political campaigns, interest groups, and research institutes. The mid-1970s brought a sharp rise in industry opposition to environmental reform, particularly regarding the energy sector. Corporate demands for cheap and profitable fossil fuel-based energy increased pressure on Congress and the executive branch to move away from environmental protection. Some have traced the upswing in industry opposition to environmental reform to the "Oil Crisis" of 1973, when fuel shortages resulted from the embargo imposed in October by the Organization of Petroleum Exporting Countries (OPEC) in response to U.S. aid to Israel during the Yom Kippur War. The OPEC action reflected broader Third World resistance to Western dominance of global energy markets and resources. Analysts tie a dip in public concern for the environment that showed up in opinion polls in the mid-1970s to the five-month oil embargo, as Americans worried about job losses, rising heating fuel prices, and long lines at the gas pump. An economic recession followed in 1974–75. These developments no doubt did constrain the debate over environmental legislation in the mid-1970s. However, the energy industry already had been maneuvering to derail regulation of fossil fuel extraction and the U.S. Senate voted in July—weeks *before* the October 1973 Yom Kippur War— to exempt the proposed trans-Alaska pipeline from preparing an environmental impact statement.[83]

In some ways, in fact, the crisis could have stimulated the drive for renewable energy. Environmentalists were "given unexpected support" by the oil crisis, argues biologist Victor Scheffer, as energy experts began "to study the potential of six kinds of renewable energy: solar (including biomass), wind, ocean tidal, ocean wave, ocean thermal energy conversion, and geothermal." However, instead of launching a big push toward renewables, Nixon proposed "Project Independence," the construction of one thousand nuclear power plants by the year 2000.[84]

In the mid-1970s, after a long string of victories, the movement began suffering legislative losses. For example, in 1974 and again in 1975, President Gerald Ford vetoed strip mine reclamation bills that had been championed by the environmental lobby. Environmentalists generally viewed Jimmy Carter as a friend to the environment. Carter supported renewables, installing solar panels on the White House. However, Carter also proposed an Energy Mobilization Board with the authority to override environmental laws to fast-track power plant construction. Nonetheless, activists rallied and, in an indication of the movement's continued strength, defeated the plan in 1979.[85]

No Nukes: "A Great Big Time Bomb"

On November 13, 1974, Karen Silkwood was on her way to meet Oil, Chemical, and Atomic Workers union representative Steve Wodka and *New York Times* reporter David Burnham to share evidence of hazardous practices at the Kerr-McGee plutonium plant near Oklahoma City where she worked. She never arrived. Her car crashed mysteriously in a single car accident. The previous September, Silkwood and two colleagues had testified before the Atomic Energy Commission alleging that Kerr-McGee endangered the lives of workers by failing to protect them from exposure to plutonium.[86] Silkwood's death became a rallying point for antinuclear protests and calls to protect whistleblowers and activist women.

State-based groups in the Northeast, West, and South opposed the construction of nuclear plants in their regions. Activists from the People's Energy Project of the Granite State Alliance formed the Clamshell Alliance in 1975 to protest construction of a nuclear plant in Seabrook, New Hampshire. More than 1,400 activists were arrested at an October 1976 protest at the proposed site. The Abalone Alliance, formed in 1977, led direct-action protests aimed at shutting down Pacific Gas and Electric's Diablo Canyon reactor on the

California coast. And in the South, the Palmetto Alliance, also founded in 1977, opposed construction of a new plutonium enrichment plant in South Carolina. At three hundred square miles, the existing Savannah River Plant in Aiken, South Carolina, was already the largest Atomic Energy Commission site. Built in the early 1950s, for a time it had been the nation's sole producer of weapons-grade plutonium and of tritium triggers for nuclear bombs. Activists organized against plans to recycle plutonium in spent nuclear fuel at the Allied General Nuclear Services radioactive waste storage site in nearby Barnwell by opposing licensing for facility expansion. Musicians Gil Scott-Heron and Brian Jackson brought national attention to plans to build the uranium enrichment plant at Barnwell with their song decrying the "great big time bomb tickin' in South Carolina." Eventually, the Carter administration blocked the proposed enrichment facility's funds.[87]

Population Growth and Population Control

The population control movement gained new momentum from Paul Ehrlich's 1971 book, *The Population Bomb: Population Control or the Race to Oblivion*, which had sold three million copies in paperback by the mid-1970s. In the book, commissioned by the Sierra Club with a foreword by David Brower, Ehrlich argued that the human population had already exceeded sustainable limits. Curbing further growth required drastic action: families should limit themselves to two children, their replacement quotient. Influenced by Fairfield Osborn, Jr. and William Vogt, Ehrlich had helped form the organization Zero Population Growth (ZPG) in 1968. ZPG's tactics included lobbying and public education. In addition, the group opened vasectomy clinics and distributed condoms labeled "Save the World: Use a Condom." Prominent among Ehrlich's critics was Barry Commoner, who declared that Ehrlich underestimated innovations in technology and production that allowed for further population growth while neglecting the impact of overconsumption of resources in developed countries.[88]

The population limits of the planet were featured in a 1972 report, *The Limits of Growth*, published by a private, business-oriented think tank, The Club of Rome. Using computer modeling techniques that were new and controversial, a group of MIT social scientists plotted economic and ecological trends that predicted an "uncontrollable decline" in the Earth's capacity to support human survival. "If the present growth trends in world population, industrialization, pollution, food production, and resource depletion continue unchanged," the MIT researchers reported, "the limits to growth on this planet will be reached sometime within the next one hundred years." Some criticized the report's authors as exaggerating the potential for decline; others, including Commoner, laid the blame not primarily on overpopulation but on the polluting technologies propagated by postwar capitalism.[89]

The Stockholm Conference, 1972

Global leaders signed more international conservation-related conventions and treaties in the decade of the 1970s than had been signed during the forty years prior to 1970. Until the Biosphere Conference held in Paris in September 1968, limited meaningful follow-up on the 1949 U.N. Lake Success conferences had taken place. Sponsored by UNESCO, the Paris Biosphere Conference convened representatives from sixty-four nations to discuss the condition of the planet. "The dramatic views of the Earth from outer space, resulting from the Apollo Program," wrote one scholar, "added an emotional impact to what men had already scientifically known regarding the singular character of the Earth and its biosphere." The first truly global conference to make recommendations for protecting the earth's resources, the Biosphere Conference called on UNESCO to begin interdisciplinary research with particular attention to socio-ecological conditions in developing countries.[90]

The U.N. Economic Commission for Europe (which predates the European Union) in 1969 made "the improvement of environmental conditions" one of its four priorities. "[M]an's impact on global climates" was an issue covered in the preparatory meetings leading up to an international meeting in Stockholm. The 1972 United Nations Conference on the Human Environment, referred to as the Stockholm Conference, was the first in a series of decennial conferences that would provide a focal point for international cooperation—and debate—on the global environmental consequences of human activity. Interest in the Stockholm meeting was so great among activists that the Swedish government created "The Forum," a conference for non-governmental organizations to confer, strategize, and showcase alternative energy products. The conference proper, however, upheld that each nation had the "sovereign right to exploit their own resources." Developed countries grudgingly recognized the distinct interests of developing nations. The conference led directly to the creation in 1975 of the United Nations Environment Programme (UNEP), based—significantly—in Nairobi, Kenya.[91]

Grassroots Anti-Toxics Campaigns

The conventional narrative of the environmental movement suggests that the turn toward legislative action, litigation, and reliance on scientific expertise to the exclusion of protest left larger mainstream groups out of touch with many of the environmental concerns that were emerging directly out of the experiences of local communities. In broad strokes, that conclusion is certainly merited. But, in fact, the realities on the ground were more complicated. Local groups turned to EDF, NRDC, or Earthjustice for legal representation; some national organizations like the Sierra Club built chapters and several sought to build lobbying networks within the states.

In addition, toward the end of the 1970s, a new environmentalism sprouted from the bottom up, in local grassroots anti-toxics struggles. Polluters often tried to brand these local struggles as NIMBY—Not in My Backyard—protests, characterizing these activists as selfish, seeking only to protect their own homes and neighborhoods. If residents did not oppose toxic dumps or noxious industries in their neighborhoods, who would? Activists countered the critique with the term NIABY, Not in Anybody's Backyard.

In 1978, a group of residents in the suburban working-class neighborhood of LaSalle in Niagara Falls, New York, grew concerned after several children were diagnosed with leukemia. Parents began to investigate, targeting the noxious smells and toxic substances their children encountered at the 99th Street Elementary School. Homemaker Lois Marie Gibbs began talking with her neighbors and in August 1978 helped to form the Love Canal Homeowners Association (LCHA), which grew to represent more than 500 families. Love Canal activists discovered that before selling the site to the school district for one dollar in 1953, the Hooker Chemical Company had buried more than 21,000 tons of chemical waste in an abandoned canal. When New York State health officials finally investigated, they identified in the black tarry substance bubbling up on the school playground one of the most highly toxic chemicals created: dioxin. The state's August 1978 public health order for the immediate evacuation of pregnant women and children under age two raised further alarm. How could the site be considered safe for older children and adults?[92]

Over the next two years, residents of Love Canal fought for permanent relocation, to be paid for with state aid, for everyone who wanted to leave the neighborhood. The women activists argued that, in failing to protect them from toxic chemicals entering their bodies, the Department of Health was interfering with a most basic right, their right to become mothers. The Homeowners Association used creative tactics, on one occasion sending a pair of coffins—one for an adult and one for a child—to the governor. After a seven-year-old child died of kidney failure, children played an important role in the demonstrations, confronting Governor Hugh Carey, holding protest signs, reading "Help My Brothers and Sister; It's Too Late for Me." Love Canal residents enjoyed strong support from organized labor. The UAW Conservation Committee, OCAW, and the United Steelworkers provided tactical advice as well as tangible assets—money, space, and copiers. The Love Canal activists engaged in "citizen science," identifying their own experts, doing research, and collecting data. In addition, they made skillful use of the media and direct action, including briefly holding hostage two EPA representatives in May 1980.[93]

Love Canal highlighted the extent to which women led grassroots environmentalism in the late 1970s. Like their Progressive Era counterparts, the female activists at Love Canal deployed maternalist arguments, framing their activism as an extension of traditional women's concerns: children, family, home, and health. They focused attention on reproductive harm from pollution—miscarriage rates ten percentage points above the norm, birth defects, and possible genetic damage. (Women activists sent a Father's Day card to the governor with the names of women of Love Canal who had endured miscarriages.) Men's rhetoric and actions were more likely to stress economic concerns, like the lost value of their homes; one male activist called for a tax and mortgage boycott. Roles were evolving and soon, some men, too, would frame their environmental concerns in terms of caring for family. Even as women took on leadership roles that embodied feminist principles, the women at Love Canal declared that they were not feminists and did not explicitly challenge gender inequality. "They became feminists while vocally rejecting the [feminist] movement itself," writes historian Elizabeth Blum.[94]

"The contradiction between their progressive demands and tactics versus their public rhetoric supporting traditional female gender roles demonstrated two things," explains historian Amy Hay, "the mixed progressive legacy of America's postwar social movements and a foreshadowing of the 1980s conservative ideology, which emphasized the traditional nuclear family and heterosexual reproduction as the basis of citizenship." Invoking their concerns as mothers, the women at Love Canal also stressed the *state's obligation* to provide a safe environment, to "protect reproduction, children, and homes," notes Hay. Their rhetoric "consistently stressed their citizenship rights and their rights as taxpaying Americans to justify the provision of environmental health and safety," explains Blum. "Their pleas expressed an intrinsic belief that citizenship includes the right to a healthy environment."[95]

As a visible manifestation of the toxics crisis, the Love Canal disaster helped to recast environmentalism, challenging the lingering, if mistaken, perception that the environment was a cause for the elite. Sociologist Thomas Szasz has argued that the grassroots anti-toxics movement arose not out of the environmental movement, but out of a broader tradition of American dissent. Working-class families in this upstate New York community took the lead in pressuring government officials at every level to demand their right to a healthy neighborhood. However, the LCHA activists' approach was both "empowering and exclusionary," notes Blum. The LCHA was only the most visible of the organizations working to redress pollution at Love Canal. The Concerned Love Canal Renters Association represented tenants, most of whom lived at Griffon Manor, the federal housing project adjacent to the site, where 60 percent of residents were African American. As one historian notes, these residents faced both political marginalization and "a broader environment of discrimination and neglect." By casting the Love Canal crisis as a "homeowner's" fight, white middle-class LCHA members left out the African American and other low-income Griffon Manor residents, implicitly limiting the rights of citizenship to whites. Also active on behalf of the Love Canal residents was the Ecumenical Task Force of the Niagara Frontier, comprised of more than 200 largely middle-class religious activists, who framed the Love Canal situation as "an American spiritual crisis" and a question of racial and class justice.[96]

Pursuing a determined fight against Hooker Chemical and state and federal officials, the residents of Love Canal won relocation and modest compensation. Convinced that "ordinary citizens" could make a difference, Gibbs continued her environmental advocacy. After moving to northern Virginia, she founded the Citizens' Clearinghouse on Hazardous Waste (CCHW) in 1981. The group, later known as the Center for Health, Environment and Justice (CHEJ), operates an information clearinghouse serving grassroots groups. Within a decade, the organization's newsletter, "Everyone's Backyard," reached more than eight thousand subscribers nationally. In 1994, Occidental Chemical Company, successor to Hooker Chemical, reached a $98 million settlement with the EPA and FEMA for cleanup and relocation costs incurred at Love Canal.[97]

Three Mile Island

"The China Syndrome," a popular film portraying a nuclear power plant accident, opened in mid-March 1979. The film's title was a reference to a fictional meltdown so severe that it bored through the earth. A news reporter (Jane Fonda) and cameraman (Michael Douglas) endeavor to report on the accident, while company officials attempt a cover-up and portray the shift supervisor (Jack Lemmon), who is anxious about plant safety, as mentally unbalanced.[98]

Just two weeks later, a real-life partial core meltdown occurred at the Unit 2 reactor at the Three Mile Island nuclear plant, operated by Babcock and Wilcox, near the state capital of Harrisburg, Pennsylvania. Local activists had led sporadic protests of the Three Mile Island (TMI) plant for a decade, but most residents of the area had gladly accepted the facility, which created jobs and contributed to regional prosperity. The 1979 accident was the most serious nuclear reactor failure in the world to date. (Of reactor accidents, only the Chernobyl disaster in the Soviet Union in 1986 and the tsunami-damaged reactors at Fukushima, Japan, in 2011 have surpassed TMI in threat level). A leak of coolant surrounding the reactor core went unchecked for several hours; in responding to the leak, operators released radioactive water into the Susquehanna River, which feeds the rich estuary of the Chesapeake Bay. If public attention to environmental issues had waned over the course of the decade, Three Mile Island was a brutal reawakening.[99]

For a nation that had been told that nuclear power was both non-polluting and safe, the Three Mile Island accident was devastating. Families in the vicinity of the reactor were concerned about the intimate and unseen consequences of radiation: exposure that had the potential to alter genes and disrupt reproduction. Like Love Canal, because it threatened children's health and women's reproductive capacity, the disaster yielded "a distinct gender politics that combined women's heightened agency with ecological anxieties about motherhood, reproduction, and species continuity," as historian Natasha Zaretsky argues.[100] Hoping to calm the public's fears, President Jimmy Carter visited the Three Mile Island site, his wife Rosalynn accompanying him. But the TMI disaster, followed by the meltdown at Chernobyl eight years later, forever changed Americans' attitudes toward nuclear power.

Both the Love Canal fight and the Three Mile Island disaster exposed what Amy Hay identifies as "ordinary Americans' mistrust of political structures" borne of the Vietnam era and Watergate. Love Canal activists like Lois Gibbs had become disillusioned with government inaction but also experienced their fight as empowering. For Three Mile Island residents in a largely conservative area of Pennsylvania, the near meltdown was a source of disillusionment with not only the nuclear power industry, but also the government in its inability to protect them from environmental hazards. As Zaretsky notes, the anxieties of the atomic age were rekindled by the TMI nuclear accident. The reaction to Three Mile Island was illustrative of the political realignment underway with the decline of New Deal liberalism. In the forefront at hearings in Harrisburg and demonstrations at the plant gates in the early 1980s were conservative business leaders and Republican Party committeewomen, protesting not only reactor restart but also "big government." The inadequate official response contributed to a pessimistic view of the nation as a weakened and vulnerable body, Zaretsky notes, hastening the turn toward "ethno-nationalism that mobilizes images of community endangerment, demarcates sharp lines between insiders and outsiders, and creates a climate of paranoia, fear, and distrust."[101]

Nonetheless, the Love Canal fight spurred the passage in 1980 of the Comprehensive Environmental Response, Compensation, and Liability Act (CERCLA, or cir-clah), capping an extraordinary decade and a half of environmental legislation. The Superfund Law, as it is known, created a fund for cleaning up some of the worst environmental damage of the postwar era and instituted the *polluter pays* principle. A pool of money to be provided by polluting industries would pay for the messy and dangerous job of containing and managing industrial wastes. Though its limitations would later become apparent, the law's passage was a tremendous victory for the anti-toxics movement. [102]

The legislative successes of the 1970s were due to a combination of strong grassroots momentum, high levels of popular concern, widespread media coverage, well-developed organizational infrastructure, active litigation, and well-placed allies and bipartisanship in Congress. These legislative achievements illustrate philosopher and social critic Noam Chomsky's observation that activists have "created the rights that we enjoy."[103] No social movement in the U.S. had been so successful so quickly in achieving its legislative goals. By the end of the decade, professional staffs, not volunteer efforts, sustained the large national campaigns. Ironically, the very success of the movement in winning a robust legislative response led on the one hand to public complacency borne of a sense that government was addressing pollution. In a paradox, however, the movement won unprecedented federal oversight at a time when distrust in government to provide environmental protection was growing. This situation left activists particularly vulnerable to the sweeping reversal sought by the Reagan administration. In fact, the backlash had already begun.

Notes

1 Rome, *The Genius of Earth Day*, 11; Sutter, "The World with Us," 105.
2 Fox, *The American Conservation Movement*, 259; Harvey, *Wilderness Forever*, 193–94, 206, 209, 55, 250.
3 Harvey, *Wilderness Forever*, 229, 5; Turner, "'The Specter of Environmentalism,'" 126.
4 Section 2 (c), Public Law 88-577 (16 U.S.C. 1131–1136) 88th Congress, Second Session, September 3, 1964; Wallace Stegner to David E. Pesonen, "Wilderness Letter," December 3, 1960, in Stegner, *The Sound of Mountain Water*, 153. By 2016, wilderness areas covered 109 million acres. The Wilderness Society, "National Wilderness Preservation System," http://wilderness.org/article/national-wilderness-preservation-system (accessed May 4, 2017).
5 Sellers, *Crabgrass Crucible*, 268; Wurster, *DDT Wars*, 18, 27.
6 Pulido, *Environmentalism and Economic Justice*, 79, 97, citing *El Malcriado*, "Reflections on the Poisoning of Food and Man," *El Malcriado* 3, no. 4 (October 15–31, 1969): 4, Box 1965–76. EL MAL.
7 Pulido, *Environmentalism and Economic Justice*, 94, 111, 59, 90.
8 Pulido, *Environmentalism and Economic Justice*, 60, 87–88, 86, 105; Pursell, *Technology in Postwar America*, 146, citing "Farmworkers Used as Pesticide Guinea Pigs," *Los Angeles Times*, February 11, 1971.
9 Pulido, *Environmentalism and Economic Justice*, 100.
10 Pulido, *Environmentalism and Economic Justice*, 118–19; Gottlieb, *Forcing the Spring*, 315–17.
11 Isaac, "Movement of Movements," 55; Tom Lehrer, "That Was the Year That Was," Reprise/Warner Bros. Records (1965), reprinted in the *Sierra Club Survival Songbook*, ed. Jim Morse and Nancy Mathews (San Francisco, 1971), 18–21; Malvina Reynolds, "What Have They Done to the Rain?" *Ear to the Ground* (Smithsonian Folkways, 2000); Richie Havens, "Follow," lyrics by Jerry Merrick, "Mixed Bag," Verve, 1966; Joni Mitchell, "Ladies of the Canyon," Reprise Records, 1970; James E. Perone, *The Album: A Guide to Pop Music's Most Provocative, Influential, and Important Creations*, The Praeger Singer-Songwriter Collection. 4 vols. (Santa Barbara: Praeger, 2012), 120.
12 Roszak, *The Making of a Counter Culture*, 42, 66; Marcuse, *One-Dimensional Man*; Gottlieb, *Forcing the Spring*, 143, 132–34.
13 Carole Cadwalladr, "Whole Earth Catalog: The Book that Changed the World," *The Guardian*, May 4, 2013; Steinberg, "Can Capitalism Save the Planet?," 9; Jundt, *Greening the Red, White, and Blue*, 3, 5.
14 Schumacher, *Small Is Beautiful*, 178, 184; Wood, *E.F. Schumacher*, 241, 363.
15 Nader, *Unsafe at Any Speed*; Nader, "The Profits in Pollution," 19.
16 Dowie, *Losing Ground*, 28.
17 Gottlieb, *Forcing the Spring*, 128–29; Merchant, *Radical Ecology*, 9; Egan, *Barry Commoner*, 81.
18 Gottlieb, *Forcing the Spring*, 139.
19 Rep. David Ross Obey, a Democrat from Wisconsin, who served from 1969 to 2011, read Seeger's entire poem into the *Congressional Record* on October 20, 1998 during an appropriations debate, Taylor, "Deep Ecology to Radical Environmentalism," 183.

The poem was later set to music by world musician Elise Witt. Taylor, *Dark Green Religion*, 18ff.

20 Joseph Sittler, Jr., "A Theology for Earth." *The Christian Scholar* 37, no. 3 (September 1954): 367–74, 372; White, "Historical Roots of Our Ecologic Crisis," 1207. See, for example, Ellen Fenzel Arnold, *Negotiating the Landscape: Environment and Monastic Identity in the Medieval Ardennes* (Philadelphia: University of Pennsylvania Press, 2013), 5.

21 Jacobs, *The Death and Life of Great American Cities*.

22 Guha and Martinez-Alier, *Varieties of Environmentalism*, 61, 186, 200, (emphasis in original); Mumford, *The City in History*.

23 Zimring, *Clean and White*, 212.

24 Goldstein, "'The Search for New Forms,'" 391, 382, 386, 377.

25 Udall, *The Quiet Crisis*, 172; "Udall Calls Conference on Man, Nature in City," *Bridgeport Sunday Post*, October 22, 1968, 22; Sterling Tucker, "Nature and the Ghetto Dweller," in *Man and Nature in the City: A Symposium Sponsored by the Bureau of Sport Fisheries and Wildlife*, U.S. Department of the Interior, October 21–22, 1968 (Washington, D.C.: U.S. Govt. Print. Office, 1969), 46–48.

26 Alfredo Morabia, "Unveiling the Black Panther Party Legacy to Public Health," *American Journal of Public Health* 106, no. 10 (October 2016): 1732–33; Alondra Nelson, "The *Longue Durée* of Black Lives Matter," *American Journal of Public Health* 106, no. 10 (October 2016): 1734–37, 1735, 1736.

27 Rickford, "'We Can't Grow Food on All This Concrete,'" 956. Rickford is referencing SNCC leader Stokely Carmichael (Kwame Ture), Malcolm X University director Owusu Sadaukai, Amiri Baraka, Eldridge Cleaver, writer Ann Cook, and economist Robert S. Browne.

28 Tom Levin, Adam Gifford, Ellen Gifford, "A Chance for Change," *Science Film Services*, 1965; Edge, *The Potlikker Papers*, 62–63.

29 Telegram from Martin Luther King, Jr. to Dick Gregory, Martin Luther King, Jr. Papers, Civil and Human Rights Museum, Atlanta, Georgia, on view March 14, 2015; "Gregory and Wife Guilty in Indian Fishing Protests," *New York Times*, December 2, 1966, 69.

30 Wilkinson, *Messages from Frank's Landing*, 55–56; *U.S. v. Washington*, 384 F. Supp. 312 (W.D. Wash. 1974). Aff'd 520 F. 2d 676 (9th Cir. 1975). Also see, Grossman, *Unlikely Alliances*, 37–63. John Eligon, "'This Ruling Gives Us Hope': Supreme Court Sides with Tribe in Salmon Case." *The New York Times*, June 11, 2018.

31 Stradling and Stradling, *Where the River Burned*, 146, 79, 194.

32 McCormick, *Reclaiming Paradise*, 58; Gottlieb, *Forcing the Spring*, 180; Lynton Caldwell, "Implementing NEPA: A Non-Technical Political Task," in Clark and Canter, eds. *Environmental Policy and NEPA*, 337.

33 Victor Yannacone, Jr., "Can Law Reclaim Man's Environment?," *Trial: The National Legal Newsmagazine* 5 (August 1969): 10; Hay, "Dispelling the 'Bitter Fog,'" 184; Carson, *Silent Spring*, 278; Fiege, *Republic of Nature*, 428; Blackstone, "Ethics and Ecology" in Blackstone, ed., *Philosophy and Environmental Crisis*, 16–42; *Sierra Club v. Morton*, 405 U.S. 727, 741 (1972); Staci Rubin and Phelps Turner, "Massachusetts Is Making Strides toward Environmental Justice," *Environmental Justice* 8, no. 5 (2015): 181–84, 181; Moberg, *René Dubos, Friend of the Good Earth*, 172; Title I: Congressional Declaration of National Environmental Policy, Sec. 101, 42 USC § 4331.

34 Bob Monroe, Associated Press, "Dirty World Cranks Back Up after 'Spic and Span' Effort," *The Birmingham News*, April 23, 1970, 1; Egan, *Barry Commoner*, 79; Hays and Hays, *Beauty, Health, and Permanence*, 52.

35 Gottlieb, *Forcing the Spring*, 36; Jundt, *Greening the Red, White, and Blue*, 203ff.; Monroe, "Dirty World Cranks Back Up," 1.

36 Jundt, *Greening the Red, White, and Blue*, 204; Sale, *Green Revolution*, 25; Denis Hayes, Interview by Scott Schang, Environmental Law Institute, September 14, 2011; Rome,

The Genius of Earth Day, 72, 90. UAW Flyer, "What We've Done," www.nelsonearth-day.net/docs/nelson_47-26_uaw_env_flyer.pdf (accessed May 7, 2017).

37 Denis Hayes, Interview by Scott Schang, Environmental Law Institute, September 14, 2011; Environmental Teach-In, Inc. "Environmental Action: April 22," *Environmental Action* 1, no. 1 (January 31, 1970), Gaylord Nelson papers; Rome, *The Genius of Earth Day*, 58.

38 Jundt, *Greening the Red, White, and Blue*, 212.

39 McCormick, *Reclaiming Paradise*, 67, citing *TIME*, February 2, 1970, 56; Environmental Teach-In, Inc., "Discord Likely to Grow, says Hayes: Soothing Effect a Myth," *Environmental Action* 1, no. 1 (January 31, 1970) in Gaylord Nelson, Speeches and other documents on Earth Day, 1970 (from the Gaylord Nelson Papers, MSS 1020, in the Archives of the Wisconsin Historical Society) online facsimile at: www.wisconsinhistory.org/turningpoints/search.asp?id=1671 (accessed April 29, 2017), 2; "Statement of Denis Hayes, National Coordinator, Environmental Action," U.S. Congress, House Committee on Government Operations, "The Environmental Decade (Action Proposals for the 1970s)," Ann Arbor, Michigan, March 13, 1970; Denis Hayes, in Daniel Schorr, "CBS News with Walter Cronkite," April 22, 1970, archived at An Earth Day Scrapbook, https://midcenturymodernmag.com/an-earth-day-scrapbook-3777357a8340 (accessed May 1, 2017).

40 Commoner, *The Closing Circle*, 9; I.F. Stone, "How Earth Day Was Polluted," *I.F. Stone's Bi-Weekly*, Washington, D.C., May 4, 1970, 1.

41 Daniel Schorr, "CBS News with Walter Cronkite," April 22, 1970, archived at An Earth Day Scrapbook, https://midcenturymodernmag.com/an-earth-day-scrap-book-3777357a8340 (accessed May 1, 2017).

42 Lonnie Bunch, "Black and Green: The Forgotten Commitment to Sustainability," 83–86, 83, in Kress and Stine, eds., *Living in the Anthropocene.*

43 Hare, "Black Ecology," 2.

44 Washington, "Ball of Confusion," 206, 212; Rome, "What Really Matters in History," 310–11; Rome, *The Genius of Earth Day*, 5; "Environment: The Rise of Anti-Ecology," *TIME*, August 3, 1970; Washington, "Ball of Confusion," 208, citing *Business Week*, November 14, 1970; Whitney Young, Jr., *Call and Post*, April 25, 1970, cited in Stradling and Stradling, *Where the River Burned*, 175.

45 Rome, *The Genius of Earth Day*, 5; Rome, "What Really Matters in History," 310–11; "Environment: The Rise of Anti-Ecology." *TIME*, August 3, 1970; Rome, *The Genius of Earth Day*, 143; Stradling and Stradling, *Where the River Burned*, xi; Larry Gabriel, "Detroit's Urban Farms Are Nothing New," *Detroit Free Press*, June 4, 2013; Washington, "Ball of Confusion," 207, in Egan and Crane, eds., *Natural Protest.*

46 Environmental Teach-In, Inc. "Interruption," *Environmental Action* 1, no. 1 (January 31, 1970), Gaylord Nelson papers.

47 Krech, *The Ecological Indian*. Much later, the New Orleans *Times-Picayune* revealed that Cody was in fact Oscar DeCorti, an Italian-American actor born of immigrant parents in Kaplan, Louisiana, who played more than a dozen roles as a Native American. Angela Aleiss, "Native Son: After a Career as Hollywood's Noble Indian Hero, Iron Eyes Cody is Found to Have an Unexpected Heritage," The New Orleans *Times-Picayune*, May 26, 1996. The "Crying Indian" ad was resurrected in 2016 by the Ad Council, which touted it as "one of the most memorable and successful campaigns in advertising history," so named by *Ad Age Magazine*. www.adcouncil.org/Our-Campaigns/The-Classics/Pollution-Keep-America-Beautiful-Iron-Eyes-Cody (accessed May 10, 2017). Steinberg, "Can Capitalism Save the Planet?," 14.

48 Ted Perry, "Home," Southern Baptist Convention Radio and Television Commission, 1972; Zelko, *Make It a Green Peace!*, 88. See Chief Seattle, "Every Part of this Country is Sacred to My People," https://suquamish.nsn.us/home/about-us/chief-seattle/#tab-id-5 (accessed May 10, 2017).

49 Ogden Doremus, as quoted by William Buzbee, Public talk, Greenlaw, Atlanta, Ga., October 7, 2016.

50 Adams et al., *A Force for Nature*, 18, 39; *Scenic Hudson Preservation Conference v. Federal Power Commission*, 354 F. 2d 608 (2d Cir. 1965).

51 J. Gustave Speth, Interview by John C. Cruden, Environmental Law Institute, April 13, 2012; Harvey, *Forever Wilderness*, 173–74, 176; Lear, *Rachel Carson*, 561n43; *Sierra Club v. Morton*, 405 U.S. 727, 741 (1972); Stone, "Should the Trees Have Standing?"

52 Adams et al., *A Force for Nature*, 18, 89; J. Gustave Speth, Interview by John C. Cruden, Environmental Law Institute, April 13, 2012.

53 Roy L. Ash, President's Advisory Council on Executive Organization, *CQ Almanac Online Edition*, https://library.cqpress.com/cqalmanac/document.php?id=cqal70-1293675 (accessed September 16, 2016); Reorganization Plan No. 3 of 1970, 35 FR 15623, 84 Stat. 2086, July 9, 1970.

54 Liroff, *A National Policy for the Environment*, 211.

55 Solid Waste Disposal Act, 42 U.S.C. §6901 et seq. (1965); Environmental Education Act, 20 U.S.C. §5501; Clean Air Act, 42 U.S.C. §7401 et seq. (1970); Federal Water Pollution Control Act, 33 U.S.C. §1251 et seq. (1972); Endangered Species Act, 16 U.S.C. §1531 et seq. (1973);

56 Toxic Substances Control Act, 15 U.S.C. §2601 et seq. (1976); Resource Conservation and Recovery Act, 42 U.S.C. §6901 et seq. (1976); McNeill, *Something New Under the Sun*, 29.

57 Rome, "What Really Matters in History," 304; Matthew Connelly, "Seeing Beyond the State: The Population Control Movement and the Problem of Sovereignty," *Past and Present* 193 (November 2006): 197–233.

58 The five groups all had been founded before World War II: the Izaak Walton League, the National Audubon Society, the National Wildlife Federation, the Sierra Club, and the Wilderness Society. Annual growth continued in the early 1970s, but at a lower annual rate, between 6 and 8.5 percent between 1971 and 1974 as compared with 12–18 percent annual increase from 1966 through 1970, Fox, *The American Conservation Movement*, 315; Mitchell et al., "Twenty Years of Environmental Mobilization," 228.

59 Dowie, *Losing Ground*, 1.

60 Adams et al., *A Force for Nature*, 44; Dowie, *Losing Ground*, 49, 47; Mark Stoll, *Inherit the Holy Mountain*, 191–92; Adams et al., *A Force for Nature*, 92–94, 96.

61 Payne, *I've Got the Light of Freedom*, 156; Cathy Hinds, Heeten Kalan, Jane McAlevey, Baldemar Velasquez, Diane Tavorian, Pam Tau Lee, and Anthony Thigpen, "The National Toxics Campaign: Some Reflections and Thoughts for the Movement," 8, www.ejnet.org/ej/ntcf.pdf (accessed June 18, 2017); Dowie, *Losing Ground*, 46; Brulle, *Agency, Democracy, and Nature*, 264.

62 Wellock, *Critical Masses*, 42, 49.

63 McPhee, *Encounters with the Archdruid*, 160; Fox, *The American Conservation Movement*, 349; Rome, *The Genius of Earth Day*, 211.

64 By 2016, FOE had chapters in sixty-six countries. Glen Canyon Institute, www.glen canyon.org/about/david-brower (accessed January 27, 2018).

65 Gottlieb, *Forcing the Spring*, 183.

66 Zelko, *Make It a Green Peace!*, 30–31; Zelko, "The Politics of Nature," 716–42, 733 in Isenberg, *The Oxford Handbook of Environmental History*; Zelko, *Make It a Green Peace!*, 322; Weyler, *Greenpeace*, 10; Sharp, *The Politics of Nonviolent Action*, as summarized in Zelko, *Make It a Green Peace!*, 14, 16.

67 Zelko, *Make It a Green Peace!*, 98–100, 67.

68 Melosi, *The Sanitary City*, 14; McNeill and Engelke, *The Great Acceleration*, 184.

69 Churchill, *Struggle for the Land*, 239.

70 Churchill, *Struggle for the Land*, 242; Esther Yazzie-Lewis and Jim Zion, "*Leetso*, the Powerful Yellow Monster," in Brugge, *The Navajo People and Uranium Mining*, 4;

Doug Brugge, Jamie L. deLemos, and Cat Bui, "The Sequoyah Fuels Corporation Release and the Church Rock Spill: Unpublicized Nuclear Releases in American Indian Communities," *American Journal of Public Health* 97, no. 9 (September 2007): 1595–600, 1597; Churchill, *Struggle for the Land*, 245; Gottlieb, *Forcing the Spring*, 323–25.

71 Doug Brugge and Rob Goble, "A Documentary History of Uranium Mining and the Navajo People," in Brugge et al., *The Navajo People and Uranium Mining*, 36; Southwest Research and Information Center, www.sric.org/index.php (accessed May 3, 2017).

72 Churchill, *Struggle for the Land*, 242–43; U.S. House, Select Subcommittee on Labor of the Committee on Education and Labor in the House of Representatives, April 1, April 4, and May 1, 1968. https://babel.hathitrust.org/cgi/pt?id=uc1.$b655015;view =1up;seq=7; Churchill, *Struggle for the Land*, 246.

73 Jundt, "Dueling Visions," 63, citing J.I. Rodale's 1945 book *Pay Dirt: Farming & Gardening with Composts* (New York: Devin-Adair Company, 1945); Jundt, "Dueling Visions," 69.

74 Nearing and Nearing, *Living the Good Life*; Lappé, *Diet for a Small Planet*.

75 Smith, *Wendell Berry and the Agrarian Tradition*, 1, 14–15, 9, 2.

76 Jedediah Purdy, "Environmentalism Was Once a Social-Justice Movement," *The Atlantic*, December 7, 2016.

77 Mazzocchi, quoted in Druley and Ordway, *Toxic Substances Control Act*, 19; Sheehan, quoted in Druley and Ordway, *Toxic Substances Control Act*, 15; Environmental and Natural Resources Policy Division, Legislative History of TSCA, 94th Congress, 2nd session, edited by House Committee on Interstate and Foreign Commerce. Washington, D.C.: Library of Congress, 1976, 210.

78 Brulle, *Agency, Democracy, and Nature*, 216; Gottlieb, *Forcing the Spring*, 151–52.

79 Rector, "The Spirit of Black Lake," 45–47, 53.

80 Rector, "The Spirit of Black Lake," 52, 54–55, 58, 66.

81 Rector, "The Spirit of Black Lake," 60–61.

82 Jundt, *Greening the Red, White, and Blue*, 200.

83 Piketty, *Capital in the Twenty-First Century*, 330, 335; Dunlap, "Trends in Public Opinion," 296; Jacobs, *Panic at the Pump*, 3–5; "Congress Completes Action on Alaskan Pipeline Bill." *CQ Almanac* 1973, 29th ed. 596–614. (Washington, D.C.: Congressional Quarterly, 1974) http://library.cqpress.com/cqalmanac/cqal73-1227237 (accessed October 14, 2018).

84 Scheffer, *The Shaping of Environmentalism*, 70; Wellock, *Preserving the Nation*, 194; Dunlap, "Trends in Public Opinion toward Environmental Issues," 292. According to the U.S. Energy Information Administration, in 2016, 61 nuclear power plants operate in 30 states, with a total of 99 nuclear reactors. www.eia.gov/tools/faqs/faq. php?id=207&t=21 (accessed May 12, 2017).

85 Hays and Hays, *Beauty, Health, and Permanence*, 145, 59.

86 David Burnham, "Death of Plutonium Worker Questioned by Union Official," *The New York Times*, November 19, 1974, 28.

87 Tom Corwin, "War Against Weapons: Activists Mount Protests Against SRS Nuclear Projects," *The Augusta Chronicle*, November 28, 2000; Frederickson, *Cold War Dixie*; Gil Scott Heron and Brian Jackson, "South Carolina (Barnwell)," "From South Africa to South Carolina," Arista Records, November 1975; Caroline Rose Peyton, "Radioactive Dixie: A History of Nuclear Power and Nuclear Waste in the American South, 1950–1990." Ph. D. Diss., University of South Carolina, 2016, 210.

88 Ehrlich, *The Population Bomb*; McCormick, *Reclaiming Paradise*, 70. ZPG is now known as Population Connection, www.populationconnection.org/us/30-years-of-zpg/ (accessed May 10, 2017); McCormick, *Reclaiming Paradise*, 71–73.

89 Meadows et al. and Club of Rome. *The Limits to Growth*, ix–x; Egan, *Barry Commoner*, 118–19.

90 Lynton K. Caldwell, "Concepts in Development of International Environmental Policies." *Natural Resources Journal* 13 (April 1973): 190–202, 198; UNESCO, *The Biosphere Conference: 25 Years Later* (Paris: UNESCO, 1993), 5.

91 Kai Hünemörder, "Environmental Crisis and Soft Politics: Détente and the Global Environment, 1968–1975." in McNeill et al., *Environmental Histories of the Cold War*, 257–76, 262; Sale, *The Green Revolution*, 41; Principle 21, Declaration of the United Nations Conference on the Human Environment, Stockholm, 1972.

92 Gibbs, *Love Canal: The Story Continues*, 21–23; Blum, *Love Canal Revisited*, 22, 26–27.

93 Hay, "Recipe for Disaster," 115–19; Blum, *Love Canal Revisited*, 57–58; Gibbs, *Love Canal: The Story Continues*, 172–82.

94 Blum, *Love Canal Revisited*, 97–102; Hay, "Recipe for Disaster," 115, 122–23, 126–27; Blum, *Love Canal Revisited*, 48.

95 Hay, "Recipe for Disaster," 125, 111; Blum, *Love Canal Revisited*, 50.

96 Szasz, *Ecopopulism*, 6, 69ff.; Blum, *Love Canal Revisited*, 51; Newman, *Love Canal*, 121–22, 160–61.

97 Gibbs, *Love Canal: The Story Continues*, 19; Newman, *Love Canal*, 212–13; Matthew L. Wald, "Out-of-Court Settlement Reached Over Love Canal," *The New York Times*, June 22, 1994.

98 James Bridges, Mike Gray, and T.S. Cook, "The China Syndrome," *Columbia Pictures*, 1979.

99 Zaretsky, *Radiation Nation*, 60, 186–88.

100 Zaretsky, *Radiation Nation*, 2.

101 Hay, "Recipe for Disaster," 126; Zaretsky, *Radiation Nation*, 2, 7, 13.

102 42 U.S.C. 103.

103 Noam Chomsky, "Requiem for the American Dream," directed by Peter D. Hutchison, Kelly Nyks, and Jared P. Scott, *Netflix*, 2015.

4

THE CONSERVATIVE COUNTERMOVEMENT AND THE UPSURGE OF ENVIRONMENTAL JUSTICE (1980–1990)

Former California governor Ronald Reagan ascended to the presidency in 1981 vowing to undo almost every major environmental legislative achievement of the 1970s and "set business free again." The conventional narrative of anti-environmentalism dates the revolt against federal environmental protections to this moment. In fact, Reagan's presidency anchored a counterrevolution that had begun much earlier. The Reagan administration slashed the EPA budget, slowed implementation of toxic substances regulation and Superfund, and gutted environmental enforcement. These actions were devastating. Nonetheless, the backlash against environmental reform had deep roots. The Reagan counterrevolution is best understood within the much longer trajectory of the conservative movement in the U.S., a movement that placed opposition to environmental reform at its center. In fact, as environmental historian Mark Fiege has argued, "The modern conservative movement might be understood fundamentally as an argument about nature."[1]

Neoliberal economic policies introduced in the 1970s weakened the labor-environment coalition that had seemed so promising at the 1976 Black Lake meeting. The shift in the political landscape would also deepen the divide between Washington, D.C.-based environmental groups on the one hand and grassroots and newly emergent environmental justice groups on the other.

Political geographer David Harvey defines neoliberalism as "a theory of political economic practices that proposes that human well-being can best be advanced by liberating individual entrepreneurial freedoms and skills within an institutional framework characterized by strong private property rights, free markets, and free trade."[2] In practice, neoliberal economics meant deregulating industry, exporting factories and jobs, undermining unions, freezing or slashing wages, and eliminating environmental regulations. As a result of long-term employment trends and assaults on organized labor, union membership in the U.S. peaked in 1979 and then began a sharp decline. Fewer union members meant less support for labor-environment initiatives.[3]

Reagan was largely unsuccessful in reversing the legislative mandates of the 1970s, in part because Democrats controlled the House throughout his two terms. Nonetheless, by appointing agency heads hostile to environmental regulation, Reagan was able to slow or block implementation of rules protecting public lands and wilderness areas, restricting toxic chemicals, and limiting coastal drilling. The Reagan administration also used severe budget cuts to stymie environmental protection. The effects resonated globally. In 1981, Reagan cut U.S. contributions to the U.N. Environment Programme by 80 percent, from $10 million to $2 million. (Congress restored three-fourths of the global commitment in 1982).[4]

The Rise of the Conservative Movement

Conservatives had long focused on limiting the role of government in regulating industry and natural resources. In the late 1940s and 1950s, to thwart government control of public lands, some elements of the "New Right" accused conservationists of subversion. Nevada Senator Pat McCarran, best known for a law restricting immigration and travel by "subversives," led a series of hearings during World War II aimed at reducing grazing fees on public lands. At a 1947 hearing on public lands policy held by Wyoming congressman Frank Barrett, who had tried unsuccessfully to abolish the Jackson Hole National Monument in his state, one committee member opined: "The power of the government to regulate grazing seems more nearly modeled on the Russian way of life. . .To protect the ranges, the forest and watersheds is communism." In the 1950s, McCarthyites and the John Birch Society, founded in 1958, undermined environmental reform by targeting communists and other progressives.[5]

Although arch-Republican Barry Goldwater supported private preservation of wild places, he strenuously opposed the Wilderness Act on the grounds of federal overreach. Goldwater's 1964 presidential campaign helped to capture a segment of the electorate and consolidate a "New Right" devoted to the sanctity of private property over public land, states' authority vis-à-vis the federal government, and broad resistance to regulation. Underlying overt arguments about limiting the role of government was a poorly disguised subtext about race and the rights of citizenship. Reagan's election campaign used overt racial appeals to motivate a white, conservative base, emulating Nixon's so-called "southern strategy." (In fact, both men had honed their electoral strategies first in California.) White constituencies—not only in the South, but also in northern and western locales—incensed by government enforcement of desegregation and voting rights resisted the expansion of federal environmental protections.[6]

Arch-conservatives constituted a distinct minority within the Republican Party before the late-60s. Then, conservatives' ascendance capitalized on a backlash against the 1960s protests, whites' objections to busing to achieve racial integration in schools, Watergate and the resignation of President Nixon, rising crime, and the Iran hostage crisis. The conservative constituency grew as a result of the perceived loss of American power after the U.S. withdrew from the Vietnam War. Economic factors included mounting unemployment, inflation, and increasing wealth disparities, that brought resistance to policies that appeared to be redistributive in favor of the poor.

In the 1970s, politicians in the West and South, including Republican senators Goldwater (Arizona), James Eastland and John Stennis (Mississipi), John Tower (Texas), and Strom Thurmond (South Carolina) opposed every major initiative that environmentalists offered. In a highly influential 1971 blueprint for conservatives, corporate attorney Lewis Powell, whom Nixon appointed to the Supreme Court in 1972, advised the U.S. Chamber of Commerce to copy the tactics of environmentalists and establish "public interest legal firms" to challenge environmental laws. By the late 1970s, a half-dozen regional legal firms were coordinated by the benignly-named National Legal Center for the Public Interest, with funding from major oil companies, including Amoco, Chevron, Marathon, Phillips, and Shell, as well as from Joseph Coors of the Coors brewing company. Among those regional firms active in the West was the Mountain States Legal Foundation in Denver, established in 1977, which challenged state regulation of oil and gas industries, Endangered Species Act designations, and anti-discrimination laws, among other cases. The law firm's first president was former Chamber of Commerce lobbyist and attorney James Watt.[7]

Responding to laws such as the Clean Air Act, energy industries helped to fund additional infrastructure for the conservative movement. Architects of efforts to reverse environmental gains included billionaire oil and banking magnate Richard Mellon Scaife and conservative political strategist Paul Weyrich, head of the Free Congress Foundation. Conservative think tanks emerged, such as the Heritage Foundation (founded in 1973 with support from Scaife) and the Cato Institute (founded in 1977 with support from foundations associated with Koch Industries, the diversified oil and chemical companies that would be headed by Charles and David Koch). Funding researchers who penned briefing papers spurning ecologists' scientific studies, these think tanks would provide talking points for a generation of politicians and appointed officials. The conservative American Legislative Exchange Council (ALEC), formed in 1973, primarily aims to influence state legislatures in favor of "limited government, free markets and federalism." Conservatives were also building a mass base, through organizations such as the Moral Majority, founded by televangelist Jerry Falwell in 1979.[8]

Conservatives took the dismantling of environmental laws and regulations as part of their core mission. A special 1982 report prepared for the Republican Study Committee, "The Specter of Environmentalism: The Threat of Environmental Groups," warned that "Extremist environmentalism threatens to undermine natural resource and economic development." Circulated among Republican lawmakers, the report acknowledged growing popular support for the environmental lobby but saw a political opportunity for conservatives in opposing environmental measures, particularly among voters in the American West.[9]

Although significant bipartisan support had been crucial to the passage of environmental reforms in the 1960s and 1970s, Republican enthusiasm for environmental reform had not matched that of the Democrats since World War II. By 1973, Democratic members of Congress were twice as likely as Republicans to vote for environmental reform. Historian James Morton Turner cites social scientists Riley E. Dunlap and Michael Patrick Allen in reporting that, "Republicans voted for the environmental reform agenda 27 percent of the time in 1973, 19 percent in 1994, and 10 percent in 2004. In contrast, Democrats voted for the same agenda 56 percent, 68 percent, and 86 percent of the time, respectively."[10]

However, local or regional interests as much as party affiliation seemed to govern legislators' stances on bills affecting natural resources. Key Democrats opposed environmental legislation and many Republicans supported protective measures. Colorado congressman Wayne Aspinall, who so vehemently opposed the 1964 Wilderness Act, for example, was a Democrat. Senator Edmund Muskie, Earth Day supporter and a Maine Democrat, found an ally in first term Tennessee Republican Howard Baker to forge and pass the 1970 Clean Air Act (*unanimously* in the Senate) and the Clean Water Act.[11] The significant margin of Republican support for environmental legislation was crucial; the decline of that support proved debilitating.

With the creation of an infrastructure of conservative institutions and the expansion of their influence in Congress, bipartisan support for environmental legislation had begun to decline by the end of Nixon's presidency, certainly by the start of the Reagan years. The irony, wrote historian Brian Allen Drake, "is that in rejecting the federal role in environmental protection, the Republican Party turned its back on its own legacy, much as it did when it dropped the mantle of civil rights in favor of the Southern Strategy."[12]

A small but influential group of western anti-environmentalists, dubbed the "Sagebrush Rebellion"—ranchers, loggers, and grazing outfits who opposed expanding wilderness areas in the West—surfaced in 1979. Sagebrush was in part a reaction to the Federal Land Policy and Management Act of 1976, which reinforced the multiple uses policy on federal lands. The multiple uses policy valued "scientific, scenic, historical, ecological, environmental, air and atmospheric, water resource, and archeological" uses of public lands alongside mining, grazing, and timber harvesting.[13] The stockholders, mine operators, and timber company officials who held profitable low-cost leases on public lands, viewed the multiple use policy as an encroachment.

The architects of Sagebrush raised state's rights arguments to challenge federal land policy. Their activism was one manifestation of a broader countermovement— a populist revolt devoted to transferring federal control of public lands and wilderness areas to the states or the private sector. The rebellion was relatively short-lived, however, faltering on the realization that if the land were offered for public sale, the states would have to allocate substantial funds to maintain big tracts of land and farmers and grazers would likely lose out to wealthy mining interests. The Sagebrush Rebellion lasted only until 1984, but its proponents did not disappear.[14]

Reagan Administration Actions

One symbol of Reagan's level of environmental concern was his refusal to reaffix solar panels to the White House roof after it was repaired. During the Carter administration, the panels had supplied solar-heated water for the cafeteria and the laundry. But Reagan went well beyond symbolism in his opposition to renewable energy, slashing funding for research on alternative sources of energy.[15]

A primary Reagan administration thrust was to devolve responsibility for environment, health, and social welfare from the federal government to the states. The "New Federalism," as it was called, branded as "unfunded mandates" federal regulations requiring the states to provide environmental protection without federal resources to defray the cost. Labeling regulations "command and control" measures put a pejorative spin on the 1970s environmental legislation.

Having briefly considered abolishing the Council on Environmental Quality, Reagan settled instead "on dismissing half the staff and halving the budget." His Task Force on Regulatory Relief—headed by Vice President George H.W. Bush—solicited businesses and trade groups to devise a "hit list" of regulations to be "relaxed or eliminated." The Clean Air Act was an explicit target. The administration temporarily froze all pending regulations, requiring they be submitted to the Office of Management and Budget (OMB) for cost-benefit assessments, and issued a directive not to publish proposed rule changes until the OMB had commented. Shrouding procedures for regulatory review in secrecy "sometimes serve[d] merely to launder industry arguments on their way to the EPA," noted one study of Reagan-era rule-making.[16]

Most significantly, Reagan appointed a quartet of anti-environmentalists from the West to key administrative posts. Most prominent were Sagebrush rebel and extractive industry attorney James Watt as Secretary of the Interior, who, as director of the Mountain States Legal Foundation, came directly out of the conservative infrastructure built in the 1970s, and conservative Colorado attorney Anne Gorsuch as head of the EPA. Reagan also named Louisiana-Pacific timber company general counsel John Crowell as Assistant Secretary of Agriculture overseeing the U.S. Forest Service and Colorado rancher Robert Burford to lead the Bureau of Land Management (BLM). Each appointee was hostile to the missions of their respective agencies; most of them did not last a full term.

After James Watt promoted opening eighty million acres of federal land to oil extraction and mining, he was featured on the cover of *TIME* magazine in 1982, under the headline "Going, Going. . .! Land Sale of the Century." In a

1983 speech, Watt compared environmentalists to Nazis *and* Bolsheviks. The Sierra Club, Friends of the Earth, the Wilderness Society, and other groups gathered more than one million signatures on a petition—"What's Wrong? Watt's Wrong!"—calling for Watt's ouster. Watt also came under fire from Congress, which blocked his attempts to increase federal land leases to coal companies and expand offshore oil and gas drilling. His resignation was hastened by a comment that he made about the composition of a coal industry advisory committee. "We have every kind of mixture you can have," he said, "I have a black, I have a woman, two Jews and a cripple. And we have talent." Watt resigned in late 1983 to avoid being ousted by Congress.[17]

Mainstream environmental groups managed to arrange a meeting with Anne Gorsuch in July 1981, but upon asking for regular communication with the EPA and environmental leaders, the group was rebuffed. Gorsuch reportedly replied, "I don't have time to keep everybody informed in town who wants to be informed."[18]

Agency directors seldom seek to *decrease* their budgets, but Gorsuch slashed the EPA budget by more than 20 percent, specifically cutting funding for enforcement. She, too, was forced to resign. Congress cited her with contempt for refusing to turn over records of the Superfund program "amid charges of political manipulation and mismanagement," *The New York Times* reported. Her aide at the EPA, Rita Lavelle, went to prison for lying to Congress and obstructing a federal investigation of a former employer's waste dumping practices at California's Stringfellow Acid Pits.[19]

Six hundred displaced EPA personnel formed a "SAVE EPA" group, working alongside environmental groups, EPA staff unions—the American Federation of Government Employees (AFGE) Council 238 and the newly chartered National Federation of Federal Employees Local 2050—and allies in Congress to restore funding and return the agency to its mission. When the first administrator of the agency, Republican moderate William D. Ruckelshaus, returned to head the agency, EPA staff cheered.[20]

Environmental Activism Swells

Under fire, the environmental movement swelled. Though the conservative countermovement brought setbacks in the regulatory arena, the hostilities of the Reagan era proved a boon to environmental organizations. The threat of losing environmental protections prompted public concern that aided in recruiting new members, catalyzed collaboration, spurred robust fundraising, and sparked local conservation efforts. The environmental movement reshaped itself in response to the conservative countermovement in ways that would ultimately prove both constructive and detrimental.

Environmental organizations had experienced record growth rates in the late 1960s, especially in 1969 and 1970. The rate of membership growth in five major groups slowed between 1971 and 1975. All told, however, over the two decades between 1965 and 1985, membership in the ten largest environmental groups increased more than six-fold (from 500,000 to 3.3 million). After Reagan was re-elected, membership doubled again by 1990 (7.2 million). Over the twenty-five-year period between 1965 and 1990, organizational assets grew from less than $10 million to $514 million.[21]

Growth appeared to be related to the groups' platforms. Between 1970 and 1980 the Wilderness Society and the Izaak Walton League, both traditional wilderness groups, experienced slight declines in membership. Groups that had expanded their agendas to take on pollution-related concerns grew: the Sierra Club (by 46 percent) and the National Wildlife Federation (by 51 percent). The National Wildlife Federation was by far the largest of the older wilderness groups, with 612,000 members in 1975 (almost double the National Audubon Society, and four times the Sierra Club membership). The Manhattan-based Audubon Society, known as a group of bird watchers, revamped its identity by campaigning against DDT, and grew by a whopping 330 percent.[22]

Even as overall membership in environmental organizations grew significantly, movement support flagged among some constituencies. In addition, a deliberate strategy drove a wedge between historic allies. Fishers and hunters had formed a key constituency on issues of wilderness protection: the Izaak Walton League, Ducks Unlimited, Trout Unlimited, the Bass Anglers, and countless local hunting and fishing clubs. Several factors contributed to some supporters falling away. Animal liberation activists' rejection of hunting and challenge to unlimited gun rights alienated some fishermen and hunters, historian Thomas Wellock has noted. The themes of individual liberty and rejection of federal authority that were motivating the conservative upsurge had long resonated among many conservationists, some of whom then gravitated to more conservative positions. Also, however, Carl Pope, of the Sierra Club, identified "a conscious political strategy to separate rural hunters and fishers from urban environmentalists." Anti-Sierra Club articles started appearing in hunting magazines. Said Pope, "It wasn't about hunting and fishing. It was about politics."[23]

For the most part, however, environmental activists were galvanized by the offensive against hard-won advances. The nationals and grassroots groups battled the administration, successfully pressing Congress to preserve legislative gains. In the face of conservative power in the executive branch and the Senate, some nationals sought compromise, even accommodation, with industrialists. By contrast, other groups expanded grassroots organizing.

The 1980s saw the articulation of increasingly diverse variants of environmental thought and action: ecofeminism, radical libertarianism, and various biocentric approaches, including deep ecology. This period saw the advent of an environmental justice movement that began to reframe the very definition of environmentalism.

On the one hand, the chilling political climate sparked an unprecedented level of collaboration among environmental groups. Leaders of several national environmental organizations, many of them actively pressuring Congress to hold the line against environmental rollbacks, came together in Washington, D.C. in 1981. Philanthropist Robert Allen of the Kendall Foundation invited CEOs of some of the largest and most effective environmental organizations to join a group that became known as the "Group of Ten." Some of the groups had affiliated informally for various campaigns during the 1970s, but several of the leaders had never met prior to the 1981 gathering.[24]

The "Group of Ten"

1981 Member Organizations of the "Group of Ten," with CEOs at the time:

National Audubon Society, Russell Peterson

Sierra Club, J. Michael McCloskey

Izaak Walton League, Jack Lorenz*

National Parks Conservation Association, Paul C. Pritchard*

National Wildlife Federation, Thomas Kimball

The Wilderness Society, William (Bill) Turnage

Environmental Defense Fund, Janet Brown†

Environmental Policy Institute, Louise Dunlap†

Friends of the Earth, Rafe Pomerance

Natural Resources Defense Council, John H. Adams

*The Izaak Walton League and the National Parks Conservation Association joined after first meeting.
†The chief executives of the Group of Ten included two women when the group was founded.[25]

The combined lobbying efforts of the Group of Ten would prove important to limiting the damage to the regulatory scaffolding built in the 1970s. However, the exclusivity of the new alliance created tensions within the movement. Major groups, including the World Wildlife Fund and The Nature Conservancy, were not invited because they were not considered "active," that is, they were not involved in lobbying Congress. Greenpeace and Environmental Action were excluded because they engaged in direct action protests. The Conservation Foundation declined membership because director William Reilly (who later became EPA Administrator under George H.W. Bush) was concerned about associating with "adversarial" litigation groups. Bill Turnage of The Wilderness Society has said that, even within the Group, the "territoriality and rivalry" was intense.[26]

Charges of elitism arose from groups not invited to the table and the divide between Beltway environmentalists and grassroots movements deepened. Tensions rose as the national groups increasingly hired managerial leaders, people who had not necessarily come up through the ranks as environmental activists. In 1990, all the top leaders of the Group of Ten organizations were men. Even after the group doubled in size in the 1990s to become "the Green Group," as noted by Robert Gottlieb, the group "still functioned as if they had proprietary rights to the development of environmental policy."[27]

In 1982, several national groups jointly published *Ronald Reagan and the American Environment: An Indictment.* The report critiqued, for example, projections of a nearly 50 percent hike in timber sales from national forests, but cuts to trail maintenance by 30 percent. The publication recommended electoral strategies: Invite candidates to environmental forums. Offer to speak or debate about the book before local clubs. Carry out a "Plan of Fifteen": discuss action steps with "five friends, five relatives, and five people where you work."[28] While this and other educational efforts were directed at supplying information and tools to grassroots groups and individuals, national entities maintained limited staff devoted to local organizing, a major strategic failure.

Grassroots groups were often less willing to compromise than the national groups, as illustrated by their respective positions on Arizona senator Morris Udall's 1981 bill to create a permanent national repository for high-level radioactive waste. Radioactive waste—discards from bomb plants and from nuclear electricity-generating plants—was a mounting ecological problem with no obvious solution. Everyone was anxious to address the problem of decentralized, poorly monitored dumps. National groups, including Environmental Action, the Environmental Policy Center, Friends of the Earth, and the Sierra Club, supported the bill because it committed to establishing a permanent national repository. (The Sierra Club later withdrew its support.) But as it evolved, the bill gave the nuclear industry protection from both citizen complaints and EPA oversight and authorized storage options for reprocessed spent fuel, which longtime grassroots anti-nuclear activists at the Clamshell Alliance and the Abalone Alliance opposed. With endorsement from the key national groups, however, the Nuclear Waste Policy Act of 1982 passed easily. It was the only major new environmental law to be passed between 1981 and 1986. The law remains controversial, prompting battles, for example, over siting the radioactive dump abutting Western Shoshone land at Yucca Mountain, Nevada. Opposition from tribes, from Nevadans (in 1989, the Nevada legislature made it illegal to dump high-level nuclear waste in the state), and from environmental groups has stalled the project for decades.[29]

Grassroots activists and the EPA were identifying more and more hazardous sites. Lois Gibbs estimated that the Center for Health, Environment, and Justice was providing advice on organizing and financial support to five thousand local groups nationwide in the late 1980s. Activists near hazardous sites were conducting 'popular epidemiology'—doing their own research into local patterns of exposure and disease—often in collaboration with academic scientists. Like the women who carried out the Baby Tooth Survey in the 1950s, these groups employed "citizen science" to locate and confront environmental hazards to human health, sometimes explicitly critiquing the use of science to create hazardous "military technologies and synthetic agrochemicals."[30]

Times Beach, Missouri, Residents Forced Out by Dioxin Exposure

In late 1982, at homes located along a stretch of Route 66 just seventeen miles west of St. Louis, scientists found high levels of highly toxic dioxin. Dioxin-laced oil had been sprayed on unpaved roads to keep down dust in the vicinity. (A 1979 National Wildlife Federation survey listed Missouri second only to Georgia in hazardous waste; twenty-six sites contaminated with dioxin, a probable carcinogen, were located in a chemical-industry intensive area of eastern Missouri.) "The Beach," a former summer resort turned white working-class suburb, lay along the Meramec River, which flooded in December 1982, putting residents' homes under ten or more feet of water. Tests of water and soil showed levels of dioxin registering one hundred or more times the EPA standard. An EPA "Christmas letter" advised the more than two thousand residents of Times Beach: "If you are in town it is advisable for you to leave, if you are out of town do not go back."[31]

Times Beach Mayor Marilyn Leistner described the impact of the discovery of dioxin exposure: "For us it has meant loss of property values, community, neighbors, friends, identity, and security, and most of all, loss of our health. It has meant marital discord, discipline problems in school children, a type of forced bankruptcy, redlining by insurance companies, loss of liability insurance on property." Like residents of Love Canal and Three Mile Island, residents of Times Beach, "lost control of their lives; the choices were no longer theirs, many of us no longer had faith in the government or in the system."[32] EPA recalcitrance in the wake of the disaster was central to that loss of faith.

It soon became clear that dumping of dioxin- and polychlorinated biphenyl (PCB)-laced oil had been going on for more than a decade. Fifty miles northwest in Moscow Mills, Shenandoah Arena horse park owner Judy Piatt had traced the deaths of her fifty horses to a waste hauler, Russell Bliss, who had sprayed the horse track, among other locales, with wastes from several companies. One area plant had produced Agent Orange, the dioxin-based defoliant the U.S. had used to destroy tropical forests in Vietnam. Bliss Oil Co. was still dumping wastes on the roadsides, and neither the EPA nor state authorities had taken remedial action. Times Beach became a national symbol of hazardous waste mismanagement. Under pressure from a Congressional investigation and just weeks before she resigned, Anne Gorsuch (now Burford) came to Times Beach in February 1983 to announce a Superfund buyout and relocation plan. Compounding the exposures and despite protests, a hazardous waste incinerator was built at Times Beach. The town was disincorporated in 1985 and not until 1997 was the cleanup process declared complete. In 1999, the area was designated Route 66 State Park, a bird sanctuary.[33]

Environmental Justice

Even as the Reagan administration attempted to blunt environmental gains, a redefined environmentalism was emerging out of the civil rights and the anti-toxics struggles. Identifying a pattern of toxic facilities sited in proximity to communities of color, the Reverend Benjamin Chavis, a former chemistry teacher and black freedom movement activist from Oxford, North Carolina, coined the term, "environmental racism." Chavis defined environmental racism as "racial discrimination in environmental policymaking, the enforcement of regulations and laws, the deliberate targeting of communities of color for toxic waste facilities, the official sanctioning of the life-threatening presence of poisons and pollutants in our communities, and the history of excluding people of color from leadership of the environmental movement." The term came also to refer to the lack of amenities in neighborhoods where people of color or low-income populations reside. Reframing the focus of the movement in this way provided an important counterthrust to the Reagan-era assault on environmentalism.[34]

A struggle over a landfill in Warren County, North Carolina, was pivotal. A contractor for the state had sprayed oil containing banned chemicals—highly toxic PCBs—along highway roadsides. The chemicals were known to be hazardous to human health, causing skin lesions, liver disease, and developmental disabilities in children, and were associated with various cancers. Once the illegal roadside dumping was discovered, state officials began looking for a place to deposit the PCB-contaminated soil. After vetting several locales, officials chose to

PHOTO 4.1 Southern Christian Leadership Conference President Rev. Joseph Lowery (center) joined the North Carolina group, Warren County Citizens Concerned About PCBs, in their protest of a PCB landfill in a majority African American neighborhood. Photo credit Janet Knott/*The Boston Globe* via Getty Images, 1982.

construct a landfill near an African American neighborhood in Warren County. People living nearby were especially concerned that the local water supply could become contaminated with PCBs.[35]

Residents organized Warren County Citizens Concerned about PCBs in protest, but state officials refused to halt the dumping. Citizens Concerned sought the support of the SCLC, the civil rights organization founded in the late 1950s by the Reverend Martin Luther King, Jr. In late September, at the peak of the Warren County struggle, SCLC president the Reverend Joseph Lowery and Mrs. Evelyn Lowery participated in a human blockade against trucks bringing PCB-contaminated soil to the site and were among the 410 arrested that day. The campaign was multiracial, as indicated by the arrests: 241 African Americans, 129 whites (including local landowners), and forty Native Americans. Members of the Congressional Black Caucus joined the protest. Unsuccessful in blocking the PCB landfill, Warren County activists nonetheless helped inaugurate a new phase of the environmental movement, one in which African Americans, other activists of color, and their white allies overtly challenged second-class citizenship marked by environmental vulnerability. The landfill struggle built a multiracial campaign that led to significant black empowerment in this northeast North Carolina region. In the aftermath, African Americans were elected to the state house and senate and as county sheriff and obtained positions as county manager and registrar of deeds.[36]

Methods for documenting environmental racism grew in part out of a landfill challenge in a majority (82 percent) black neighborhood in Houston, Texas. In 1979, Margaret Bean, Patricia Reaux, and Louise Black, African American residents of Northwood Manor, Texas, learned that Southwestern Waste Management was building a landfill near the local high school. The three women and other residents—mostly homeowners—and civic groups formed the Northeast Community Action Group and sought legal help from attorney Linda McKeever Bullard to block the landfill siting as discriminatory. Bullard asked her husband, Robert Bullard, a sociologist, to investigate. Just as the activists had suspected, Bob Bullard identified a pattern: three of the four privately-owned toxic waste dumps in Houston were located in close proximity to African American and Latino neighborhoods. Though the Northwood Manor residents lost their suit, and the landfill was completed, the fight led the city to impose restrictions on landfills near public facilities, including schools, and the Texas Department of Health agreed to require detailed land use, economic, and demographic data before issuing future landfill permits. Robert Bullard went on to make the study of environmental racism the focus of his work, writing, among other books, *Dumping in Dixie: Race, Class, and Environmental Quality* (1990). In that book, Bullard outlined the pattern of environmental racism, showing that hazardous waste and other noxious facilities were disproportionately concentrated in long established communities of color and low-income neighborhoods in fourteen southern states.[37]

In 1983, in the wake of the Warren County struggle, a federal General Accounting Office (GAO) study confirmed the disparate proximity by race to hazardous waste sites. Then, in 1987, *Toxic Wastes and Race*, prepared by Charles Lee and published by the Commission for Racial Justice of the United Church of Christ, not only mapped hazardous waste sites near communities of color but also showed race to be the single most significant factor in hazardous waste siting, more important than household income, property values, or rates of home ownership. Communities of color, including Native American reservations, dominated the *Toxic Wastes and Race* map. The pattern was particularly stark in the South and Southwest.[38]

It is difficult to demonstrate the discrimination was intentional. Environmental advocates argued that the discriminatory *effect* of siting decisions was hazardous to communities of color and the poor, whether or not *intent* to discriminate could be demonstrated. One report from the California waste industry consulting firm Cerrell Associates revealed that, in siting noxious facilities, industry targeted neighborhoods least likely to resist. "All socioeconomic groupings tend to resent the nearby siting of major facilities," the Cerrell report acknowledged, "but the middle and upper-socioeconomic strata possess better resources to effectuate their opposition." The consultants recommended against siting hazardous facilities within a five-mile radius of wealthier neighborhoods, targeting instead "[o]lder people, people with a high school education or less, and those who adhere to a free market orientation."[39]

Anti-toxics campaigns were only one aspect of environmental justice. The cooperative farming movement that had led Fannie Lou Hamer to start the Freedom Farm Corporation in 1969 was part of a larger movement across the South. Headquartered in Atlanta, with a training center in Epes, Alabama, the Federation of Southern Cooperatives formed in 1967 to provide support and collective marketing opportunities to small farmers, particularly black farmers. Robert S. Browne founded the Emergency Land Fund in 1973 to combat the precipitous decline in African American land ownership, which dropped by nearly half from a peak of fifteen million acres in 1910 to 7.8 million acres in 1999. The two organizations merged in 1985, strengthening the Federation and broadening its mission. By 1990, organization leaders framed their work as "environmental justice" and "sustainable agriculture." The Federation fought the U.S. Department of Agriculture over denying loans to black farmers and eventually won major discrimination lawsuits against the agency. The Federation had a global focus, too, teaching and learning from farmers in South Africa, Cuba, and other countries about sustainable agriculture methods.[40]

Bhopal: Transnational Chemical Disaster

The transnational nature of the pollution crisis was highlighted when the pesticide production facility at a Union Carbide plant in working class neighborhood of Bhopal, India, exploded on the night of December 2, 1984. The explosion released the chemical methyl isocyanate, killing thousands of people in their beds and exposing as many as 500,000 more to the gas. The production of the pesticide in Bhopal was part of the "Green Revolution," the U.S. strategy for selling industrial agriculture to India and other developing countries. "[T]he 'Green Revolution' purposefully disrupted the small-scale, manual, multicrop, organic agriculture that had developed in India over thousands of years," writes medical anthropologist Bridget Hanna, "in favor of large-scale, monocrop, chemically and mechanically maintained agriculture."[41]

"It couldn't happen here," was the official refrain in the U.S. after Bhopal; stringent laws and regulations protected Americans from such disasters. And then it did. Just eight months after Bhopal, on August 11, 1985, an explosion at a Union Carbide plant released a toxic mix containing the same lethal pesticide in the Kanawha Valley, West Virginia. Thousands were affected, 135 seriously enough to go to the hospital. With the claim, "We all live in Bhopal," activist George Bradford both expressed solidarity with the Bhopal victims and pointed out that even without an explosion, routine and pervasive exposure to toxic chemicals was widespread in the United States and worldwide. Bhopal drove reform in the United States. "Bhopal's Babies" included new U.S. regulations requiring polluting industries to report emissions to the EPA for a public national database.[42]

The aftermath of Bhopal underscored the importance of global environmental action. Over the next thirty years, Bhopal victims and their allies helped reshape activism. The Bhopal Group for Information and Action in India and the Bhopal Action Resource Center in the U.S. continue to seek recompense and medical treatment for the survivors. The transnational—or translocal—campaign linked Bhopali activists with U.S. counterparts, including activists at the Highlander Research and Education Center in New Market, Tennessee. The organizing tradition at Highlander drew on the experiences and knowledge of participants as the core strength of any movement. Collecting histories of survivors, conducting popular epidemiology, and mapping the power dynamics among the relevant economic players were among the strategies utilized.[43]

The Bhopal disaster raised questions about human rights and the changing nature of environmentalism. The Bhopal disaster also highlighted the ever-present risk of catastrophe in modern society. "Risks are always *future* events that *may* occur, that *threaten* us," wrote German sociologist Ulrich Beck.[44]

Union Carbide reached a $470 million settlement with the Indian government in 1989 for the 600,000 affected individuals that was "a disaster in itself," later noted the *Los Angeles Times*. Bhopal also showed how movements operate at different scales over time. The prolonged fight over compensation, cleanup, and health of the Bhopal survivors began attracting more attention in the U.S. in the 1990s, as economic globalization made U.S. activists more sensitive to overseas environmental problems. The international movement picked up again in 2001 after Dow and Union Carbide merged.[45] The fight continues to the present.

Industry's Response to the Upsurge in Environmentalism

Using stealth tactics to undermine environmental activism, industry groups created entities meant to weaken or forestall environmental regulation, with names that sounded neutral or even pro-environment. The Competitive Enterprise Institute and the Thomas Jefferson Institute for Public Policy "nourish a special hostility toward the climate issue," historian Christopher Sellers explains. The National Wetlands Coalition represents the oil and gas industry. The U.S. Council for Energy Awareness was a front for pro-nuclear companies. The Alliance for America solicited access to public lands on behalf of more than 550 timber, mining, and livestock interest groups. The Heartland Institute joined these ranks in 1984. Founded by anti-tax advocate Americans for Tax Reform founder and president Grover Norquist and conservative Republican South Carolina senator Jim DeMint, the organization championed "free-market solutions to social and economic problems" through "individual liberties, limited government, and free markets." Often co-opting environmental rhetoric, these groups politicized science, dismissing environmental researchers' cautions regarding biotechnology, climate change, even dioxin. "Greenwashing" used public relations tactics to exaggerate a company's commitment to "being green."[46]

By the mid-1980s, the political opposition to environmental reform had grown more sophisticated. Using a blend of pop psychology and corporate communications, industry public relations consultants trained corporate executives in "outrage reduction" and "Dealing with Angry People." These strategies aimed to defuse protest rather than address its causes, whether toxic exposure, habitat destruction, or sprawl. After "citizen advisory councils" or "community advisory groups" were established at numerous EPA Superfund cleanup sites in response to public pressure, regulated entities and the EPA sought to "manage the movement," entangling activists in endless meetings with little follow-through and limited results.[47] Though soon exposed, these strategies were nevertheless disorienting to environmental campaigners, who had to adapt quickly.

Officials from a range of industries learned that they could limit regulation of their products simply by casting doubt about the level of hazard associated with use. In their 2010 book, *Merchants of Doubt*, Naomi Oreskes and Erik Conway explained the technique perfected by the tobacco industry. Using industry-funded science to "manufacture doubt," industry officials created just enough doubt about critical studies of their products to avoid or lessen regulation. With scientific information at the heart of many claims of ecological harm, industrial firms cultivated a network of experts to produce favorable studies. The most notorious of these efforts was exposed in the 1980s, when it was found that the Illinois-based IBT Labs had falsified hundreds of animal studies on which federal agencies such as the FDA and the EPA had relied in determining safety standards.[48]

Between 1983 and 1993, the EPA shifted its method of evaluating harms to human health and the environment to a risk assessment paradigm. Using epidemiological tools for the study of the spread of disease to its own ends, industry seized upon quantitative risk assessment techniques to posit levels of "acceptable" risk, downplaying the seriousness of environmental exposures.[49]

Favored countermovement strategies in the legal field include "takings" litigation. Relying on the Fifth Amendment of the Constitution, which promises no taking of "private property for public use, without just compensation," property owners challenged environmental restrictions on development, such as limitations on coastal construction. In "takings" litigation, property owners attempt to win compensation by claiming that the value of their property is severely decreased by environmental regulations or administrative decisions.[50]

Developers and industry officials repeatedly filed Strategic Lawsuits Against Public Participation, or SLAPP suits, countersuing those who raised concerns about their construction plans, manufacturing methods, or disposal operations.

Such cases were not necessarily designed to win, but to force environmental staffers or volunteers to hire attorneys to defend against the suit, tying up activists' valuable time and limited financial resources. In one of the first such suits directed at an environmental group, Sierra Club activists faced an $80 million lawsuit filed by a developer in 1972 after the club had successfully blocked a project to turn an historic 5,380-acre ranch outside Sacramento into "ranchettes." Sometimes SLAPP suits backfired. In the Sacramento case, the targeted Sierra Club activists filed a countersuit, a "SLAPPback" suit, and received a significant settlement from the construction company. (Many states have since instituted anti-SLAPP provisions.)[51]

After the Superfund law was amended and strengthened in 1986, the big chemical firms and other industrial manufacturers established the "Superfund Coalition" and began to seek inroads into the environmental movement. Composed of chemical and electrical giants Dow Chemical, DuPont, Monsanto, General Electric, Union Carbide, and their insurers, Hartford, Cigna, and Aetna, the group attempted to recruit environmental organizations for a collaborative study of the "problems" with Superfund. The Sierra Club, NRDC, EDF, and the Audubon Society saw the effort as a scheme to undermine the law and unanimously declined. The main problem with Superfund, they believed, was obvious: industry's failure to adequately meet their legal obligation to fund the program. The firms then chose the Conservation Foundation, which accepted a $2.5 million grant to "study" Superfund. The Superfund Coalition exemplified what journalist William Greider called "deep lobbying" and "mock democracy," a long-term strategy supported by industries with deep pockets and the ability to devote full-time staff and consultants to the effort. A 1991 *New York Times* article, "Experts Question Staggering Costs of Toxic Cleanups," gave the industries behind the Superfund Coalition precisely the headline they had hoped.[52]

Responding to the fact that public approval ratings of the U.S. chemical industry had dropped from 55 percent "mostly to very favorable" in 1965 to four percent by the end of the 1980s, the chemical industry launched a massive public relations campaign to position itself as friendly to the environment. So as to escape further regulation in the post-Bhopal environment, the chemical industry introduced the Responsible Care™ Initiative, designed by strategic communications consultants, aiming to show the American consumer that the industry was voluntarily monitoring itself.[53]

Corporations also sought to wield influence by giving directly to the Group of Ten, anticipating that their status as donors would protect them from criticism. "[S]ome of the worst environmental offenders—for example, DuPont, Chevron, Monsanto, Mobil, and WMX," writes Mark Dowie, "became some of the largest environmental donors." The National Wildlife Federation, the Conservation Foundation, the National Audubon Society, and the World Wildlife Fund, Dowie explained, were "among the largest recipients of corporate largesse."[54]

Despite the pressures external and internal to the movement, the 1980s were not without legislative progress on particular environmental initiatives. Congress passed amendments that strengthened the Safe Drinking Water Act in 1986 and the Clean Water Act in 1987. With anti-toxics groups pushing from the grassroots and Group of Ten organizations working in Washington, Democrats in Congress managed to renew and update the Superfund law in 1986. The Superfund Amendments and Reauthorization Act (SARA) extended the polluter pays principle and increased the Superfund Trust budget to $8.5 billion. SARA increased state involvement in decision-making, created additional avenues for citizen participation, and gave the EPA more power, including authority to settle with polluters. The amendments placed greater emphasis on evaluating human health near hazardous sites and updated criteria for placing sites on the National Priorities List to target for cleanup. The act was a clear victory for environmentalists.[55]

SARA Title III (the Emergency Planning and Community Right-to-Know Act (EPCRA, pronounced ĕp-cră)), known as the Right-to-Know Act, was a response to pressure by anti-toxics groups. A direct reaction to the chemical explosions in Bhopal and West Virginia, the Right-to-Know Act created the Toxic Release Inventory (TRI), requiring firms to make public data on their chemical releases.[56] The EPA has never had sufficient staff to verify the accuracy of the release reports, but the TRI does give communities one tool to better monitor emissions in their neighborhoods.

Since the 1970s, environmental litigation groups had pressed the EPA to enforce laws against pollution, preserve public lands, and protect endangered species. Under Reagan, organizations like the NRDC stepped up their enforcement efforts as well, surpassing the Department of Justice in pursuing alleged violations of the Clean Water Act, for example. (In 1982, the NRDC filed sixty-two cases compared to the more amply resourced EPA and Department of Justice's fifty-six cases.) A 1984 NRDC victory in *Chevron v. NRDC*, in which the Supreme Court held that courts owed deference to agency regulations, affirmed the EPA's authority to regulate, which would later prove fundamental to the agency's authority to regulate greenhouse gases.[57]

In a further sign of the resilience of the movement despite Reaganism and the increased salience of environmental protections in presidential campaigns, George H.W. Bush projected an image of himself as "the Environment President" during the 1988 race. Bush tapped Republican William Reilly, who had served as a senior staff member in the President's Council on Environmental Quality under Nixon and now directed the Conservation Foundation (which had merged with the World Wildlife Fund in 1985), to succeed Ruckelshaus at the EPA. However, senior Bush advisers reportedly "shoulder[ed] Reilly aside to water down critical decisions." Few positive domestic environmental policy changes occurred in a four-year term otherwise characterized as an era of "administrative neglect."[58]

Mainstream Groups Adapt

A number of leading national organizations modified their programs extensively to accommodate the conservative backlash. Some sought direct engagement with industry. For example, in 1982 the NWF initiated a series of meetings between environmental organizations and the business community, creating the Corporate Conservation Council, to identify common ground and skirt Washington gridlock. The largest of the Group of Ten organizations (with a $90 million annual budget and a staff of 630 in 1991), the NWF came under particular criticism for its cozy ties with industries like Waste Management, Inc., the world's largest waste disposal company and target of many local environmental battles. Waste Management's chairman, Dean Buntrock, was appointed to the NWF's board of directors in 1987. The NWF president, biologist Jay D. Hair, raised grassroots environmentalists' ire for drawing a $220,000 salary (approximately $492,300 in 2019 dollars) and maintaining the organization's glass and marble headquarters. Some viewed the Council's "Synergy" meetings as a much-needed and pragmatic collaboration; others considered them "the pinnacle of Washington environmentalists' accommodation to the ways of corporate America."[59]

In 1985, the Group of Ten published *An Environmental Agenda for the Future*, a pragmatic document that addressed eleven major policy areas: (1) nuclear (weapons) issues; (2) human population growth; (3) energy strategies; (4) water resources; (5) toxics and pollution control; (6) wild living resources; (7) private lands and agriculture; (8) protected land systems; (9) public lands; (10) urban environments; and (11) international responsibilities. Grassroots groups saw the document as top-down directive, composed with little input from activists outside Washington. The agenda placed a good deal of emphasis on overpopulation, while deliberately avoiding issues such as nuclear energy or the petrochemical industry that were deemed especially controversial or about which the organizations had less unanimity. By the end of the decade, noted Robert Gottlieb, the Group of Ten had "effectively redefined mainstream environmentalism less as a movement and more directly as an adjunct to the policy process."[60]

Electoral Strategies

In the 1970s, the major environmental organizations had focused on legislation and litigation; in the 1980s they moved more directly into the electoral arena. Several had already developed training programs to familiarize activists with the workings of Congress and state legislatures. Some coordinated "Lobby Days" in Washington for members to meet with representatives to press their concerns.

A number of environmental activists launched campaigns for elected office. Barry Commoner ran for president in 1980 with Native American LaDonna Harris as vice-president on the Citizens Party ticket, garnering less than one percent of the vote. Loosely following the model of Green Parties in Europe, which had begun coalescing in 1979, the U.S. Green Party began fielding candidates at the local level in 1985. Though nonprofit organizations could not directly endorse candidates, leaders of Audubon and several other Group of Ten organizations supported Democratic presidential candidate Walter Mondale in the 1984 election. In 1983, the newly formed Freeze Voter followed the League of Conservation Voters' example and began publishing scorecards of the voting records of members of Congress on nuclear issues. Freeze Voter '84 was one of seven antinuclear PACs in 1984 and raised $3.75 million of the nearly $5.5 million raised by the groups. Aligned with the Nuclear Weapons Freeze Campaign, leaders of Freeze Voter pushed for the major party platforms to adopt antinuclear positions and attempted to mobilize voters. A number of organizations incorporated separate 501(c) 4 groups, which, under the federal tax code, could conduct broader election-related activities, and which took a more active role in registering voters.[61]

In presidential campaigns launched in 1984 and 1988, the Reverend Jesse Jackson, a Martin Luther King associate and civil rights leader, challenged Reaganism and explicitly embraced environmentalism. The Jackson campaigns took organizational form in the Rainbow Coalition, a remarkable example of multiracial organizing, which brought together farmers, labor leaders, peace and environmental activists, leftists, and a sizable portion of black elected officials, whose numbers had expanded significantly since the passage of the Voting Rights Act in 1965. "[T]he emergence of the Jackson campaign in 1984," writes participant Sheila Collins, "as a progressive, black-led, multiracial, anticorporate, and anti-imperialist movement that took an electoral form must be appreciated as a daring and visionary innovation." Jackson attended environmental justice rallies around the country, supporting the farmworkers' campaign to end pesticide poisoning in the fields, the National Family Farm Coalition's efforts to support farmers, and low-wage laborers' right to organize against sweatshop practices. A number of peace movement and environmental leaders endorsed Jackson's campaign as individuals; some took on leadership roles in the coalition. Electoral politics, Collins argues, gave peace and environmental leaders access to broader publics. However, the Democratic Leadership Council (DLC), a centrist group that formed in 1985 within the Democratic Party, sidelined the Rainbow effort, nominating DLC moderate Arkansas governor Bill Clinton as its standard bearer in 1992.[62]

The Environmental Movement Expands

Despite, and in some ways because of, the hammer that the Reagan administration brought down on legislative and regulatory progress, not only were activists energized, but the field of environmental movements expanded. The environmental justice movement arose alongside multi-issue organizations like the Rainbow Coalition.

Once again, the peace movement served as a stimulus to environmental activism. The introduction of the controversial Strategic Defense Initiative (SDI), a proposal to create a missile defense shield, only escalated tensions. Nicknamed "Star Wars" after the popular series of movies, SDI drove the development of ever more powerful nuclear weapons designed to penetrate the defensive shield. Congress voted for huge increases in military spending during Reagan's tenure, $456.5 billion in 1987 as compared with $325.1 billion in 1980.[63]

Peace organizations such as the Committee for a Sane Nuclear Policy (SANE) had long been allied with the environmental movement. Spurred by Reagan's saber-rattling on nuclear arms, peace activists showed a marked resurgence, making even louder demands for a halt to the arms race with the Soviet Union. A young woman from Huntsville, Alabama, Randall Forsberg, is credited with advancing the proposal for "a mutual and verifiable halt by the United States and the Soviet Union on the testing, production and deployment of all nuclear weapons," which became known as the "Nuclear Freeze" or simply "the Freeze." Because continued nuclear testing, potential deployment, and nuclear waste posed environmental threats, the Nuclear Weapons Freeze Campaign united environmental activists and peace organizations in a coalition against the nuclear arms race. The damage to public health from the Cold War nuclear buildup was already evident at weapons building sites. For example, at the Rocky Flats production facility in Colorado, where the plutonium bomb triggers were made, plant workers and nearby residents subject to radiation releases registered elevated levels of leukemia and of lung, bronchial, ovarian, and testicular cancer.[64] Tens of thousands of new activists joined the anti-nuclear movement in the early 1980s.

The Freeze campaign's signature event was a June 12, 1982, march up Fifth Avenue to the United Nations building in New York City that attracted more than 700,000 participants. The march reflected the fact that the nuclear freeze movement had attracted mostly white activists across all age groups, especially women. However, African American leaders and cultural icons were among the June 12 speakers. Rev. Herbert Daughtry of the National Black United Front led a contingent that included Harry Belafonte, Chaka Kahn, Toni Morrison, Ossie Davis, and Ruby Dee in a separate march through Harlem that then converged with other marchers. In a victory for the campaign, the U.S. signed an Intermediate Nuclear Forces Treaty with the Soviets in 1987, with both sides agreeing to destroy ground-launched nuclear and conventional intermediate-range missiles.[65]

The reactor meltdown at the Soviet nuclear installation at Chernobyl on April 28, 1986, during the negotiations over the nuclear treaty, spurred the signing of the treaty and highlighted the hazards of nuclear energy production. More serious than the Three Mile Island accident, Chernobyl was not only a disaster for the Soviet people living nearby and downwind. The radiation drifted into Europe and to other countries around the globe. After the signing of the treaty,

Chernobyl encouraged activists to shift their focus from nuclear disarmament to the hazards of nuclear power.[66]

Women's Environmental Activism and Ecofeminism

French feminist Françoise d'Eaubonne coined the term *ecofeminism* in 1974. Ecofeminism's central insight: the subjugation of women and the degradation of nature are intertwined, and, therefore, the liberation of each requires the liberation of the other. Beyond this central point, ecofeminists hold divergent views, some nearly diametrically opposed to others. In addition, many female eco-activists neither define themselves as feminists nor embrace the language of feminism, even as they advance both causes.[67]

Environmental historian Carolyn Merchant and others have detailed the diverse vantage points from which women activists and feminist theorists have approached environmental thought and action. Liberal ecofeminists demanded greater attention to environmental issues that disproportionately affect women and critiqued environmental organizations for lacking women in leadership positions. (In the early 1980s, men headed all but two of the major national organizations who joined the Group of Ten.) Generally, liberal ecofeminism does not fundamentally question human dominion over nature or the liberal economic order. Cultural ecofeminists embrace the idea that women's biological and social roles as mothers inspire them to ensure the Earth's capacity to support future generations. Other feminist thinkers bristle at the notion that gender roles are in any way constrained by biology. The idea that "women's nature is to nurture" is, in their view, counter to the most basic tenets of feminism and gender equality.[68]

Radical ecofeminists, including Marxist and socialist feminists, regard both environmental degradation and the devaluation of women's work—both unpaid work in the home and lower-paid work elsewhere—as structural problems and call for a fundamental social and economic transformation. Urban geographer Dolores Hayden suggests that the structure of cities reinforces gender inequality by continuing to privatize women's work, and that reshaping environments through innovative living solutions such as co-housing could yield greater equality.[69]

In his indispensable history of the environmental movement, *Forcing the Spring*, Robert Gottlieb argues that ecofeminism represented "more a set of ideas than an actual set of organizations." Gottlieb suggests that after playing a strong role in the anti-nuclear activism of the early 1980s, ecofeminism faded as "a significant activist force." The evolution of Women's Action for Nuclear Disarmament (WAND, pronounced "wănd") offers an illustrative counter-example. Founded in 1982 by U.S.-based, Australia-born pediatrician Helen Caldicott, WAND focused its early work on achieving a comprehensive nuclear test ban treaty between the U.S. and the Soviet Union. That work melded peace and ecological themes.

After the nuclear weapons threat and Cold War hostilities receded, WAND explicitly embraced an environmental agenda, changing its name to Women's Action for New Directions in 1991 and tackling the problems of civilian nuclear energy and nuclear waste. Adopting the maternalist slogan, "War is not healthy for children and other living things," WAND's ecofeminist argument for activist intervention in environmental affairs was implicit: that women in their social— *not biological*—roles as mothers and caregivers represented a constituency uniquely invested in protecting the next generation from nuclear and other environmental threats. (In 2019, WAND stands as the primary group assisting the residents of Shell Bluff in 51 percent minority Burke County, Georgia, in their fight to block the only nuclear reactors presently being built in the U.S.)[70]

Like mainstream environmentalists, white ecofeminists have faced criticism for excluding women of color and failing to tackle racial and class inequalities. Incorporating race and class perspectives, social justice or intersectional ecofeminism considers environmental inequalities as inseparable from other forms of injustice. Political scientist Dorceta Taylor has documented the relatively high percentage of women in leadership roles in environmental justice activism. Of the 205 environmental justice groups Taylor examined as of 1992, 49 percent had female leaders, whereas only 27 percent of 1083 traditional environmental organizations had women in leadership roles.[71]

Environment and Labor

Organized labor had been an ally in enacting the Wilderness Act in 1964, a financial supporter of the first Earth Day, and a central coalition partner in passing the Toxic Substances Control Act in 1976. But coalitions need constant nurturing and what was at times a mutually productive alliance floundered by the early 1980s under the combined pressures from without—economic downturn, government opposition, and industry manipulation—as well as pressures from within—divergent class outlooks and genuine policy differences. The class divide was exacerbated by the conservative assault on both constituencies.

The Reagan era assault on hard-won workers' rights and environmental regulations weakened the partnership. The Reagan administration's breaking of the PATCO (Professional Air Traffic Controllers Organization) strike in 1981 and industry's practice of outsourcing to low-wage, overseas employers diminished organized labor's strength and numbers. At a time when federal laxity in enforcing Occupational Safety and Health Act (OSHA) regulations reduced safety on the job, the declining clout of unions also weakened environmental protections.[72]

The classic example of worker-environmentalist antagonism centers in California and the Pacific Northwest where environmentalists' efforts to preserve old growth redwoods and other forests put them at odds with loggers. Among forest protection activists was EarthFirst!er Judi Bari, a carpenter who built homes in Mendocino County. As a union organizer whose work utilized forest products, Bari attempted to nurture ties with loggers. She was concerned not only about sustainable forestry, but also about workers' rights and economic inequality.[73] The history of the Redwood Wars illustrates the difficulties of forging a labor-environment alliance in a globalizing industry.

Campaigns to protect the giant trees had a long history, dating to the Save the Redwoods League founded in 1918, when few laws governed logging. Conservation era strategists sought to protect the majestic groves by purchasing land that was then turned over to the state or federal government as public parks. The movement in the 1980s went further, eventually succeeding in establishing rules to protect ecosystems on land privately owned by timber companies.[74]

Structural changes in the logging industry in the 1980s, including declines in demand and the availability of cheap imported lumber, led to the loss of up to thirty thousand jobs in the Pacific Northwest. Still, logging companies sought to increase output, targeting the old growth forests. One of the few tools for environmentalists bent on saving not only the forests, but the entire ecosystem, was the Endangered Species Act. So, the spotted owl habitat became the center of the campaign to preserve old growth redwoods. Logging companies and loggers blamed the Act and the environmentalists as the source of their economic woes. For their part, environmentalists, as historian Richard White has argued, tended to view nature as "a place where leisured humans come only to visit and not to work, stay, or live." To working class loggers or miners, noted White, environmentalists' habit of condemning work in nature cast them as either "a privileged leisure class. . . [or] quaint reactionaries."[75]

In spring 1990, as anti-logging activists from EarthFirst! and the Rainforest Action Network planned Redwood Summer—modeled on Freedom Summer, the Mississippi-based voting rights campaign of 1964—to bring hundreds of volunteers to protect the redwood groves, violence against forest activists erupted. On May 24, a car-bomb exploded in Oakland, California, severely injuring Judi Bari and her partner Darryl Cherney. In a bewildering turn of events, Cherney and Bari, who advocated nonviolence, were charged in the bombing. The charges were soon dropped, but the case has never been solved. (The Center for Investigative Reporting identified 124 credible cases of violence against environmental activists in thirty-one states between 1988 and 1994.) Legal gridlock over logging persisted, but the adversaries eventually reached an uneasy compromise that protected some groves, including some designated stands on privately held land.[76]

By contrast, a 1984 lockout by the German chemical company, Badische Anilin und Soda-Fabrik (BASF) in Geismar, Louisiana, yielded a powerful alliance between workers and environmentalists. Union leaders, a broad range of willing local, national, and international partners, and parallel interests helped this coalition endure. Seeking contract concessions, the chemical company locked out workers from the Oil, Chemical, and Atomic Workers Union in 1984.

OCAW took on BASF's dismal environmental record, connecting occupational hazards with the danger of chemical exposures to the surrounding community and attracting a broad coalition of supporters in the U.S. and Germany, including the Sierra Club, Greenpeace, the German Green Party, and Catholic and Baptist religious leaders. BASF rehired the workers in 1989. William Fontenot, an environmental specialist in the Louisiana Attorney General's office, told *The New York Times* that over the five-year struggle, the union "raised the level of consciousness about the environment in Louisiana."[77]

Biocentrism and Deep Ecology

In the mid-1970s, British NASA Mars research collaborator James Lovelock had proposed the "Gaia hypothesis," that the Earth is a self-regulating system much like a single organism. His formulation and other biocentric approaches—focused not on human-centered rationales for nature preservation, but on the intrinsic value of nature itself—grew in popularity in the 1980s. Evolutionary biologist Edward O. Wilson's 1986 book *Biophilia* argued that human affection for other living systems—*biophilia*, or love of life—is pervasive and innate. Though some fellow evolutionary biologists regarded sociobiology with skepticism, Wilson's books were widely read, and the concept of biophilia registered as intuitive to many environmentalists.[78]

Bioregionalism, another biocentric approach introduced in the 1980s, is "the belief that certain material characteristics—climate, topography, indigenous flora or fauna—combine with culture to define a unity of place and people."[79] Bioregionalists argue that decisions regarding resource use should take into account biogeography; ecological, not political boundaries should guide decision-making. Regional compacts, such as the Great Lakes pollution remediation plan involving U.S. states and Canadian provinces, would be one example. Bioregionalists advocate greater regional self-sufficiency, through measures like limiting the extra-regional transport of foodstuffs and other goods to avoid energy costs, not shipping oranges to the U.S. from South Africa, for example, or kiwis from Australia.

As early as 1972, Norwegian philosopher Arne Naess was presenting the concept of "deep ecology" at international conferences. A committed hiker and mountaineer, Naess criticized mainstream environmentalists for making humans their ecological focus. Fundamentally a critique of managing the planet for human benefit, which Naess termed "shallow ecology," deep ecology sees humans as no more valuable than any other part of a larger ecosystem. The deep ecologists' moral claim, writes religious historian Bron Taylor, "is that nonhuman life is valuable, even apart from its usefulness to human beings." Because humans are a particularly destructive element of the biosphere, deep ecologists believe that human activity, including reproduction, must be severely curtailed if the planet is to flourish. During a trip in the Sierras in 1984, Naess and fellow philosopher

George Sessions crafted eight principles for human nonintervention in nature. The Deep Ecology platform celebrated the "richness and diversity of life forms" and argued that "humans have no right to reduce this richness and diversity except to satisfy vital needs." The platform demanded activism; adherents to the philosophy had an "obligation directly or indirectly to participate in the attempt to implement the necessary changes." Naess developed a modest following in the U.S.; the Foundation for Deep Ecology opened in 1990 and continues to advocate biocentrism.[80]

Animal Protection

Organized concern for animal well-being has a long history in the United States dating to the founding of the American Society for the Prevention of Cruelty to Animals in 1866. The Humane Society was established in the 1950s. By the 1970s, an impassioned animal protection movement had emerged, thanks in part to the work of engaged philosophers, including Australian bioethicist Peter Singer. Singer couched his approach to animal rights in utilitarian values, that is, the greater good afforded to humans by preventing animal suffering. Singer's 1975 book, *Animal Liberation: A New Ethics for Our Treatment of Animals*, spurred a generation of activists to alleviate the plight of animals used in medical testing.[81] Singer's perspective was less ecological than ethical. The Animal Legal Defense Fund, a law group devoted to fighting cruelty to animals through both legislative reform and the courts, formed in 1979. The Animal Liberation Front, a direct-action group, was founded in 1980.

People for the Ethical Treatment of Animals (PETA, pronounced pē-tă) formed in 1980 and organized boycotts and educational campaigns to protest the mistreatment of animals. After PETA's first major protest, the World Day for Laboratory Animals in 1980, the organization diversified its tactics to include nonviolent and direct-action protests, disrupting animal research centers and entertainment venues where animals performed. The group, which remains active, seeks to end the use of animals in laboratories operated by the food, pharmaceuticals, chemical, and cosmetic industries and to prohibit the manufacture and sale of fur and leather clothing. PETA also promotes the humane handling of animals in circuses, water parks, and the film industry. The organization claimed 6.5 million members worldwide in 2019.[82]

Campaigns to protect baby seals and pandas notwithstanding, the need to protect human health has proven more persuasive to Congress, the courts, and the broader public than protecting nonhuman species. Likewise, the EPA has long been far more likely to base a decision to regulate on harms to human health than on harms to the local ecology. In 2016, however, PETA negotiated an agreement with the EPA to reduce the agency's reliance on animal testing in its Endocrine Disruptor Screening Program, a program that evaluates the hormone disrupting effects of certain chemicals.[83]

Radical and Libertarian Environmentalism

One of the more complex and contradictory figures to claim the label environmentalist, former park ranger and fire lookout Edward Abbey gained fame in the 1960s for the novel *Fire on the Mountain* (1962) and the essay collection *Desert Solitaire* (1968). Born in the northern Appalachian coalfields of Pennsylvania in 1927, Abbey lived his adult life in the American West. He was a gruff, bearded radical who had served as a military policeman during World War II and had earned a reputation as a womanizer and boozer. As historian Brian Allen Drake has noted, in his writings and public speeches, Abbey blended right-wing orthodoxies—supporting gun rights and opposing Latino immigration and affirmative action—with traditional left-wing causes. He was against the Vietnam war, pro-choice, and anti-big business. He advocated a return to Jeffersonian agrarianism, but never practiced farming. Above all, notes Drake, Abbey was wary of centralized government.[84]

Abbey's environmentalism was a byproduct of his antipathy to the "Power Combine," as he dubbed the agriculture, mining, timber, and oil industries, which, aided by federal policies, exploited nature. "He embraced environmentalism," writes Drake, "because it struck at the Combine's heart: its dependence on the exploitation of nature." Abbey wrote that

> [i]f we can draw the line against the industrial machine in America and make it hold, then perhaps in decades to come we can gradually force industrialism underground, where it belongs, and restore to all citizens of our nation their rightful heritage of breathable air, drinkable water, open space, family-farm agriculture, a truly democratic political economy.

Abbey alienated many with his reactionary stands on race, population growth, and immigration. ("I do not wish to live in a society dominated by blacks, or Mexicans, or Orientals," he wrote.)[85]

While postwar environmentalism in the U.S. is generally associated with liberalism, which favored government restraint on corporate threats to environmental health and well-being, Abbey gives evidence of "a strong antifederalist streak" within environmentalism, writes Drake. Abbey regarded environmentalists as a bulwark against industrial exploitation of nature, and therefore likely targets of repression. Industry also had begun, Abbey wrote, "'to recognize conservationists and environmentalists—not labor leaders, not government, not Marxists—as [its] chief antagonists in shaping the character of the American future.'"[86]

One of the best known and certainly the most controversial among Abbey's more than twenty books is the 1975 novel *The Monkeywrench Gang*. The novel promoted *ecotage*, the sabotage of bulldozers, drill rigs, and other equipment used in mining and the destruction of forests. Dave Foreman, a one-time Goldwater Republican and former lobbyist for The Wilderness Society, became one of

Abbey's main disciples. Foreman and others were inspired by Abbey's book to form Earth First! in 1981. Members of the group practiced an "aggressive brand of environmentally-oriented civil disobedience." Devotees of Abbey saw themselves as Eco-Warriors, defending the planet and its nonhuman occupants. Foreman's book *Ecodefense: A Field Guide to Monkeywrenching* described tactics ranging from "tree-sits" to tree-spiking. Tree-spiking—driving metal spikes in trees to deter logging—could severely injure loggers and was rare. More benign actions included tree-sits (activist Julia Butterfly Hill famously sat in a California redwood for more than two years to protest logging) and guerilla theater, such as decorating the face of Colorado's Glen Canyon Dam with a banner that resembled a large crack.[87]

Religious Environmental Activism

Spurred in part by the hostility of the Reagan administration to environmental protection, religious and spiritual activism for environmental causes increased in the mid-1980s. The "eco-theological ethics" that took organizational form in the 1980s, sociologist of religion Laurel Kearns has argued, fell within three identifiable trends: a "Christian stewardship ethic," an "eco-justice ethic," and a "creation spirituality ethic." Eco-justice proponents tended to work directly through denominational structures. Christian stewardship and creation spirituality were organized as the North American Conference on Christianity and Ecology (NACCE) in 1985. Congregants taking the stewardship approach interpreted the passage in Genesis regarding human dominion over the earth to call for humans to act as stewards. Proponents of this view focused on combatting resource depletion, becoming involved in land and agriculture issues. Member organization Catholic Rural Life, for example, whose history dates to 1923, works with state-based Farmers Unions on food security issues. Eco-justice advocates were influenced by liberation theology and sought to redress social inequality. These activities focused on public health, anti-toxics campaigns, and land rights for indigenous populations. The creation spiritualists took a more biocentric view. Likely to be liberal, less likely to be churchgoers, this group advocated for wilderness protection and preventing extinctions.[88]

In 1990, representatives of major religions, including Christian, Jewish, Muslim, Hindu, Buddhist, Ba'hai, and Native American faiths, came together at a "Caring for Creation" conference in Washington, D.C. Hosted at the National Cathedral, the conference was a high-profile event, a "cross-disciplinary, inter-religious dialogue at high levels." Speakers included Britain's Prince Philip, long involved in the leadership of the World Wildlife Fund, astronomer Carl Sagan, Senator Al Gore, journalist Lester Brown of the Worldwatch Institute, former EPA administrator Russell Train, and EPA administrator William Reilly. A new group, the North American Conference on Religion and Ecology (NACRE) emerged from the gathering. [89]

The National Religious Partnership for the Environment (NRPE), established in 1993, included Catholics, Jews, liberal Protestants, and the conservative Protestant Evangelical Environmental Network (EEN), though they were not without church opposition. In the context of "decline in the societal influence of the mainline denominations," the NRPE became an important core of support for environmental action, lobbying Congress, working on local and state environmental issues, and conducting broad public education programs among their congregations. However, religious environmentalists' critique of Western theology evoked strong vitriol from Christian fundamentalist speakers and writers, who, noted Kearns, "suspect all environmentalism is paganism."[90]

The Sustainability Paradigm

By the 1980s, the work of U.S. environmentalists had grown increasingly transnational. Greenpeace and Friends of the Earth had offices in several countries. In 1982, the John D. and Catherine T. MacArthur Foundation provided $15 million to the World Resources Institute (WRI), headed by NRDC co-founder Gus Speth, to work with advocates, governments, and businesses to advance pragmatic, human-centered solutions to global problems of environment and development. Likewise, the Environmental Defense Fund collaborated with European counterparts to design international protocols for containing toxic substances. NRDC's intermediary role in demonstrating that secret nuclear tests could be verified scientifically proved crucial to the signing by the U.S. and the Soviet Union of the Intermediate Test Ban Treaty of 1987, as NRDC director John H. Adams and colleagues described in their 2010 account of the organization's history, *A Force for Nature*.[91]

The United Nations Environment Programme convened its second global gathering of nations in Nairobi, Kenya, in 1982. In Nairobi, U.S. activists learned about Kenyan anti-deforestation activists' efforts led by Wangari Maathai, who would later win a Nobel Peace Prize for her work. The World Commission on Environment and Development, established by the United Nations in 1984, began evaluating global environmental challenges. Led by former Norwegian Prime Minister Gro Harlem Brundtland, the commission published its report, *Our Common Future*, in 1987. The report focused on sustainable development, defined as "development that meets the needs of the present without compromising the ability of future generations to meet their own needs."[92]

The Brundtland Commission's formulation of sustainable development reframed environmentalism in the decades ahead, as the concept became a compelling framework for much environmental activism. Thousands of schools, businesses, state and local governments adopted the sustainability paradigm as the basis for ecologically protective projects ranging from "reduce, recycle, and reuse" efforts to wetland restoration. The College Board lists seventy-seven colleges and universities with sustainability studies programs in 2019.[93]

However, sustainability, as articulated by the Brundtland Commission, has its critics. On one hand, the sustainability paradigm offers a capacious tent, big enough to cover many varieties of environmentalism. However, though the original document included language spotlighting "the essential needs of the world's poor, to which overriding priority should be given," that passage rarely accompanies the oft-quoted definition. Some critics suggest that the definition of sustainability should be amended to include "in a just and equitable manner." Others claim the idea has been co-opted to endorse pro-growth neoliberal economic policies. "Sustainable development's dependence on the global market economy," notes feminist scholar Annie Rochette, "[fails] to recognize the latter's exploitation of Nature, the poor and women, especially in developing countries."[94]

International environmental gatherings brought U.S. environmental activists in contact with Third World activists working to stop forest destruction and protect indigenous land rights. Facing severe repression, Francisco Alves Mendes, Jr., known as Chico Mendes, was a Brazilian rubber worker and conservationist. As a labor leader, Mendes defended rubber workers and the Brazilian rainforest against exploitation. Mendes was murdered in 1988 for his opposition to cattle ranchers' burning in the Amazon. After Mendes's death, Marina Silva led rubber tappers in the fight against deforestation, eventually becoming Brazilian Minister of Environment (2003–2008).[95]

The wind-down of the Cold War in the late 1980s contributed to a signature international environmental achievement during the Reagan years: the signing of the first international environmental agreement to take aim at whole class of chemicals. Despite the administration's initial resistance, U.N. countries made progress on limiting chlorofluorocarbons (CFCs) that were damaging the earth's ozone layer. With *glasnost* opening up communications inside the Soviet Union and relations easing between the U.S. and the U.S.S.R., leaders of both countries wanted to appear willing to cooperate. Agreeing to reduce CFCs seemed a relatively easy way to project amenability to change. Industry cooperation was uncharacteristically strong, as chemical companies such as DuPont had developed substitutes for CFCs that they were anxious to market. Nations negotiated and signed the Montreal Protocol on Substances that Deplete the Ozone Layer in 1987, requiring participating countries to curb the release of CFCs. The agreement committed signatories to reducing their output of CFCs by 50 percent within ten years. The agreement worked because it set hard limits on CFC releases. Due to the 1987 Montreal Protocol and subsequent revisions, worldwide use of ozone-damaging chlorofluorocarbons dropped by 80 percent between 1986 and 1994, and the stratosphere showed evidence of repair.[96]

Oil Disaster

The Exxon Valdez ran aground in Prince William Sound, Alaska, on March 29, 1989, dumping nearly eleven million tons of crude oil into the sound and killing thousands of sea birds and other wildlife. Investigators blamed the ship's captain, but, for environmentalists, he was only the last in the chain linking the devastation that befell the Sound to the exploitation of the oil fields on the North Slope in Alaska and northwest Canada. National environmental groups lobbied Congress, which responded with the 1990 Oil Pollution Act, authorizing the EPA to establish a cleanup fund paid for by a tax on oil. More radical grassroots demands to shut down the pipeline or block the risky tanker transport of oil from the North Slope did not receive a hearing. By agreeing to the Valdez Principles, a set of voluntary guidelines designed to encourage good corporate behavior, the oil industry managed to skirt stronger preventive legislation.[97]

A resurgent grassroots movement not only survived but grew during the Reagan years. By 1990, the leading national environmental organizations had grown in numbers and capacity. Public opinion favored environmental protection, giving a broad base of support for environmental initiatives. However, continued economic globalization posed significant challenges for the increasingly diverse—even fragmented—movement.

Notes

1 Sale, *Green Revolution*, 49; Fiege, *Republic of Nature*, 423.
2 Harvey, *A Brief History of Neoliberalism*, 2.
3 Ioris, *The Political Ecology of the State*, 16; Craig Becker, "The Pattern of Union Decline, Economic and Political Consequences, and the Puzzle of a Legislative Response," *Minnesota Law Review* 98 (2014): 1637–50; Bureau of Labor Statistics, Economic News Release, Union Members Summary, January 19, 2018. In 2017, the U.S. Bureau of Labor Statistics reported 14.8 million union members, 10.7 percent of the workforce, as compared to 1983, when 17.7 million union members made up 20.1 percent of wage and salary workers.
4 Turner, "'The Specter of Environmentalism,'" 126; Scheffer, *The Shaping of Environmentalism in America*, 178.
5 Turner, "'The Specter of Environmentalism,'" 125; Brulle, *Agency, Democracy, and Nature*, 123.
6 Turner, "'The Specter of Environmentalism,'" 126; Drake, *Loving Nature*, 21, 181, 183, 47–49; Lassiter and Crespino, *The Myth of Southern Exceptionalism*, 6–7.
7 Drake, *Loving Nature*, 47, 50; League of Conservation Voters, Scorecards, http://scorecard.lcv.org/scorecard/archive (accessed December 1, 2018); Rowell, *Green Backlash*, 7, citing Associated Press, "Private Enterprise Also Has Its Champion," *The Tribune*, August 26, 1979; Lewis F. Powell, Jr. to Mr. Eugene B. Sydnor, Jr., Chairman, Education Committee, "U.S. Chamber of Commerce Confidential Memorandum: Attack on American Free Enterprise System," August 23, 1971; Rowell, *Green Backlash*, 8.
8 "About ALEC," American Legislative Exchange Council, www.alec.org/about/ (accessed March 21, 2018); Turner and Isenberg, *The Republican Reversal*, 49.
9 Tim Peckinpaugh, Republican Study Committee, "Special Report: The Specter of Environmentalism: The Threat of Environmental Groups," February 12, 1982, http://docs.azgs.az.gov/SpecColl/2008-01/2008-01-1765.pdf (accessed June 8, 2017); Turner, "'The Specter of Environmentalism,'" 123.
10 Turner, "'The Specter of Enviromentalism,'" 147, citing Riley E. Dunlap and Michael Patrick Allen, "Partisan Differences on Environmental Issues: A Congressional Roll Call Analysis," *Western Political Quarterly* 29 (September 1976): 384–97.

11 Harvey, *Wilderness Forever*, 273; Howard H. Baker, Jr., "Cleaning America's Air – Progress and Challenges," Speech at the University of Tennessee, Knoxville, March 9, 2005, www.muskiefoundation.org/baker.030905.html (accessed May 15, 2018).

12 Drake, *Loving Nature*, 182.

13 Lou Cannon, "Sagebrush Rebellion Challenges U.S. Grip on Western Land," *The Washington Post*, April 9, 1979; Brulle, *Agency, Democracy, and Nature*, 125; Federal Land Policy and Management Act, 43 U.S.C. 1701, §101 (8) (1976).

14 Wellock, *Preserving the Nation*, 220; Rowell, *Green Backlash*, 9–10.

15 David Biello, "Where Did the Carter White House's Solar Panels Go?" *Scientific American*, August 6, 2010, 41.

16 McCormick, *Reclaiming Paradise*, 134; Percival, *Environmental Regulation*, 693, citing Erik D. Olson, "The Quiet Shift of Power: Office of Management and Budget Supervision of Environmental Protection Agency Rulemaking Under Executive Order 12,291," *Virginia Journal of Natural Resources Law* 4, no. 1 (1984): 1–80, 40.

17 Cover, *TIME*, August 23, 1982; "The Legacy of James Watt," *TIME*, October 24, 1983; Sale, *Green Revolution*, 51; Edward Roby, "Dump Watt Petitions go to Congress," *United Press International*, October 18, 1981; Steven R. Weisman, "Watt Quits Post; President Accepts with 'Reluctance,'" *The New York Times*, October 10, 1983.

18 Lois Romano and Jacqueline Trescott, "The Rise and Fall of Anne Burford," *The Washington Post*, March 10, 1983.

19 Weisman, "Watt Quits Post"; Ronald L. Claveloux, "The Conflict between Executive Privilege and Congressional Oversight: The Gorsuch Controversy," *Duke Law Journal*, 1983, 1333–58; Philip Shabecoff, "Rita Lavelle Gets 6-Month Term and Is Fined $10,000 for Perjury," *The New York Times*, January 10, 1984.

20 Sellers et al., *The EPA Under Siege*, 19–20; Rowell, *Green Backlash*, 9–10.

21 Fox, *The American Conservation Movement*, 315. The five groups were the Izaak Walton League, the National Audubon Society, the National Wildlife Federation, the Sierra Club, and the Wilderness Society. Jay Letto, "One Hundred Years of Compromise," *Buzzworm* (March–April 1992): 26–32, 29.

22 Sale, *Green Revolution*, 33.

23 Figures from Fox, *The American Conservation Movement*, 315; Gottlieb, *Forcing the Spring*, 174; Wellock, *Preserving the Nation*, 208; Christina Larson, "The Emerging Environmental Majority," *Washington Monthly*, May 1, 2006, https://washington monthly.com/2006/05/01/the-emerging-environmental-majority-2/ (accessed June 9, 2017).

24 Gottlieb, *Forcing the Spring*, 168–71; Dowie, *Losing Ground*, 69.

25 For a listing of the 1990 leaders, see Kuzmiak, "The American Environmental Movement," 275.

26 Gottlieb, *Forcing the Spring*, 171; Dowie, *Losing Ground*, 271n5, 70.

27 Sale, *Green Revolution*, 54; Gottlieb, *Forcing the Spring*, 165.

28 The ten groups that prepared the report included Friends of the Earth, Natural Resources Defense Council, The Wilderness Society, Sierra Club, National Audubon Society, Environmental Defense Fund, Environmental Policy Center, Environmental Action, Defenders of Wildlife, Solar Lobby, *Ronald Reagan and the American Environment: An Indictment* (San Francisco: Friends of the Earth, 1982), 17, 140–42.

29 Sale, *Green Revolution*, 57, 58; Rothman, *Saving the Planet*, 202; Sam Mintz, "Appeals Court Tosses Texas Suit over Yucca Mountain," *E&E News*, June 4, 2018.

30 Brown, *Toxic Exposures*, 17; Brown and Mikkelson, *No Safe Place*, 2; Peter Taylor, *Unruly Complexity*, xv; Szasz, *Ecopopulism*, 72, citing Citizens' Clearinghouse on Hazardous Wastes, *Annual Report* (CCHW: Arlington, Va., 1988).

31 EPA, "1983 Press Release: Joint Federal/State Action Taken to Relocate Times Beach Residents," February 22, 1983, https://archive.epa.gov/epa/aboutepa/1983-press-release-joint-federalstate-action-taken-relocate-times-beach-residents.html

(accessed May 15, 2018); Marilyn Leistner, "The Times Beach Story," *Synthesis/ Regeneration* 7–8 (Summer 1995). www.greens.org/s-r/078/07-09.html (accessed July 10, 2017).

32 Leistner, "The Times Beach Story."

33 Robert Reinhold, "Missouri Dioxin Cleanup: A Decade of Little Action," *The New York Times*, February 20, 1983; William Powell, "Remember Times Beach: The Dioxin Disaster, Thirty Years Later," *St. Louis Magazine*, December 3, 2012; U.S. EPA, "Times Beach One-Page Summary," Superfund Redevelopment Initiative, November 2002 (accessed June 18, 2017).

34 Karl Grossman, "The People of Color Summit," 272–97, quoting Rev. Benjamin Chavis in Bullard, ed., *Unequal Protection*, 278; Taylor, "The Rise of the Environmental Justice Paradigm."

35 McGurty, *Transforming Environmentalism*, 57, 55.

36 McGurty, *Transforming Environmentalism*, 108, 128.

37 Blum, "The Gunfighters of Northwood Manor," 224–40, in Melosi and Pratt, eds. *Energy Metropolis*, 231ff.; *Bean v. Southwestern Waste Management*, 482 F. Supp. 673 (1979); Bullard, *Dumping in Dixie*, 44–45.

38 U.S. General Accounting Office, *Siting of Hazardous Waste Landfills*; Commission for Racial Justice, *Toxic Wastes and Race*.

39 Cerrell Associates, "Political Difficulties Facing Waste-to-Energy Conversion Plant Siting," in J. Stephen Powell, ed., *California Waste Management Board* (Los Angeles, 1984), 26.

40 Edward "Jerry" Pennick, Heather Gray, Miessha N. Thomas, "Preserving African American Rural Property: An Assessment of Intergenerational Values Toward Land," 153–73, 154, 157, in Jordan et al., *Land and Power*; *Pigford v. Glickman*, 185 F.R.D. 82 (D.D.C. 1999). A consent decree in the case was expected to provide up to $2 billion in payments for up to twenty thousand African American farmers for discrimination in USDA loans and programs. Clyde E. Chesney, "African American Environmentalism: Issues and Trends for Teaching, Research, and Extension," 179–205, 184–85, in Jordan et al., *Land and Power*.

41 George Bradford was the penname for activist David Watson. Elizabeth D. Blum, "Toxic Relationships: Two Sides of the American Relationship with Chemicals," *Reviews in American History* 45, no. 2 (June 2017): 355–61, 356; Bridget Hanna, "Unending Disaster, Enduring Resistance," 488–523 in Michel Feher, *Nongovernmental Politics*, 492–93.

42 Fortun, *Advocacy after Bhopal*, 57, 60; George Bradford, "We All Live in Bhopal," www. eco-action.org/dt/bhopal.html, (accessed November 19, 2017); Fortun, *Advocacy after Bhopal*, 15, 63–64.

43 Fortun, *Advocacy after Bhopal*, 17; Stephen Zavestoski, "The Struggle for Justice in Bhopal: A New/Old Breed of Transnational Social Movement," 129–46, in Armiero and Sedrez, eds., *A History of Environmentalism*, 136.

44 Beck, *World at Risk*, 9 (emphasis in original).

45 Larry Everest, "Union Carbide's Bhopal Settlement Is a Disaster in Itself," *Los Angeles Times*, February 23, 1989; Bridget Hanna, "Unending Disaster, Enduring Resistance," 488–523 in Michel Feher, *Nongovernmental Politics*, 514.

46 Christopher Sellers, "How Republicans Came to Embrace Anti-Environmentalism"; Ann Reilly Dowd, "Environmentalists Are on the Run," *Fortune*, September 19, 1994; The Heartland Institute website, https://heartland.org/ (accessed December 1, 2018); Rampton and Stauber, *Trust Us, We're Experts!*, 254–55.

47 Spears, *Baptized in PCBs*, 278–79.

48 Oreskes and Conway, *Merchants of Doubt*, 244–45; Spears, *Baptized in PCBs*, 155–57.

49 Oreskes and Conway, *Merchants of Doubt*, 161.

50 Dowie, *Losing Ground*, 98–101; Percival, *Environmental Regulation*, 995ff.

51 Cole and Foster, *From the Ground Up*, 99; George W. Pring and Penelope Canan, *SLAPPS: Getting Sued for Speaking Out* (Philadelphia: Temple University Press, 1996),

36–37. For anti-SLAPP provisions, see, for example, California Code of Civil Procedure § 425.16.

52 Dowie, *Losing Ground*, 89; William Greider, *Who Will Tell the People: The Betrayal of American Democracy* (New York: Simon & Schuster, 1992), 43–45; Peter Passell, "Experts Question Staggering Costs of Toxic Cleanups," *The New York Times*, September 1, 1991.

53 Chemical Manufacturers Association Public Outreach Program, *Community Awareness and Emergency Response Code of Management Practices*, December 10, 1990, http://info house.p2ric.org/ref/33/32377.pdf (accessed December 1, 2018); Spears, *Baptized in PCBs*, 278–89.

54 Dowie, *Losing Ground*, 115.

55 EPA, The Superfund Amendments and Reauthorization Act (SARA) of 1986, 42 U.S.C. § 9601 et seq.

56 Fortun, *Advocacy After Bhopal*, 63–64.

57 Percival, *Environmental Regulation*, 1078; *Chevron U.S.A. v. NRDC*, 104 S. Ct. 2778 (1984).

58 Kuzmiak, "The American Environmental Movement," 276, citing M. Hager, "How Goes the Environment?" *National Wildlife* (January 1991): 14; Sale, *Green Revolution*, 74–75.

59 John Lancaster, "The Environmentalist as Insider," *The Washington Post*, August 4, 1991; Tokar, *Earth for Sale*, 21.

60 Adams et al., *An Environmental Agenda for the Future*; Jennifer Thomson, "Surviving the 1970s: The Case of Friends of the Earth," *Environmental History* 22, no. 2 (April 2017): 235–56, 236; Sale, *Green Revolution*, 56; Dowie, *Losing Ground*, 71; Gottlieb, *Forcing the Spring*, 175.

61 Pam Solo, *From Protest to Policy: Beyond the Freeze to Common Security* (Cambridge: Ballinger, Solomon, Fredric and Jacob Fishman, 1988), 169; Dunlap, "Trends in Public Opinion," 299.

62 Sheila D. Collins, *The Rainbow Challenge: The Jackson Campaign and the Future of U.S. Politics* (New York: Monthly Review Press, 1986), 86, 217–19.

63 Greg Schneider and Renae Merle, "Reagan's Defense Buildup Bridged Military Eras: Huge Budgets Brought Life Back to Industry," *The Washington Post*, June 9, 2004, E1. According to the Center for Strategic and Budgetary Assessments in projected 2005 dollars.

64 Dennis Hevesi, "Randall Forsberg, 64, Nuclear Freeze Advocate, Dies," *The New York Times*, October 26, 2007, B6; Iversen, *Full Body Burden*, 168.

65 Kinchy, "African Americans in the Atomic Age," 313.

66 Gottlieb, *Forcing the Spring*, 242–43.

67 Merchant, *The Death of Nature*, 2; Blum, *Love Canal Revisited*, 47.

68 Merchant, *Earthcare*, 8; Mies and Shiva, *Ecofeminism*.

69 Hayden, "What Would a Non-Sexist City Be Like?"

70 Gottlieb, *Forcing the Spring*, 272; Becky Rafter, Mary Olson, Jumana Master, "Community Impacts at the Crossroads of Nuclear and Climate Injustices in the U.S. South," Atlanta, Ga.: Georgia Women's Action for New Directions and the Nuclear Information and Resource Service (NIRS), December 2017, https://gawand.org/wp-content/uploads/2017/12/GA-WAND_Climate_Nuclear_Report_Dec_2017.pdf.

71 Taylor, "Women of Color, Environmental Justice, and Ecofeminism," 38–81, in Warren, *Ecofeminism*, 60.

72 Gottlieb, *Forcing the Spring*, 373–75.

73 Loomis, *Empire of Timber*; Richard White, "Are You an Environmentalist or Do You Work for a Living?" 171–85, in Cronon, ed. *Uncommon Ground*; Speece, *Defending Giants*, 159.

74 Speece, *Defending Giants*, 48–49.

75 Speece, *Defending Giants*, 138; Richard White, "Are You an Environmentalist?" 171–85, in Cronon, *Uncommon Ground*, 173, 181.

76 Speece, *Defending Giants*, 148; Rowell, *Green Backlash*, 157–64; Center for Investigative Reporting study cited in C.D. Stelzer, "Fighting Fire with Fire: The Torching of an Environmentalist's Home," from the *Riverfront Times* [St. Louis], reprinted in *The Times Beach Chronicles, stlreporter* 4, July 22, 1994; Speece, *Defending Giants*, 251–52.

77 Minchin, *Forging a Common Bond*; Gottlieb, *Forcing the Spring*, 376–81; Frances Frank Marcus, "Labor Dispute in Louisiana Ends with Ecological Gain," *The New York Times*, January 3, 1990.

78 Lovelock, *Gaia: A New Look at Life on Earth*; Wilson, *Biophilia*.

79 Klingle, "Spaces of Consumption," 103.

80 Taylor, *Ecological Resistance Movements*, 15 (emphasis in original); Arne Naess and George Sessions, "The Deep Ecology Platform," 1984, *Foundation for Deep Ecology*. The eight principles can be accessed at www.deepecology.org/platform.htm (accessed June 12, 2017).

81 Singer, *Animal Liberation*.

82 "About PETA," People for the Ethical Treatment of Animals website, www.peta.org/about-peta/ (accessed January 14, 2019).

83 Russell, "Lost among the Parts Per Billion," 30–31; "About PETA," People for the Ethical Treatment of Animals, www.peta.org/about-peta/ (accessed January 14, 2019).

84 Drake, *Loving Nature*, 4–6.

85 Drake, *Loving Nature*, 160, 168; Edward Abbey, "The Conscience of the Conqueror," *Abbey's Road*, 137; Drake, *Loving Nature*, 161; Keith Goetzman, "Was Edward Abbey Racist and Sexist?" *The UTNE Reader*, reprinted from *Earth First*, July/August 2009.

86 Drake, *Loving Nature*, 178, 169, citing Abbey, "The Conscience of the Conqueror," in *Abbey's Road*, 135.

87 Foreman, *Eco-Defense*; Drake, *Loving Nature*, 173, 175.

88 Kearns, "Saving the Creation," 56; "Catholic Rural Life," *The Forum on Religion and Ecology at Yale,* http://fore.yale.edu/religion/christianity/projects/Catholic_Rural_Life/ (accessed June 29, 2018).

89 Kearns, "Saving the Creation," 62.

90 Kearns, "Saving the Creation," 59, 64, 60.

91 "History," World Resources Institute, www.wri.org/about/history (accessed May 18, 2017); Adams et al., *A Force for Nature*, 112–23.

92 United Nations, *Our Common Future*, 41.

93 "Major: Sustainability Studies," College Board, https://bigfuture.collegeboard.org/college-search?major=2248_Sustainability%20Studies (accessed January 31, 2019).

94 Agyeman et al., *Just Sustainabilities*, 5; Barber, *A House in the Sun*, 254; Rochette, "Stop the Rape of the World," 162.

95 Revkin, *The Burning Season*; Dauvergne, *Environmentalism of the Rich*, 85.

96 Uekotter, "The End of the Cold War," 343–51 in McNeill and Unger, *Environmental Histories of the Cold War*, 346; "J. Gustave Speth," Interview by John C. Cruden, Environmental Law Institute, April 13, 2012; Fortun, *Advocacy after Bhopal*, 359–60n4; McCormick, *Reclaiming Paradise*, 188–89; Uekotter, "The End of the Cold War," 343–51, 346; McNeill, *Something New under the Sun*, 114. The agreement was revised in 1990 to cut CFCs entirely by 2000.

97 Oil Pollution Act, 33 U.S.C. §2701 et seq. (1990); Steinberg, *Down to Earth*, 260.

5

GLOBALIZING ENVIRONMENTALISM (1990–2000)

Earth Day 1990

Earth Day 1990 embodied the promise of environmentalism as well as the internal and external challenges facing the movement. The anniversary opened a decade in which environmental activists extended their campaigns globally, reacted to the spread of market-oriented environmentalism, and countered another round of challenges from increasingly well-funded opponents. Social justice environmentalism surged, moving some national organizations to respond to calls for diversifying their staffs and enlarging their missions. Hopes ran high that avowedly pro-environment administrations would deliver on environmental promises.

Much had changed since the grassroots upsurge manifested on the first Earth Day twenty years earlier. The 1970 events had taken place amid the ferment of the civil rights revolt and the fight to end U.S. involvement in Vietnam. Over the ensuing two decades, environmentalists had won sweeping federal measures to clean the nation's air and water, to protect wilderness and endangered species, and to hold polluters accountable for hazardous waste. Activists had built organizational powerhouses to lobby, sue, and campaign for broadening environmental protection, and had won regulatory reforms, even under hostile administrations.

On the eve of Earth Day 1990, however, mobilizing Congressional support for environmental protection was so difficult that planners recognized a need "to create a political mandate for tougher environmental laws." Yet, the 1990 Earth Day's "Green Pledge" offered a considerably tamer message than the earlier calls for "an environmental revolution." Earth Day 1990 targeted individual action, focusing on recycling and eco-sensitive consumerism. As one *New York Times* reporter wrote, organizers hoped "to steer millions of investors and consumers toward companies judged to be most sensitive to environmental concerns."[1]

The focus on altering consumer behaviors—important as that was—overlooked industrial production and transport, failing to address the largest contributors to the waste stream. Scores of corporate sponsors eager to burnish their green credentials funded rallies and clean-up campaigns. Their participation tended to moderate organizers' demands. While the 1990 rallies were larger than ever—nearly one million people participated in New York City alone—follow-up actions translated into limited policy gains.

Much to their credit, Earth Day 1990 planners extended the call to action internationally, ultimately garnering roughly 200 million participants in 140 countries. "It has to be international this time because of the nature of the issues," said Denis Hayes, chairman of Earth Day 1990, on returning from an organizing trip to Europe. Transnational concerns such as exported wastes, deforestation, genetically engineered crops, and the steadily warming climate required global action. Globalization—a decades-long process characterized by increased mobility of capital, outsourcing of production, downward pressure on wages, privatization, and deregulation—restricted the ability of individual nation-states to limit environmental hazards to human health and the destruction of natural landscapes. At the same time, given the global extent of concern, environmentalists seemed poised to build on earlier successes to safeguard the future of the planet and the rights of its inhabitants.[2]

A New Era of Transnational Activism

The decline of the Cold War had lifted global prospects for negotiations, creating a "window of opportunity" for transnational environmental reform. The success of international treaties negotiated in the late 1980s in reducing the nuclear threat and limiting ozone-depleting chemicals augured well. The formation of the European Union (EU) in 1986 "gave the European Community formal authority on environmental issues for the first time."[3] In fact, one rationale for the formation of the EU, championed by Green parties in Germany and elsewhere, had been the need for consistent environmental policies across national borders for which air and water pollution had little respect. EU countries were now an influential pro-environment bloc.[4]

In the U.S., environmental causes enjoyed public support at "unprecedented levels," with 74 percent of respondents in a 1990 *New York Times/CBS* poll agreeing that "Environmental improvements should be made regardless of cost." More than one-fifth of the population chose "environment" as one of the two most important problems facing the country.[5]

Pro-environment groups were growing in number, sophistication, and resources. "[E]nvironmentalism's vitality has been sustained by the continuity and skill of its political base," political scientist Walter Rosenbaum has argued. By the early 1990s, the Washington, D.C.-based lobby network, now known as the "Green Group," had expanded to include twenty-seven organizations. New members included groups with an international focus, such as the World Resources Institute (WRI) and ZPG, as well as the Union of Concerned Scientists (UCS) and Marian Wright Edelman's social justice-oriented Children's Defense Fund (CDF). By the mid-1990s, the environmental movement was "larger and financially better off" than either the civil rights movement or the peace movement," sociologist Robert Brulle has noted. More than ten thousand environmental groups existed around the country.[6] Many local and state-based groups were motivated by environmental justice concerns.

By the early 1990s, most large American environmental organizations had developed significant international programs; several were involved in transnational collaborations between governments and NGOs. Greenpeace was instrumental in negotiations among environmental NGOs and developing countries that led to an agreement limiting the export of wastes from rich countries to poor ones.[7]

Toxic Colonialism: Developing Nations and ENGOs Tackle International Dumping of Hazardous Wastes

In the 1970s, the U.S. and western Europe had turned to Mexico, Southeast Asia, and African nations as dumping sites for the waste and detritus of industrial production and the consumption-driven lifestyles of the developed world. Greenpeace activist Jim Puckett (later with the Basel Action Network) called the practice of shipping waste to developing countries in no economic position to refuse: "toxic colonialism." By the late 1980s, the volume of hazardous waste shipped from the developed world had reached 30 to 45 million metric tons annually; more than half went to non-OECD nations and one-fifth of the total was dumped in Third World countries. In addition, multinational corporations often located their most hazardous production processes in developing nations. Acknowledging this practice in a 1971 advertisement, Standard Oil Company had boasted, "We take sulfur out of the oil in Venezuela to keep it out of the air at home."[8]

In 1991, World Bank chief economist Larry Summers justified dumping hazardous wastes in developing countries in a controversial memo that began: "Just between you and me, shouldn't the World Bank be encouraging MORE migration of the dirty industries to the LDCs [less developed countries]?" The Summers memo suggested that people in countries with lower life expectancy were unlikely to live long enough to contract cancer from the toxic exposures generated by such facilities. "[T]he economic logic behind dumping a load of toxic waste in the lowest wage country," the memo continued, "is impeccable and we should face up to it." Greenpeace faxed the leaked memo all over the world. Though Summers disputed the memo's intent, its appearance heightened concerns about the environmental impact of World Bank projects in developing nations just as the U.N. Environment Programme prepared to hold its decennial conference in a developing nation, at Rio di Janeiro, Brazil, in 1992.[9]

Many countries had agreed to limit transboundary wastes with the signing in 1989 of the Basel Convention on the Control of Transboundary Movements of Hazardous Wastes and Their Disposal. Conceived in concert with environmental non-governmental organizations (ENGOs), the Basel Convention stood as a prominent example of a multilateral agreement to address a problem of global environmental injustice. The Basel agreement restricted transboundary transfers of waste without the knowledge of destination governments. However, the political reality facing environmentalists in the U.S. was that even when presidential administrations were willing to negotiate and sign international agreements, an increasingly hostile Congress was not. Though George H. W. Bush authorized the signing of the Basel treaty in 1989, as of 2019, the U.S. Congress has not ratified it. The Basel Action Network (BAN), an international watchdog group based in Seattle formed in 1997, monitors waste shipping and the treaty's implementation.[10]

Obstacles for Environmentalism

The period from the fall of the Berlin Wall in November 1989 to the launch of the new millennium was characterized by disappointments for U.S. environmentalists, even with self-described pro-environment administrations and, after a mild recession in 1990–1991, a relatively robust economy for much of the decade. Both Congress and regulators showed diminishing willingness to curb industry. Increasing globalization and the integration of world markets yielded intense resource extraction and the continued transfer of production, pollution, and waste from developed to developing nations, sharpening inequality both within and between nations. The demise of the Soviet Union and state socialism in general left capitalism apparently triumphant and reinforced American exceptionalism—which held the U.S. system to be uniquely superior to other nations—leaving few checks on American power and U.S. corporations' actions around the world. The U.S. tendency to unilateral action, to act alone or to abandon multilateral alliances and agreements, increased, especially regarding climate concerns. As a result, non-state actors—NGOs, civil society, consumers, and pro-environment businesses—became even more important in shaping environmental practices and policy.[11]

Several trends in finance and trade hindered environmentalism in the early 1990s. As global trade burgeoned, so did competition, environmental historian

Frank Uekoetter has noted, creating "a strong incentive to favor short-term gains at the expense of long-range sustainability," which eroded protective regulations. Globalization accelerated the spread of new technologies, many of which appeared clean and innovative to the user, despite relying on polluting production processes and toxic components. Income inequality, which had dropped significantly in the U.S. during World War II and held stable between 1950 and 1970, rose sharply in the U.S., especially after the Reagan era tax breaks for the highest earners took effect in the early 1980s.[12] The consequent reduction in real earnings for many workers made environmental rules an easy scapegoat.

Fossil fuel dependence continued to create global instability and environmental disaster. The 1990–1991 Gulf War brought a rise in oil prices that contributed to an economic recession at home as well as the worst oil disaster in history—a deliberate release by Iraqi forces in January 1991 of more than 300 million gallons of crude oil, which fouled the Persian Gulf.[13] As demonstrations against the Gulf War broke out across the U.S. and in Europe, antiwar and environmental activists joined once again in protest. "No Blood for Oil," read the protesters' signs.

Corporate mobility and the power of transnational corporations increased, undermining the power of nation-states to regulate them. Historian Susannah Rankin Bohme describes the case of U.S. and Central American fruit grove workers exposed to the chemical dibromochloropropane (DBCP), a pesticide used to kill tiny worms in the soil and known to cause serious health problems, including sterility in men. With backing from California Rural Legal Assistance, the Migrant Legal Action Program, and the National Association of Farmworker Organizations, U.S. fruit grove workers had brought a halt to DBCP use in the U.S. in the mid-1980s and would eventually win compensation for U.S. workers exposed to the chemical. Central American laborers—*los afectados*—also sued for damages. Nicaraguan workers won their claims against producers Dow and Dole in U.S. courts in 2007 only to have the relief they won denied because their claims arose on foreign soil.[14]

Market-Based Environmental Reform: The Clean Air Act of 1990

Centralized regulation through clean air laws of the 1970s had resulted in dramatic improvements in air quality in the U.S. New cars produced by U.S. automakers in 1990 emitted 96 percent less carbon dioxide and 75 percent less nitrogen oxide than cars made two decades earlier. However, a decade of administrations hostile to environmental regulation had greatly weakened federal enforcement of environmental laws. The 1970 Clean Air Act had aimed for an overall reduction of 90 percent in "carbon monoxide, hydrocarbons, and ozone over major U.S. urban areas by 1977," and by 1990, had achieved reductions of only about 30 percent.[15] Winning further reductions in air pollution through existing regulatory mechanisms appeared unlikely. Industry chafed against regulatory restraints, decrying so-called "command-and-control" legislation. The "polluter pays" principle faced increasing fire from regulated industries, which resisted paying for Superfund cleanups. Proposals for market-based reforms, such as emissions offsets and pollution trading schemes, were gaining traction.

Negotiations over the Clean Air Act of 1990 reflected a divide in the mainstream environmental movement. One wing had begun advocating collaboration with industry and market-based solutions to environmental problems in response to the Reagan Era counterrevolution. In the two decades since its founding in 1967, for example, the Environmental Defense Fund abandoned its "sue the bastards" motto to become one of several major environmental organizations advocating "coalitions with former enemies," in the words of EDF executive director Fred Krupp. In a 1986 op ed strategically placed in the business-oriented *Wall Street Journal* (to the ire of his movement colleagues), Krupp called for a new "third stage of environmentalism," with "the increased use of market-oriented incentives" to realize "growth, jobs, taxpayer and shareholder interests." Likewise, National Wildlife Foundation President and CEO Jay Hair's Corporate Conservation Council convened off-the-record meetings between environmental organization executives and business leaders, which continued to be held in the 1990s. Such shifts in strategy created a lasting rift in the environmental movement. Groups squared off over strengthening "polluter pays" regulation versus supporting market-based reforms. Among the most visible and vocal leaders, Hair and Krupp advocated of market-based reforms, while Greenpeace director Peter Bahouth and Sierra Club chair Michael McCloskey remained skeptical.[16]

Market-based reforms treat pollution as a commodity. Cap emissions, EDF policy analysts suggested, specifically the sulfur dioxide (SO_2), and nitrogen oxides (NO_x) components of acid rain and allow the trade of pollution credits. Polluting companies would have to reduce emissions by a set amount. If a company achieved greater reductions than the law required, its pollution credits could be traded or sold. Environmental movement opponents of creating emissions markets feared that the arbitrary emissions levels established by "cap-and-trade" programs would perpetuate pollution and exacerbate unequal exposures to toxics. Policy differences over the legislation were further aggravated by the fact that EDF had negotiated elements of the plan in secret with the White House, without consulting its partners in the National Clean Air Coalition, a coordinated lobbying effort.[17]

The system, as enacted in the 1990 revisions to the Clean Air Act, no longer required polluting industries to use the best available control technology (BACT), which might have yielded greater reductions in pollution. Ultimately, the cap-and-trade mechanism did significantly reduce SO_2—the EPA reported in 2015 reductions of 80 percent over 1990 levels—and reduced costs. However, the Act significantly limited democratic participation by short-circuiting the public hearing process, instituted a risk-based rather than a health-based paradigm for measuring pollution impact, and did not address co-occurring emissions. Furthermore, according to one study, companies' ability to transfer pollution credits from one plant to another did indeed result in heavier concentrations of pollution in "poorly educated communities."[18]

The Clinton Administration

On the federal level, environmentalists' hopes soared with the election of William Jefferson Clinton and vice president Al Gore, a pro-environment senator who was knowledgeable about the changing climate. Like Carter before him, Clinton tapped senior staff of national environmental organizations for top environment-related posts. At least four key administration staffers came from the NRDC alone. As administrator of the United Nations Development Programme, World Resources Institute director Gus Speth became "the highest-ranking American in the UN system."[19] Former Arizona governor Bruce Babbitt left the leadership of the League of Conservation Voters to become Secretary of the Interior. In June 1993, Clinton established the President's Council on Sustainable Development, with Vice-President Gore as convener.

Ultimately, the Clinton administration let down environmental allies on several fronts. The president chose as members of the Council on Sustainable Development several chief executives of major companies with poor environmental records—chemical firms Dow and DuPont, oil giant Chevron, timber corporation Georgia Pacific, and waste company Browning-Ferris. Environmental representatives on the Council were heavily weighted toward the market-oriented wing of the movement. Clinton cut the EPA budget, failed to set stringent CAFÉ (corporate average fuel economy) standards for vehicles, and did little to control carbon emissions from coal-fired power plants. Activists felt betrayed when Vice President Gore supported a trial run of a hazardous waste incinerator they had been fighting in Liverpool, Ohio.[20]

Although environmentalists were generally pleased with attorney Carol Browner, who served as EPA administrator throughout Clinton's presidency, her support for rescinding the longstanding Delaney Clause—the zero-tolerance standard for cancer-causing food additives and pesticides in food—angered many. The chemical industry-allied think tank, the American Council on Science and Health (ACSH), had since its founding in 1978 pressed to eliminate the standard. The NRDC fought the change, winning a settlement in 1992 that would have forced the EPA to ban more than thirty chemicals that left pesticide residues in food. Nevertheless, after a determined long-term public relations campaign by the ACSH, Congress passed and President Clinton in 1996 signed a bill relaxing the standard.[21]

Achieving movement goals became even harder after the 1994 election, when a Republican majority swept into the U.S. House. The partisan divide in Congress and many state legislatures widened. Republicans coalesced around an oppositional strategy that rejected even traditionally bipartisan arenas, such as environmental protection.

Movement Challenges

Not only did the globalizing economy and partisan politics constrain further environmental reform. A shift in the nature and extent of environmental problems weakened the U.S. movement's ability to translate widespread popular support into significant legislative gains. Internal factors, including the failure of the large national environmental organizations to nurture relationships with grassroots groups and sharp strategy differences among environmental groups, also contributed.

Many environmental problems were less spectacular and less visible than fiery rivers and deadly smog; the effects of biotechnology, non-point source pollution, climate change, and hormone-disrupting chemicals were incremental and complex. Asthma rates soared, but officials were slow to acknowledge particulate air pollution as a major cause. Climate scientists were predicting serious problems ahead, but global warming gained little traction with the public because the signs were subtle and difficult to observe without technical equipment. These chronic or "slow motion technological disasters," as sociologist Stephen Couch and colleagues have termed them, developed over long periods, with *cumulative* effects that only gradually became evident.[22]

At the same time, major Washington-based groups continued to pursue a top-down mobilizing strategy over grassroots organizing. Once again, Earth Day 1990 was emblematic. As movement historian Adam Rome explained, organizers "sought to 'enlist' people in a well-defined movement, not to empower them to work out their own vision of how they might make a difference."[23]

Free Market Environmentalism or "Green Capitalism"

The Clean Air Act's cap-and-trade provision was a part of a larger trend toward "free-market environmentalism." Also called "green capitalism," "corporate environmentalism," or "green liberalism," free market environmentalism solicits voluntary action by industry and by individual consumers. Drawing on Indian environmentalist Sunita Narain, international relations scholar Peter Dauvergne calls this stance "environmentalism of the rich," that is, environmentalism that "manifests as business partnerships, eco-product fundraising, and market solutions," often based in the illusory notion that smart consumption will rescue the planet. The spectrum of free market environmentalists includes businesses with varying commitments to "going green." At one pole are businesses pursuing sustainable production as good for the environment and good for the bottom line, including eco-business innovators working in solar or green-building design. At the other are "greenwashers," poll-savvy corporate executives seeking to obscure polluting operations through "greenspeak." Often, these are companies with poor environmental records who seek out partnerships with major environmental groups. Some corporations, through large donations, earn the title "Million

Dollar Pandas" to polish their corporate images. Coca-Cola, for example, is a major sponsor of the World Wildlife Fund but continues to deplete water supplies in locales where potable water is scarce.[24]

Of course, large national and international environmental organizations with staffs of two hundred or more like NRDC and WRI depend on large donors. The bind created by relying on significant corporate donations is acknowledged even by their critics. "[I]t's virtually impossible to do public interest work of any scale—in academia or journalism or activism," writes Canadian journalist Naomi Klein, "without taking money of questionable origin, whether the origin is the state, corporations, or private philanthropy." What matters, Klein states, is whether "that funding is having undue influence—shaping the kinds of research undertaken, the kinds of policies advanced, as well as the kinds of questions that get asked in the first place."[25]

Free market environmentalism was not new. Physicist Amory Lovins had been advocating such an approach since the late 1970s. Friends of the Earth published his *Soft Energy Paths: Toward a Durable Peace* in the U.S. in 1977 and David Brower backed the approach, which "combine[d] a serious commitment to efficient use of energy with the use of renewable resources." In a series of books and essays, Lovins and entrepreneur Paul Hawken outlined the challenges and opportunities environmentalism presented to entrepreneurs. In *The Ecology of Commerce: A Declaration of Sustainability*, Hawken, co-owner of Smith & Hawken garden supply company, critiqued corporate practices from a business owner's perspective. "Quite simply," wrote Hawken, "our business practices are destroying life on earth." His 1999 book, *Natural Capitalism*, written with Amory and L. Hunter Lovins, suggested that businesses should create a restorative economy, "close the loop" in the production process by eliminating waste, and practice "capitalism as if living systems mattered." The authors outlined the dilemma:

> There is still a yawning gulf between the kind of 'green' environmentalism that business wants to promote—one that justifies growth and expansionary use of resources—and the kind that actually deals with the core issues of carrying capacity, drawdown, biotic impoverishment, and extinction of species.

They spoke frankly of and to their peers, "Business, despite its newly found good intentions with respect to the environment, has hardly changed at all."[26]

In a 2017 essay, Adam Rome offers several models companies use to reduce the environmental impact of their operations and save costs: waste prevention instead of pollution abatement; reengineering and reuse of raw materials; more ecological sourcing and sustainability indexing for suppliers; and redesigning the industry model to promote reuse. However, practices have sometimes fallen short of goals. For example, Minnesota manufacturer 3M instituted a Pollution Prevention Pays program in 1975 that encouraged employees to focus on waste prevention, redesigning processes to cut waste. Nevertheless, the company was forced in 2018 to settle a water pollution lawsuit in its home state for $850 million. In a successful effort to redesign an industry model, after reading Hawken's *Ecology of Commerce*, Interface owner Ray Anderson revamped his LaGrange, Georgia-based carpet business. Recognizing the carpet industry as a major producer of waste, Anderson developed recyclable carpet that could be leased to institutional clients and green builders in replaceable modular squares. By doing so, Interface diverted 154,000 tons of carpet from landfills over a twenty-year period, while also minimizing the use of new raw materials. Anderson became an outspoken advocate of sustainable business practices, lecturing at business and environmental conferences nationwide.[27]

Environmental economists began challenging the pro-growth assumptions underlying both the globalization of consumerism and free-market environmentalism. Herman Daly, a senior environmental economist at the World Bank before becoming one of that institution's foremost critics, advocated for what he termed "steady state economics" and against never-ending growth. Daly's work spawned the Center for Advancement of the Steady State Economy (CASSE), with chapters in several U.S. cities and countries around the world aimed at working to stabilize both population and consumption and to achieve a just distribution of resources. "Sustainability is achieved when the human economy fits within the capacity provided by Earth's ecosystems," CASSE members believe.[28] Economists such as Daly argue for considering ecological limits and impact on the physical world when choosing among infrastructure and investment options.

Environmental Justice Surges

By the late 1980s, environmental justice activism had gained momentum, especially in southern cities and small towns that were subject to noxious chemical facilities and waste dumps. In November 1988, hundreds joined the Great Louisiana Toxics March against the degradation caused by chemical plants sited along the Mississippi between Baton Rouge and New Orleans, where roughly one-fourth of U.S. chemical manufacturing is based. Beginning at Devil's Swamp, a biodiverse wetland turned Superfund site, and proceeding along a winding 150-mile route along River Road, the ten-day march called attention to the severely impacted stretch of river labeled "Cancer Alley" for the high rates of disease among its predominately African American and low-income residents. Chemical contamination displaced whole towns along the river. Morrisonville, Sunrise, and Reveilletown, towns originally founded by free persons of color or former slaves were bought out by Dow, Placid Refining Company, and Georgia Gulf Corporation, respectively.[29]

Co-sponsors of the 1988 march included the Louisiana Toxics Project, the Louisiana Environmental Action Network (LEAN), the Gulf Coast Tenants Organization, the Delta Chapter of the Sierra Club, and the Oil, Chemical, and

Atomic Workers Union. Greenpeace piloted one of its ships, the Beluga, up the river, bringing water testing equipment. The protest marked a new upsurge of activism centered on the ecological damage and hazards to human health from chemical pollution. Although the impetus for the march was local, organizers also aimed to pressure the incoming George H.W. Bush administration to make good on its environmental promises.

Activists at the forefront of environmental justice campaigns critiqued not only corporations and government policies that ignored communities of color but also major environmental organizations. In March 1990, the Southwest Organizing Project (SWOP)—a multiracial group in New Mexico formed in 1980 with a strong base in the Chicano/Latino community—sent a letter signed by SWOP director Richard Moore and more than one hundred co-signers to major U.S. environmental and conservation organizations, demanding they address the environmental concerns of communities of color. The letter called for the "Group of Ten" organizations to hire activists of color. At the time, the Sierra Club had one person of color on its 250-member professional staff; the Audubon Society employed three African Americans out of 315 employees. But as activist Dana Alston later said, "diversification of boards and staffs alone [would] not guarantee accountability." The environmental justice movement also critiqued the national environmental groups on their organizing style, characterized by one historian as reliant on "technocratic rationality and top-down managerialism." The letter went much further, specifying ways in which mainstream groups routinely overlooked communities of color and laying out an agenda for reorienting environmentalism.[30]

The letter cited America's history of "racist and genocidal practices including the theft of lands and water, the murder of innocent people, and the degradation of our environment." The U.S. military, especially, placed "minority workers in the most highly radioactive and toxic worksites." Signers argued that environmental groups were complicit with government and industry. "[Y]our organizations play an equal role in the disruption of our communities," the letter continued, "our survival needs and cultures are ignored." The Sierra Club and the Wilderness Society, for example, were supporting legislation to annex thirteen thousand acres considered to be ancestral holdings of the Acoma people to form El Malpaís National Monument in New Mexico. Signatories protested the Nature Conservancy and the National Audubon Society for their opposition to "a local, highly successful economic development project" operated by Chicanos in northern New Mexico that supported sheep grazing in the Humphries and Sargent Wildlife areas. Globally, proponents of environmental justice opposed "debt-for-nature swaps" whereby Third World countries signed over lands to conservation groups in exchange for reductions in their national debts. Despite the letter's scathing rebuke, the real goal was to seek "dialogue and mutual strategizing. . .[to] create a global environment that protects us *all*."[31]

In October 1991, the People of Color Environmental Justice Summit convened in Washington, D.C. Adding organizational clout to the letter's demands, three hundred Native American, African American, Latino, Asian American, and Pacific Islander activists from fifty states and Puerto Rico, Canada, Central and South America, and the Marshall Islands attended the Summit; another 250 representatives of peace, environmental, public health, civil rights, and religious organizations joined in on the second day. The conference approved a broad set of principles, including the demand that "public policy be based on mutual respect and justice, for all peoples, free from any form of discrimination or bias" and "affirm[ing] the sovereignty and self-determination of the indigenous peoples whose land [the U.S. government] occupies and holds in trust." The document explicitly invoked human rights and internationalism: "Environmental justice considers governmental acts of environmental injustice a violation of international law, the Universal Declaration of Human Rights, and the United Nations Convention on Genocide." The purpose of the gathering was "not in reaction to the environmental movement" but rather to "reaffirm their traditional connection to and respect for the natural world, and to speak for themselves on some of the most critical issues of our times," wrote Dana Alston, director of the Environment, Community Development, and Race Program at the Panos Institute in Washington, D.C. Reporting on the conference, Alston summed up that "the environment is woven into an overall framework and understanding of social, racial, and economic justice." Attendees' redefinitions of "environment," she explained, "are deeply rooted in culture and spirituality, and encompass all aspects of daily life—where we live, work, and play."[32]

Environmental justice groups gravitated toward "bottom-up" modes of organizing. Many adopted the Jemez Principles for Democratic Organizing, introduced at a meeting on globalization and trade convened in December 1996 by the Southwest Network for Economic and Environmental Justice in Jemez, New Mexico:

1) Be Inclusive
2) Emphasis on Bottom-Up Organizing
3) Let People Speak for Themselves
4) Work Together in Solidarity and Mutuality
5) Build Just Relationships Among Ourselves
6) Commitment to Self-Transformation.[33]

In the wake of the People of Color Summit, local environmental justice organizations proliferated. A 1992 conference in New Orleans at historically black Xavier University attracted more than two thousand attendees. Conferees included Jesus People Against Pollution, formed after a chemical plant explosion in Columbia, Mississippi, and Native Americans for a Clean Environment, who were seeking redress for a uranium release at Kerr-McGee's Sequoyah Fuels nuclear plant in Oklahoma. Designed to bring labor, civil rights, and environmental activists together, the conference was sponsored by the Southern Organizing Committee for Social and Economic Justice (known as SOC, pronounced *sock*), long active in racial justice activism and labor organizing, and co-sponsored by Jobs with Justice, the Coalition of Black Trade Unionists (CBTU), and seven international unions. Also present were staffers from the Highlander Research and Education Center, likewise rooted in labor and civil rights movements, which had been holding workshops for environmental organizers since the late 1980s. The Center's Stop the Pollution or alternatively, Save the Planet (STP), workshops trained activists from two-thirds of U.S. states, as well as Ecuador, South Africa, and India.[34]

Church networks were a major source of institutional support for the environmental justice movement. The Commission for Racial Justice of United Church of Christ had published the 1987 *Toxic Wastes and Race* report, sponsored the first People of Color Summit, and led "toxic tours" to expose the hazards communities of color faced. African American church leaders established the National Black Church Environmental and Economic Justice Network in 1993.[35]

Like their Washington-based counterparts, environmental justice activists had entered the Clinton years on a hopeful note. Major players like Rev. Benjamin Chavis and sociologist Robert Bullard participated in the Clinton transition team, proposing natural resource and environmental policies for the departments of Energy, Interior, and Agriculture and for the EPA. Civil rights veteran and Georgia congressman John R. Lewis and then-Tennessee senator and vice-presidential candidate Al Gore had co-sponsored the Environmental Justice Act of 1992, during the previous session of Congress. The bill proposed to designate and protect from further toxic development Environmental High Impact Areas, which tended to be communities of color and low-income neighborhoods.[36] However, white tolerance for race-based remedies to discrimination had declined, and the proposed legislation, though repeatedly introduced, never made it out of committee.

Environmental Justice and the EPA

From its beginnings in 1970, the EPA, like other federal agencies, was charged with ensuring non-discrimination within its programs. An EPA report of that year had noted that "fulfillment of civil rights responsibilities is one approach to alleviating the burdensome environmental problems of the poor." However, not until the 1990s, and then only under pressure from environmental justice activists, did the agency take steps toward achieving what the agency itself defined as "the fair treatment and meaningful involvement of all people regardless of race, color, national origin, or income, with respect to the development, implementation, and enforcement of environmental laws, regulations, and policies."[37]

In 1992, environmental justice advocates began filing complaints with the EPA based on Title VI of the Civil Rights Act of 1964, which prohibits discrimination in the administration of federal programs. Of the first two hundred Title VI complaints the EPA received, the agency immediately rejected 70 percent.

In 1998, when the EPA finally issued its intent to begin investigating complaints of discrimination, Congress repeatedly blocked funding for the effort.[38]

Nonetheless, environmental justice organizing garnered greater attention from the EPA to local toxics struggles. EPA's Office of Environmental Equity became the Office of Environmental Justice (OEJ) in 1994 and the EPA hired as its director Charles Lee, one of the authors of the 1987 *Toxic Wastes and Race* report. The EPA also formed the National Environmental Justice Advisory Council (NEJAC, pronounced knee-jack) that year, appointing environmental justice leaders to serve, including Bob Bullard, who chaired the Health and Research Subcommittee; Richard Moore of SWOP; and Pam Tau Lee, a California-based labor and public health advocate. Business representatives were also appointed, including a consultant for the agribusiness giant, Monsanto, Michael Pierle. NEJAC's role is advisory only. However, its regional meetings and national briefings by the EPA facilitated environmental justice networking and cross-fertilization of strategies.

Environmental justice advocates won a signature policy achievement with the issuance of Executive Order 12898 by President Clinton in 1994. The order required not just the EPA, but all federal agencies, to identify and address "disproportionately high and adverse human health or environmental effects of its programs, policies, and activities on minority populations and low-income populations." The order was designed to promote non-discrimination in federal programs as well as provide minority and low-income communities access to public information and opportunities to participate in environmental decision-making. The Executive Order gave advocates a new tool for protecting areas already heavily polluted. Citing the order, the Nuclear Regulatory Commission in 1997 denied a permit for a uranium enrichment facility in an already impacted African American neighborhood in rural Louisiana.[39]

The environmental justice movement remained decentralized, exercising its power through networks rather than establishing a national center or hiring lobbyists in Washington, D.C. Leading individuals include Carl Anthony, an architect and urban planner who directed the Urban Habitat Program he founded in 1989 with Karl Linn and David Brower of the Earth Island Institute, with the aim of highlighting strategies for ecologically sound urban development. Some environmental justice scholar-activists founded research and advocacy centers, many of which were located at historically black colleges and universities. For example, environmental sociologist Beverly Wright launched the Deep South Center for Environmental Justice in 1992 at Xavier University. Robert Bullard established an Environmental Justice Resource Center at Clark Atlanta University in 1992. The University of Michigan School for Environment and Sustainability (SEAS), originally founded in 1927, established a Masters' certificate in Environmental Justice in the late 1990s, the first U.S. school to do so.[40]

Much as the civil rights movement has come to be understood as countless local movements, social justice environmentalism comprises thousands of local organizations. Some focus on a discrete goal and are temporary; others are durable, taking on multiple community concerns. Among the vast network is West Harlem Environmental Action (WeAct) in New York City, formed by journalist Peggy Shepard and others in 1988 to oppose construction of a sewage treatment plant in north Manhattan. WeAct works with the Mailman School of Public Health at Columbia University, conducting community-based research on children's environmental health to stop lead paint poisoning and combat high asthmas rates in Harlem. The group has employed diverse tactics—from civil disobedience to a lawsuit that resulted in a multi-million-dollar pollution abatement plan.[41]

A major win for environmental justice came in 1995 in Hawai'i, when the Pele Defense Fund blocked construction of a planned giant geothermal energy plant. Joined by several other Hawaiian organizations as well as the Rainforest Action Network, the Sierra Club, Friends of the Earth, Greenpeace, and Earth First!, the Pele Defense Fund challenged plans by the state of Hawai'i to allow the major geothermal project to bore under Wao Kele o Puna rainforest into a live volcano to harvest steam energy. Named for the Hawaiian spiritual goddess of volcanoes, Pelehonuamea, "Pele of the sacred land," the Pele Defense Fund's work addressed an important element of the environmental justice paradigm: cultural and religious freedom. Contesting commercial exploitation of the sacred site, the Pele Defense Fund noted that drilling would have led to devastation of 22,000 acres of rainforest and industrialization of the Big Island and Oahu. The Defense Fund and its allies successfully halted the project in 1995. (Despite the State of Hawai'i's agreement in 1995 "not to support, proceed with, participate in, or directly facilitate the production of geothermal energy on the Island of Hawai'i," proposals for tapping the geothermal source surfaced again in 2010. The battle took on fresh salience in 2018 when the eruption of the Kilauea volcano threatened to engulf another geothermal plant.)[42]

Some national organizations heeded the environmental justice movement's demand for hiring more people of color, strengthening both local organizing and the national groups. Greenpeace, for example, hired African American anti-apartheid activist Damu Smith, leader of the National Black Environmental Justice Network, as southern regional field organizer. Smith helped to lead a key environmental justice battle to block the Japanese firm Shintech from siting a major polyvinylchloride plant in Convent, Louisiana. Working with LEAN and the Gulf Coast Tenants, the campaign organized rallies and built alliances. Law students from the Environmental Law Clinic at Tulane University, headed by attorney Robert Kuehn, assisted residents in filing lawsuits to block the facility and require the EPA to consider alternatives, but met with vigorous opposition. A state judge blocked the Law Clinic from representing the residents, on the grounds that the clinic was mandated to represent low-income clients and not all of the plaintiffs qualified as such. Eventually, however, the coalition succeeded; Shintech dropped its plans to locate the facility in Convent. The company proposed a smaller plant at a less populous site in Plaquemine, Louisiana, thirty-five miles upriver. The new group that formed in Plaquemine, People Reaching Out to Stop Shintech's Toxins (PROTEST), was unsuccessful in blocking construction of that plant.[43]

Nature Preservation Versus Land Justice

The limited policy successes of environmental advocacy groups under an ostensibly supportive Democratic administration prompted considerable rethinking of the movement's goals and strategies. "The Trouble with Wilderness," a provocative 1995 essay by University of Wisconsin environmental historian William Cronon, outlined a central challenge facing late twentieth-century environmentalism. One of the founding generation of contemporary environmental historians, Cronon critiqued mainstream U.S. environmentalism for focusing on wilderness preservation to the neglect of the environments in which most people live. The essay elicited a sharp rebuttal from wilderness advocates who had been working to protect endangered places and species. However, Cronon's admonition buttressed the environmental justice movement's critique.[44]

Program initiatives advanced by mainstream groups and environmental justice activists continued to differ. A 1992 EPA study examined organizational literature and convened focus groups, determining that mainstream organizations prioritized "ecosystems, environmental education, and environmental laws and legislation" over environmental justice concerns such as "toxic wastes, human health, and technology."[45] These divergent priorities could be difficult to reconcile.

For example, whereas mainstream groups continued to target nuclear power, Native American environmental groups pushed for redress for nuclear exposure, winning the Radiation Exposure Compensation Act (RECA) in 1990. The law applied not only to miners, but also to workers and downwinders from the Nevada nuclear weapons test site in certain counties in Utah, Colorado, and Arizona. RECA conveyed a tepid apology from Congress to uranium miners "for the hardships they have endured." The law provided compensation for miners with medical proof of lung cancer or other respiratory disease who could prove exposure prior to 1971. A coalition of grassroots Native groups and uranium workers' organizations continued to push to increase compensation levels and expand the groups covered, winning amendments signed into law in 2000.[46]

Native populations working to end "radioactive colonization" within the U.S. connected with indigenous peoples from around the world at the World Uranium Hearings in Salzburg, Austria, in 1992. Conveners demanded "No more exploitation of lands and people by uranium mining, nuclear-power generation, nuclear testing, and radioactive waste dumping." Other demands included cleanup and restoration, an end to government secrecy, and full compensation and independent health monitoring for affected humans and other living things. In 2005, the Navajo Nation Council voted sixty-three to nineteen to ban uranium mining and processing within its borders. Despite support in Congress for ending research and development grants for the mining companies, Eastern Navajo Diné Against Uranium Mining and the Southwest Research and Information Center have had to go to court to enforce the ban.[47]

At times, the environmental demands of communities of color have directly conflicted with those of mainstream environmental organizations. A 1990s conflict over forest policy in New Mexico pitted community foresters, Chicano and Hispano environmental justice advocates against ultraconservative "Wise Use" groups and right-wing militia members, as well as mainstream environmental organizations and the Forest Service. The region had seen centuries of contention between Hispanos, Native Americans, and Anglos over land rights. Always present in struggles over land are "colonial legacies," geographer Jake Kosek has noted. "Every time La Floresta [the Forest Service] tries to save the forest," local activist Max Córdova told Kosek in 1999, "we end up losing our lands." In the 1960s, Reies López Tijerina, a Chicano activist in the Alianza Federal de las Mercedes (Federal Alliance of Land Grants) and others sought to regain access to land promised to inhabitants of the region in the 1848 Treaty of Guadeloupe Hidalgo, which ended the Mexican-American war. The Forest Service's resource management policies favored commercial loggers over Native subsistence needs, and in the early 1990s, local Hispano foresters and environmental activists coalesced to protest constraints on indigenous access to forest resources such as firewood and small logging operations. However, the Sierra Club introduced the Zero Cut Initiative, designed explicitly to more aggressively block logging and grazing in national forests. Although credited with revitalizing the club's membership base, the campaign also revealed a sharp divide between indigenous activists and mainstream environmentalists over land use.[48]

In northern New Mexico's Carson National Forest (named not for Rachel Carson but for wilderness trapper, guide, and "Indian agent" Kit Carson), controversy erupted when the most influential environmental group in the region, Forest Guardians (which included many Sierra Club members) filed lawsuits to block all logging on federal land in northern New Mexico. The community forestry movement was led by local Hispano activists, whose communities confronted "loss of land, racial inequalities, and rural poverty" and depended on the forests for firewood, as well as for logging jobs. At a confrontation on November 22, 1995, competing signs told the story. Indigenous activists carried signs reading: "We Refuse to Be Endangered" and "The Owl or *La Gente* *[the People]*: The Choice is Easy." Hispano leaders hung in effigy stuffed images of two Forest Guardians. Forest Guardian supporters' signs read: "Stop Scape-Goating Environmentalists." The issue was divisive within the Sierra Club. Some members of the Santa Fe chapter supported the community forestry movement against the club's zero-cut campaign. An accommodation of local residents' firewood needs eventually was reached, but the fight had the effect, writes Kosek, of "forcing people to choose between two very different strains of the environmental movement."[49]

The Arctic National Wildlife Refuge

Early in the 1990s, wilderness advocates managed once again to forestall efforts to open the Arctic National Wildlife Refuge (ANWR—pronounced "an-wăr") to oil and gas drilling. First set aside under President Eisenhower in 1960, just one year after Alaska became a state, ANWR comprises 19.6 million acres in the northeast corner of the state. Lauded by John Muir in *Travels in Alaska* (1915), by Bob Marshall in *Arctic Village* (1933), and called a "place of enchantment" by Wilderness Society leaders Olaus and Margaret "Mardy" Murie, who pressed to have the Refuge designated, ANWR is regarded as an iconic wilderness site, a rare holdout against fossil fuel-based industrialization. Ever since oil was discovered by the ARCO Corporation in nearby Prudhoe Bay on Alaska's north shore in December 1967, oil and gas companies have targeted the region for drilling.[50] Advocates for the Refuge have faced several battles in Congress to maintain its protected status.

Legislative and executive actions in the 1970s both addressed indigenous claims and established a larger reserve. The Alaska Native Claims Settlement Act of 1971 rescinded Native Alaskan claims to most of the land in exchange for forty-four million acres and nearly one billion dollars for Native groups. The settlement laid "the basis for autonomous development of indigenous economies and societies on an unprecedented scale," environmental historian Carolyn Merchant has observed. The legislation protected eighty million acres of the forest until 1978. At that time, President Jimmy Carter exercised presidential authority under the American Antiquities Act of 1906 to protect two-thirds of the eighty million acres. The remainder was secured through the passage of the Alaska National Interest Lands Conservation Act of 1980, signed by Carter that December, setting aside what one writer described as "more wild country than had been preserved anywhere in the world up to that time."[51]

However, potential rich on- and off-shore oil reserves have kept ANWR under threat. Tribal groups in Alaska have taken divergent positions on drilling in the Arctic region. The indigenous Gwich'in have long opposed efforts to open ANWR to drilling. Many Iñupiat, who also inhabit the region, support drilling and see economic benefits in opening the reserve. Two coalitions, the Alaska Coalition, including the NRDC, the Sierra Club, and the Wilderness Society, and Americans for Alaska, have long lobbied against drilling. Opening the Refuge to drilling was a priority for former oil company owner George H.W. Bush. However, aided by public outrage over the Exxon Valdez oil disaster in 1989, Congress blocked drilling in 1991.[52]

The Power of Philanthropy

Foundations remained influential in setting program priorities, but foundations contributed only about seven percent of the funding for national environmental groups in 1995. Individual donors, giving large and small amounts, generally provided the bulk of funding. The Nature Conservancy had the largest income and net worth by far, due in part to its large investment in land; a study using 1995 data found that among eighty-four leading organizations, the Conservancy garnered nearly 30 percent of the income. A significant funding gap separated the large and small organizations. The vast majority of grassroots and environmental justice groups had "no reportable income."[53]

Recognizing that the environmental justice paradigm enriched the movement's perspective and broadened its base, foundations with a history of underwriting mainstream environmental groups gradually began supporting environmental justice work. Several national groups themselves established well-intentioned environmental justice projects, some of which had the perverse effect of tapping resources that might otherwise have gone to smaller, less well-known, local or regional environmental groups.[54]

In 1997, Dana Alston, then president of the National Black United Fund, outlined a new model for funding. Instead of giving grants to large organizations to distribute among local groups, Alston suggested to foundation leaders that they fund grassroots organizations directly and then support the technical assistance that local groups determined would be needed to help them succeed. Progressive funders in the National Network of Grantmakers, among others, adopted the model, directly donating to environmental justice groups.[55]

Still, garnering sufficient funding was tough, even for big name environmental groups. Between 1990 and 1994, amid economic recession, Greenpeace lost almost a million members and 40 percent of its revenue. The economic downturn was only one factor. Internal debates raged over whether to continue as a largely direct-action organization or pursue partnerships with business and a more traditional lobbying role. Bailed out by the international office, which discouraged environmental justice work, Greenpeace pulled back from its work with local grassroots organizations after the Shintech campaign. Greenpeace continued to refuse funding from "corporations, political parties, unions, or large corporate endowments" but regained financial health in the 2000s, attracting millions of new members across forty countries.[56]

Rio: The Earth Summit

"Think Globally, Act Locally" had long been a slogan of the environmental movement. The 1990s brought increased international action. Amid expanding globalization and the collapse of the Soviet bloc, the U.N. Environment Programme held the third in its series of decennial conferences on environment and development in Rio di Janeiro, Brazil, in 1992. Known as the Earth Summit, the Rio Conference was the largest U.N. environmental conference to date, gathering most of the world's nations—more than 170 of 195 countries—around a shared agenda. The aim: to promote and sustain economic growth within environmental limits. Sustainable development dominated the conversation at Rio. Sustainable growth meant not only funding for solar energy or safe drinking water projects, but also technology transfers to support renewables and green infrastructure. Of particular concern to developing nations was gaining political support of wealthy, developed nations for addressing the Third World debt crisis.

The Rio Conference produced several agreements, or conventions, on climate and on biodiversity and introduced Agenda 21, a plan for "an open, equitable, secure, non-discriminatory and predictable multilateral trading system that is consistent with the goals of sustainable development." President George H.W. Bush attended, signing the United Nations Framework Convention on Climate Change (UNFCCC) that has provided the scaffolding for subsequent international meetings on the subject. In a press conference in Rio, President Bush vowed, "The United States fully intends to be the world's preeminent leader in protecting the global environment."[57] Concurring, the Senate ratified the treaty by a two-thirds vote.

Rio encouraged U.S. participants to look outward, to consider global problems, and to underscore the links between poverty and inequality and the environment. However, the priorities of U.S.-based organizations abroad and the needs of marginalized groups in developing countries were sometimes at odds. Conflicts surfaced, for example, when rainforest protection or land reserves resulted in displacement of local populations.[58]

Still, the Rio conference stimulated greater information-sharing among NGOs and the G-77 alliance of developing nations. Rio, and the agreements negotiated by the attending parties, signaled also that "states do not monopolize environmental policy," argues Joan Martínez-Alier. Environmentalism was becoming more definitively transnational, with nongovernmental environmental organizations playing a larger role than before Rio.[59] The Rio gathering invigorated U.S. environmental justice advocates, who learned of kindred struggles from newly democratic South Africa to South Asia, and who would increasingly frame their work in the context of not just civil, but international, human rights.

Coming as it did, just before the first International Year of the World's Indigenous People in 1993, the Rio Conference helped to highlight the environmental devastation facing indigenous populations in the Global South. For example, the Yanomami of the Amazon basin suffered from malaria, other diseases, and incursions by land developers, gold mining interests, and agricultural colonists. The EDF and other major international environmental organizations threatened to boycott Rio in protest, which aided the Yanomami in securing an agreement from the Brazilian government to designate a region of 96,000 square kilometers as a reserve for the tribe. Indigenous activists frequently faced extraordinary danger of violent reprisal. In 1995, Nigeria executed Ogoni human rights leader Ken Saro-Wiwa along with eight other members of the Ogoni tribe who had been pressing for clean water, reduced air pollution, and protection of their land from the multinational oil companies drilling in the Niger Delta.[60]

As the decade wore on, activists and academics from the developing world advanced a forceful social justice critique of environmentalism in wealthy countries. Indian scholar Ramachandra Guha and Spanish economist Joan Martínez-Alier urged greater attention to the ecological needs of the poor and marginalized, which they termed "environmentalism of the poor." The formulation, also called "livelihood ecology," focuses attention on "ecological distribution conflicts" and "the uncertain hazards from new technologies" affecting the majority of the world's population, "whose livelihoods are threatened by mines, oil wells, dams, and tree plantations to feed the increasing throughput of energy and materials of the economy within or outside their own countries."[61]

The "Wise Use" Movement

If the fight by environmentalists in the 1980s was waged against the executive branch, the battle of the 1990s was with Congress. The Sagebrush Rebellion had faltered in the mid-1980s, but a successor had soon begun taking shape in Reno, Nevada, at a conference sponsored by the Center for the Defense of Free Enterprise (CDFE) in 1988. Taking its name from the Progressive Era conservationists' slogan, the anti-environmentalist "Wise Use" campaign built a stronger institutional infrastructure than its predecessors and a larger base, drawing support not only from timber, oil, and mining interests, but also from ranchers, farmers, and ordinary citizens. The Wise Use movement was also better funded, with considerable financial support from extractive industries. Conservative think tanks honed messaging and built a strong media presence for the Wise Use campaign. Wise Use candidates took advantage of gerrymandered districts to win partisan advantage in congressional elections in 1994. The movement was especially strong in the West. Wise Use groups gained influence within the Western Governors Association, though they also found allies among Republicans in the South. By 1994, CDFE had a mailing list of 125,000 and support from conservative heavyweights Senator Jesse Helms of North Carolina, Senator Ted Stevens of Alaska, and former Defense Secretary Dick Cheney from Wyoming.[62]

The goals were not new. The twenty-five-point "Wise Use Agenda" included prospecting for oil and gas in the Arctic National Wildlife Refuge (ANWR), logging on three million acres of the Tongass National Forest in Alaska and mining on all public lands, and gaining "standing to sue" for industries "threatened or harmed by environmentalists." In contrast to that of the Sagebrush rebels, Wise Use rhetoric focused not on state's rights, but on individual rights and freedoms.

Wise Users framed their bid to turn federal lands to more profitable private use as an appeal for limiting the "coercive force of government." Extremists within the movement attacked both environmentalists and federal natural resource officers, bombing homes and federal offices. As described by the League of Conservation Voters, the Wise Use "movement rest[ed] on a radical (and fundamentally anti-democratic) reinterpretation of the private property rights already guaranteed by state and federal constitutions, in a barely disguised attempt to evade environmental protection laws."[63]

Intensifying the rhetoric, radio talk show hosts amplified the heavy drumbeat against environmentalists as extremists, socialists, elitists, and anti-human. Author Andrew Rowell cites a 1994 incident on Paul Weyrich's satellite and cable TV network when a commentator urged listeners to "'spread the alarm and alert America to the growing oppression by rule and regulation which over-zealous bureaucracies and 'EEEGs'—extremist environmentalist elitist groups—have imposed on basic and supposedly inalienable citizen rights."[64]

Window of Opportunity Closing

The window of opportunity that opened with the decline of the Cold War and the election of a pro-environment administration soon narrowed. The mid-1990s found environmentalists unexpectedly playing defense despite popular support and positions of influence in the administration. The Democratic Party had embraced a centrist posture. The 1994 election brought to Congress a Republican majority bent on reducing the size and power of the federal government and cutting regulations and funding for environmental protection. Historian Christopher Sellers attributes Republican white flight from environmental causes in part to racialization of environmental reform in this era. As awareness of environmental racism increased and black representatives became the staunchest supporters of environmental concerns in Congress, environmentalism was coded as a "race" issue as part of a broader campaign against the regulatory state.[65]

After 1994, Clinton administration plans to elevate the EPA to a cabinet department were dropped, because many believed putting the initiative to a vote would invite Republican attempts to weaken the agency. Environmental leaders with positions of power within the administration found it more difficult to challenge members of Congress than they had been able to do from outside government. Even prominent Democrats who had run as environmentalists defected on key votes. For example, a proposed tax on non-renewable energy resources passed the Republican-led House and then died in the Democratic-led Senate Finance Committee. Leading Democrats supported wasteful spending on new roads in national forests.[66]

Nonetheless, environmentalists managed to defeat the worst assault on environmental regulation of the Clinton years: Senator Bob Dole's regulatory reform bill targeting the EPA, OSHA, and Food and Drug Administration regulations.

With assistance from advocates as diverse as Robert Kennedy, Jr., and cartoonist Garry Trudeau, the Green Group mapped the strategy that won sixty-three House Republican votes and defeated the Regulatory Relief Act. Activists flooded Congress with eighty-five sacks of mail and a million signatures on petitions supporting environmental laws. In retaliation for the defeat, Republicans slapped dozens of anti-environment riders on the 1996 budget bill, which Clinton vetoed.[67]

At issue in the regulatory reform debate was the role of the federal government in limiting environmental hazards and protecting public health. Since the Progressive Era, reigning in the worst corporate environmental abuses had been considered an appropriate role for government. Now, many in Congress were backing away from that responsibility. Still, as in the 1980s, the congressional assault on environmental regulation once again backfired, strengthening public resolve in support of environmental protection. Giving just one example, John Adams of the NRDC explained that the fight against the 104th Congress brought that organization 85,000 new members.[68]

Kyoto Protocol Fails to Gain Official U.S. Support

The biggest disappointment on environmental issues of the Clinton years, and likely the most consequential, was the failure of the United States to adopt the Kyoto Protocol on climate. The 1997 Kyoto climate talks led to an international agreement to reduce greenhouse gases. Acknowledging that the vast majority of greenhouse gas emissions had been produced by developed nations, the agreement allotted rich and poor nations "common but differentiated" responsibilities for reducing carbon emissions and gave developing nations more time to reach their targeted reductions. Vice President Gore signed the Kyoto Protocol on behalf of the U.S., but the U.S. Senate refused to ratify the agreement.

Ultimately, the failure to ratify the Kyoto Protocol can be traced to the Global Climate Coalition (GCC). Representing the "Big Three" U.S. automakers—GM, Ford, and Chrysler—and an array of multinational coal, oil, and gas companies (including Exxon, Shell, Amoco, and Texaco), the GCC opposed international climate targets and policies. The GCC had pressured Congress to pre-emptively restrict U.S. negotiators at Kyoto. Democrats as well as Republicans in the U.S. Senate had voted ninety-five to zero five months *before* the meeting, to reject any agreement that did not require developed and developing countries, including China and India, to restrict emissions in similar fashion. The U.S. failure to ratify the Kyoto agreement exemplified the perceptible shift toward unilateralism since the decline of the Cold War.[69]

Tackling Military Toxics

Toxic legacies of World War II and the Cold War at military production and weapons storage sites in the U.S. remained an environmental health concern and a focus of organizing in the 1990s. In addition to their nuclear arsenals, both the U.S. and the Soviets had maintained substantial stockpiles of chemical weapons. Deadly nerve agents—sarin, VX—and the blister agent, mustard gas, had been stockpiled since the early 1960s. Superseded as a weapon of war, this Cold War arsenal was stored in aging containers in danger of leaking. Signing the Chemical Weapons Convention in 1993, the U.S. and the Soviets agreed to destroy their respective chemical arsenals.

A grassroots coalition, the Chemical Weapons Working Group (CWWG), demanded safe disposal of the chemical weapons stored in both countries. Active from the early 1990s into the second decade of the twenty-first century, CWWG included groups from the eight chemical stockpile sites around the continental U.S. as well as representatives from Guam and, notably, from Russia. The coalition was founded by Vietnam War veteran Craig Williams of Berea, Kentucky, who won the prestigious Goldman Prize for the effort.

Concerned not only about explosions during destruction of the chemicals, but also about potential long-term environmental health effects of leaks and releases, CWWG members succeeded in pressuring the U.S. to put in place safety measures around chemical weapons incinerators constructed at the Anniston, Alabama, and Tooele, Utah, stockpile sites. The coalition blocked incineration of the weapons at sites in Maryland, Colorado, Indiana, and Kentucky, convincing the Army to use the safer option of chemical neutralization instead. Activists also succeeded in forcing the Army to adhere to its promise to dismantle the Alabama incinerator once destruction of the local chemical weapons stockpile was complete.[70]

Precautionary Action in a Risk Society

While environmentalists are uniquely dependent on science for understanding the anthropogenic changes to the earth and in human bodies, science has not provided easy solutions. The problems are technically complex and politically contested. During the 1980s, an entire consulting industry emerged to counter the movement's claims, diverting the practice of risk assessment and risk management to undermine regulation.[71]

During the 1990s, a sector of the environmental movement pressed for the adoption of a precautionary approach, in contrast to the "after the event" doctrine that had prevailed in much of U.S. law. The precautionary approach reframed risk and uncertainty. It had been adopted as part of the Rio Declaration on Environment and Development. Principle 15 states:

> In order to protect the environment, the precautionary approach shall be widely applied by States according to their capabilities. Where there are threats of serious or irreversible damage, lack of full scientific certainty shall not be used as a reason for postponing cost-effective measures to prevent environmental degradation.[72]

In January 1998, more than two dozen scientists, attorneys, foundation leaders, and representatives of environmental organizations gathered at the Wingspread Center in Racine, Wisconsin, headquarters of the Johnson Foundation, to discuss applying this paradigm to environmental regulation in the U.S. The Wingspread Statement, as the resulting manifesto came to be called, adopted a precautionary approach to protecting environmental health. The concept built on a longstanding principle, which dates to Greek physician Hippocrates, loosely translated as "First, do no harm." Drawing also on the German concept *vorsorge*, meaning foresight, the "better safe than sorry" approach, advocates urged the U.S. to protect people from untested chemicals by requiring strict evaluation of the health impact of new chemicals before permitting them to be marketed. Wingspread attendees would author several publications designed to promote the precautionary approach in local, state, and national legislation. The City of San Francisco, an early convert, adopted a precautionary principle ordinance in 2003, committing the city to "making choices based on the least environmentally harmful alternatives." The European Union would take the lead globally, adopting a precautionary approach to toxic chemicals in 2007, despite strong opposition from the chemical industry and the George W. Bush administration, which exercised pressure via the U.S. Department of State.[73]

Media and Environmental Activism

Popular news coverage of environmental issues broadened in the 1990s, both in the mainstream media and via targeted programing. Since the 1970s, major city newspapers had been assigning reporters to the "environmental beat," contributing significantly to public awareness. Environmental groups understood the importance of media and publishing and spawned a robust collection of periodicals that highlighted issues of concern. Each major organization had a newsletter, which served a networking function. Specialized news magazines and investigative journals appeared as well. *Orion Magazine* (formerly *Orion Nature Quarterly*) has been publishing since 1982. Peter Montague of the Environmental Research Foundation published *Rachel's Hazardous Waste News* (later *Rachel's News* and *Rachel's Precaution Reporter*) from 1986–2009, withstanding a legal challenge from industry to do so.[74]

The 1990s saw an increase in targeted print and broadcast media. In 1991, the Institute for Southern Studies in Durham, North Carolina, publisher of *Southern Exposure*, published the "Green Index," evaluating states' performances on various environmental measures, including handling of air and water pollution, toxic chemicals, and hazardous waste. (Oregon and Maine ranked highest, with Louisiana and Alabama falling at the bottom of the rankings.)[75]

Public Radio International began producing the radio series "Living on Earth" in 1991. (By 2018, more than 270 stations carried the program.) Dedicated eco-news wire services developed. *Energy and Environment News*, a newswire service, began publishing in 1998. Pete Myers, who co-authored *Our Stolen Future* with Theo Colborn, launched in 2002 the Science Communications Network, which publishes *Environmental Health News,* an online news aggregator that provides links to the top environmental stories each day. A host of professional associations devoted to the environment formed, including the Society of Environmental Journalists. A wealth of peer-reviewed academic journals covering environmental subjects appeared; there would be nearly 300 such publications in 2018. Academic journals included the Forest History Society's *Forest and Conservation History* (previously *Forest History*), which merged in 1996 with *Environmental History* published by the American Society for Environmental History. *Race, Poverty, and the Environment*, co-founded by architect and urban planner Carl Anthony and attorney Luke Cole, appeared in 1990. An eponymous journal dedicated to *Environmental Justice,* founded by Sylvia Hood Washington, came later, in 2007. In a further indication of the growing importance of global environmental issues, two journals on the subject began publishing in 1990, *Global Planetary Change* and *Global Environmental Change.*[76]

Hollywood movies played a role in popularizing environmental causes. Feature films helped to spread awareness of the health consequences of environmental pollution and highlighted the role of legal activism. In "A Civil Action" (1998) John Travolta played the flamboyant personal injury lawyer Jan Schlichtmann who brought wrongful death lawsuits against several companies for polluting the wetlands that served the water supply for Woburn, Massachusetts, a working-class suburb of Boston. Several residents had died from leukemia. "Erin Brockovich" (2000), starring Julia Roberts, portrayed the story of Hinkley, California, which had been polluted with hexavalent chromium (chromium VI) by the Pacific Gas and Electric Company. More than six hundred residents sued PG&E and won a $333 million settlement in 1996. (Fifteen years later, the *Los Angeles Times* reported that the plume that initially brought the toxic chemical into people's wells was still migrating, contaminating additional wells in Hinkley as it moved.)[77]

Globalization, Direct Action, and the WTO

The globalization of production and the consequent decline in workers' rights and environmental protection led to intense debate over U.S. trade policy and a marked radicalization of some sectors of the labor and environmental movements. The 1993 North American Free Trade Agreement (NAFTA) lowered tariffs on goods traded between the U.S., Canada, and Mexico. Side agreements to the trade pact on labor and environmental standards fell far short of offering job protections for U.S. workers or equal environmental protection for laborers in developing economies. To the disappointment of labor allies, most of the environmental leaders on Clinton's Council on Sustainable Development supported NAFTA. Only the Sierra Club opposed the Council's endorsement of the pact.[78]

The creation of the World Trade Organization (WTO) in January 1995, an outgrowth of the 1947 General Agreement on Tariffs and Trade (GATT), signaled intensifying globalization. A forum for negotiating international trade agreements, the WTO was dominated by large multinational corporations that wished to take advantage of cheap labor markets and weaker environmental regulations by moving production and even corporate headquarters overseas. "The WTO has proven to be profoundly anti-environmental both procedurally and substantively, handing down environmentally damaging decisions whenever it had the opportunity to do so," writes interdisciplinary scholar Ken Conca. The first major ruling issued by the WTO struck at the EPA requirement that both domestic and foreign gasoline refineries make cleaner gas. In addition, as researchers from the San Francisco-based International Forum on Globalization have pointed out, the WTO allows the patenting and commodification of seeds, medicinal botanicals, and the genetic components of life.[79]

When Service Employees International Union president John Sweeney came to lead the AFL-CIO in 1995, he reinvigorated an alliance with environmentalists. Most of organized labor staunchly opposed NAFTA, predicting that the rush of jobs out of the country would only increase, leaving workers in the U.S. unemployed and workers in developing countries vulnerable to exploitation. It was already clear that laborers in the *maquiladoras*—the assembly plants along the southern U.S. border where poorly paid Mexican workers assemble products duty-free and tariff-free—were exposed to hazardous levels of dust and toxic chemicals. It was also clear that competition from these factories placed downward pressure on wages and environmental standards in the U.S.[80]

At the 1999 meeting of the World Trade Organization in Seattle, Washington, the labor and environmental movements allied to challenge these trade policies. This third meeting of the WTO's highest decision-making body was to have begun negotiations on tariffs and trade in agriculture, services, and other arenas between 135 participating countries, about 80 percent of which were developing nations. In what became known as "the battle in Seattle," labor and environmental activists joined in protesting the effects of globalization, including the decline in manufacturing jobs in the U.S. and the low pay and poor environmental records in the Third World economies to which multinationals had moved their factories. Activists staged direct action protests, using confrontation and spectacle to direct attention to injustices and inequalities perpetuated by state actors. Building upon the mass anti-sweatshop campaigns against companies such as Nike and GAP that had been underway since the late 1980s, anti-globalization activists used selective buying, boycotts, and educational efforts focused on worker rights with a strong environmental component. The demands of activists ranged from those who sought the demise of the WTO to those who sought genuinely free trade with a world minimum wage, guarantees for workers' rights to organize, safe working conditions, and environmental protections.

David Brower, founder of Friends of the Earth and the Earth Island Institute, then nearly ninety, and David Foster, of the Steelworkers District 11, led a new enviro-steelworker alliance, the Alliance for Sustainable Jobs and the Environment. While National Wildlife, Sierra Club, and World Resources Institute leaders lobbied President Clinton (unsuccessfully) on the global logging trade, direct action groups protested outside. Protestors included:

> Earth First!, the Ruckus Society (a direct-action training center), Food Not Bombs, Global Exchange, a small contingent of anarchists dressed in black, with black masks, plus a hefty international contingent including French farmers, Korean Greens, Canadian wheat growers and British opponents of genetically modified food.[81]

According to the Associated Press, roughly forty thousand demonstrators rallied on the opening day of the conference, as environmentalists joined with steelworkers, mineworkers, and a host of AFL-CIO unions. However, "pockets of rioting overshadowed peaceful demonstrations," the Associated Press reported, as a small group of self-identified anarchists smashed storefronts of retailers McDonald's, Starbucks, the Gap, and Nike. Using tear gas, pepper spray, rubber bullets, and concussion grenades, the Seattle police brutally suppressed the protest.[82]

That the protests had an impact was undeniable. In the end, mass demonstrations blocked the opening and closing sessions, preventing scheduled meetings.

PHOTO 5.1   Labor and environmental groups opposed World Trade Organization policies on globalization of trade with few protections for workers and the environment in Seattle, 1999. Photo by Eric Draper, Associated Press.

Internal pressures within the WTO also helped to collapse the talks. The major trading partners differed over export subsidies and farm price supports. Developing and developed countries disagreed over wage and labor standards and over which countries were entitled to full participation in the conference negotiations. African and Caribbean delegates refused to yield to U.S. pressure to accept an agreement that did not recognize the rights of developing nations.[83]

The Seattle protests exposed rifts over tactics within the environmental movement and between environmentalists and labor. But the joint protests also represented a move toward greater intersectionality between social justice movements and demonstrated once again the power of an alliance between labor and environmentalists. Though the two movements have at times been at odds, the relationship would continue. However, the decline of the labor movement as a reliable base of the Democratic Party weakened pro-labor, pro-environment Democrats in Congress. As the size and strength of the labor movement has weakened, so has the political clout of the environmental movement.

Due to the rise of the conservative wing of the Republican Party, the centrism of key Democrats, the increasing sophistication and strength of the anti-environmental forces, and a deep chasm within the movement over strategy, the Clinton years did not produce the hoped-for gains. Environmental groups forestalled some of the worst anti-regulatory moves but achieved few legislative advances at the national level on the issues that mattered most, including environmental justice concerns and climate. Hard-won successes, such as the Shintech victory in Louisiana and the Pele Defense Fund's win in Hawai'i, came at the local level and were led by experienced social justice leaders who steered strategic partnerships with national environmental groups. Climate and climate justice activism would take center stage in the new millennium. The global challenges to environmentalism would only increase.

Notes

1 Barnaby J. Feder, "The Business of Earth Day," *The New York Times*, November 12, 1989.
2 Hayes quoted in Barnaby J. Feder, "The Business of Earth Day," *The New York Times*, November 12, 1989; McNeill, *Something New under the Sun*, 339.
3 Uekoetter, "The End of the Cold War," in McNeill et al., *Environmental Histories of the Cold War*, 343–51, 345, 348.
4 Clapp and Dauvergne, *Paths to a Green World*, 158–59.
5 Dunlap, "Trends in Public Opinion," 285, 300, 305.
6 Rosenbaum, *Environmental Politics and Policy*, 47; Brulle, *Agency, Democracy, and Nature*, 106, 102–03.
7 Caldwell, "Globalizing Environmentalism," 259, 265; Clapp, "The Toxic Waste Trade," 510.
8 McNeill, *Something New Under the Sun*, 29; Dowie, *Losing Ground*, 119–21; Tam Dalyell, "Thistle Diary: Toxic Wastes and Other Ethical Issues," *New Scientist*, July 4, 1992; Clapp, "The Toxic Waste Trade," 506; Jundt, *Greening the Red, White, and Blue*, 6.
9 Harvey, *Justice, Nature and the Geography of Difference*, 366–67.
10 Basel Action Network, www.ban.org/ (accessed January 22, 2019).

11 Clapp, "The Toxic Waste Trade," 516.

12 Uekoetter, "The End of the Cold War," in McNeill et al., *Environmental Histories of the Cold War*, 343–51, 349; Piketty, *Capital in the Twenty-First Century*, 291, 335.

13 Kayvan Farzaneh, "The Biggest Oil Spills in History," *Foreign Policy*, April 30, 2010, https://foreignpolicy.com/2010/04/30/the-biggest-oil-spills-in-history/ (accessed December 28, 2018) .

14 Bohme, *Toxic Injustice*, 15, 33–35, 96, 74, 204.

15 "A Monumental Day," *New York Times,* Editorial, April 22, 1990; Dowie, *Losing Ground*, 86.

16 Frederic D. Krupp, "New Environmentalism Factors in Economic Needs," *Wall Street Journal*, November 20, 1986, 34; Gottlieb, *Forcing the Spring*, 191, 215–16; Dowie, *Losing Ground*, 116.

17 Brian Tokar, "The Myths of 'Green Capitalism,'" *New Politics* XIV, no. 4 (Winter 2014); Claude Engle and Hawley Truax, "The Carrot or the Stick?," *Environmental Action* 21, no. 6 (May 1990): 12.

18 Environmental Protection Agency, *20th Anniversary of the Acid Rain Program: 2015 Program Progress* (Washington, D.C.: Environmental Protection Agency, 2015); Evan J. Ringquist, "Trading Equity for Efficiency in Environmental Protection: Environmental Justice Effects from the SO_2 Allowance Trading Program," *Social Science Quarterly* 92, no. 2 (June 2011): 297–323, 297.

19 Gore, *Earth in the Balance*; Adams et al., *A Force for Nature*, 199.

20 Dowie, *Losing Ground*, 184, 181.

21 American Council on Science and Health, "The Delaney Clause: The Beginning of the End," Delaney Special Media Update, ACSH Press Release, September 1996.

22 Rosenbaum, *Environmental Politics and Policy*, 47; Mitman, *Breathing Space*, 196; Stephen Couch and J. Stephen Kroll-Smith, "Patterns of Victimization and the Chronic Technological Disaster," in *The Victimology Handbook: Research Findings, Treatment, and Public Policy*, edited by Emilio Viano, 159–76 (New York: Garland, 1990).

23 Rome, *The Genius of Earth Day*, 279.

24 Dauvergne, *Environmentalism of the Rich*, 4; Steinberg, "Can Capitalism Save the Planet?" 8; Rowell, *Green Backlash*, 110; Dauvergne, *Environmentalism of the Rich*, 90, 127, 134.

25 Klein, *This Changes Everything*, 198.

26 Lovins, *Soft Energy Paths*; Sale, *Green Revolution*, 23; Scheffer, *The Shaping of Environmentalism in America*, 70; Hawken, *The Ecology of Commerce*, 4, 2; Hawken et al., *Natural Capitalism*, 9; Hawken, *The Ecology of Commerce*, 30–31.

27 Rome, "The Ecology of Commerce," in Berghoff and Rome, *Green Capitalism?*, 5–7; Julia Horowitz, "3M will pay $850 million in Minnesota to end water pollution case," *CNN.com*, February 21, 2018, https://money.cnn.com/2018/02/20/news/companies/3m-minnesota-environmental-settlement/index.html (accessed October 26, 2018); Heather Clancy, "Interface Steps Up Carpet Recycling," *GreenBiz*, February 1, 2016, www.greenbiz.com/article/interface-steps-carpet-recycling (accessed December 28, 2018); Anderson, *Mid-Course Correction: Toward a Sustainable Enterprise*.

28 "Herman Daly," The Center for the Advancement of the Steady State Economy (CASSE), http://steadystate.org/herman-daly/ (accessed November 30, 2016).

29 Jordan Flaherty, "Fears of Cultural Extinction along the Gulf Coast," *Facing South*, Institute of Southern Studies, June 15, 2010, www.facingsouth.org/2010/06/fears-of-cultural-extinction-on-louisianas-gulf-coast.html (accessed November 30, 2017).

30 Richard Moore, Southwest Organizing Project, to Jay D. Hair, President, National Wildlife Federation, March 16, 1990; Gottlieb, *Forcing the Spring*, 336; Dana Alston, "The Summit: Transforming a Movement," 29; Di Chiro, "Nature as Community," in Cronon, *Uncommon Ground*, 298–320, 306.

31 Richard Moore, Southwest Organizing Project, to Jay D. Hair, President, National Wildlife Federation, March 16, 1990, emphasis added.

32 The full list of principles can be accessed at Principles of Environmental Justice, www. ejnet.org/ej/principles.html (accessed October 26, 2018); Alston, "The Summit: Transforming a Movement," 1, 28.

33 "Jemez Principles on Democratic Organizing," Environmental Justice Network, December 1996, www.ejnet.org/ej/jemez.pdf (accessed October 14, 2017).

34 Ellen Spears, "Freedom Buses Roll Along Cancer Alley," *Southern Changes* 15, no. 1 (Spring 1993): 1–11; Nader, "The Profits in Pollution," 21; Barbara Israel, Mark A. Chesler, Beth Baker, Elaine Wellin, Sham Langer, and Bill Forderer, "Environmental Activists Share Knowledge and Experiences: Description and Evaluation of STP Schools at the Highlander Research and Education Center" (working paper #20, University of Michigan Program in Conflict Management, Ann Arbor, 1991).

35 Mark Stoll, *Inherit the Holy Mountain*, 239.

36 Camacho, *Environmental Injustices, Political Struggles*, 42. Bunyan Bryant and Paul Mohai further documented the disparities in *Race and the Incidence of Environmental Hazards* (1992).

37 Task Force on the Environmental Problems of the Inner City, *Our Urban Environment and Our Most Endangered People: A Report to the Administrator of the Environmental Protection Agency* (Washington, D.C.: U.S. Govt. Print. Office, 1971); "Environmental Justice," Environmental Protection Agency, www.epa.gov/environmentaljustice (accessed November 6, 2017).

38 Data from the EPA Office of Civil Rights, "Title VI Complaints Listing" (Washington, D.C.: Environmental Protection Agency, 2007), 1–17; Margaret Kriz, "Environment: Coloring Justice Green," *National Journal* 33, no. 30 (July 28, 2001): 2419ff.

39 Exec. Order No. 12898, 59 FR 7629 §§1–101–02 (February 16, 1994); Cole and Foster, *From the Ground Up*, 74, 161–62.

40 Interview with Carl Anthony by Carl Wilmsen, "The Civil Rights Movement and Expanding the Boundaries of Environmental Justice in the San Francisco Bay Area, 1960–1999," 1999, Regional Oral History Office, Bancroft Library, University of California, Berkeley, 42. The Deep South Center moved with Wright to Dillard University, also in New Orleans, in 2005. "History," School for Environment and Sustainability, https://seas.umich.edu/about/history (accessed January 22, 2019).

41 Gottlieb, *Forcing the Spring*, 163–64; "Community Engagement Core," The NIEHS Center for Environmental Health in Northern Manhattan, www.mailman.columbia. edu/programs/niehs-center-environmental-health-northern-manhattan/community-outreach (accessed May 5, 2018).

42 Davianna Pōmaika'i McGregor and Noa Emmett Aluli, "Wao Kele O Puna and the Pele Defense Fund," in Goodyear-Kàōpua, Hussey, and Wright, *A Nation Rising*, 180–98; Simon Romero, "Madame Pele, Hawai'i's Goddess of Volcanoes, Awes Those Living in Lava's Path," *The New York Times*, May 21, 2018.

43 Markowitz and Rosner, *Deceit and Denial*, 265–86; Allen, *Uneasy Alchemy*, 84–87ff.

44 Cronon, "The Trouble with Wilderness," in Cronon, ed., *Uncommon Ground*, 69–90.

45 Dowie, *Losing Ground*, 32, citing Elaine Koerner, *Science Rules: Priority Setting Within Environmental Organizations* (Washington, D.C.: EPA Office of Public Liaison, n.d.).

46 Pasternak, *Yellow Dirt*, 165; Brugge and Goble, "The Radiation Exposure Compensation Act," in Brugge et al., *The Navajo People and Uranium Mining*, 138, 146.

47 Yazzie-Lewis and Zion, in Brugge et al., *The Navajo People and Uranium Mining*, 9; Interview with Rita and Mitchell Capitan, "Eastern Navajo Diné Against Uranium Mining," Brugge et al., *The Navajo People and Uranium Mining*, 172–74.

48 Kosek, *Understories*, 8, xiv, 14; David Correia, "The Sustained Yield Forest Management Act and the Roots of Environmental Conflict in Northern New Mexico," *Geoforum* 38 (2007): 1040–51, 1041; Brulle, *Agency, Democracy and Nature*, 202; Kosek, *Understories*, 324–25n145.

49 Kosek, *Understories*, 128, xii, 129, 324–25.

50 Adams et al., *A Force for Nature*, 218.

51 Merchant, *American Environmental History*, 172; Adams et al., *A Force for Nature*, 218–21, quoting T.H. Watkins on 221.

52 Shepard Krech III, "Beyond *The Ecological Indian*," in Harkin and Lewis, *Native Americans and the Environment*, 3–31, 21–23; Jacobs, *Panic at the Pump*, 294.

53 Dowie, *Losing Ground*, 49; Brulle, *Agency, Democracy, and Nature*, 240–41, 103.

54 Dowie, *Losing Ground*, 81.

55 Adisa Douglas, "Dana Alston: Activist and Funder," *Network News*, National Network of Grantmakers, 1999, 1, 4. Alston remained an influential leader in the environmental justice movement until her untimely death in 1999 at age forty-seven.

56 Dowie, *Losing Ground*, 46; Zelko, *Make It a Green Peace!*, 317; Dauvergne, *Environmentalism of the Rich*, 79.

57 Agenda 21: Programme of Action for Sustainable Development, § 2.5; "The President's News Conference in Rio de Janeiro," The American Presidency Project, June 13, 1992, www.presidency.ucsb.edu/documents/the-presidents-news-conference-rio-de-janeiro (accessed December 21, 2017).

58 Mark Dowie, "Conservation Refugees," *Orion Magazine*, November/December 2005, https://orionmagazine.org/article/conservation-refugees/ (accessed July 5, 2018).

59 Clapp, "The Toxic Waste Trade," 510; Martínez-Alier, *The Environmentalism of the Poor*, 196.

60 Alison Brysk, *From Tribal Village to Global Village: Indian Rights and International Relations in Latin America* (Stanford: Stanford University Press, 2000), 134–36; Roy Doron and Toyin Falola, *Ken Saro-Wiwa*, Ohio Short Histories of Africa (Athens: Ohio University Press, 2016).

61 Guha and Martínez-Alier, *Varieties of Environmentalism*; Martínez-Alier, *Environmentalism of the Poor*, 14, 10, 12–13.

62 Dowie, *Losing Ground*, 102, 93–98; Sellers, "How Republicans Came to Embrace Anti-Environmentalism."

63 Wellock, *Preserving the Nation*, 240; Rowell, *Green Backlash*, 17–18, 16; Brulle, *Agency, Democracy, and Nature*, 130, 127; Turner, "The Specter of Environmentalism," 125; League of Conservation Voters, "National Environmental Scorecard," 103rd Congress, February 1994.

64 Rowell, *Green Backlash*, 47, citing NET [National Empowerment Television, Paul Weyrich's satellite and cable TV network], One if by Land. . ., Washington, 1994.

65 Sellers, "How Republicans Came to Embrace Anti-Environmentalism."

66 League of Conservation Voters, "National Environmental Scorecard," 103rd Congress, February 1994, 4, 6.

67 Adams et al., *A Force for Nature*, 215.

68 Adams et al., *A Force for Nature*, 216.

69 Pursell, *Technology in Postwar America*, 226; Rowell, *Green Backlash*, 86; Malone and Khong, *Unilateralism and U.S. Foreign Policy*, 2.

70 Spears, *Baptized in PCBs*, 174–201.

71 Oreskes and Conway, *Merchants of Doubt*.

72 United Nations Educational, Scientific and Cultural Organization, The Rio Declaration on Environment and Development (1992), www.unesco.org/education/pdf/RIO_E.PDF.

73 Report on the Wingspread Conference on the Precautionary Principle, January 26, 1998, www.sehn.org/wing.html (accessed December 1, 2018); San Francisco Precautionary Principle Ordinance, July 2003, https://sfenvironment.org/policy/environment-code (accessed July 18, 2017); Gareth Harding, "EU Chemicals Law Causes Stink," United Press International, Brussels, September 30, 2003, www.upi.com/Analysis-EU-chemicals-law-causes-stink/98741064943790/ (accessed October 14, 2018). See also, Raffensperger and Tickner, *Protecting Public Health and the Environment*.

74 Peter Montague, "Slapped," *Rachel's Hazardous Waste News* #370, December 30, 1993.

75 Hall and Kerr, *1991–1992 Green Index*, 4.

76 PRI's "Living on Earth" Facebook Page, www.facebook.com/pages/category/ Environmental-Conservation-Organization/PRIs-Living-on-Earth-117348464962280/ (accessed October 1, 2018). Journals count obtained by searching in SCOUT, ejournals, on "environment" adding delimiter "peer reviewed journals" on February 3, 2018. Lowenthal, *George Perkins Marsh*, 415.

77 Steven Zaillian, "A Civil Action," Burbank, Calif.: Touchstone Pictures, 1998, based on the book *A Civil Action*, by Jonathan Harr (New York: Vintage, 1995); Steven Soderbergh. "Erin Brockovich," Hollywood: Universal Pictures, 2000; Paloma Esquivel, "15 Years after 'Erin Brockovich,' Town Still Fearful of Polluted Water," *Los Angeles Times*, April 12, 2015.

78 Dowie, *Losing Ground*, 184.

79 Ken Conca, "The WTO and the Undermining of Global Governance," *Review of International Political Economy* 7, no. 3 (Autumn 2000): 484–94, 484; Debi Barker and Jerry Mander, "The WTO and Invisible Government," *Peace Review* 12, no. 2 (2000): 251–55, 254, 252.

80 Dowie, *Losing Ground*, 188; Rafael Moure-Eraso, Meg Wilcox, Laura Punnett, Leslie MacDonald, and Charles Levenstein, "Back to the Future: Sweatshop Conditions on the Mexico-U.S. Border. II. Occupational Health Impact of Maquiladora Industrial Activity," *American Journal of Industrial Medicine* 31 (1997): 587–99.

81 St. Clair, "Seattle Diary," 91, 88.

82 Associated Press, "Protests Disrupt WTO Session, But Ministers Insist They Will Carry On," *The* [Centralia, Washington] *Chronicle*, December 1, 1999; St. Clair, "Seattle Diary," 82.

83 Susan S. Westin, "World Trade Organization, Seattle Ministerial: Outcomes and Lessons Learned," Testimony before the Subcommittee on Trade, Committee on Ways and Means, U.S. House of Representatives (Washington, D.C.; U.S. General Accounting Office, 2000); St. Clair, "Seattle Diary," 96.

6

INTERSECTIONAL ACTIVISM AND CLIMATE JUSTICE (2001–PRESENT)

Climate change, the defining environmental concern of the early twenty-first century, has re-anchored a sprawling movement. As new climate-focused advocacy groups have sprung up and existing environmental organizations shifted course to address climate realities, activism became at once more global and more decentralized. The annual Conferences of the Parties (COPs) that have been held since the establishment of the UNFCCC in 1992 have intensified international collaboration, not only among participating countries, but also among environmental organizations attending concurrent events. Actions at the local level have multiplied as place-based groups increasingly pressured county commissions, city councils, and state governments to be proactive on the issue of climate.

Climate is entangled with virtually every other environmental concern—energy use, access to clean water, food security, protection of land and oceans, biodiversity, desertification. Climate activists increasingly frame their work as intersectional, strengthening alliances with related causes. Sectors of the labor movement and proponents of immigrant justice, peace, gender equity, and racial justice often work in parallel with environmentalists, if not together. The result is a field of movements of unprecedented breadth and diversity.

According to one Gallup poll, the number of Americans who identified as environmentalists declined sharply in the twenty-five years between 1991 and 2016, from 78 percent to 42 percent. At the same time, concern about global warming has never been higher. Moreover, most Americans polled say they want government action on climate change.[1] Nevertheless, partisan politics and climate denialism continue to hamper government intervention to reduce harmful emissions. Oil and gas industrialists and their think tanks, lobbyists, and sympathizers in Congress deny—publicly at least—that climate warming is caused by human activities, especially the burning of fossil fuels.

During the Obama years, the U.S. participated in a global climate agreement, acted to block the Dakota Access and Keystone oil pipelines, and designed a Clean Power Plan to reduce reliance on coal. The Obama administration continued to restrict drilling in the Arctic National Wildlife Refuge, and EPA paid greater attention to environmental injustice. However, the rising electoral clout of right-wing populism ushered in a third wave of anti-environmentalism and the Trump administration gutted each of these measures soon after taking office.

"A Common Concern of Mankind"

Climate concerns are not new in U.S. policy. Extreme partisanship on the issue is a recent development. As early as 1965, President Lyndon Johnson sent a special message to Congress: "This generation has altered the composition of the atmosphere on a global scale through radioactive materials and a steady increase in carbon dioxide from the burning of fossil fuels." Later that year, the President's Science Advisory Committee, acting on Cold War research and a Conservation Foundation report, issued warnings on the "Possible Effects of Increased Atmospheric Carbon Dioxide on Climate." The report forewarned of the "melting of the Antarctic ice cap," the "rise of sea level," "the warming of sea water," and "increased acidity of fresh water."[2]

The first congressional action on climate warming came during the Carter administration, with the passage in 1978 of the National Climate Program Act, which sought "to improve the understanding of climate processes, natural and man induced, and the social, economic, and political implications of climate change." At the suggestion of Rafe Pomerance of Friends of the Earth and environmental scientist Gordon MacDonald, Carter's chair of the Council on Environmental Quality Gus Speth pressed the administration to address "global climate disruption." Sierra Club program director Patricia Scharlin placed "Climate" in the center of her Venn diagram of the organization's proposed five-year plan in 1976. (However, members of the chapter-based organization did not choose to focus on climate at the time, Sierra Club director Michael McCloskey later surmised, because the issue was "impossibly large" and not yet "ripe.") By 1979, a core group of scientists were beginning to question "the future habitability of the planet," explained *New York Times* writer Nathaniel Rich in 2018. In 1980, the *Global 2000 Report* prepared for President Carter by the Council on Environmental Quality and the Department of State indicated a need to limit greenhouse gas emissions (GHGs) to curb the global rise in temperature.[3]

Initially, climate policy was neither polarizing nor politicized. Climate research and the scientists who conducted it were recognized as playing a crucial role in national decision-making. In 1987, during Reagan's tenure, Congress passed the Global Climate Protection Act, directing the EPA to develop a "coordinated national policy on global climate change" and the Department of State to coordinate related "multilateral diplomacy." In 1988, a NASA scientist, Goddard

Institute for Space Studies director James Hansen, testified to Congress that a warming trend driven by carbon emissions would be widely evident by the year 2000 but was already underway. "The earth is warming by an amount which is too large to be a chance fluctuation," said Hansen, "the greenhouse effect has been detected, and it is changing our climate now."[4]

The probability that human-caused climate change threatens the planet has appeared on the agenda of every U.N. Conference on the Human Environment since Stockholm in 1972. In 1988, the U.N. labeled climate "a common concern of mankind." According to Nathaniel Rich, an international agreement on reducing carbon emissions, modeled on the successful Montreal Protocol, appeared possible in 1989, but negotiators for the George H.W. Bush administration blocked the setting of binding targets. The Climate Change Convention agreed to at the Rio conference in 1992, a non-binding plan to reduce GHGs, was approved by 154 countries, including the U.S. By 1995, the Intergovernmental Panel on Climate Change (IPCC), established in 1988 by the UNEP and the World Meteorological Organization to review and conduct scientific research on climate, reported that the evidence already showed a "discernible human influence on global climate."[5]

Climate activism has been global from its inception. The Climate Action Network (CAN), an international coalition of NGOs that do not represent industry, formed in 1989. Committed to sustainable development and climate change action, CAN works both inside and outside of international climate conferences. At the Kyoto negotiations in 1997, CAN activists were among the nearly four thousand nongovernmental observers who outnumbered governmental representatives nearly two to one. Facilitated by new technologies—live internet feeds, sessions simulcast on TV, and cell phones—activists gained unprecedented access to the proceedings; observer advocates and scientists were able to communicate instantaneously with official delegations on the conference floor.[6]

The Kyoto agreement was modest: it acknowledged anthropogenic climate change, set small but binding cuts on GHGs for developed nations, and permitted market trading of emissions allowances. Nevertheless, climate mitigation faced increasingly partisan opposition. When George W. Bush came into office in 2001, narrowly edging past pro-environment Democrat Al Gore, Bush cut support for promoting energy-efficiency programs. Bush, who had strong ties to the oil and gas industry, announced that the U.S. would not abide by Kyoto limits soon after taking office.[7] The protocol went into effect without U.S. support on February 16, 2005.

With little prospect of dislodging federal inertia, activists have sought to persuade cities and states to reduce greenhouse gases. In 2001, six New England states and four Canadian provinces established a bioregional compact to cap emissions. In 2005, the U.S. Conference of Mayors and members of the National Governors Association decided to adhere to the Kyoto recommendations, creating what one study termed "a de facto transnational alliance through translocal action."[8]

Working both through negotiation and direct action, environmental groups also aimed to directly influence corporate and consumer behavior through boycotts, divestment efforts, and selective buying campaigns.

9/11: Global Geopolitics Alter the Terrain of Protest

After the September 11, 2001 bombing of the World Trade Center in New York City by Al Qaeda militants, publicly questioning U.S. policy became more difficult. Local policing became far more militarized, constraining domestic protest. The U.S. Patriot Act of 2001 redefined domestic terrorism, such that even nonviolent protestors could be subject to domestic terrorism charges. Calls for energy independence in the wake of the attack prompted renewed efforts to drill in ANWR, but once again, in 2002, the proposal was defeated, by Senate vote of fifty-four to forty-six.[9]

The 9/11 assault also had immediate environmental consequences for the more than 37,000 first responders, cleanup crews, and others exposed, some severely, to toxic dust from the explosions. For a decade, a determined group would fight for recognition of and compensation for injuries from dust exposure, including respiratory disease and cancer. Ten years after the bombings, Congress finally acknowledged the claims and allocated $4.2 billion to establish the World Trade Center Health Program to provide testing, treatment, and compensation to 9/11 first responders. Congress extended the program in 2015 for another seventy-five years.[10]

Hurricane Katrina Rips Away the Veil

Americans witnessed what many understood as evidence of changing climate patterns when hurricane Katrina slammed into the Gulf Coast on August 29, 2005. The storm itself forced mass evacuations and left tens of thousands homeless. The following day, levees weakened by generations of neglect failed to hold. In addition to the loss of life—more than 1,800 people died—Katrina triggered an estimated $110 billion in damage, uprooting 1.2 million people from cities and towns along the Gulf Coast. Most areas of New Orleans flooded; the Lower Ninth Ward, 98 percent African American, was devastated.[11]

Slow violence borne of manmade disaster gave way to spectacular violence in the face of natural disaster. "Katrina tore the veil away to reveal the persistence of poverty and race-based disadvantage in America," wrote former *Times-Picayune* editor Jed Horne, though the realities that were "startling from a distance came as no great surprise on the ground." The mishandling of the relief efforts revealed racial and class inequalities exacerbated by the disaster and raised basic concerns about environmental human rights.[12]

The handling of recovery and rebuilding by government at all levels was disastrous. It was hard for residents not to view the neglect as purposeful. FEMA

(Federal Emergency Management Agency) trailers were rendered uninhabitable by interior cabinets and furnishings containing formaldehyde, a toxic substance that made residents sick. Amid massive displacement, government was slow to act and even then, HUD grants for replacement housing were capped at an inadequate $150,000, with no benefits for renters. New Orleans' African American communities were hardest hit when the levees broke, but other marginalized groups also suffered. Vietnamese Americans in the Versailles neighborhood organized Citizens for a Strong New Orleans East to prevent the city from targeting their community for a dump of post-hurricane waste.[13]

Much of the effective response to Katrina came from voluntary efforts by individuals, churches, and other nonprofits, including environmental organizations. The Louisiana Environmental Action Network, a longstanding environmental justice group, collected and distributed food, water, medical, and baby supplies and housed displaced residents in their Baton Rouge office for several months. The New Orleans Survivor Council and Residents of Public Housing attempted to get public housing restored. The New Orleans-based advocacy group Common Ground set up a relief station in the Ninth Ward. The Sierra Club launched a Gulf Coast Restoration project, raising $250,000 to help local chapters in Louisiana, Mississippi, and Alabama restore coastal ecosystems. An NRDC study of toxic contamination resulting from the floods found significantly elevated levels of arsenic in soils at six elementary schools persisting a year and a half after the storm.[14]

Advocates for Environmental Human Rights, a public interest law firm formed in 2003 by Monique Harden and Nathalie Walker co-authored a report in 2007 to the U.N. Committee for the Elimination of Racial Discrimination, charging the U.S. government, including the departments of Justice and of Health and Human Services, with "failure to protect the rights of displaced people." The discriminatory environmental conditions and treatment, they argued, violated fundamental human rights.[15]

While few single disasters can be definitively attributed to climate alteration, the increase in the *frequency* of storms, droughts, and floods resulting from climate shifts was becoming much harder to dismiss. Warmer seas yielded stronger and more frequent hurricanes. A 2015 analysis by James Hansen, the former NASA scientist who had sounded the alarm in 1988, and colleagues notes that a 2°C increase in average temperature above preindustrial levels is "highly dangerous," and would prompt additional ice shelf melt, causing oceans to rise even more than previous IPCC predictions.[16]

Climate Action and Climate Justice

A reconvening of environmental justice activists in 2002 on the ten-year anniversary of the People of Color Summit resulted in "Ten Principles for Just Climate Change Policies in the U.S." Among them were the reduction of greenhouse gases and demands for major emitters like the U.S. to act.[17] The climate justice principles adopted at the 2007 U.N. conference in Bali point out that marginalized populations who are the least responsible for greenhouse gas emissions are also the most vulnerable to climate warming.

Bali Principles of Climate Justice (excerpt) (2007)

- A demand for a moratorium on all new fossil fuel exploration and exploitation, nuclear power plant construction, and large hydroelectric dam construction;
- Opposition to the role of corporations both in shaping unsustainable practices, and in unfairly influencing policy;
- The subordination of 'market-based or technological solutions to climate change' to principles of democracy, sustainability, and social justice;
- The principles of 'common but differentiated responsibilities' [between developed and developing nations] and democratic accountability that governments must hold to in responding to the climate crisis;
- The principle of the 'ecological debt' owed by the Global North to the rest of the world for its disproportionate share of historical CO_2 emissions;
- The right of workers in fossil-fuel industries to a safe, healthy work environment, and the need for a 'just transition' to a clean energy economy;
- The rights of women, youth, the poor, and rural peoples to have an equal voice in decision-making processes, without facing discrimination; and
- The right of Indigenous peoples and affected communities 'to represent and speak for themselves,' to control all their traditional lands, to protect themselves from any threat to their territories or their 'cultural way of life,' and to exercise 'free, prior, and informed consent' over project decision-making.

A summary of the twenty-seven Bali Principles, which were based on the Principles of Environmental Justice from the 1991 People of Color Summit, NAACP et al., *Coal Blooded*, 5.

Concurrent with the Bali U.N. conference, as climate justice activists grew increasingly impatient with the lack of government action, new climate-oriented organizations formed. Climate Justice Now! (CJN!) formed in 2007, as did a counterpart in Europe, Climate Justice Action. New groups included: the Climate Reality Project, led by former vice-president Al Gore; the Citizens' Climate Lobby (CCL); Rising Tide, with fifty chapters in the U.S. and Mexico in 2018; and, ecoAmerica. Existing groups such as the Indigenous Environmental Network (founded 1990) refocused on climate. The Rainforest Action Network (RAN), founded in 1985, redefined its mission, now demanding corporate accountability at the intersection of forest protection, climate change, and human rights. As the baby boomer leadership of many environmental organizations approached retirement, some organizations set about training the new generation of activists.

The youth-focused climate justice organization, Power Shift, held its first biennial conference in November 2007 in Washington, D.C. Environmentalists targeted coal-fired electricity-generating plants as the most significant emitters of GHGs and sought to shift public subsidies from fossil fuels to renewables. In 2010, the Sierra Club initiated an international "Beyond Coal" campaign, training activists not only in the U.S. but also in Australia, India, and South Africa.[18]

Scholar and author Bill McKibben, who helped to put climate change on the public's radar in 1989 with his book *The End of Nature*, joined with other university-based activists to found 350.org in 2008. The group's name refers to the goal of reducing carbon dioxide (CO_2) in the atmosphere from the already dangerously high 400 parts per million (ppms) reached in 2013 to 350 ppms. The group mounted the International Day of Climate Action in 2009. A multiorganization "Keep It in the Ground" campaign, supported by the British newspaper, *The Guardian*, Greenpeace, and others, sought to move energy policy away from dependence on fossil fuels. Leaders of 350.org developed a road show on climate change, hosting town hall meetings and rallies featuring locally-based activists across the U.S. and around the globe. By 2017, the group had affiliates in 188 countries.[19]

Again, local actions were significant. The Little Village Environmental Justice Organization (LVEJO) successfully shut down two Edison International coal-fired power plants near their neighborhood on Chicago's southwest side in 2012. Led by Kimberly Wasserman, the campaign's multi-year effort included door-to-door health surveys that found asthma to be prevalent, letters to city hall, and body bag protests at the mayor's office. LVEJO collaborated with national social justice organizations—the Indigenous Environmental Network and the NAACP—to systematically examine the link between coal-fired power plants, climate, and environmental injustice. The result, *Coal Blooded: Putting Profits Before People*, noted that out of 378 U.S. coal-fired power plants studied, seventy-five failed basic environmental safety standards. Four million people lived within three miles of a failing plant. Of these, 53 percent were people of color. The average per capita income of people living near a failing plant was $17,500, which was 25 percent below the state average in Illinois.[20]

Stakeholders Sue EPA to Address Climate Change

In 2007, the U.S. Supreme Court ruled the Clean Air Act required the EPA to regulate greenhouse gas emissions that contribute to climate change. Obama-era EPA administrator Lisa P. Jackson called the Supreme Court's decision "perhaps the most significant decision ever reached in environmental law."[21] The sequence of events leading to this landmark decision illustrates the importance of litigation in advancing environmental protection, the increasing politicization of science, and the crucial role states and localities play in pressing for climate action.

During the final years of the Clinton administration, having grown impatient with the EPA's failure to address climate change, twenty environmental, technology, and solar energy groups filed a petition with the EPA to require the agency to regulate greenhouse gases. In September 2003, with the George W. Bush administration in office, the EPA responded. Though an overwhelming majority of climate scientists agreed that the climate was warming, that human activity was the cause, and that immediate action would be necessary to reverse the consequences, EPA officials refused to act. The EPA denied having statutory authority to regulate greenhouse gas emissions, including CO_2, claiming GHGs were not air pollutants and that a causal link to climate change "cannot be unequivocally established." (The Bush administration also stepped up pressure on climate scientists, demanding, for example, in 2004, that James Hansen submit to politically-appointed public affairs officers prior to publication all lectures, academic papers, website postings, and requests for interviews.)[22]

A dozen states, led by Massachusetts, and several cities sought review of the agency's decision in federal court. Joining the lawsuit were the Center for Biological Diversity, the Center for Food Safety, the Conservation Law Foundation, Environmental Advocates, Environmental Defense, Friends of the Earth, Greenpeace, the International Center for Technology Assessment, the National Environmental Trust, the NRDC, the Sierra Club, the Union of Concerned Scientists, and the U.S. Public Interest Research Group. Intervening on the side of the EPA were the governments of ten oil and gas industry states, several industry trade associations, the Alliance of Automobile Manufacturers, the National Automobile Dealers Association, the Engine Manufacturers Association, the Truck Manufacturers Association, the CO_2 Litigation Group, and the Utility Air Regulatory Group.[23]

In *Massachusetts et al. v. EPA*, decided in 2007, the Supreme Court held that "greenhouse gases fit well within the [Clean Air] Act's capacious definition of 'air pollutant'" and that EPA has the statutory authority to regulate them. In a five to four decision, crafted by Justice John Paul Stevens, a conservative Republican and independent thinker, the Court explicitly noted that, "The harms associated with climate change are serious and well-recognized." Meanwhile, the climate crisis was growing ever more dire. Carbon emissions grew at a much faster annual rate between 2000 and 2008 (3.5 percent) than in the previous decade (0.9 percent).[24]

In August 2015, after holding public hearings around the country, the EPA put forward a Clean Power Plan designed to reduce carbon emissions from coal. Six months later, in a surprise decision, the Supreme Court ruled five to four along ideological lines to freeze implementation of the plan while lower courts considered a challenge mounted by twenty-seven states and various business groups. Nevertheless, climate and health activists succeeded in shuttering coal-powered polluters; they were aided by market pressures—abundant low-cost natural gas and a growing job sector in renewables. More than 250 coal-fired power plants were shut down or slated for closure between 2012 and 2017.[25]

Climate Justice and the Environmentalism of the Poor

Tensions between the old conservationism and the new social justice environmentalism have replicated themselves in the climate movement, with supporters of reform-oriented technocratic solutions set against those who seek a fundamental shift away from fossil fuels to renewable energy. Technocratic solutions include sequestration, which takes various forms, including pumping carbon wastes into underground wells. Carbon offsets allow users, whether individuals or corporations, to purchase "carbon sinks" that absorb CO_2, a patch of forest perhaps, to "offset" their carbon emissions. Critics of carbon trading suggest that commodifying carbon is at best a temporary solution that only prolongs fossil fuel dependence, when the climate problem demands more sweeping, structural change. In addition, carbon sinks are often located in territories occupied by indigenous peoples, who have been subjected to various abuses as a result of carbon trading, noted Tom Goldtooth, director of the Indigenous Environmental Network, including "land grabs, killings, violent evictions and forced displacement, violations of human rights, threats to cultural survival, militarization, and servitude." Other technocratic proposals include geoengineering—seeding the atmosphere with sunlight-reflecting particles or treating the ocean with iron dust to trap more carbon, for example. Critics consider such options short-sighted and likely to unwittingly introduce new environmental hazards.[26]

Direct action tactics of the climate justice movement have included blocking pipeline construction and bidding on oil and gas leases with no intention to pay for them. At a time when the administration resists change, the dispersed structure of the climate justice movement is an asset. Activists are focusing on local actors: public service commissions, coal-fired and nuclear power plants, and the planning and zoning commissions that authorize sprawl and other "climate-threatening projects."[27]

Opposing free-market environmentalism and challenging "the unsustainability of the world politics of growth," the climate justice movement has become a sprawling network, with no one center. Constituents include U.S. environmental justice organizations, the Jubilee movement seeking reductions in Third World nations' crushing debts so that they may direct resources to climate mitigation, and the intersectional movement that links labor, environment, and human rights activists, partly an outgrowth of the 1999 WTO protests in Seattle.[28]

At times, "ecological violence" visited upon the poor results directly from over-consumption among the wealthy. Authors Lisa Sun-Hee Park and David Pellow observe an increasing trend among the well-to-do of establishing enclaves protected from the effects of climate change. Exercising "environmental privilege," the wealthy buy their way out of otherwise inescapable environmental crises that affect the poor.[29]

Global Climate Action

The 15th UNFCCC Conference of the Parties convened in Copenhagen in 2009 with high expectations. The external conference, Klimaforum09, evidenced a robust movement, convening an estimated fifty thousand people from NGOs and other groups, who exchanged strategies and formed alliances. But the official meeting yielded little.

After the disappointment at Copenhagen, in April 2010, Bolivian president Evo Morales convened a People's Conference on Climate Change and the Rights of Mother Earth in Cochabamba, Bolivia. Cochabamba articulated the environmentalism of the poor and rallied climate justice activists. Roughly thirty thousand people attended; one-third came from outside Bolivia, mostly from Latin American countries. Represented were "[g]overnment delegations from countries all over the world, summit-hopping autonomists, UN-bureaucrats, Andean coca farmers." Protecting Pachamama, or Mother Earth, was the focus, especially of Latin American groups, who formed the Pachamama Alliance in the wake of the conference. By 2014, the People's Climate March would bring several hundred thousand marchers to Manhattan and a total of more than 2,500 events in 162 countries.[30]

In December 2015, U.N. climate talks in Paris (COP-21) finally negotiated a solution to the impasse between developed and developing nations that had heretofore hampered an international climate accord. The accord required each participating nation to make a *voluntary* but *binding* commitment to limit emissions. Wealthy nations promised one billion dollars in funding to mitigate climate change, to be paid annually through 2020, when contributions might be increased. Climate specialists had hoped for a commitment to holding the rise in global average temperature to well below the two degrees Celsius above pre-industrial levels deemed necessary to avoid wholesale disaster. But pledges to reduce emissions fell short of that goal. Nevertheless, the agreement ignited hopes for immediate and concerted action to reduce greenhouse gases. In an indication of the collective sense of urgency, fifty-five countries signed on within a year, making the agreement effective on November 4, 2016.[31]

Responses to Global Climate Warming

- 1965 – President Johnson's Science Advisory Committee Report, *Restoring the Quality of Our Environment* is released
- 1972 – U.N. Conference on Environment and Development at Stockholm launches the U.N. Environment Programme
- 1978 – U.S. National Climate Program Act seeks to improve understanding of climate climate

- 1987 – U.S. Global Climate Protection Act mandates a coordinated national policy
- 1988 – The U.N. Environment Programme (UNEP) and the World Meteorological Society establish the Intergovernmental Panel on Climate Change (IPCC)
- 1988 – NASA scientist James Hansen testifies to Congress about the warming trend
- 1988 – Oil and gas industry forms the Global Climate Coalition (GCC)
- 1989 – Climate Action Network (CAN) forms
- 1992 – Rio "Earth Summit" adopts the UNFCCC
- 1994 – UNFCCC enters into force
- 1997 – Kyoto Protocol negotiated, U.S. Senate pre-emptively rejects Kyoto Protocol
- 2001 – George W. Bush formally withdraws U.S. from Kyoto Protocol
- 2003 – U.S. states, cities, and environmental groups sue EPA to regulate GHGs
- 2005 – U.N. labels climate change a human rights issue
- 2007 – Bali Conference (COP-13) yields Principles of Climate Justice
- 2007 – Climate Justice Now! forms
- 2007 – U.S. Supreme Court rules in *Massachusetts v. EPA*, 549 U.S. 497 (2007) that the EPA has authority to regulate GHGs
- 2009 – Fifty thousand attend Copenhagen Conference of the Parties (COP-15) and Klimaforum09
- 2010 – People's Conference on Climate Change and the Rights of Mother Earth, Cochabamba, Bolivia
- 2014 – The People's Climate March, September 14
- 2015 – EPA issues final rule on its Clean Power Plan
- 2015 – Pope Francis issues *Laudato Sí, Papal Encyclical on Climate Change*
- 2015 – The Paris Conference (COP-21) negotiates an international commitment to mitigate climate change
- 2016 – The Paris Agreement enters into force, November 4
- 2017 – U.S. President Donald J. Trump announces plan to withdraw U.S. from the Paris Agreement and rejects the Clean Power Plan
- 2017 – More than 1,400 U.S. cities, states, and NGOs pledge to honor the Paris Agreement

Since the nineteenth century, scientists and scholars have warned repeatedly of the need for "amelioration of climate." Global climate activism has continued to broaden to meet this twenty-first century challenge to keep global temperature rise below two degrees Celsius to prevent disaster.

Climate Denialism Forestalls Action

Efforts to address climate change have met fierce opposition from a top-down campaign bankrolled by many of the same oil and gas industrialists and think tanks behind the Sagebrush and "wise use" movements. These counter-strategies have institutionalized delay, blocking federal efforts to reduce carbon emissions. A vast, well-funded public relations machine seeks to elect anti-climate protection candidates, undermine science, and poison popular opinion through disinformation. According to *E&E News*, coal industry officials and their public relations teams have mounted particularly aggressive public relations campaigns attempting, ironically, to discredit the environmental movement as a bastion of white privilege.[32]

The Union of Concerned Scientists and investigative reporting by the *Los Angeles Times* and the Energy and Environment Reporting Project at Columbia University reported in 2015 that "the fossil fuel industry was well aware of the scientific understanding of climate change even as it continued to sow doubt about the science and block climate action." Oil and gas giant Exxon's internal research dating to the late 1980s acknowledged that the global warming trend was anthropogenic and due primarily to CO_2 emissions from fossil fuels. Between 1998 and 2005, however, according to the *Los Angeles Times*, Exxon was spending more than $16 million on a campaign involving at least forty-three other organizations to promote doubt about climate science and shift attention to the negative economic aspects of restricting CO_2 emissions. The exercise was a classic case of "manufacturing doubt," sowing skepticism to forestall regulation.[33]

The Global Climate Coalition, the industry group that helped derail U.S. support of the Kyoto agreement in the 1990s, folded in 2002, as many of its funders, including Exxon, recognized that outright denial was becoming less tenable. Industry propaganda began claiming instead that global warming, while real, was not that big a problem, and could even yield some benefits. The free-market think tank, the Competitive Enterprise Institute, launched a campaign in 2006 with the slogan: "Carbon dioxide: They call it pollution, we call it life."[34]

After the demise of the GCC, visible funding for climate denial operations from Koch Affiliated Industries and ExxonMobil began declining precipitously. Now the largest portion of funding—$78.8 million or 14 percent of the total between 2003 and 2010—comes from untraceable sources via two donor-advised funds, Donors Trust and Donors Capital Fund. The industry groups the GCC once represented—the pro-industry think tanks, including the Competitive Enterprise Institute, the Heartland Institute, the CATO Institute, and the Marshall Institute—along with the U.S. Chamber of Commerce and the American Petroleum Institute continue to oppose regulating GHGs.[35]

Recent political science research suggests that countering the politics of white racial resentment is crucial to advancing efforts to address climate change. DePauw University political scientist Salil Benegal analyzed public opinion data and found that while many factors, including ideology, education level, economic recession, personal experiences with weather, and media legitimation of climate denial views affect attitudes about climate, "narratives of white grievance and resentment [are] being frequently employed in the context of climate change and energy policy." Partisan slogans such as "Obama is Costing You $1,300 Per Vehicle," circulated in May 2009, cause "a racial spillover effect," argues Benegal. Polling data show that "higher levels of racial prejudice and resentment are highly correlated with lower levels of agreement that climate change is occurring, and that climate change is anthropogenic."[36]

Climate change denialists have also attacked individual climate scientists by various means, from censoring their reports to outright harassment. Censorship of climate change reports prepared by NASA climate scientists, including James Hansen, led to hearings in 2007 by the U.S. House Committee on Oversight and Government Reform, on "Allegations of Political Interference with the Work of Government Climate Change Scientists." After geographer Richard Heede in 2013 developed a method of "carbon accounting," which directly challenged the claim that "everyone's to blame" for climate change by documenting that just ninety companies are responsible for 63 percent of greenhouse gases emitted worldwide, Tennessee Republican congressman Lamar Smith, a climate denialist, subpoenaed Heede to face questioning before a U.S. House committee that bordered on harassment. Photographers from the right-wing opposition research group, America Rising Squared, routinely tail 350.org co-founder Bill McKibben, hoping for embarrassing photographs that might discredit him with supporters.[37]

Worldwide, violence against environmental advocates continued—including those outspoken on climate warming. The human rights group Global Witness traced 200 deaths in 2016 alone of land rights and environmental activists to paramilitary, government police, and private security personnel, among others.[38]

Climate Action Efforts Redouble

In face of opposition, climate activism has continued to broaden. The American Public Health Association, for example, declared 2017 the year of Climate Change and Health. "Climate change is our greatest public health challenge," APHA Executive Director Georges C. Benjamin wrote to members early that year. Evidence mounts that communities of color in the U.S. are particularly vulnerable to climate change. Scientist Andrew Geller of EPA's Sustainable and Healthy Communities Research Program reported that, "of the U.S. residents within .25 miles of Superfund sites with a very high Coastal Vulnerability index, 40% are people of color." Kim Knowlton, of the Natural Resources Defense Council and the Mailman School of Public Health at Columbia University, noted that workers in construction and landscaping, the majority of whom are Hispanic, already face three times higher risk of occupational mortality from heat-related causes than workers in other jobs.[39]

Evidence that climate change was already contributing to global instability and mass dislocation underscored the urgent need for action. In August 2016, the Alaskan island village of Shishmaref voted to relocate to the mainland, at least five miles inland. Due to rising sea levels, frequent storms, and melting ice floes, the Iñupiat villagers' homes were falling into the sea.[40] But funding to assist with climate migration is lacking, even as these American climate refugees expose climate warming to be a pressing problem not a future concern.

Climate activists are pursuing an array of creative strategies to prompt government action. Our Children's Trust, a group of twenty-one youth plaintiffs, Earth Guardians, and James Hansen, on behalf of Future Generations, sued the Obama administration EPA in 2015 for inaction that harmed their civil rights to life, liberty, and the pursuit of happiness. "I have no doubt that the right to a climate system capable of sustaining human life is fundamental to a free and ordered society," wrote U.S. District Court Judge Ann Aiken in the case, *Juliana v. U.S.*, refusing to dismiss the lawsuit. In late October 2018, supported by 350. org and the Citizens' Climate Lobby, Our Children's Trust mounted sixty-two rallies at sites in the U.S., including the Supreme Court and every state. That November, the Supreme Court refused to halt the case, allowing the youths' challenge to continue.[41]

Other tactics aimed directly at the fossil fuels industry. In 2012, activists launched an international campaign for divestment of stocks in fossil fuel companies. Organizations such as the Ceres' Investor Network for Climate Risk and the Interfaith Center on Shareholder Responsibility reported in early 2016 a record number of stockholder resolutions on mitigating climate change. By that time, campus-based fossil fuel divestment campaigns had persuaded universities and other institutions to divest $50 billion in fossil-fuel assets.[42]

When the dependence on fossil fuels destroyed sensitive ecologies and threatened human health, place-based movements countered:

- The Gulf Restoration Network, founded in the mid-1990s, and the Gulf Restoration Watch, swung into gear to monitor cleanup and promote resilience planning for human well-being and habitat recovery after a British Petroleum (BP) oil rig exploded in the Gulf of Mexico in April 2010, killing eleven oil workers, and spewing nearly five million barrels of crude into the Gulf. The disaster exposed once again the costs of continued fossil fuel dependence and the risky infrastructure that delivers oil to American consumers. A bipartisan presidential commission concluded in 2011 that the companies involved—BP, Halliburton, and Transocean—made preventable mistakes.[43]
- Protestors picketed the headquarters of Texas-based Plains All American Pipeline, after a rupture in 2015 dumped 140,000 gallons of crude in the biologically rich Santa Barbara Channel, forty-six years after the spill in the same locale that helped inspire the National Environmental Policy Act.

A California grand jury indicted Plains All-American on forty-six criminal charges, including four felonies. However, capped at roughly $3 million, the maximum penalties were easily absorbed by a company that reported earning $43 billion in revenue and $878 million in profits in 2014. Activists won passage of three bills tightening the state's pipeline regulations in 2015.[44]

- A transborder coalition of farmers, Native groups, environmental organizations, and municipalities opposing the Keystone XL pipeline extension cited fossil fuel extraction as both a direct contributor to climate change and a pollution threat to land and aquifers. Moreover, extending the pipeline network committed to another generation of fossil fuel dependence. Campaigners in Canada, many of whom were First Nations activists, opposed the oil shale extraction industry's encroachment on treaty lands in the Alberta Tar Sands region. Canceled by the Obama administration, the XL pipeline reopened early in the Trump administration. (A major leak spilled more than 210,000 gallons in November 2017.)[45]

Because nuclear power generation does not produce significant GHGs, even some climate activists consider nuclear power a viable energy option. The environmental consequences of nuclear power were questioned, however, when on March 11, 2011, an earthquake measuring 9.0 on the Richter scale, centered in the Pacific Ocean east of Japan, struck that country's northeast coast. The earthquake propelled a tsunami that engulfed the coastal city of Fukushima and set off meltdowns at the Fukushima Daiichi nuclear power plant. More than fifteen thousand people died from the tsunami; 573 died evacuating from the reactor disaster. In the U.S. by 2018, building of new reactors had halted, with the exception of a single site in eastern Georgia, near the majority African American community of Shell Bluff, where residents continue attempts to halt plant expansion on environmental safety grounds.[46]

Energy industrialists and their supporters often invoke national security and the need for "energy independence" to justify exploitation of oil and gas. Environmentalists counter that fossil fuel dependence and extreme extraction make impacted communities—and the nation—*less* safe. Protests emerged in the early 2000s in New York, Pennsylvania, Texas, and other locales, soon after hydraulic fracturing, or "fracking," entered widespread use. The technique involves pumping a toxic mixture of water, sand, and chemicals into the ground with sufficient pressure to crush shale, loosening pockets of natural gas. The resulting slurry contaminates wells and aquifers. Industry supporters in Congress pushed through an amendment limiting the EPA's authority to regulate hydraulic fracturing in the Energy Policy Act signed by President Bush in 2005.[47]

With little prospect of federal action, anti-fracking activists applied pressure at the state and local level. New York Governor Andrew Cuomo banned fracking in that state in 2014, citing health concerns and increased risk of earthquakes.

In Texas, home to nearly a quarter of the nation's projected oil reserves, oil and gas interests have a powerful hold over state government. In November 2014, urged by the Denton Drilling Awareness Group, people in the city of Denton voted by a wide margin (59 to 41 percent) to ban fracking within the town's borders. The Texas legislature promptly overruled Denton voters, raising what *NBC News* called a "War on Local Democracy."[48]

Indigenous people continued to resist environmental threats to Native rights and tribal sovereignty. Since 1990, the Indigenous Environmental Network (IEN) has sought to "educate and empower Indigenous Peoples to address and develop strategies for the protection of our environment, our health, and all life forms—the Circle of Life." The IEN affirms traditional knowledge and Native cultural and spiritual beliefs. The network also works on policies from the tribal to the international level and to "recognize, support, and promote environmentally sound lifestyles, economic livelihoods, and to build healthy sustaining Indigenous communities." For example, the Women's Water Commission of the Anishinabek Nation, influenced by writer/activists Winona Laduke, Deborah McGregor, and Debra White Plume, hiked the perimeter of the Great Lakes beginning in the early 2000s to raise awareness of the need for water quality improvements in the region.[49]

PHOTO 6.1   The Standing Rock Sioux and their allies linked tribal sovereignty, water protection, and climate change activism in their fight against the Dakota Access pipeline, 2016. Photo credit JIM WATSON/AFP/ Getty Images.

Mni wičoni!: Water is life

No recent campaign captured more national attention regarding tribal sovereignty and environmental rights than that against the DAPL. Indigenous activists and allies stood up to corporate plans to construct a pipeline that threatened the sacred sites and drinking water sources of the Standing Rock Sioux in North Dakota. The more than $3.7 billion, 1,200-mile DAPL project was designed to transport half a million barrels of crude oil daily from the Bakken oil shale fields underlying Montana, North Dakota, and central Canada to a shipping terminal in Illinois. Residents of the Standing Rock reservation, home to 8,200 people, were particularly angered by the plans to place the pipeline one-half mile *upstream* of the reservation especially since a route ten miles upstream of the city of Bismarck had been rejected for fear it might contaminate the city's drinking water supply. As pipeline construction neared Standing Rock in April 2016, members of the tribe established the Sacred Stone base camp on public land, taking a nonviolent stand as "water protectors." Earthjustice (formerly the Sierra Club Legal Defense Fund) filed suit on behalf of the tribe, charging that in approving the project, the Army Corps of Engineers violated the National Historic Preservation Act and encroached on Indian land rights.[50]

An intersectional grassroots movement linking indigenous rights, climate change, and water protection, the NO DAPL campaign drew thousands of protesters, scores of North American tribes, environmental organizations, human rights groups such as Amnesty International, and several entertainers, including actors Susan Sarandon, Mark Ruffalo, and Leonardo DiCaprio. Greenpeace and 350.org supported the fight. Tactics included not only direct action, but also prayer and delicate negotiations with federal representatives from the Army Corps of Engineers, the Department of Justice, and the Bureau of Indian Affairs. Reacting to "the brutality of the police response," especially the police use of weaponized water against the protesters, U.S. military veterans also rallied to support the Standing Rock Sioux, as did Black Lives Matter. (A Native Lives Matter movement predates the pipeline struggle.)[51]

The campaign strengthened native unity. Native Solidarity, a new group, was born of the NO DAPL fight. A Dallas, Texas, protest at pipeline company Energy Transfer Partners headquarters united Choctaw, Sioux, indigenous Mexican, Cherokee, and Lakota tribes along with the Sierra Club, the Dallas Peace and Justice Center, and the Green Party.[52]

During the fall of 2016 as many as five thousand supporters swelled the ranks at protest sites in North Dakota. Protestors withstood helicopter and drone surveillance; police also used noise bombardment to harass the Standing Rock encampments. On September 3, police deployed attack dogs and

(continued)

(continued)

pepper spray against protestors, provoking outrage nationally. During the week of October 24, law enforcement arrested more than four hundred. In late November, police fired rubber bullets, tear gas, and icy water from cannons at nonviolent protestors on public land. Three hundred were injured; twenty-six went to the hospital. In December, the Standing Rock Sioux, Cheyenne River Sioux, and Yankton Sioux appealed to the Inter-American Commission on Human Rights, citing human rights violations and police violence.[53]

The Standing Rock tribe won an eleventh-hour victory soon thereafter. Responding to a directive from the Obama White House, the U.S. Army Corps of Engineers announced its decision not to grant an easement for the pipeline. The victory at Standing Rock, however transitory, was momentous. Standing Rock Sioux won a new review of the alternatives to the proposed route and a recommendation from the White House Council on Environmental Quality that federal agencies "'heighten agency attention to alternatives' in some cases 'where environmental effects on tribal resources are at stake.'" In early 2017, however, the Trump administration summarily reversed the Corps' decision, allowing the pipeline to open. Five spills occurred along the route over the next six months.[54]

In conjunction with the University of Arizona Indigenous Peoples Law and Policy Program and civil rights lawyers around the country, the Water Protector Legal Collective is pursuing lawsuits that challenge police violence and the criminalization of protesters. In November 2018, one protestor won a reversal of her felony conviction for participating in a peaceful vigil against abuse of indigenous women in areas surrounded by the "man camps" at pipeline construction sites.[55]

The State of the Movement

By 2015, the top ten environmental organizations by membership totaled fifteen million, with two thousand staff members and a combined budget of $525 million. Despite their strength, real challenges exist to enforcing environmental laws and enacting additional protections, challenges emanating from the courts as well as the executive and legislative branches. Environmental groups had enjoyed extraordinary success through litigation since 1970. "The courts were profoundly important," noted NRDC co-founder Gus Speth told an interviewer in 2012. "But it is more complicated today. The Supreme Court has put down some bad decisions." The conservative bloc on the court has halted many equal protection claims, requiring proof of intent to discriminate rather than demonstrating a pattern of discriminatory effect, and seeks to restrict the deference due agency environmental regulations and limit who deserves standing to sue. The High

Court's decision in 2010 in the *Citizens United* campaign finance case opened a floodgate for huge sums of money to influence elections.[56]

Some argue that the retreat from strong environmental policies is due in part to the failure of major national groups to connect policy work with political organizing and electoral campaigns. A gap exists "between where the public is now and where the sort of mainline environmental organizations are," Speth continued. "We pay a high price for neglect of electoral politics and real grassroots movement building [and] organizing, [for] inside-the-Beltway wonkishness."[57]

In a much-debated 2004 essay and subsequent book, environmental consultants Ted Nordhaus and Michael Shellenberger proclaimed "the death of environmentalism." These authors dismissed the need to address environmental injustice, promoting instead reliance on high-tech businesses and the creative class to solve environmental problems.[58] Invoked just as the climate justice movement was infusing new energy into environmentalism, their critique represented a fundamental misreading of the movement's vitality. Multiple environmental justice campaigns, a few of which are highlighted below, attracted broad attention and support, though public officials often failed to provide adequate redress.

How well has the environmental movement addressed environmental injustice? Historian Eileen McGurty, writing in 2007, argued that the "'marriage of social justice with environmentalism' remains a rocky union between ambivalent partners." Many environmentalists do now "think more critically about the ways environmental and social justice issues intersect." However, large national environmental organizations have made little progress in diversifying their ranks and leadership. In a 2014 interview Bob Bullard described the relationship between environmental justice and mainstream organizations as "parallel movements. . . [W]here there's overlap in terms of issues and agendas and strategies for getting things done as a collective, we're seeing groups come together. . . But for the most part these groups are pretty much the same as they were 20 years ago." Former EPA staffer Mustafa Ali concurred. "The big greens are giving more attention to frontline communities," Ali said in 2017, "[but] more needs to happen, there's no way to sugar coat it."[59]

Organizations had mixed records in addressing social justice concerns. Within the Sierra Club, for example, pockets of anti-immigrant fervor lingered. A slate of unsuccessful candidates for the Club's Board of Directors in 2004 advocated barring immigration to the U.S., with one member, also of Californians for Population Stabilization, suggesting that "over-immigration leads to environmental decay." On the other hand, the Sierra Club's ambitious Environmental Justice and Community Partnerships Program (initially the National Environmental Justice Grassroots Organizing Program) launched in 2007 and directed by African American attorney Leslie Fields conducts grassroots organizing and assists local groups, with an annual budget of about $1 million.[60]

Despite initial promises and specific projects, a 2014 study of 191 environmental organizations led by political scientist Dorceta Taylor, *The State of*

Diversity in Environmental Organizations, concluded that, while the preservation and conservation organizations studied have made significant progress toward gender diversity, "ethnic minorities occupy less than 12 percent of the leadership positions." At the same time, many states have seen a proliferation of local and statewide environmental justice groups. Since 2012, the National Environmental Justice Conference has held annual trainings on environmental justice; the March 2017 event had 650 attendees.[61]

Within the EPA, a 2015 study noted some successes in capacity building through its small grants program, but concluded that, despite the emphasis that the Obama-era agency placed on environmental justice, the agency has largely failed to deliver distributive, procedural, and corrective justice. The agency's *Plan EJ 2014*, timed to coincide with the twentieth anniversary of the Clinton executive order on environmental justice, had acknowledged the need for improvement in cross-agency rulemaking, compliance, and enforcement; in analysis and technical assistance to overburdened communities; and in integrating environmental justice with other initiatives.[62]

A 2015 assessment of the environmental justice movement based on interviews with thirty-one of the nation's most prominent environmental justice activists and scholars found

> growing numbers of groups needing financial resources, an increased competition for political legitimacy, and an evolution toward more networking and increased cooperation between groups and with government agencies, with relatively less radicalism and tension within the movement than in the earlier days of the movement.[63]

Flint, Michigan: A Denial of Democracy

The persistence of environmental racism came vividly to national attention in 2015 when the dogged efforts of a local physician and residents identified lead contamination of the water supply in Flint, Michigan. Citizen activist LeeAnne Walters journeyed from her home in Flint, Michigan, to testify on Capitol Hill before the House Oversight and Government Reform Committee in early February 2016 about the link between the poisoned water coming from her tap and the rashes on her boys' skin. A scandal had erupted the previous year in Flint over lead leaching into the drinking water after the city began drawing its water from the Flint River rather than from Lake Huron. Area children tested positive for elevated levels of lead, a neurotoxin that causes cognitive and behavioral difficulties, especially in young children.[64]

In a declining Rust Belt city with more than 40 percent of people in poverty, the Flint crisis was a classic case of environmental injustice.

More than 61 percent of residents were African American, Latino, Asian, or Native American. Conditions in Flint bluntly illustrated the disparate environmental impact by race and class of aging infrastructure, a common problem nationwide. The city faced multiple problems related to deindustrialization—pollution, segregated housing, under-resourced schools, and lack of employment.[65]

Often, people in affected communities themselves identify toxic contamination and pressure authorities to act. Such was the case in Flint, where several local environmental justice groups formed; Flint Rising and FlintH$_2$OJustice were among those who brought attention to the lead contamination. A key whistleblower was pediatrician Dr. Mona Hanna-Attisha, the director of the pediatric residency program at Flint's Hurley Children's Hospital, who refused to back down from her findings that the percentage of children with unsafe blood lead levels more than doubled after the city switched its water source.[66]

Although President Obama declared a national emergency and made five million dollars available to Flint, three years after the lead contamination was acknowledged, the water remained unsafe for food preparation and drinking. Some residents filed civil lawsuits aiming to win compensation to provide remediation and health care for those who suffered exposure. Only the most egregious environmental violations see even the *pursuit* of corrective justice, that is, punishment of violators. However, criminal charges—including willful neglect, misconduct in office, tampering with evidence, and involuntary manslaughter—were filed against no fewer than fifteen individuals, including several Michigan Department of Environmental Quality officials.[67]

The Flint crisis resulted in part from a denial of democracy: Michigan law had enabled an unelected city manager to be placed in charge of Flint. "We don't have just a water problem," Claire McClinton of the Flint Democracy Defense League told the news outlet *Democracy Now!* "We've got a democracy problem." Environmental justice scholar David Pellow called it a "democracy deficit." Black Lives Matter activists went further, condemning the denial of access to clean drinking water as a human rights violation, an act of "state violence."[68]

"Slow Violence" at Camp Lejeune, North Carolina

A case of chemical contamination at a Marine base in North Carolina shows the impact of incremental, insidious buildup of pollution over time, which scholar Rob Nixon has termed "slow violence." Marine Master Sgt. Jerry Ensminger lost his daughter Janey, age nine, in 1985 to a rare form of leukemia. Ensminger learned that, for nearly thirty-five years, from 1953 to 1987, Camp Lejeune, the Marine

Corps base where his family had lived, had been contaminated with industrial solvents that were known to cause various health conditions, including leukemia, bladder, liver, and kidney cancer, non-Hodgkin's lymphoma, and Parkinson's disease. The Veterans' Administration had known about the presence of some of the chemicals since the 1980s. With the advocacy group called "The Few, The Proud, The Forgotten," Ensminger pressed for more than a decade to get health care coverage and compensation for veterans and their families exposed at Camp Lejeune.[69]

In a Senate hearing in 2015, North Carolina Republican senator Richard Burr acknowledged the Camp Lejeune exposures as one of the worst incidents of environmental exposure in the nation's history, chastising the government for "negligently poisoning [servicemembers] and their families" and "engaging in a decades long cover-up." The Agency for Toxic Substances and Disease Registry (ATSDR) later confirmed that perchloroethylene, trichloroethylene, vinyl chloride, benzene, and other contaminants had entered the drinking water supply. Congress passed legislation, the Janey Ensminger Act, signed by President Obama in 2012, which is largely responsible for requiring the Veterans Administration (VA) to cover health costs for a total of fifteen ailments, including male breast cancer, renal toxicity, neuro-behavioral effects, female infertility, and miscarriage. Under pressure from veterans, the VA rewrote its guidelines in 2016 to provide a "presumptive service connection" and thereby disability coverage to veterans stationed at Lejeune during the decades in question.[70]

Labor/Environment Alliance Tackles Green Jobs and Toxics Policy

"We need to create a green economy that Dr. King would be proud of. . .[one] that includes everybody," environmental and social justice activist turned television commentator Van Jones declared at PowerShift 2009. Jones founded Green for All in Oakland, California in 2007 to promote green jobs and ecologically-sound community development for people of color and working families. Jones's book with Ariane Conrad, *The Green-Collar Economy: How One Solution Can Fix Our Two Biggest Problems*, was published in 2008. Author of *Rebuild the Dream* and founder of the Dream Corps, which involves young people in social justice work, Jones served briefly in the Obama White House as green jobs advisor, before earning a national voice as a CNN political analyst. In 2011, the Bureau of Labor Statistics reported 3.4 million green jobs—defined as jobs that "produce goods or provide services that benefit the environment or conserve natural resources." Sustainable South Bronx, led by Majora Carter, hosts another green jobs effort. A national campaign for green jobs is supported by the BlueGreen Alliance, a labor-environment coalition formed by the United Steelworkers Union and the Sierra Club in 2006. By 2018, the Alliance had grown to include several of the largest unions in the U.S., including the American Federation of Teachers, the Communications Workers of America, the Plumbers and Pipefitters Union, and the Service Employees International Union along with the largest environmental groups, including NRDC, NWF, the Union of Concerned Scientists, and the Environmental Defense Fund Action Committee.[71]

A labor-environment alliance was instrumental to the 2016 reforms to the Toxic Substances Control Act. The law, which authorizes the EPA to regulate exposure to toxic chemicals, was weak to begin with and had not been updated since it was passed in 1976. The intervening decades had yielded considerable new knowledge about the dangers of low level exposures, reproductive toxicity, and endocrine disruption—the chemical interference with hormone regulation. The EPA was in dire need of additional resources to monitor the thousands of new chemicals on the market. U.S. policy reform was also impelled by a new system for regulating toxic chemicals instituted in Europe in 2007. Known as REACH, the Regulation, Evaluation, and Authorisation of Chemicals, the European protocol takes a precautionary approach, aiming to prevent new chemicals from being released into the environment until they are proven to be safe. While the protocol was under negotiation, the George W. Bush administration pushed hard to weaken it, but U.S. environmental, public health and labor groups had argued the European legislation would "address profound gaps in public health protections against toxic chemicals." The fact that chemical manufacturers were obligated after 2007 to meet REACH requirements in order to sell chemicals in Europe pushed the American chemical industry, which had long resisted, to consider TSCA reform.[72]

So, in 2010, with leadership from Senator Frank Lautenberg, a Democrat from the pollution-plagued state of New Jersey, reformers launched an ambitious campaign to overhaul TSCA. Safer Chemicals, Healthy Families—a coalition of environmental, public health, consumer, and labor organizations—lobbied for strong provisions, including precautionary language, comparable to REACH. After Sen. Lautenberg passed away in 2013, Republicans in Congress axed these provisions and substituted a weaker version of the legislation that the chemical industry preferred. The final bill, signed by President Obama in 2016, gave the EPA more authority to regulate certain highly toxic chemicals but in some ways regressed by preventing states from crafting their own precautionary laws.[73] This outcome of prolonged and difficult negotiations indicated the difficulties faced by even a well-organized, highly mobilized, intersectional campaign in the face of a Congress hostile to environmental regulation.

Food Justice Activism

Exacerbated by climate shifts, concern over global food insecurity has increased since the mid-1990s and food justice activists have stepped up within the U.S. and globally. Other food and food justice concerns include: food deserts, areas where access to healthy food is limited, and industrial agriculture's widespread use of genetically modified organisms. Food insecurity affects one in eight U.S. households.[74]

A resurgence of organic farming and a "buy local" food movement have been underway in the 2000s. The proliferation of organic farming testifies to growing awareness of the social costs of industrial, monocrop agriculture—including the destruction of pollinators, dead aquatic zones due to fertilizer runoff, and the health hazards of herbicides and pesticides. Though the volume of organic food grown and sold remains small relative to produce from industrial agriculture, food justice activism has pushed the major grocery store chains to offer more organic and healthy alternatives.

Activists call for decentralizing food production to better meet nutritional needs; localizing food production can also reduce the energy impact of long-distance shipping. The early twenty-first century has seen a dramatic increase in home gardens, school and urban-lot garden projects in the U.S. Such efforts were boosted when First Lady Michelle Obama installed a vegetable garden on the White House lawn as part of an anti-obesity campaign. By 2017, the American Community Gardening Association estimated that there were more than eighteen thousand community gardens in the U.S. and Canada. Community gardens build cooperation, strengthen neighborhoods, and raise awareness about healthy eating. By promoting food security in disadvantaged neighborhoods, the urban agriculture movement, as food systems researchers Kristin Reynolds and Nevin Cohen argue, can also provide an arena for addressing systemic racism, gender inequality, and economic disparities.[75]

A diverse and extensive food movement around the globe connects U.S. activists to locales where the crisis is dire. The Oakland, California-based Institute for Food and Development Policy, or Food First, analyzes inequalities in food systems and links U.S. activists and Central America food justice activists in support of community-based movements for land equity, sustainability, public health, and economic equality. Indian scholar and ecofeminist Vandana Shiva has gained worldwide influence through speaking tours for food sustainability. Seed-saving of non-GMO seeds is an important part of Shiva's work at Navdanya Biodiversity Conservation Farm in India, where she engages women in developing food security, teaching agricultural practices that help ensure adequate, local food production. Food justice activists like Shiva critique capitalist economic structures as perpetuating inequalities in food production and distribution.[76]

The International Peasants' Movement, *La Via Campesina*, represents 200 million small farmers and 150 local and national organizations in seventy countries. Formed in Belgium in 1993, La Via Campesina has focused on food sovereignty—"the right of peoples to healthy and culturally appropriate food produced through sustainable methods and their right to define their own food and agriculture systems." The organization's work in agroecology and peasants' rights brought the network into the climate justice movement.[77]

When U.S. firms started producing GMO foods in the mid-1990s, they met with immediate opposition, particularly from Europe. Scientific uncertainties surround the long-term health risk for humans and the indeterminate effects on ecosystems. Concerns range from antibiotic resistance in humans to reduction in biodiversity, as GMO crops displace existing varieties that thrive better in low rainfall conditions, for example. Also at stake are "farmer livelihoods, rural communities, international trade relations, [and] the structure of the food industry." Opposition to GMO foods is stronger in Europe, Mexico, and India than in the U.S., which accounts for more than 50 percent of GMO crops. Since 2003, the Cartagena Protocol on Biosafety, an international treaty, has sought to protect biodiversity against genetically modified organisms introduced through international trade, but the U.S. has not ratified the agreement. Organizations in the U.S. protesting GMO crops include Food and Water Watch, founded in 2005, which now has 100 staffers across the U.S. and around the world. Moms Across America and the Non-GMO Project are among those who have held demonstrations and boycotts, demanding at minimum that GMO foods be labeled, a step many GMO producers oppose vigorously.[78]

Intersectional Movements

The 2010s brought new upsurges of intersectional grassroots campaigns that highlighted access to public space as an environmental justice issue. On September 17, 2011, Occupy Wall Street took over Zuccotti Park in Manhattan's financial district, and renamed it Liberty Park. Targeting America's wealthiest one percent—whose share of wealth in 2010 was greater than one-third the total wealth—Occupy activists popularized the slogan, "We are the 99%." Pushing discussion of income inequality into mainstream U.S. politics, the Occupy movement at its peak reached 100 U.S. cities and spurred protests in more than 1,500 locations worldwide. As occupations waned the following year, many Occupy activists joined the climate change movement, bringing their direct action experience to the Keystone pipeline protests and to successful campus fossil fuel divestment campaigns. Core Occupy activists founded the Sunrise Movement, a broad-based campaign to urge Congress to pass a carbon tax and other measures to slow global warming.[79]

Black Lives Matter, a campaign to stop police brutality and end violence against black communities, arose first in 2013 on social media and then in street demonstrations in Ferguson, Missouri, after resident Michael Brown was shot to death by police. The Movement for Black Lives swept public consciousness, inspired a new generation of activists, especially in large cities. The organization's work included broadening the call for divestment from fossil fuels. Black Lives Matter reframed environmental justice concerns to include "the criminalization of urban space," as African American historian Yohuru Williams has noted. Some traditional environmental organizations expressed support. "It is impossible not to be outraged," wrote the Sierra Club.[80]

Power and Light: Church Engagement with Climate Activism

Influenced in part by the international climate change movement, a religious trend toward "eco-justice" identified in the 1990s by sociologist of religion Laurel Kearns, has grown. In May 2015, newly vested Pope John Francis issued *Laudato Sí: Papal Encyclical on Climate Change.* "O Lord, seize us with your power and light, help us to protect all life, to prepare for a better future. . ." proclaimed the document, casting the weight of the Catholic Church behind the global campaign on climate change.[81] Religious institutions of many denominations have developed environmental stewardship committees. Some focus on greening their churches through reduce, reuse, and recycle projects. Others have created neighborhood energy-saving programs or urban gardening projects.

Though many religious groups across the political spectrum actively pursue pro-environment legislative agendas, others do not. In the 1990s, the Evangelical Environmental Network defended the Endangered Species Act. Congregation-based groups lobby in favor of climate change action in concert with national organizations such as the Friends National Committee on Legislation (FNCL). By contrast, the National Association of Evangelicals—which claims to reach thirty million members or roughly one-fourth of the electorate—tends to support conservative legislators with poor environmental scorecards.[82]

Different denominations and faiths are working toward climate awareness and action and clean energy. Interfaith Power and Light, formed in 1998 as an Episcopal organization by Rev. Sally Bingham, grew by 2016 to include some eighteen thousand congregations in forty states. That year, more than 220 evangelical leaders signed onto "Climate Change: An Evangelical Call to Action," calling for moral witness and political action by participating churches and their members. Evangelical Christian Katharine Hayhoe, a climate scientist at Texas Tech, dedicated herself to communicating facts about climate science with audiences skeptical on religious grounds. The Creation Care Ministry at the historic Ebenezer Baptist Church in Atlanta has adopted environmental stewardship as a goal. Only 8.2 percent of Muslim Americans belong to an "environmental group" but fully 97 percent favor strong environmental laws. Green Muslims, formed in Washington, D.C., in 2007, conducts "spiritually inspired environmental education, reflection, and action."[83]

The Trump Era: A "Third War" on Environmentalism

The ascendance to power of the extreme Right has accelerated what had been gradual chipping away at environmental laws and enforcement. Anti-regulatory fervor in Congress and the Trump White House has brought what historian Christopher Sellers dubs "the third war against the federal environmental state" and poses the most severe stress test yet for the resilience of environmental protections established by law in the U.S.—protections put in place by mass engagement and the bipartisan actions of presidents, Congress, and the courts over more than five decades.[84]

Trump cabinet appointments echoed those of Reagan, whose selections were made "largely on the basis of ideology or loyalty rather than environmental or governmental experience," as one analysis noted.[85] Trump appointed Scott Pruitt, who as attorney general of Oklahoma sued the EPA to block enforcement of federal clean air and clean water protections more than a dozen times, to lead that agency. Montana property development and oil pipeline company executive Ryan Zinke was tapped to head the Department of the Interior. An American Chemistry Council lobbyist, Nancy Beck, was appointed to head the EPA's Office of Chemical Safety and Pollution Prevention.

The Trump administration quickly dismantled several environmental initiatives of the Obama administration and issued hasty approvals of the Keystone XL and Standing Rock pipelines. The administration overturned portions of the "methane rule," which regulates emissions from new oil and gas wells, and attempted to rescind the Clean Power Plan, which was designed to clean up coal-fired power plants and help reach U.S. climate targets.[86] The administration withdrew from major trade agreements, endangering the already limited international protections that environmentalists and labor leaders have successfully negotiated. Moreover, Republican majorities in both houses of Congress during the first two years of the Trump administration left no effective congressional check on executive overreach.

The Trump administration professes support for a "back to basics" approach to environmental management, claiming to focus on clean air and clean water but protecting neither. Under proposal is reversing the Mercury and Air Toxics rule, which has decreased hazardous mercury pollution since it was implemented in 2015. A labeling rule promulgated in December 2018 obscures genetically modified ingredients in foods, popularly known as GM foods, replacing the well-recognized reference to genetic modification with the unfamiliar descriptor "bioengineered." By December 2018, two years into the Trump presidency, "on the way out" were nearly eighty environmental rules. "Regulatory sabotage," one analyst called it. The changes made to air quality, water quality, and toxic chemical regulations alone could result in as many as eighty thousand premature deaths over the next ten years, noted a report by Harvard researchers published in the *Journal of the American Medical Association* in May 2018.[87]

Trump administration tactics have been tried before: slashing funding for ecological testing and environmental enforcement, appointing department heads who seek to destroy the agencies they lead, targeting civil servants who remain committed to their agency's mission, and opening federal lands to wanton, below-market mineral, oil, and gas extraction. But this assault on environmental protections differs. Basic elements of democracy are in the cross-hairs. Speaking at the Conservative Political Action Committee in February 2017, white nationalist Stephen Bannon, a close advisor to the president, called for "the deconstruction of the administrative state." Regular attacks on the press as an institution threaten the free flow of ideas. According to the State Innovation Exchange, anti-democratic, anti-protest legislation surfaced in at least twenty state legislatures, a disturbing response to recent mass protests. Proposed restrictions on demonstrators ranged from increased penalties and fines to forcing convicted protestors to pay the costs of policing public rallies. Arkansas, Oklahoma, North Dakota, South Dakota, and Georgia succeeded in passing anti-protester legislation.[88]

Congressional opponents of environmentalism took the assault on democracy one step further in June 2018, with what Center for Biological Diversity Director Kierán Suckling called "amateurish McCarthy tactics." Chair of the House Natural Resources Committee Utah Republican Rob Bishop initiated an effort to uncover "undue foreign influence" on environmental organizations "as knowing or unknowing proxies to engage in environmental lawfare." Explicitly targeted were the NRDC, the Center for Biological Diversity, and Earthjustice. In mid-2018, Bishop targeted lawsuits filed by these organizations that aim to hold U.S. military installations accountable to the nation's environmental laws.[89]

A hostile executive branch is not the only cause for concern among environmentalists in 2019. Concentration of capital is as intense as it has been since prior to antitrust legislation of the early twentieth century, making environmental campaigns for corporate responsibility more difficult. The move to privatize many functions of government transfers decision-making on important issues from arenas in which citizens exercise a modicum of influence to corporate entities, where, argues philosopher and activist Noam Chomsky, "voters have no say at all."[90]

The Trump Administration EPA

The administration's assault on the regulatory state has proved extreme at the EPA. Reductions in EPA staffing were plainly intended to undermine the agency. At the close of 2015, EPA staff levels stood at around fifteen thousand, already down from the agency's peak staffing (under Clinton) of eighteen thousand. In 2017, EPA set aside $12 million for staff buyouts. Moreover, cuts target personnel in "climate, international collaborations, environmental justice, and enforcement programs; scientific research; and grants to states for implementation and enforcement," wrote Christopher Sellers and colleagues. The newly formed Environmental Protection Network (EPN), a research group established by ex-EPA staffers, estimates that "the actual cuts to programs for clean air, water, and climate protection would be 43%."[91]

A Sierra Club FOIA request revealed that Administrator Pruitt used EPA staff to attempt to secure for his wife a Chick-fil-A franchise. More than a dozen ethics investigations into Pruitt's first-class travel, spending on office furniture, a

$43,000 secure phone booth, and $3 million spent on a round-the-clock security detail forced his resignation in July 2018.[92]

Meanwhile, Pruitt had delayed implementation of, or quickly overturned, rules essential to public health and safety. For example, the EPA's Office of Chemical Safety and Pollution Prevention delayed indefinitely a rule restricting some uses of trichloroethylene (TCE), one of the cancer-causing chemicals to which the Camp Lejeune military personnel, among others, were exposed. Cozy relationships with regulated industries were evidenced by Pruitt's delay of "a rule barring coal-powered plants from dumping toxic metals into rivers, a move requested by a coal industry group," *The New York Times* reported in June 2018. So much had the agency tilted toward industry that an independent team of analysts raised concerns about "regulatory capture," that is, that the EPA had become almost wholly beholden to the interests of the entities it regulates.[93]

Particularly troubling has been the administration's "animosity toward science, the evidentiary foundation for the vast majority of agency actions," wrote Sellers and colleagues. Data for tracking climate fluctuations were slated for removal from the EPA website. Career scientists who raised concerns about policy directions were targeted for "monitoring." Members of the EPA's Science Advisory Board have been dismissed. An industry-supported "Secret Science" initiative would bar the EPA from relying on peer-reviewed studies if the raw data have not been made public, ruling out many authoritative epidemiological studies. At the same time, the EPA maintained secrecy about its own operations. Environmental organizations, good government groups, and even conservative organizations had to file numerous Freedom of Information Act (FOIA) lawsuits in 2017 to obtain basic information about the agency's current operations.[94]

On June 1, 2017, President Trump announced plans to withdraw the U.S. from the Paris Climate Agreement. Accompanied by a call for U.S. "energy dominance," the move isolated the U.S. In a related action, the EPA announced plans to halt scheduled improvements in fuel efficiency standards for six years. Paradoxically, states' rights advocates in charge at the federal level challenge states' authority to enact state environmental laws more protective than those at the federal level, threatening to revoke the waiver California has relied upon to implement its own stringent fuel and emissions standards.[95]

Pruitt's successor at the EPA, former coal industry lobbyist Andrew Wheeler, has pursued "a quieter but no less destructive approach," according to an independent November 2018 report. Under Pruitt and Wheeler, the EPA has shifted enforcement to the states, which are ill-equipped to carry out investigations and cannot impose fines as high as those levied by the EPA.[96]

Resistance Erupts

Official hostility to environmental protection proved a membership boon to environmental organizations, as it had during the Reagan era. Donations soared.

In the *week* following the 2016 election, 7,500 signed on as monthly donors with Greenpeace, more than had done so in the previous *ten months* combined. The Sierra Club brought in eleven thousand new members and three million dollars in the month following the election, nearly nine times the contributors than the previous December. Environmental Defense Fund took in ninety thousand new members in the first nine months of 2017.[97]

The Trump reversal has also activated new constituencies. As opposition to climate science has become a political tool, "a central litmus test for the American right," scientists have joined with other activists to counter anti-scientific bias in policy making. The March for Science in Spring 2017 launched an Action Network whose goals include "increasing evidence based input into policy making" and "sustaining public funding of science." The Action Network works "for science advocacy, mobilizing people around net neutrality, the budget, science education, [and] federally funded research."[98]

Immediately after President Trump announced the withdrawal from the Paris Climate Agreement, more than 1,400 U.S. cities, states, and businesses declared their commitment to the Paris targets. The United States Climate Alliance, which includes sixteen states plus Puerto Rico, is "committed to upholding Barack Obama's Paris pledge to reduce United States GHGs 26 percent to 28 percent by the 2025 target date." At COP-23, a follow-up meeting to the Paris Accords in November 2017, representatives of U.S. states, cities, and the civil society sector set up the U.S. Climate Action Center bearing the hashtag, #WEARESTILLIN. Hundreds walked out of the official U.S. delegation's presentation on nuclear, coal, and fossil fuels. The same month, civil war-torn Syria announced that it would join the Accords, leaving the U.S. as the only outlier.[99]

Multiple actors have sought to limit presidential power to block climate mitigation. States and cities have sued to hasten the hearing of lawsuits over the Clean Power Plan. The State of California has filed suit to block the proposed delay in raising fuel efficiency standards.[100]

Environmental litigation groups have used citizen suits to mount a formidable legal defense against Trump administration rollbacks. During the first year of the Trump presidency, the NRDC alone filed almost one lawsuit per week in response to nearly fifty anti-environment policy reversals and rule changes. Legal successes include an August 2018 court ruling obtained by the South Carolina Coastal Conservation League, Clean Water Action, the Southern Environmental Law Center, and other groups. The ruling blocked a Trump administration change in rules governing the "waters of the United States" (WOTUS) that would have removed from federal Clean Water Act protection more than half the nation's wetlands and 18 percent of intermittent or seasonal streams, endangering not only human health, but numerous other species, including salamanders, trout, ducks, and deer.[101]

Though EPA staff risked being sidelined for speaking out, the two EPA unions, the American Federation of Government Employees Council 238, representing eight thousand employees, and the National Federation of Federal Employees Local 2050, representing an additional 110,000, launched "Save the U.S. EPA Day" on September 13, 2017 to advocate for a fully funded EPA. Through the Environmental Protection Network, former EPA staff from multiple administrations provided information and analysis to legislators and the public "to provide an informed and rigorous defense against efforts to undermine the protection of public health and the environment." Mustafa Ali, who resigned in Spring 2017 after more than twenty years at the EPA Office of Environmental Justice, went to work with the justice group, Hip Hop Caucus, and the Super PAC Climate Hawks Vote, which supports office seekers who make addressing climate change their top priority.[102]

Most major environmental organizations have political action committees (PACs). The newly formed PAC 314.org (a reference to the math symbol Pi), for example, seeks to elect candidates drawn from STEM (Science, Technology, Engineering, and Math) professions. The League of Conservation Voters Action Fund, a traditional PAC, has been contributing to candidates since 1992 and gave more than $750,000 to candidates for federal office in 2016. The LCV Victory Fund, a Super PAC, is not obligated to disclose its donors but cannot make direct contributions to candidates. The LCV Victory Fund spent more than $20 million in 2016, including over $7.5 million on broadcast and web advertising.[103]

The conservative electoral victories in 2016 also stimulated a renewed commitment among environmentalists and other progressives to seek electoral office. Pro-environment candidates from nearly every region of the country met with success in the 2018 midterm elections. Seven of the candidates endorsed by Climate Hawks Vote won their races. Nineteen candidates who refused to accept campaign funds from the fossil fuel industry likewise won. Electoral victories occurred in places where people least expected. Majorities in Montana, New Mexico, and Nevada elected Democrats who supported retaining federal control over public lands, preserving national monuments, and expanding renewable energy. In Arizona, a Republican candidate who favored opening the Arctic National Wildlife Refuge and offshore waters to drilling lost; in Nevada, two Democratic House candidates defeated Republican opponents who advocated devolving federal lands to the states. Nevadans also voted in favor of a ballot measure to raise renewable energy standards. In South Carolina's 1st congressional district, voters supported the Democratic candidate, Joe Cunningham, an ocean engineer, who opposes oil drilling in Atlantic coastal waters and promptly filed a bill to protect the coast.[104]

The shift in the political landscape in the U.S. House after the 2018 midterms heartened activists. A swath of progressive Democrats is committed to holding accountable the EPA and other federal agencies responsible for protecting the environment and public health—Interior, the Forest Service, Agriculture, the Bureau of Land Management, among others. In one positive sign in early 2019, the U.S. Senate passed a sweeping package of bills expanding public lands.[105]

Nevertheless, the task of maintaining and extending environmental protections remains daunting.

Notes

1 Jeffrey M. Jones, "Americans' Identification as 'Environmentalists' Down to 42%," Gallup, April 22, 2016, www.gallup.com/poll/190916/americans-identification-environmentalists-down.aspx (accessed April 25, 2017); Lydia Saad, "Global Warming Concern at Three-Decade High in U.S.," Gallup, March 14, 2017, https://news.gallup.com/poll/206030/global-warming-concern-three-decade-high.aspx (accessed May 26, 2017); Lydia Saad and Jeffrey M. Jones, "U.S. Concern About Global Warming at Eight-Year High," *Gallup Politics*, March 16, 2016, www.gallup.com/poll/190010/concern-global-warming-eight-year-high.aspx (accessed August 2, 2017); Gallup, "Environment, In Depth: Topics A to Z," news.gallup.com/poll/1615/environment.aspx (accessed August 2, 2017).

2 Lyndon B. Johnson, "Special Message to Congress on Conservation and Natural Beauty," *The American Presidency Project*, www.presidency.ucsb.edu/ws/?pid=27285 (accessed January 8, 2017); Howe, *Making Climate Change History*, 10–11; President's Science Advisory Committee, *Restoring the Quality of Our Environment, Report of the Environmental Pollution Panel* (Washington, D.C.: The White House, 1965), 111.

3 15 U.S. Code §2904, Sec. (d) (2); Speth, *Red Sky at Morning*, 2; Patricia Scharlin, "The Sierra Club International Committee Questionnaire—Five-Year Plan," and Michael McCloskey, "Criteria for International Campaigns," in Howe, *Making Climate Change History*, 119, 121–22; Rich, "Losing Earth," 20; Council on Environmental Quality and U.S. Department of State, *The Global 2000 Report to the President: Entering the Twenty-First Century* (Washington, D.C.: U.S. Government Printing Office, 1980).

4 15 U.S. Code §2901, Sec. 1103 (b), (c); James E. Hansen, NASA Goddard Center for Space Studies, Testimony to the U.S. Senate Committee on Energy and Natural Resources, June 23, 1988.

5 U.N. General Assembly, A/RES/43/53, Protection of Global Climate for Present and Future Generations of Mankind, December 6, 1988, www.un.org/documents/ga/res/43/a43r053.htm (accessed January 20, 2019); Rich, "Losing Earth," 58–59; Intergovernmental Panel on Climate Change, *Climate Change 1995: The Science of Climate Change* (Cambridge; New York: Cambridge University Press, 1996), 4.

6 Oberthür and Ott, *The Kyoto Protocol*, 83.

7 Aaron M. McCright and Riley E. Dunlap, "Defeating Kyoto: The Conservative Movement's Impact on U.S. Climate Policy," *Social Problems* 50, no. 3, (2003): 348–73, 349.

8 Jennifer S. Lee, "The Warming is Global, But the Legislating in the U.S. Is All Local," *The New York Times*, October 29, 2003; Judith Resnik, Joshua Civin, Joseph Frueh, "Ratifying Kyoto at the Local Level: Sovereigntism, Federalism, and Translocal Organizations of Government Actors (TOGAs)," *Ariz. L. Rev.* 50 (2008): 709–86, at 717n25, 711.

9 ACLU, "How the USA Patriot Act Redefines Domestic Terrorism," www.aclu.org/other/how-usa-patriot-act-redefines-domestic-terrorism (accessed August 5, 2017); Mark J. Palmer, "Oil and the Bush Administration," *The Earth Island Journal*, The Earth Island Institute (Fall 2002).

10 World Trade Center Health Program, Research Meeting Proceedings, June 17–18, 2014; Joanna Walters, "9/11 Health Crisis: Death Toll from Illness Nears Number Killed on Day of Attacks," *The Guardian*, September 11, 2016.

11 Edward B. Barbier, "Hurricane Katrina's Lessons for the World," *Nature* 524 (August 20, 2015): 285–87, at 285; Thomas Craemer, "Evaluating Racial Disparities in

Hurricane Katrina Relief Using Direct Trailer Counts in New Orleans and FEMA Records." *Public Administration Review* 70, no. 3 (2010): 367–77, 367.

12 Horne, *Breach of Faith*, 85.

13 Harden et al., "Racial Discrimination in the Aftermath of Hurricane Katrina," 7; S. Leo Chiang, "A Village Called Versailles," distributed by New Day Films, 2009; Gulf Coast Reconstruction Watch and Southern Exposure, *Blueprint for Gulf Renewal* (Durham: Institute for Southern Studies, August/September 2007), 25.

14 Gulf Coast Reconstruction Watch and Southern Exposure, *Blueprint for Gulf Renewal* (Durham: Institute for Southern Studies, August/September 2007), 23–24, 28; Leslie Fields, Albert Huang, Gina Solomon, M.D., M.P.H., Miriam Rotkin-Ellman, M.P.H., Patrice Simms, "Katrina's Wake: Arsenic-Laced Schools and Playgrounds Put New Orleans Children at Risk," 1–35 (New York: Natural Resources Defense Council, 2007).

15 Harden et al., "Racial Discrimination in the Aftermath of Hurricane Katrina," i.

16 J. Hansen et al. "Ice Melt, Sea Level Rise, and Superstorms: Evidence from Paleoclimate Data, Climate Modeling, and Modern Observations that 2°C Global Warming is Highly Dangerous," *Atmospheric Chemistry and Physics* 15 (2015): 20059–179.

17 PowerShift, "Ten Principles for Just Climate Change Policies in the U.S.," https://powershift.org/sites/wearepowershift.org/files/10%20Principles%20for%20Just%20Climate%20Change%20Policies%20in%20the%20U.S..pdf (accessed May 23, 2018).

18 The Sierra Club, "Milestone 250th and 251st American Coal Plants Announce Retirement," news release, March 20, 2017, https://content.sierraclub.org/press-releases/2017/03/milestone-250th-and-251st-american-coal-plants-announce-retirement (accessed January 4, 2019).

19 "Our History," 350.org, https://350.org/our-history/ (accessed January 4, 2017).

20 Author's notes, Little Village Environmental Justice Tour, American Society for Environmental History, March 31, 2017; NAACP et al., *Coal Blooded*, 24, 27; Audrey Haynes, "Coal-Fired Power Plants Disproportionately Impact Communities of Color, says NAACP," *Earth Island Journal*, November 15, 2012.

21 *Massachusetts v. EPA*, 127 S. Ct. 1438 (2007); Lisa P. Jackson, "Remarks on the Endangerment Finding on Greenhouse Gases, as prepared," December 7, 2009, https://yosemite.epa.gov/opa/admpress.nsf/dff15a5d01abdfb1852573590040b7f7/b6b7098bb1dfaf9a85257685005483d5!OpenDocument (accessed January 13, 2017).

22 *International Center for Technology Assessment v. Carol Browner*, Petition for Rulemaking and Collateral Relief Seeking the Regulation of Greenhouse Gas Emissions from New Motor Vehicles under §202 of the Clean Air Act, October 20, 1999, www.ciel.org/Publications/greenhouse_petition_EPA.pdf (accessed January 7, 2017); *Massachusetts v. EPA*, 127 S. Ct. 1438 (2007), quoting National Research Council, *Climate Change Science, An Analysis of Key Questions*, (2001), 17; EPA, "EPA Denies Petition to Regulate Greenhouse Gas Emissions from Motor Vehicles," news release, August 28, 2003, https://archive.epa.gov/epapages/newsroom_archive/newsreleases/694c8f3b7c16ff6085256d900065fdad.html (accessed October 6, 2018). On September 8, 2003, EPA entered an order denying the rulemaking petition, "Control of Emissions from New Highway Vehicles and Engines," 68 FR 173, 52922–33. Andrew Revkin, "Climate Expert Says NASA Tried to Silence Him," *The New York Times*, January 29, 2006.

23 *Massachusetts v. EPA*, 127 S. Ct. 1438 (2007).

24 *Massachusetts v. EPA*, 127 S. Ct. 1438 (2007), 1455; "Carbon Emissions Grow Faster than in the '90s," *Atlanta Journal-Constitution*, February 15, 2009, A16.

25 SCOTUSblog, "Carbon Pollution Controls Put on Hold," by Lyle Denniston in *SCOTUSblog*, a blog about the U.S. Supreme Court, February 9, 2016; Dominic Rushe, "Top U.S. Coal Boss Robert Murray: Trump 'Can't Bring Mining Jobs Back,'" *The Guardian*, March 27, 2017; Jon Kamp and Kris Maher, "Coal's Decline Spreads Far Beyond Appalachia," *Wall Street Journal*, June 20, 2017; The Sierra Club, "Milestone 250th and 251st American Coal Plants Announce Retirement," March 20, 2017.

26 Bond, *Politics of Climate Justice*, 21–22, xv; Klein, *This Changes Everything*, 57–58.

27 Wen Stephenson, "Dispatches from the Front Lines of the Climate Justice Movement," *The Nation* (October 26, 2015): 17–21; Bond, *Politics of Climate Justice*, 202–03.

28 Maurie J. Cohen, "The Death of Environmentalism: Introduction to the Symposium," *Organization Environment* 19 no. 1 (March 2006): 74–81; Bond, *Politics of Climate Justice*, 187.

29 Park and Pellow, *The Slums of Aspen*, 3.

30 Tadzio Mueller, "The People's Climate Summit in Cochabamba: A Tragedy in Three Acts," *Ephemera: Theory & Politics in Organization* 12, nos. 1–2 (2012): 70–80; Dauvergne, *Environmentalism of the Rich*, 82.

31 Sergey Paltsev, "The Complicated Geopolitics of Renewable Energy," *Bulletin of the Atomic Scientists* 72, no. 6 (2016): 390–95, 391. United Nations, The Paris Agreement, The United Nations Framework Convention on Climate Change, entered into force October 5, 2016, http://unfccc.int/paris_agreement/items/9485.php (accessed July 29, 2017). Erika Bolstad, "2016: The Year in Climate Change," *E&E News*, December 23, 2016.

32 Robert J. Brulle, "Institutionalizing Delay: Foundation Funding and the Creation of U.S. Climate Change Counter-Movement Organizations," *Climatic Change* 122 (2014): 681–94, 690, 687; Dylan Brown, "'The Voice' of Coal Bids Adieu to Washington," *E&E News*, April 30, 2018.

33 Mulvey and Shulman, *The Climate Deception Dossiers*, 25; Katie Jennings, Dino Grandoni, and Susanne Rust, "How Exxon Went from Leader to Skeptic on Climate Change Research," *Los Angeles Times*, October 23, 2015; Oreskes and Conway, *Merchants of Doubt*, 246–47.

34 Neela Banerjee, "How Big Oil Lost Control of Its Climate Misinformation Machine," *Inside Climate News*, December 22, 2017; Morton, *The Planet Remade*, 232.

35 Robert J. Brulle, "Institutionalizing Delay: Foundation Funding and the Creation of U.S. Climate Change Counter-Movement Organizations," *Climatic Change* 122 (2014): 681–94, 690, 687; Dunlap and Jacques, "Climate Change Denial," 700.

36 Salil D. Benegal, "The Spillover of Race and Racial Attitudes into Public Opinion About Climate Change," *Environmental Politics* 27, no. 4 (March 2018): 733–56, 736, 751, 752.

37 Committee on Oversight and Government Reform, U.S. House of Representatives, *Allegations of Political Interference with the Work of Government Climate Change Scientists*, January 30, 2007 (Washington, D.C.: Government Printing Office, 2007); Douglass Starr, "Just 90 Companies Are to Blame for Most Climate Change, This 'Carbon Accountant' Says," *Science*, August 25, 2016; Richard Heede, "Tracing Anthropogenic Carbon Dioxide and Methane Emissions to Fossil Fuel and Cement Producers, 1854–2010," *Climatic Change* 122, nos. 1/2 (January 2014): 229–41; Bill McKibben, "Embarrassing Photos of Me, Thanks to My Right-Wing Stalkers," *New York Times Sunday Review*, August 5, 2016, SR4.

38 Global Witness, *Defenders of the Earth Killed in 2016*.

39 Georges C. Benjamin, American Public Health Association, Email message to members, January 5, 2017; Dr. Andrew Geller, "Environmental Justice Research Roadmap and Interagency Efforts on Climate Justice," Council of State and Territorial Epidemiologists (CSTE), Webinar, August 16, 2016; Author's notes, Climate and Health Meeting, *The Carter Center*, February 16, 2017.

40 Christopher Mele and Daniel Victor, "Alaskan Island Village Votes to Relocate to the Mainland," *The New York Times*, August 20, 2016, A14.

41 Judge Ann Aiken, Opinion and Order, *Juliana et al. v. U.S. et al.*, Case No. 6:15-cv-01517-TC, U.S. District Court, Oregon, November 10, 2016, 32; Benjamin Hulac, "Kids Rally As Climate Trial's Fate Remains Murky," *E&E News*, October 30, 2018; Order in Pending Case, 18A410, *In re United States et al.*, November 2, 2018.

42 Peyton Fleming, "Investors Raising Heat on Fossil Fuel Companies and Their Strategies for Emerging Low-carbon Economy," *Ceres*, March 7, 2016; Michael Levitin, "The Triumph of Occupy Wall Street," *The Atlantic*, June 10, 2015.

43 National Commission on the BP Deepwater Horizon Oil Spill, *Deep Water*, vii.

44 Kirk Siegler, "Santa Barbara Oil Spill Reopens Fierce Environmental Debate," *NPR Weekend Edition Saturday*, May 23, 2015; Kirk Siegler, "Texas Oil Company Faces Criminal Charges over Southern California Oil Spill," *NPR All Things Considered*, May 17, 2016; Doug Smith and Brittny Mejia, "Pipeline Company Indicted in 2015 Santa Barbara County Oil Spill," *Los Angeles Times*, May 17, 2016.

45 Steven Mufson and Chris Mooney, "Keystone Pipeline Spills 210,000 Gallons of Oil on Eve of Permitting Decision for TransCanada," *Washington Post*, November 16, 2017.

46 Becky Oskin, "Japan Earthquake and Tsunami of 2011: Facts and Information," *Live Science*, September 13, 2017, www.livescience.com/39110-japan-2011-earthquake-tsunami-facts.html (accessed June 8, 2018); "573 Deaths 'Related to Nuclear Crisis,'" *The Yomiuri Shimbun*, February 5, 2012; Jim Galloway, "Behind the Great Plant Vogtle Rebellion of 2018," *The Atlanta Journal-Constitution*, October 2, 2018.

47 Section 322 of the Energy Policy Act of 2005 limits EPA regulation of hydraulic fracturing, "Key Environmental Issues in the Energy Policy Act of 2005 (P.L. 109-58; H.R. 6)" (Washington, D.C.: Congressional Research Service, September 15, 2005).

48 Peggy Heinkel-Wolfe, "Denton Voters Pass Proposition by 59 percent," *Denton Record-Chronicle*, November 5, 2014; Peggy Heinkel-Wolfe, "Ban on Hydraulic Fracturing Repealed," *Denton Record-Chronicle*, June 17, 2015; Zachary Roth, "What Happened in Denton: The War on Local Democracy," *NBC News*, August 2, 2016.

49 The goals of the Indigenous Environmental Network are outlined at www.ienearth. org/about/ (accessed December 1, 2018). Gregory D. Smithers, "Beyond the 'Ecological Indian': Environmental Politics and Traditional Ecological Knowledge in Modern America," *Environmental History* 20, no. 1 (2015): 83–111, 103, 99. See also, Winona LaDuke, *All Our Relations: Native Struggles for Land and Life*.

50 Jack Healy, "North Dakota Oil Pipeline Battle: Who's Fighting and Why," *The New York Times*, August 26, 2016; Earthjustice, "The Standing Rock Sioux Tribe's Litigation on the Dakota Access Pipeline," https://earthjustice.org/features/faq-standing-rock-litigation (accessed January 20, 2019).

51 Louise Erdrich, "Holy Rage: Lessons from Standing Rock," *The New Yorker*, December 22, 2016.

52 Jeffrey Weiss, "Protestors Assail Oil Pipeline," *The Dallas Morning News,* September 3, 2016, 1D, 3D.

53 "Dakota Access Pipeline Company Attacks Native American Protesters with Dogs & Pepper Spray," *Democracy Now*, September 3, 2016; Blake Nicholson, "Army Corps Petitions Dakota Access Company," *Atlanta Journal Constitution*, November 11, 2016, A9; Derek Hawkins, "Activists and Police Trade Blame after Dakota Access Protester Severely Injured," *The Washington Post*, November 22, 2016; Seánna Howard, Robert A. Williams Jr., Michelle Cook, Terry Janis, and Andrea Carter, "Indigenous Resistance to the Dakota Access Pipeline: Criminalization of Dissent and Suppression of Protest," Report to the United Nations Special Rapporteur on the Rights of Indigenous Peoples, Victoria Tauli-Corpuz (Tucson: University of Arizona Rogers College of Law, 2018), 9n9.

54 Ellen M. Gilmer, "Dakota Access: Activists Hail 'Historic Decision' Stopping Pipeline," *E&E News*, December 5, 2016; Alleen Brown, "Five Spills, Six Months in Operation," *The Intercept*, January 9, 2018, https://theintercept.com/2018/01/09/dakota-access-pipeline-leak-energy-transfer-partners/ (accessed November 30, 2018).

55 Jeff Brady, "Two Years After Standing Rock, Tensions Remain," *NPR*, November 29, 2018, www.npr.org/2018/11/29/671701019/2-years-after-standing-rock-protests-north-dakota-oil-business-is-booming (accessed November 30, 2018); *Dundon v.*

Kirchmeier, 1:16–cv–00406, U.S.D.C., N.D., filed November 28, 2016.Water Protector Legal Collective, "Water Protector Wins Appeal at North Dakota Supreme Court," November 7, 2018, https://waterprotectorlegal.org/water-protector-wins-appeal-at-nd-supreme-court/ (accessed November 30, 2018); *North Dakota v. Jessee,* 2018 ND 241, No. 20180047, November 6, 2018.

56 Katharine Bagley, "A Field Guide to the U.S. Environmental Movement," *InsideClimate News*, April 7, 2014, https://insideclimatenews.org/print/31294 (accessed February 5, 2018); J. Gustave Speth, Interview by John C. Cruden, Environmental Law Institute, April 13, 2012. For example, *Alexander v. Sandoval*, 532 U.S. 275 (2001) limited cases in which proof of disparate impact was sufficient to show discrimination. Philip Dane Warren, "The Impact of Weakening *Chevron* Deference on Environmental Deregulation," *Columbia Law Review* 118, no. 2 (March 2018); John D. Echeverria and Jon T. Zeidler, "Barely Standing: The Erosion of Citizen 'Standing' to Sue to Enforce Federal Environmental Law" (Washington, D.C.: Georgetown Environmental Law Project, 1999); *Citizens United v. Federal Elections Commission et al.*, 558 U.S. 310 (2010).

57 J. Gustave Speth, Interview by John C. Cruden, Environmental Law Institute, April 13, 2012.

58 Nordhaus and Shellenberger, *Break Through.*

59 McGurty, *Transforming Environmentalism,* 15; Wells, *Environmental Justice in Postwar America,* 10; Marty Durlin, "The Shot Heard Round the West: What Resulted from Activists' 1990 Challenge to the Big Greens," *High Country News*, February 1, 2010; Mary Hoff, "Robert Bullard: The Father of Environmental Justice," Interview, *Ensia,* 4, June 12, 2014; Mustafa Ali, public lecture, Women's Action for New Directions, Decatur, Georgia, May 21, 2017.

60 Gottlieb, *Forcing the Spring*, 24; Clapp and Dauvergne, *Paths to a Green World*, 246; Ben Zuckerman, "Nothing Racist about It," (Toronto, Canada) *Globe and Mail*, January 28, 2004; The Sierra Club Annual Report, 2007, 30, www.sierraclubfoundation.org/..

61 Dorceta E. Taylor, "The State of Diversity in Environmental Organizations," 192, 4; "Past Conferences," National Environmental Justice Conference and Training Program, http://thenejc.org/?page_id=698 (accessed December 16, 2017).

62 Konisky, *Failed Promises;* U.S. EPA, *Plan EJ 2014,* www.epa.gov/environmental justice/plan-ej-2014 (accessed January 2, 2018).

63 Bernadette Grafton, Alejandro Colsa Perez, Katy Hintzen, Paul Mohai, Sara Orvis and Rebecca Hardin, "From the Michigan Coalition to Transnational Collaboration: Interactive Research Methods for the Future of Environmental Justice Research," *Journal of Politics, Groups, and Identities* 3, no. 4 (September 2015): 684–91, 690.

64 Ron Fonger, "'My Home is Ground Zero' for Lead, Flint Woman Tells Congressional Committee," *mlive.com*, Feburary 3, 2016; Centers for Disease Control and Prevention, *Managing Elevated Blood Lead Levels Among Young Children: Recommendations from the Advisory Committee on Childhood Lead Poisoning Prevention* (Atlanta: CDC, 2002), 81.

65 U.S. Bureau of the Census, Quick Facts, www.census.gov/quickfacts/table/PST045215/2629000, estimates based on July 1, 2015.

66 Brown and Mikkelson, *No Safe Place,* 3; David Wahlberg, "Flint Doctor Used EPIC System Records to Expose Lead Crisis," *Wisconsin State Journal*, January 30, 2016.

67 Mark Brush, "These Are the 15 People Charged for their Connection to the Flint Water Crisis," Michigan Public Radio, June 16, 2017. Several have pled no contest to greatly reduced charges. Beth LeBlanc, "State Officials Plead No Contest in Flint Crisis," *The Detroit News*, December 26, 2018.

68 Richard Schragger, "Flint Wasn't Allowed Democracy," *Slate*, February 8, 2016; Claire McClinton, in "Thirsty for Democracy: The Poisoning of an American City: Special Report on Flint's Water Crisis." *Democracy Now*, February 17, 2016; Sylvia Hood Washington and David Pellow, "Water Crisis in Flint, Michigan, Interview with David Pellow, Ph.D." *Environmental Justice* 9, no. 2 (2016): 53–58; Raven Rakia, "Black Lives Matter Calls the Flint Water Crisis an Act of 'State Violence,'" *Grist*, January 26, 2016.

69 "U.S. to pay billions to Marines affected by contaminated drinking water," PBS.org, January 13, 2017.

70 Sen. Richard Burr, *Examining the Impact of Exposure to Toxic Chemicals on Veterans and the VA's Response*, U.S. Senate Committee on Veterans' Affairs, September 2, 2015 (Washington D.C.: U.S. Government Printing Office, 2016); Agency for Toxic Substances and Disease Registry, *ATSDR Assessment of the Evidence for the Drinking Water Contaminants at Camp Lejeune and Specific Cancers and Other Diseases* (Atlanta: ATSDR, January 13, 2017), 2; U.S. Department of Veterans' Affairs, "Camp Lejeune: Past Water Contamination," www.publichealth.va.gov/exposures/camp-lejeune/#sthash.B7Gu5KMB.dpuf (accessed May 17, 2018).

71 Van Jones, PowerShift 2009, March 10, 2009, www.youtube.com/watch?v=xlOv8RCkcXE (accessed January 5, 2019); U.S. Bureau of Labor, "Employment in Green Goods and Services 2011," March 19, 2013. www.bls.gov/news.release/ggqcew.nr0.htm (accessed September 29, 2017); BlueGreen Alliance website, www.bluegreenalliance.org (accessed October 21, 2018).

72 "European Commission's REACH Proposal Comes Under Fire from Bush Administration," *Bureau of National Affairs Chemical Regulation Reporter* 27, no. 28 (July 14, 2003): 867; Dirk A. Heyen, "Influence of the EU Chemicals Regulation on the US Policy Reform Debate: Is a 'California Effect' within REACH?," *Transnational Environmental Law* 2, no. 1 (April 2013): 95–115.

73 Kalyn Behnke, "Toxic Preemption: Why the Lautenberg Chemical Safety Act's Erosion of State Authority Contaminates Environmental Law," *Jurimetrics: The Journal of Law, Science & Technology* 57, no. 4 (Summer 2017): 459–82.

74 Roughly 12 percent of U.S. households were food insecure in 2016, a slight downward trend, but still higher than the pre-2008 recession levels of 11 percent, Alisha Coleman-Jensen, Matthew P. Rabbitt, Christian A. Gregory, and Anita Singh, *Household Food Security in the United States in 2016: Economic Research Service Summary Report* (Washington, D.C.: U.S. Department of Agriculture, September 2017), 1.

75 Klein, *This Changes Everything*, 85–86; FAQs, American Community Gardening Association; https://communitygarden.org/resources/faq/ (accessed December 1, 2018); Reynolds and Cohen, *Beyond the Kale*, 12–13.

76 "About Us," Food First, Institute for Food & Development Policy, https://foodfirst.org/about-us/ (accessed October 20, 2018); Shiva, *Stolen Harvest*.

77 "The International Peasant's Voice," La Via Campesina, https://viacampesina.org/en/international-peasants-voice/ (accessed August 5, 2017).

78 Kinchy, *Seeds, Science, and Struggle*, 25; Robert Falkner, "The Global Bio-Tech Food Fight, Why the United States. Got It So Wrong," *The Brown Journal of World Affairs* 14, no. 1 (Fall/Winter 2007): 99–110, 101–02; "The Cartagena Protocol on Biosafety," Convention on Biological Diversity, https://bch.cbd.int/protocol/parties/ (accessed December 4, 2018): "Anti-GMO Groups – United States," *GMO Awareness.com*, https://gmo-awareness.com/resources/anti-gmo-groups-america (accessed November 13, 2017).

79 Occupy Wall Street website, http://occupywallst.org/about/ (accessed November 30, 2018); Ron Scherer, "Opening Day for Occupy Wall Street: Act 2," *CSMonitor*, April 30, 2012; Piketty, *Capital in the Twenty-First Century*, 349; Karla Adam, "Occupy Protests Go Global," *The Washington Post*, October 15, 2011; Mark K. Matthews, Nick Bowlin, and Benjamin Hulac, "Inside the Sunrise Movement," *E&E News*, December 3, 2018.

80 Purdy, "Environmentalism Was Once a Social-Justice Movement"; Williams, *Rethinking the Black Freedom Movement*, 115; The Sierra Club, "Sierra Club Statement on Police Killings of Alton Sterling and Philando Castile," news release, July 7, 2016.

81 Kearns, "Saving the Creation," 56; Catholic Church and Francis, *Laudato Sí: On Care for Our Common Home* [Encyclical], May 24, 2015, http://w2.vatican.va/content/francesco/en/encyclicals/documents/papa-francesco_20150524_enciclica-laudato-si.html (accessed July 29, 2017).

82 Tik Root, "An Evangelical Movement Takes on Climate Change," *Newsweek*, March 9, 2016; Hochschild, *Strangers in Their Own Land*, 123.

83 Tik Root, "An Evangelical Movement Takes on Climate Change," *Newsweek*, March 9, 2016; John Schwartz, "Katharine Hayhoe: A Climate Explainer Who Stays above the Storm," *The New York Times*, October 10, 2016; "Historic Atlanta Church is Going Green," *Atlanta Journal Constitution*, August 2, 2016; Jumana Vasi, "Environmentalism and Islam: A Study of Muslim Women in the United States," *Research in Social Problems and Public Policy* 18 (2010): 451–84, 475; "Religious Environmentalism Timeline," *Chesapeake Quarterly* 15, no. 3 (October 2016) (accessed June 29, 2017).

84 Sellers, "How Republicans Came to Embrace Anti-environmentalism."

85 Sellers et al., *The EPA Under Siege*, 13.

86 Peter Baker and Coral Davenport, "Trump Revives Keystone Pipeline Rejected by Obama," *The New York Times*, January 24, 2017; Sellers et al., *The EPA Under Siege*, 54; Lisa Friedman, "Trump Wants to Repeal Obama's Climate Plan," *The New York Times*, September 28, 2017.

87 Nadja Popovich, Livia Albeck-Ripka, and Kendra Pierre-Louis, "78 Environmental Rules on the Way Out Under Trump," *The New York Times*, December 19, 2019; Joe Goffman, on Twitter, December 22, 2018; David Cutler and Francesca Dominici, "A Breath of Bad Air: Trump Environmental Agenda May Lead to 80,000 Extra Deaths per Decade," *JAMA*, May 10, 2018.

88 Philip Rucker and Robert Costa, "Bannon Vows a Daily Fight for 'Deconstruction of the Administrative State,'" *The Washington Post*, February 23, 2017; State Innovation Exchange, *2017 End-of-Session Report*, https://stateinnovation.org/wp-content/uploads/2017/08/2017-SiX-EOSR.pdf (accessed June 21, 2018).

89 Jennifer Yachnin, "Greens Decry Bishop's 'Amateurish McCarthy Tactics," *E&E News*, June 20, 2018; Kellie Lunney, "GOP Lawmakers Amplify Security Concerns of Enviro Suits," *E&E News*, June 14, 2018.

90 Noam Chomsky and David Barsamian, "Noam Chomsky Diagnoses the Trump Era," *The Nation*, October 3, 2017.

91 Kevin Bogardus, "EPA: 15,000 Employees in the 'Pipeline' at Agency," *Greenwire*, December 14, 2015; Kevin Bogardus, "EPA: Agency Sets Aside $12M for Buyouts," *E&E News*, May 19, 2017; Sellers et al., "The EPA under Siege," 5, 47, citing Environmental Protection Network, "Analysis of Trump Administration Proposals for FY2018 Budget for the Environmental Protection Agency," March 22, 2017, www.4cleanair.org/sites/default/files/Documents/EPA_Budget_Analysis_EPN_3-22-2017.pdf (accessed May 5, 2017).

92 Doreen Cantor Pastor et al. to Arthur A. Elkins, May 16, 2018, www.environmentalinteg rity.org/wp-content/uploads/2018/05/EPA-Veterans-Pruitt-Investigation-Letter.pdf (accessed May 21, 2018); Kevin Bogardus and Jeff Koss, "Pruitt's Chick-fil-A 'Opportunity' Grabs Inhofe's Attention," *E&E News*, June 5, 2018; Juliet Eilperin, Brady Dennis, Josh Dawsey, "Scott Pruitt Enlisted an EPA Aide to Help His Wife Find a Job – With Chick-fil-A," *Washington Post*, June 5, 2018; Steve Eder, Hiroko Tabuchi, and Eric Lipton, "EPA Chief Has Cozy Ties to Coal Baron," *The New York Times*, June 3, 2018, 1; Lisa Friedman, "13 Scott Pruitt Investigations: The Running List of E.P.A. Troubles," *The New York Times*, April 18, 2018.

93 Steve Eder, Hiroko Tabuchi, and Eric Lipton, "EPA Chief Has Cozy Ties to Coal Baron," *The New York Times*, June 3, 2018, 16; Dillon et al., "The EPA in the Early Trump Administration," S89.

94 Sellers et al., *The EPA Under Siege*, 38, 5; Sean Reilly, "EPA: 38 Science Advisers Get Pink Slips — Internal Email," *E&E News*, June 20, 2017; Sean Reilly, "Democrats Demand Answers on Quick 'Secret Science' Review," *E&E News*, May 9, 2018; Marianne Lavelle, "How Pruitt's 'Secret Science' Policy Could Further Undermine Air Pollution Rules," *Inside Climate News*, March 22, 2018; Emily Holden, "Anti-Secrecy Lawsuits Soaring against Pruitt's EPA," *Politico*, February 26, 2018.

95 Jack Gerard, "API's Gerard Talks 'Energy Dominance,' Administration's Oil and Gas Strategy," interview by Monica Trauzzi, *E&E TV*, August 1, 2017, www.eenews.net/ tv/videos/2243/transcript; Camille von Kaenel, "Trump Willing to Deal with Calif. on Auto Rules," *E&E News*, May 14, 2018.

96 Frederickson, Sullivan et al., *A Sheep in the Closet*, 9, 7; Timothy Cama, "EPA to Pursue Final 'Science Transparency' Rule in 2019," *The Hill*, December 14, 2018.

97 Brian Eckhouse, "Money Pours in to Sierra Club at Frantic Pace after Trump Victory," *Bloomberg*, November 16, 2016; Email message, Environmental Defense Fund Membership Director Sam Parry, September 23, 2017.

98 Sellers et al., *The EPA Under Siege*, 39; Teresa Myers, John Kotcher, John Cook, Lindsey Beall, Ed Maibach, *March for Science 2017: A Survey of Participants and Followers*, Fairfax: George Mason University Center for Climate Change Communication, April 2018, 6; Email message, March for Science, May 17, 2018.

99 Georgina Gustin, "Over 1,400 U.S. Cities, States and Businesses Vow to Meet Paris Climate Commitments," *Inside Climate News*, June 6, 2017; Editorial Board, "Hope in the Era of Trump's Climate Foolishness," *The New York Times*, June 2, 2018, A22; Joshua Busby, "3 Things We Learned at This Week's U.N. Climate Change Meeting," *The Washington Post*, November 17, 2017.

100 Amanda Reilly, "Clean Power Plan: States, Cities Oppose Trump Bid to Stall Litigation," *E&E News*, May 9, 2018; Camille von Kaenel, "Trump Willing to Deal with Calif. on Auto Rules," *E&E News*, May 14, 2018.

101 Adele Peters, "This Environmental Group Has Sued the Administration Every 8 Days," *Fast Company*, April 20, 2018; Jennifer Peters, "A Big Win for Clean Water," Clean Water Action, August 16, 2018, www.cleanwateraction.org/2018/08/16/ big-win-clean-water (accessed January 2, 2019); Ariel Wittenberg, "Salamanders to Whales: How Trump Rule Might Affect Wildlife," *E&E News*, December 19, 2018.

102 "About Us," Environmental Protection Network website, www.environmental protectionnetwork.org/about/ (accessed July 8, 2018); "About Save the U.S. EPA," https://savetheusepa.org/ (accessed May 21, 2018); "We Are Climate Hawks," Climate Hawks Vote, http://climatehawksvote.com/about/ (accessed June 18, 2018).

103 Email message, March for Science Action Network, May 17, 2018; "Mission," 314 Action, www.314action.org/mission-1 (accessed October 20, 2018); "League of Conservation Voters: Expenditures, 2016 cycle," Open Secrets, Center for Responsive Politics, www. opensecrets.org/pacs/expenditures.php?cycle=2016&cmte=C00486845 (accessed June 14, 2018).

104 Climate Hawks Vote supported candidates who won in California, Florida, Illinois, Michigan, New Mexico, Nevada, and Virginia, "Congrats Fossil Free Caucus," Climate Hawks Vote, November 8, 2018, http://climatehawksvote.com/news/congrats-fossil-free-caucus/ (accessed December 2, 2018); Chris D'Angelo, "Protecting Public Lands Was a Winning Platform in Elections Out West," *Grist*, November 17, 2018; Caitlin Byrd, "Amid Shutdown, U.S. Rep. Joe Cunningham Promises to File Bill Banning Offshore Drilling," [Palmetto, S.C.] *Post and Courier*, January 8, 2019, www.postand courier.com/politics/amid-shutdown-u-s-rep-joe-cunningham-promises-to-file/ article_f486951e-135a-11e9-923b-275a6c8f5d1e.html (accessed January 23, 2019).

105 Rob Hotakainen, "Sweeping Bill Creates Many Winners: 'This is a Big Deal,'" *E&E News*, February 15, 2019.

7

HOPE IN A STRANGE SEASON

The nation's growth has relied on the exploitation of nature and human labor but throughout American history diverse constituencies have also championed the natural rights of both. Twenty-first-century environmental activists draw on a long tradition of rights advocacy to frame their goals. From Benjamin Franklin's advocacy of the public's right to streams free of polluting wastes, to the framers' adoption of "natural rights," which as a guiding principle eventually exceeded their intent, to Cherokee women's embrace of "common rights" to the soil, and to the United Nations' declaration in 2005 that climate change is a human rights issue, ecological well-being has been framed as a question of rights. The young *Juliana v. U.S.* plaintiffs extend the demand to the right of future generations to be free of the environmental consequences of our current carbon economy.

Since at least the Progressive Era, America's civic leaders have recognized the government's duty to constrain the unchecked corporate exploitation of land, resources, and human health. Until the recent past, environmentally protective federal initiatives not only found bipartisan support but were often led by Republicans. In their long assault on environmental regulation, corporations have found fertile ground in a deindustrializing economy of their own making. Upon the spoils of rising inequality, the intense concentration of corporate wealth, and aided by lax campaign spending laws, corporations and conservative think tanks, law firms, and foundations demolished bipartisan support for environmental protections. Over the past few decades, most Republican office-holders have not only broken with their own tradition but reversed it, claiming that environmental laws and regulations represent federal overreach, are based in dubious science, and erect an unnecessary barrier to individual freedom and free enterprise.[1] Efforts to pack the courts with conservative judges who favor limited government underway since the Reagan era may constrain the judicial system as an effective arena for guaranteeing environmental protection for decades to come.

Under Trump, the executive branch has launched an assault on the administrative state itself, taking unilateral actions—in defiance of Congressional authority and public will—to undermine not only the most basic protections of clean air and clean water but also the rule of law. Offered free rein, oil and gas industrialists have begun helping themselves to formerly protected areas and offshore drilling sites with an abandon that harks to the Gilded Age. Before it ended in early 2019, the government shutdown over Trump's proposed border wall disproportionately impacted the EPA. Thirteen thousand of the agency's remaining 13,972 employees faced furloughs, effectively bringing the agency's critical environmental oversight functions to a halt. The shutdown highlighted the essential nature of the EPA's work. For example, the shutdown suspended cleanup at Superfund hazardous sites, and left the agency unable to respond to a Montana tribe's request to monitor contaminants in drinking water.[2]

Many activists now believe that demands for environmental protection must be paired with campaigns to fight economic and racial inequality, not only because justice demands it, nor even because such alliances are essential for building consensus for environmental protection, though they are. At root, structural inequalities sustain pollution and undermine environmental health. Deindustrialization often leaves disadvantaged communities more exposed to toxics than when factories were operating. The lead-polluted water supply in Flint, for example, cannot be separated from disinvestment in cities.[3]

Rebuilding bipartisanship is tied to fighting inequality. Environmental protection was a bipartisan aim in the rising economy of the 1960s. Republicans in Congress were in many cases almost unanimously in favor of environmental laws (the Clean Air Act of 1970, for example, passed seventy-three to zero in the Senate and 375 to one in the House.) But as income inequality sharpened beginning in the 1970s, consensus flagged.[4] Wielding anti-environmental rhetoric and legislative proposals among their political tools, conservatives bolstered their status within the party by building a political base among white working-class voters to capitalize on perceived decline.

In response to the Reagan era assault on environmental protections and numerous highly visible human-caused disasters—including Bhopal, Chernobyl, and the Exxon Valdez—public support for environmental protection was high again in the early 1990s, with 74 percent of the population favoring environmental improvements regardless of cost.[5] However, changes in both parties since that time—the decline of moderates and the rise of arch-conservatives in the Republican Party and the dominance of centrists in the Democratic leadership—has meant that activists found it difficult to advance environmental reforms even in Democratic administrations.

The U.S. once played a leadership role in the world on environmental issues. Now, the U.S. has fallen behind in key areas. The European Union in 2007 implemented an innovative precautionary plan for evaluating and regulating toxic chemicals before they are marketed. Powerful U.S. chemical interests ensured that hard-won toxics reform in the U.S. remains weak by comparison. Two decades into the twenty-first century, nowhere is the absence of U.S. leadership more consequential than in the arena of climate. Meanwhile, the Chinese government, for example, has invested heavily in the development and production of affordable renewable energy technologies, especially solar.[6]

Many environmental problems require global solutions, but increasingly contentious international politics make achieving environmentalists' goals more difficult. American triumphalism after the decline of the Cold War in the early 1990s has given way to unilateralism. China, Russia, and the U.S. are engaged in a "New Cold War," characterized by trade disputes, as well as intense cyber-spying and hacking. The trilateral arms race and economic battle for global power over fossil fuels have led to increasing uncertainty.[7] A rise in the quantity and technical capacity of nuclear weapons has made the world less safe against nuclear destruction. Terrorism destabilizes global conditions. Right-leaning nationalist movements have gained traction in the U.S., Europe, and Brazil. Repression of journalists and verbal and physical assaults on news outlets threaten freedom of the press and its ability to shine light on social problems, including environmental degradation.

Regaining the Initiative

In this strange season, the environmental movement is standing up to reclaim federal authority on the side of environmental protection, to defend science, and to protect policy gains. Can the environmental policy infrastructure that environmentalists and their allies have constructed over the past fifty years withstand the current onslaught? Pro-environment lawmakers shrewdly built in safeguards: EPA rules cannot be summarily changed; rulemaking procedures take time, require public hearings, and must consider written comment. By the terms of the Paris agreement, the U.S. cannot formally withdraw until November 4, 2020—one day after that year's presidential election. In the meantime, however, the U.S. has stopped contributing to the U.N. Green Climate Fund, threatening to scuttle major projects to mitigate anticipated damage from global warming.[8]

"In the very long view of biological evolution," writes environmental historian John R. McNeill, "the best survival strategy is to be adaptable, to pursue diverse sources of subsistence—and to maximize resilience." A resilient movement continues to strategically circumvent federal opposition through mass mobilizations, consumer boycotts and divestment campaigns, litigation, and green entrepreneurship, through personal commitments, and through pressure for government action at the local, state, and international levels. These strategies are creative and expand the reach and effectiveness of the movement. They are also essential, as organizations like the Sierra Club expect little environmental progress in the short term to come from the feds.[9]

Yet, if a healthy environment is a basic human right and nation-states exist to protect human rights, then restoring and extending a federal commitment to a healthy environment for all remains the central task. To that end, to cite one effort, in fall 2016, independent policy analysts and academics formed the Environmental Data and Governance Initiative (EDGI). The EDGI group monitors Trump administration reversals and works to preserve basic functions of government, including data collection. Based in part on interviews with present and former EPA staff, EDGI identified strategies that proved effective in resisting past assaults on legislative protections. The EDGI team calls for reviving the bipartisan pro-environment coalition in Congress and for spotlighting the regressive environmental and anti-science actions committed by federal agencies during the Trump administration. The movement itself must better articulate the need for protecting human health and the environment, they point out. In an agenda that underscores the power of protest, EDGI calls for activists to "[m]obilize effectively to support the EPA's environmental protections, science, and integrity, via media, protests, courtrooms, and the ballot box."[10]

Strengthening Alliances

Environmentalists have had the most wide-ranging impact when they have forged strong alliances among environmental organizations and with other constituencies, as when the labor–civil rights–environmental coalition defeated corporate polluters in the BASF and Shintech campaigns in Louisiana in the 1980s and 1990s. Promising intersectional initiatives exist on local and regional levels. In North Carolina, for example, the Moral Monday campaign, comprising 200 organizations, is anchored by the NAACP and led by state NAACP President Rev. William J. Barber, who calls his work "a moral fusion movement." Such coalitions recognize that protection of the environment is linked to the preservation of democracy, which requires renewed defense of the right to vote. Included in the group's fourteen-point People's Agenda, along with expanding voting rights, ending police assaults on African American men and women, and maintaining equal access to the state's once exemplary system of higher education, is an environmental justice job corps that seeks to "Put Young People to Work to Save the Environment and Work for Environmental Justice." In part as a result of their work, North Carolina has established an Environmental Justice and Equity Advisory Board to assist the state Department of Environmental Quality. Many other efforts also focus on training new activists. The group 350.org recently launched its Heart and Muscle Grassroots Climate Leadership training at the Highlander Research and Education Center in Tennessee, aligning its environmental work with the Center's nearly ninety-year history of labor and civil rights organizing.[11]

"[O]nly mass social movements can save us now," writes author and activist Naomi Klein. Meeting the present challenge calls for uniting the centrist technocratic and progressive social justice wings of the movement. A promising intersectional campaign attracting recent attention is the Green New Deal, inspired by the green jobs movement and climate activism. Outlined in Van Jones and Ariane Conrad's 2008 book, *The Green-Collar Economy*, and promoted by the Sunrise movement and others, the Green New Deal calls for achieving net-zero greenhouse gas emissions, creating high-wage jobs in the renewable energy sector, constructing a nationwide energy-efficient, "smart" grid, upgrading the built environment, and building resiliency against climate change using green technology and expertise. The Green New Deal has taken legislative form as a resolution introduced in early February 2019 in the U.S. House. Newly elected Rep. Alexandria Ocasio-Cortez advanced the proposal, which in early 2019 has the support of at least sixty Democratic members of Congress. The proposal seeks to make the United States "the international leader on climate action."[12]

A survey by researchers from Yale and George Mason University in late 2018 found that four out of five Americans would support such a proposal to move to 100 percent renewables within ten years and invest in green technology research, development, and job training. The Green New Deal garnered majority support in both parties, 92 percent of registered Democrats and 64 percent of registered Republicans.[13]

Though much of their focus is on climate change mitigation, Green New Deal proponents are advancing a broad agenda aimed at providing living wages and basic income, universal health care, and safe and affordable housing. The initiative specifically aims "to promote justice and equity. . .[for] 'frontline and vulnerable communities.'"[14]

"[W]e live in unnatural times," wrote Nigerian poet Ben Okri, in honor of Ken Saro-Wiwa before the Ogoni activist's 1995 execution, "and we must make them natural again with our singing and our intelligent rage." Ultimately, environmentalism not only asks us to reflect on the choices we make as individuals and the decisions we make as a society, but also urges us to act. Though it is impossible to predict which policy achievements of the past will survive in the short term, the field of movements has considerable strengths: a robust infrastructure of national and grassroots organizations, multiple constituencies, and a considerable history of collaborating with allied social movements in intersectional campaigns. More often than not, environmentalism has served to expand democracy. Movement participants have experience, deep roots in American culture, and willing global partners upon which to draw. Despite weaknesses, environmentalism has been and remains a remarkably resilient and multi-faceted force for progressive social change. In the Anthropocene, protecting the environment is both a sprint and a marathon. Sen. Gaylord Nelson's words, delivered at the first celebration of Earth Day, still resonate: continuing to transform human relationships with the environment for the better "will take a commitment beyond anything we have done before."[15]

Notes

1 Turner and Isenberg, *The Republican Reversal*, 6–7.
2 U.S. EPA, "Contingency Plan for Shutdown," December 31, 2018, www.epa. gov/sites/production/files/2019-02/documents/epa_contingency_plan_decem ber_31_2018-508.pdf (accessed January 4, 2019); Associated Press, "Shutdown Suspends Federal Cleanups at Contaminated Superfund Sites," *NBC News*, January 11, 2019.
3 Kevin T. Smiley, "Industrial Pollution and Civic Capacity in Metropolitan America," Ph.D. Diss., Rice University, 2017, 11.
4 Turner and Isenberg, *The Republican Reversal*, 12; Purdy, "Environmentalism Was Once a Social-Justice Movement."
5 Dunlap, "Trends in Public Opinion," 300.
6 "Solar: Italy makes last-ditch attempt to catch China," *E&E News*, August 20, 2018.
7 Michael Klare, "The New Geopolitics," *Monthly Review* 55, no. 3 (July–August 2003), www.monthlyreview.org/0703klare.htm, (accessed January 23, 2019); Robert D. Kaplan, "A New Cold War Has Begun," *Foreign Policy.com*, January 7, 2019, https:// foreignpolicy.com/2019/01/07/a-new-cold-war-has-begun/ (accessed January 23, 2019).
8 Congress voted for and the President signed a spending bill that includes climate funding, but not through the Green Climate Fund. Jean Chemnick, "Climate Aid Survives in Trump-signed Spending Plan," *E&E News*, February 22, 2019.
9 John R. McNeill, *Something New Under the Sun*, xxii; Jason Mark, "The Most Important Environmental Stories of 2018," *Sierra*, December 18, 2018, www.sierraclub.org/ sierra/most-important-environmental-stories-2018 (accessed January 3, 2019).
10 Sellers et al., *The EPA Under Siege*, 5.
11 Rev. Dr. William Barber (@RevDrBarber), "It's time for a moral fusion movement to take direct action to reconstruct America. It's time for a #PoorPeoplesCampaign," Twitter, April 10, 2018, 6:39 p.m.; Rev. Dr. William Barber, "Ask Anything: 10 questions with NAACP President Rev. William Barber," interview by WRAL, *WRAL. com*, December 16, 2008, www.wral.com/ask-anything-10-questions-with-naacp-president-rev-william-barber/4142989/?comment_order=forward; Claudia Geib, "Environmental Problems Go Hand In Hand With Social Injustice. North Carolina Wants to End That," *Futurism*, May 7, 2018, https://futurism.com/environmental-injustice-north-carolina.
12 Klein, *This Changes Everything*, 450; Jones and Conrad, *The Green-Collar Economy*, 79ff; House Resolution 109, Recognizing the Duty of the Federal Government to Create a Green New Deal, H.R. Res. 109, 116th Cong. (2019).
13 Abel Gustafson et al., "The Green New Deal."
14 House Resolution 109, Recognizing the Duty of the Federal Government to Create a Green New Deal, H.R. Res. 109, 116th Cong. (2019).
15 "For Ken Saro-Wiwa," Ben Okri, cited in Andrew Rowell, *Green Backlash*, xv; Jundt, *Greening the Red, White, and Blue*, 16; Bob Monroe, Associated Press, "Dirty World Cranks Back Up after 'Spic and Span' Effort," *The Birmingham News*, April 23, 1970, 1.

BIBLIOGRAPHY

Special Reports

Adams, John H., Louise C. Dunlap, Jay D. Hair, Frederic D. Krupp, Jack Lorenz, J. Michael McCloskey, Russell W. Peterson, Paul C. Pritchard, William A. Turnage, and Karl Wendelowski, edited by Robert Cahn. *An Environmental Agenda for the Future.* Washington, D.C.: Island Press, 1985.

Agenda 21: Programme of Action for Sustainable Development, United Nations Conference on Environment and Development (UNCED), June 3–14, 1992, Rio De Janeiro, Brazil. New York: United Nations Dept. of Public Information, 1993.

Alston, Dana A. *Taking Back Our Lives. A Report to the Panos Institute on Environment, Community Development and Race in the United States.* Washington, D.C.: Panos Institute, 1990.

———. *We Speak for Ourselves: Social Justice, Race, and the Environment.* Washington, D.C.: Panos Institute, 1990.

Bullard, Robert D., Paul Mohai, Robin Saha, Beverly Wright. *Toxic Wastes and Race at Twenty: 1987–2007: Grassroots Struggles to Dismantle Environmental Racism in the United States.* Cleveland: United Church of Christ Justice and Witness Ministries, 2007.

Catholic Church and Francis. *Laudato Si': On Care for Our Common Home.* Rome: Vatican Press, 2015.

Commission for Racial Justice, United Church of Christ. *Toxic Wastes and Race in the United States: A National Report on the Racial and Socioeconomic Characteristics of Communities with Hazardous Waste Sites.* New York: United Church of Christ, 1987.

Frederickson, Leif, Marianne Sullivan, Christopher Sellers, Jennifer Ohayon, Ellen Kohl Sarah Lamdan, Alissa Cordner, Alice Hu, Katarzyna Kaczowka, Natalia Navas, and Linda Wicks. *A Sheep in the Closet: The Erosion of Enforcement at the EPA.* Environmental Data & Governance Initiative (EDGI), November 2018.

Gustafson, Abel, Seth Rosentahl, Anthony Leiserowitz, Edward Maiback, John Kotcher, Matthew Ballew, and Matthew Golldberg. "The Green New Deal Has Strong Bipartisan Support." Yale Center for Climate Change Communication and the George Mason University Center for Climate Change Communication, December 14, 2018.

Hall, Bob and Mary Lee Kerr. *1991–1992 Green Index: A State-by-State Guide to the Nation's Environmental Health.* Institute for Southern Studies. Washington, D.C.: Island Press, 1991.

Harden, Monique, Nathalie Walker, and Kali Akuno. *Racial Discrimination and Ethnic Cleansing in the United States in the Aftermath of Hurricane Katrina: A Report to the United Nations' Committee for the Elimination of Racial Discrimination.* New Orleans: Advocates for Environmental Human Rights, 2007.

National Association for the Advancement of Colored People, Indigenous Environmental Network, Little Village Environmental Justice Organization. *Coal Blooded: Putting Profits Before People.* Baltimore: NAACP, 2012.

National Commission on the BP Deepwater Horizon Oil Spill and Offshore Drilling. *Deep Water: The Gulf Oil Disaster and the Future of Offshore Drilling, Report to the President.* Washington, D.C.: Government Printing Office, January 2011.

Sellers, Christopher, Lindsey Dillon, Jennifer Liss Ohayon, Nick Shapiro, Marianne Sullivan, Chris Amoss, Stephen Bocking, Phil Brown, Vanessa De la Rosa, Jill Harrison, Sara Johns, Katherine Kulik, Rebecca Lave, Michelle Murphy, Liza Piper, Lauren Richter, Sara Wylie. *The EPA under Siege: Trump's Assault in History and Testimony.* Environmental Data & Governance Initiative (EDGI), June 2017.

Taylor, Dorceta E. *Diversity in Environmental Organizations: Reporting and Transparency.* Report No. 1. University of Michigan, School for Environment and Sustainability, January 2018.

_____. *The State of Diversity in Environmental Organizations,* edited by Green 2.0. Ann Arbor: School of Natural Resources and the Environment, University of Michigan, 2014.

United Nations, *Our Common Future – Brundtland Report.* Cambridge; New York: Oxford University Press, 1987.

UNESCO. *Proceedings and Papers, International Technical Conference for the Protection of Nature (ITCPN).* Lake Success, N.Y., August 22–29, 1949, edited by the Secretariat of the International Union for the Protection of Nature. Paris: United Nations Educational, Scientific, and Cultural Organization, 1950.

UNSCCUR. *Proceedings of the United Nations Scientific Conference on the Conservation and Utilization of Resources. Plenary Meetings.* Lake Success, N.Y., August 17–September 6, 1949. Lake Success, N.Y.: United Nations Department of Economic Affairs, 1950.

U.S. General Accounting Office. *Siting of Hazardous Waste Landfills and Their Correlation with Racial and Economic Status of Surrounding Communities.* RCED-83–168: June 1, 1983.

Books

Abbey, Edward. *Abbey's Road.* New York: Dutton, 1979.

_____. *The Monkey Wrench Gang.* Philadelphia: Lippincott, 1975.

Adams, John H., Patricia Adams, and George Black. *A Force for Nature: The Story of NRDC and the Fight to Save Our Planet.* San Francisco: Chronicle Books, 2010.

Agyeman, Julian, Robert D. Bullard, and Bob Evans. *Just Sustainabilities: Development in an Unequal World.* Cambridge: MIT Press, 2003.

Alaimo, Stacy. *Bodily Natures: Science, Environment, and the Material Self.* Bloomington: Indiana University Press, 2010.

_____. *Undomesticated Ground: Recasting Nature as Feminist Space.* Ithaca: Cornell University Press, 2000.

Allen, Barbara L. *Uneasy Alchemy: Citizens and Experts in Louisiana's Chemical Corridor Disputes.* Cambridge: MIT Press, 2003.

Ammon, Francesca Russello. *Bulldozer: Demolition and Clearance in a Postwar Landscape.* New Haven and London: Yale University Press, 2016.

Anderson, Ray C. *Mid-Course Correction: Toward a Sustainable Enterprise: The Interface Model.* Atlanta: Peregrinzilla Press, 1998.

Andrews, Richard N. L. *Managing the Environment, Managing Ourselves: A History of American Environmental Policy.* 2nd ed. New Haven: Yale University Press, 2006.

Armiero, Marco, and Lise Sedrez. *A History of Environmentalism: Local Struggles, Global Histories.* London; New York: Bloomsbury Academic, 2014.

Armitage, Kevin C. *The Nature Study Movement: The Forgotten Popularizer of America's Conservation Ethic.* Lawrence: University Press of Kansas, 2009.

Barber, Daniel A. *A House in the Sun: Modern Architecture and Solar Energy in the Cold War* Oxford: Oxford University Press, 2016.

Beck, Ulrich. *World at Risk.* Malden: Polity Press, 2009.

Berghoff, Hartmut, and Adam Rome, eds. *Green Capitalism? Business and the Environment in the Twentieth Century.* Philadelphia: University of Pennsylvania Press, 2017.

Bigelow, Albert. *The Voyage of the Golden Rule; An Experiment with Truth.* Garden City: Doubleday, 1959.

Blackstone, William T., ed. *Philosophy and Environmental Crisis.* Athens: University of Georgia Press, 1972.

Blum, Elizabeth D. *Love Canal Revisited: Race, Class, and Gender in Environmental Activism.* Lawrence: University Press of Kansas, 2008.

Bohme, Susanna Rankin. *Toxic Injustice: A Transnational History of Exposure and Struggle.* Oakland: University of California Press, 2015.

Bond, Patrick. *Politics of Climate Justice: Paralysis Above, Movement Below.* Scottsville, South Africa: University of Kwazulu-Natal Press, 2012.

Boyer, Paul S. *By the Bomb's Early Light: American Thought and Culture at the Dawn of the Atomic Age.* Chapel Hill: University of North Carolina Press, 1994.

Brinkley, Douglas. *Rightful Heritage: Franklin D. Roosevelt and the Land of America.* New York: HarperCollins, 2016.

———. *The Wilderness Warrior: Theodore Roosevelt and the Crusade for America.* New York: HarperCollins, 2009.

Brown, Phil. *Toxic Exposures: Contested Illnesses and the Environmental Health Movement.* New York: Columbia University Press, 2007.

Brown, Phil, and Edwin J. Mikkelson. *No Safe Place: Toxic Waste, Leukemia, and Community Action.* Berkeley: University of California Press, 1990. Reprint, 1997.

Brugge, Doug, Timothy Benally, and Esther Yazzie-Lewis. *The Navajo People and Uranium Mining.* Albuquerque: University of New Mexico Press, 2006.

Brulle, Robert J. *Agency, Democracy, and Nature: The U.S. Environmental Movement from a Critical Theory Perspective.* Cambridge: MIT Press, 2000.

Bryant, Bunyan I., and Paul Mohai. *Race and the Incidence of Environmental Hazards: A Time for Discourse.* Boulder: Westview Press, 1992.

Buell, Lawrence. *The American Transcendentalists: Essential Writings.* The Modern Library Classics. New York: Modern Library, 2006.

Bullard, Robert D., ed. *Confronting Environmental Racism: Voices from the Grassroots.* Boston: South End Press, 1993.

———. *Dumping in Dixie: Race, Class, and Environmental Quality.* Boulder: Westview Press, 1990.

———, ed. *Unequal Protection: Environmental Justice and Communities of Color.* San Francisco: Sierra Club Books, 1994.

Camacho, David E. *Environmental Injustices, Political Struggles: Race, Class, and the Environment.* Durham: Duke University Press, 1998.

Carson, Rachel. *Silent Spring.* 40th anniversary ed. Introduction by Linda Lear. Boston: Houghton Mifflin, [1962], 2002.

Chaplin, Joyce E. *The First Scientific American: Benjamin Franklin and the Pursuit of Genius.* New York: Basic Books, 2006.

Cherniack, Martin. *The Hawk's Nest Incident: America's Worst Industrial Disaster.* New Haven: Yale University Press, 1986.

Churchill, Ward. *Struggle for the Land: Native North American Resistance to Genocide, Ecocide, and Colonization.* San Francisco: City Lights, 2002.

Clapp, Jennifer, and Peter Dauvergne. *Paths to a Green World: The Political Economy of the Global Environment.* 2nd ed. Cambridge: MIT Press, 2011.

Clark, Claudia. *Radium Girls, Women and Industrial Health Reform: 1910–1935.* Chapel Hill: University of North Carolina Press, 1997.

Clark, Ray and Larry Canter, eds. *Environmental Policy and NEPA: Past, Present and Future* Boca Raton: St. Lucie Press, 1997.

Clarke, Robert. *Ellen Swallow: The Woman Who Founded Ecology.* Chicago: Follett, 1973.

Colborn, Theo, John Peterson Myers, and Dianne Dumanoski. *Our Stolen Future: Are We Threatening Our Fertility, Intelligence, and Survival? A Scientific Detective Story.* New York: Dutton, 1996.

Cole, Luke W., and Sheila R. Foster. *From the Ground Up: Environmental Racism and the Rise of the Environmental Justice Movement.* New York: New York University Press, 2001.

Collins, Sheila D. *The Rainbow Challenge: The Jackson Campaign and the Future of U.S. Politics.* New York: Monthly Review Press, 1986.

Commoner, Barry. *Science and Survival.* New York: Viking Press, 1966.

———. *The Closing Circle; Nature, Man, and Technology.* New York: Knopf, 1971.

Crane, Jeff and Michael Egan, eds. *Natural Protest: Essays on the History of American Environmentalism.* New York; London: Routledge, 2009.

Cronon, William. *Changes in the Land: Indians, Colonists, and the Ecology of New England.* New York: Hill and Wang, 1983.

———. ed. *Uncommon Ground: Rethinking the Human Place in Nature.* New York: W.W. Norton & Co., 1996.

Crosby, Alfred W. *Ecological Imperialism: The Biological Expansion of Europe, 900–1900.* Cambridge; New York: Cambridge University Press, 1986.

Darwin, Charles. Introduction and Notes by George Levine. *The Origin of Species by Means of Natural Selection.* New York: Barnes & Noble, 2004, orig. publ. 1859.

Dauvergne, Peter. *Environmentalism of the Rich.* Cambridge: MIT Press, 2016.

Davis, Devra Lee. *When Smoke Ran Like Water: Tales of Environmental Deception and the Battle against Pollution.* New York: Basic Books, 2002.

Davis, Jack E. *An Everglades Providence: Marjory Stoneman Douglas and the American Environmental Century.* Athens: University of Georgia Press, 2009.

———. *The Gulf: The Making of an American Sea.* New York: Norton, 2017.

Doron, Roy, and Toyin Falola, *Ken Saro-Wiwa.* Athens: Ohio University Press, 2016.

Dowie, Mark. *Losing Ground: American Environmentalism at the Close of the Twentieth Century.* Cambridge: MIT Press, 1995.

Downs, Jim. *Sick from Freedom: African-American Illness and Suffering During the Civil War and Reconstruction.* New York: Oxford University Press, 2012.

Drake, Brian Allen. *Loving Nature, Fearing the State: Environmentalism and Antigovernment Politics before Reagan.* Seattle: University of Washington Press, 2013.

Druley, Ray M., and Girard Lanterman Ordway. *The Toxic Substances Control Act*. Rev. ed. Washington, D.C.: Bureau of National Affairs, 1981.

Dunlap, Riley E., and Angela G. Mertig. *American Environmentalism: The U.S. Environmental Movement, 1970–1990*. Philadelphia: Taylor & Francis, 1992.

Edge, John T. *The Potlikker Papers: A Food History of the Modern South 1955–2015*. New York City: Penguin Press, 2017.

Egan, Michael. *Barry Commoner and the Science of Survival: The Remaking of American Environmentalism*. Cambridge: MIT Press, 2007.

Ehrlich, Paul R. *The Population Bomb*. Rev. & expanded ed. New York: Ballantine Books, 1971.

Ekbladh, David. *The Great American Mission: Modernization and the Construction of an American World Order*. Princeton: Princeton University Press, 2010.

Emerson, Ralph Waldo, Oliver Wendell Holmes Collection (Library of Congress) and John Davis Batchelder Collection (Library of Congress). *Nature*. Boston: J. Munroe and Company, 1836.

Emmett, Robert S. *Cultivating Environmental Justice: A Literary History of U.S. Garden Writing*. Amherst: University of Massachusetts Press, 2016.

Feher, Michel. *Nongovernmental Politics*. New York; Cambridge: Zone Books; distributed by MIT Press, 2007.

Fiege, Mark. *The Republic of Nature: An Environmental History of the United States*. Seattle: University of Washington Press, 2012.

Finney, Carolyn. *Black Faces, White Spaces: Reimagining the Relationship of African Americans to the Great Outdoors*. Chapel Hill: University of North Carolina Press, 2014.

Finseth, Ian Frederick. *Shades of Green: Visions of Nature in the Literature of American Slavery, 1770–1860*. Athens: University of Georgia Press, 2009.

Fischer, Frank. *Citizens, Experts and the Environment: The Politics of Local Knowledge*. Durham; London: Duke University Press, 2000.

Foreman, Dave. *Ecodefense: A Field Guide to Monkeywrenching*. Tucson: Earth First! Books, 1985.

Fortun, Kim. *Advocacy after Bhopal: Environmentalism, Disaster, New Global Orders*. Chicago: University of Chicago Press, 2001.

Fox, Stephen R. *The American Conservation Movement: John Muir and His Legacy*. Madison: University of Wisconsin Press, 1985.

Frederickson, Kari A. *Cold War Dixie: Militarization and Modernization in the American South, Politics and Culture in the Twentieth-Century South*. Athens: University of Georgia Press, 2013.

Furmansky, Dyana Z. (Zaslowsky, Dyan). *Rosalie Edge, Hawk of Mercy: The Activist Who Saved Nature from the Conservationists*. Athens: University of Georgia Press, 2009.

George, Henry. *Progress and Poverty*. New York: J. W. Lovell Company, 1882.

Gibbs, Lois Marie. *Love Canal: My Story*, with Murray Levine. Albany: State University of New York Press, 1982.

Gibbs, Lois Marie. *Love Canal: The Story Continues. . .* Gabriola Island: New Society Publishers, 1998.

Giddens, Anthony. *The Politics of Climate Change*. Cambridge; Malden: Polity, 2009.

Glave, Dianne D., and Mark Stoll. *To Love the Wind and the Rain: African Americans and Environmental History*. Pittsburgh: University of Pittsburgh Press, 2006.

Global Witness. *Defenders of the Earth: Killings of Land and Environment Defenders in 2016*. London: Global Witness, 2017.

Goodwin, Jeff, and James M. Jasper. *The Social Movements Reader: Cases and Concepts*. Malden; Oxford: Wiley Blackwell, 2015.

Goodyear-Kàōpua, Noelani, Ikaika Hussey, and Erin Kahunawaikàala Wright. *A Nation Rising: Hawaiian Movements for Life, Land, and Sovereignty.* Durham: Duke University Press, 2014.

Gore, Albert. *Earth in the Balance: Ecology and the Human Spirit.* Boston: Houghton Mifflin, 1992.

Gottlieb, Robert. *Forcing the Spring: The Transformation of the American Environmental Movement.* Washington, D.C.: Island Press, 1993, 2005.

Gregg, Richard Bartlett. *The Power of Nonviolence.* [2d rev. ed. Nyack: Fellowship Publications, 1959. [1st. ed. Philadelphia: J.B. Lippincott, 1934.]

Grossman, Zoltán. *Unlikely Alliances: Native and White Communities Join to Defend Rural Lands.* Seattle: University of Washington Press, 2017.

Grove, Richard. *Green Imperialism: Colonial Expansion, Tropical Island Edens, and the Origins of Environmentalism, 1600–1860.* Cambridge; New York: Cambridge University Press, 1995.

Guha, Ramachandra, and Joan Martínez Alier. *Varieties of Environmentalism: Essays North and South.* 1st Indian ed. Delhi; New York: Oxford University Press, 1998.

Hardenberg, Wilko Graf von. *The Nature State: Rethinking the History of Conservation.* Routledge Environmental Humanities. London; New York: Routledge, Taylor & Francis Group, 2017.

Harkin, Michael Eugene, and David Rich Lewis. *Native Americans and the Environment: Perspectives on the Ecological Indian.* Lincoln: University of Nebraska Press, 2007.

Harris, Robert, and Jeremy Paxman. *A Higher Form of Killing: The Secret Story of Chemical and Biological Warfare.* New York: Hill and Wang, 1982.

Harvey, David. *A Brief History of Neoliberalism.* Oxford; New York: Oxford University Press, 2005.

———. *Justice, Nature and the Geography of Difference.* Malden: Blackwell Publishers, 1996.

Harvey, Mark W.T. *A Symbol of Wilderness: Echo Park and the American Conservation Movement.* Albuquerque: University of New Mexico Press, 1994.

———. *Wilderness Forever: Howard Zahniser and the Path to the Wilderness Act.* Seattle: University of Washington Press, 2005.

Hawken, Paul. *The Ecology of Commerce: A Declaration of Sustainability.* New York: HarperCollins Publishers, 1993.

Hawken, Paul, Amory B. Lovins, and L. Hunter Lovins. *Natural Capitalism: Creating the Next Industrial Revolution.* 1st ed. Boston: Little, Brown and Co., 1999.

Hays, Samuel P. *Conservation and the Gospel of Efficiency: The Progressive Conservation Movement, 1890–1920.* Cambridge: Harvard University Press, 1959.

———. *A History of Environmental Politics since 1945.* Pittsburgh: University of Pittsburgh Press, 2000.

Hays, Samuel P., in collaboration with Barbara D. Hays. *Beauty, Health, and Permanence: Environmental Politics in the United States, 1955–1985.* Cambridge; New York: Cambridge University Press, 1987.

Hersey, John. *Hiroshima.* New York: A.A. Knopf, 1946.

Hersey, Mark D. *"My Work Is That of Conservation": An Environmental Biography of George Washington Carver.* Athens: University of Georgia Press, 2011.

Hochschild, Arlie Russell. *Strangers in Their Own Land: Anger and Mourning on the American Right.* New York: New Press, 2016.

Horne, Jed. *Breach of Faith: Hurricane Katrina and the near Death of a Great American City.* New York: Random House, 2006.

Howard, Ebenezer, and Frederic James Osborn. *Garden Cities of to-Morrow.* Cambridge: MIT Press, 1965 [first publ. 1902].

Howe, Joshua P., ed. *Making Climate Change History: Documents from Global Warming's Past*. Seattle: University of Washington Press, 2017.

Intondi, Vincent J. *African Americans against the Bomb: Nuclear Weapons, Colonialism, and the Black Freedom Movement*. Stanford: Stanford University Press, 2014.

Ioris, Antonio Augusto Rossotto. *The Political Ecology of the State: The Basis and the Evolution of Environmental Statehood*. London: Routledge, 2014.

Isenberg, Andrew C., ed., *The Oxford Handbook of Environmental History*. Oxford; New York: Oxford University Press, 2014.

Iversen, Kristen. *Full Body Burden: Growing up in the Nuclear Shadow of Rocky Flats*. New York: Crown Publishers, 2012.

Jacobs, Jane. *The Death and Life of Great American Cities*. New York: Modern Library, 1993, orig. publ., 1961.

Jacobs, Meg. *Panic at the Pump: The Energy Crisis and the Transformation of American Politics in the 1970s*. New York: Hill and Wang, 2016.

Jones, Karen R. *Epiphany in the Wilderness: Hunting, Nature, and Performance in the Nineteenth-Century American West*. Boulder: University Press of Colorado, 2015.

Jones, Van, and Ariane Conrad. *The Green-Collar Economy: How One Solution Can Fix Our Two Biggest Problems*. New York: HarperOne, 2008.

Jordan, Jeffrey L., Edward Pennick, Walter A. Hill, Robert Zabawa, *Land and Power: Sustainable Agriculture and African Americans*. Waldorf: Sustainable Agriculture Research and Education Program, 2009.

Jundt, Thomas. *Greening the Red, White, and Blue: The Bomb, Big Business, and Consumer Resistance in Postwar America*. Oxford: Oxford University Press, 2014.

Kiechle, Melanie A. *Smell Detectives: An Olfactory History of Nineteenth-Century Urban America*. Seattle: University of Washington Press, 2017.

Kilcup, Karen L. *Fallen Forests: Emotion, Embodiment, and Ethics in American Women's Environmental Writing, 1781–1924*. Athens: University of Georgia Press, 2013.

Kinchy, Abby J. *Seeds, Science, and Struggle: The Global Politics of Transgenic Crops*. Food, Health, and the Environment. Cambridge: MIT Press, 2012.

Kingsland, Sharon E., *The Evolution of American Ecology, 1890–2000*. Baltimore: Johns Hopkins University Press, 2005.

Kirby, Jack Temple. *Rural Worlds Lost: The American South, 1920–1960*. Baton Rouge: Louisiana State University Press, 1987.

Klare, Michael T. *Resource Wars: The New Landscape of Global Conflict*. New York: Metropolitan, 2002.

Klein, Naomi. *This Changes Everything: Capitalism Vs. The Climate*. New York: Simon & Schuster, 2014.

Konisky, David M. *Failed Promises: Evaluating the Federal Government's Response to Environmental Justice*. Cambridge: MIT Press, 2015.

Kosek, Jake. *Understories: The Political Life of Forests in Northern New Mexico*. Durham: Duke University Press, 2006.

Krech, Shepard. *The Ecological Indian: Myth and History*. 1st ed. New York: W.W. Norton & Co., 1999.

Kress, W. John and Jeffrey Stine, eds. *Living in the Anthropocene: Humanity in the Age of Humans*. Washington, D.C.: Smithsonian Books, 2017.

LaDuke, Winona. *All Our Relations: Native Struggles for Land and Life*. Cambridge; Minneapolis: South End Press; Honor the Earth, 1999.

Langston, Nancy. *Toxic Bodies: Hormone Disruptors and the Legacy of DES*. New Haven: Yale University Press, 2010.

Lappé, Frances Moore. *Diet for a Small Planet*. New York: Ballantine Books, 1971.

Lear, Linda J. *Rachel Carson: Witness for Nature*. 1st ed. New York: Henry Holt, 1997.

Leopold, Aldo. *A Sand County Almanac: With Essays on Conservation from Round River*. New York: Ballantine Books, 1966 [1949].

Leopold, Aldo and Allan Brooks, *Game Management*. New York; London: C. Scribner's Sons, 1933.

Lerner, Steve. *Sacrifice Zones: The Front Lines of Toxic Chemical Exposure in the United States*. Cambridge: MIT Press, 2010.

Liroff, Richard A. *A National Policy for the Environment: NEPA and Its Aftermath*. Bloomington: Indiana University Press, 1976.

Loewen, James W. *Sundown Towns: A Hidden Dimension of American Racism*. New York: New Press: Distributed in the United States by Norton, 2005.

Loomis, Erik. *Empire of Timber: Labor Unions and the Pacific Northwest Forests*. New York: Cambridge University Press, 2016.

Lovelock, James. *Gaia: A New Look at Life on Earth*. London; New York: Oxford University Press, 1979.

Lovins, Amory B. *Soft Energy Paths: Toward a Durable Peace*. San Francisco; Cambridge: Friends of the Earth International, 1977.

Lowenthal, David. *George Perkins Marsh, Prophet of Conservation*. Seattle: University of Washington Press, 2000.

Macdonald, Peggy. *Marjorie Harris Carr: Defenders of Florida's Environment*. Gainesville: University Press of Florida, 2014.

Maher, Neil M. *Nature's New Deal: The Civilian Conservation Corps and the Roots of the American Environmental Movement*. Oxford; New York: Oxford University Press, 2008.

Malone, David, and Yuen Foong Khong, *Unilateralism and U.S. Foreign Policy: International Perspectives*. Center on International Cooperation Studies in Multilateralism. Boulder: Lynne Rienner Publishers, 2003.

Mann, Charles C. *The Wizard and the Prophet: Two Remarkable Scientists and Their Dueling Visions to Shape Tomorrow's World*. New York: Alfred A. Knopf, 2018.

Marcuse, Herbert. *One-Dimensional Man; Studies in the Ideology of Advanced Industrial Society*. Boston: Beacon Press, 1964.

Markowitz, Gerald E. and David Rosner. *Deceit and Denial: The Deadly Politics of Industrial Pollution*. Berkeley; Los Angeles: University of California Press, 2002.

Marsh, George P., and David Lowenthal. *Man and Nature: Or, Physical Geography as Modified by Human Action*. Seattle: University of Washington Press, 2003, orig. publ. 1864.

Martínez-Alier, Joan, *The Environmentalism of the Poor: A Study of Ecological Conflicts and Valuation*. Northampton; Cheltenham: Edward Elgar, 2002.

Marx, Leo. *The Machine in the Garden; Technology and the Pastoral Ideal in America*. New York: Oxford University Press, 1964.

Mauch, Christof, Nathan Stoltzfus, and Douglas R. Weiner. *Shades of Green: Environmental Activism around the Globe, International Environmental History*. Lanham: Rowman & Littlefield Publishers, 2006.

Maysilles, Duncan. *Ducktown Smoke: The Fight Over One of the South's Greatest Environmental Disasters*. Chapel Hill: University of North Carolina Press, 2011.

McCammack, Brian. *Landscapes of Hope: Nature and the Great Migration in Chicago*. Cambridge; London: Harvard University Press, 2017.

McCormick, John. *Reclaiming Paradise: The Global Environmental Movement*. Bloomington: Indiana University Press, 1989.

McGirr, Lisa. *Suburban Warriors: The Origins of the New American Right. Politics and Society in Twentieth-Century America.* 2nd ed. Princeton: Princeton University Press, 2015.

McGurty, Eileen Maura. *Transforming Environmentalism: Warren County, PCBs, and the Origins of Environmental Justice.* New Brunswick: Rutgers University Press, 2007.

McKibben, Bill. *The End of Nature.* 1st ed. New York: Random House, 1989.

McKibben, Bill, and Albert Gore. *American Earth: Environmental Writing since Thoreau.* New York: Literary Classics of the United States: Distributed to the trade by Penguin Putnam, 2008.

McNeill, John Robert. *Something New under the Sun: An Environmental History of the Twentieth-Century World.* 1st ed. New York: W.W. Norton & Company, 2000.

McNeill, John Robert, Corinna R. Unger, and German Historical Institute. *Environmental Histories of the Cold War.* Washington, D.C.; New York: German Historical Institute; Cambridge University Press, 2010.

McNeill, John Robert, and Peter Engelke. *The Great Acceleration: An Environmental History of the Anthropocene since 1945.* Cambridge: The Belknap Press of Harvard University Press, 2014.

McNeur, Catherine. *Taming Manhattan: Environmental Battles in the Antebellum City.* Cambridge: Harvard University Press, 2014.

McPhee, John, *Encounters with the Archdruid.* New York: Farrar, 1971.

Meadows, Donella H., Dennis L. Meadows, Jorgen Randers, William W Behrens III, and Club of Rome. *The Limits to Growth: A Report for the Club of Rome's Project on the Predicament of Mankind.* New York: A Potomac Associates Book, New American Library, 1974.

Melosi, Martin V. *The Sanitary City: Urban Infrastructure in America from Colonial Times to the Present.* Baltimore: Johns Hopkins University Press, 2000.

Melosi, Martin V. and Joseph A. Pratt, eds. *Energy Metropolis: An Environmental History of Houston and the Gulf Coast.* Pittsburgh: University of Pittsburgh Press, 2007.

Merchant, Carolyn. *American Environmental History: An Introduction.* New York: Columbia University Press, 2007.

———. *Earthcare: Women and the Environment.* New York: Routledge, 1996.

———. *Radical Ecology: The Search for a Livable World.* New York: Routledge, 1992.

———. *The Death of Nature: Women, Ecology, and the Scientific Revolution.* 1st ed. San Francisco: Harper & Row, 1980.

Mies, Maria, and Vandana Shiva. *Ecofeminism.* Halifax, N.S. London; Atlantic Highlands: Fernwood Publications; Zed Books, 1993.

Minchin, Timothy J. *Forging a Common Bond: Labor and Environmental Activism During the BASF Lockout.* Gainesville: University Press of Florida, 2003.

Misrach, Richard, and Kate Orff. *Petrochemical America.* New York: Aperture, 2012.

Mitman, Gregg. *Breathing Space: How Allergies Shape Our Lives and Landscapes.* New Haven: Yale University Press, 2007.

Moberg, Carol L. *René Dubos, Friend of the Good Earth: Microbiologist, Medical Scientist, Environmentalist.* Washington, D.C.: ASM Press, 2005.

Montrie, Chad. *The Myth of Silent Spring: Rethinking the Origins of American Environmentalism.* Oakland: University of California Press, 2018.

Morris, Aldon D., and Carol McClurg Mueller. *Frontiers in Social Movement Theory.* New Haven: Yale University Press, 1992.

Morton, Oliver. *The Planet Remade: How Geoengineering Could Change the World.* Princeton: Princeton University Press, 2016.

Muir, John. *My First Summer in the Sierra*. New York: Penguin Books, 1987, orig. publ. 1911.

Mulvey, Kathy and Seth Shulman. *The Climate Deception Dossiers: Internal Fossil Fuel Industry Memos Reveal Decades of Corporate Disinformation*. Cambridge: Union of Concerned Scientists, 2015.

Mumford, Lewis. *The City in History: Its Origins, Its Transformations, and Its Prospects*. 1st ed. New York: Harcourt Brace & World, 1961.

Nader, Ralph. *Unsafe at Any Speed; the Designed-in Dangers of the American Automobile*. New York: Grossman, 1965.

Nash, Linda. *Inescapable Ecologies: A History of Environment, Disease, and Knowledge*. Berkeley: University of California Press, 2007.

Nearing, Helen, and Scott Nearing. *Living the Good Life*. Harborside: Social Science Institute, 1954.

Newman, Richard S. *Love Canal: A Toxic History from Colonial Times to the Present*. New York: Oxford University Press, 2016.

Nixon, Rob. *Slow Violence and the Environmentalism of the Poor*. Cambridge: Harvard University Press, 2011.

Nordhaus, Ted, and Michael Shellenberger. *Break Through: From the Death of Environmentalism to the Politics of Possibility*. Boston: Houghton Mifflin, 2007.

Oberthür, Sebastian and Hermann Ott. *The Kyoto Protocol: International Climate Policy for the 21st Century*. New York: Springer, 1999.

Odum, Eugene Pleasants, in collaboration with Howard T. Odum. *Fundamentals of Ecology*. Philadelphia: Saunders, 1953.

Opie, John. *Nature's Nation: An Environmental History of the United States*. Fort Worth: Harcourt Brace College Publishers, 1998.

Oreskes, Naomi, and Erik M. Conway. *Merchants of Doubt: How a Handful of Scientists Obscured the Truth on Issues from Tobacco Smoke to Global Warming*. New York: Bloomsbury Press, 2010.

Osborn, Fairfield. *Our Plundered Planet*. Boston: Little, Brown, 1948.

_____. *The Limits of the Earth*. Boston: Little, Brown, 1953.

Painter, Nell Irvin. *Exodusters: Black Migration to Kansas after Reconstruction*. Lawrence: University Press of Kansas, 1986.

_____. *The History of White People*. New York: W.W. Norton, 2010.

Park, Lisa Sun-Hee, and David N. Pellow. *The Slums of Aspen: Immigrants Vs. The Environment in America's Eden*. New York: New York University Press, 2011.

Pasternak, Judy. *Yellow Dirt: An American Story of a Poisoned Land and a People Betrayed*. New York: Free Press, 2010.

Payne, Charles M. *I've Got the Light of Freedom: The Organizing Tradition and the Mississippi Freedom Struggle*. Berkeley: University of California Press, 1995.

Percival, Robert V. *Environmental Regulation: Law, Science, and Policy*. 2nd ed. Boston: Little Brown, 1996.

Piketty, Thomas, and Arthur Goldhammer, trans. *Capital in the Twenty-First Century*. Cambridge: The Belknap Press of Harvard University Press, 2014.

Pinchot, Gifford. *The Fight for Conservation*. New York: Doubleday, Page & Co., 1910.

Powell, Miles A. *Vanishing America: Species Extinction, Racial Peril, and the Origins of Conservation*. Cambridge: Harvard University Press, 2016.

Princen, Thomas. *The Logic of Sufficiency*. Cambridge: MIT Press, 2005.

Pulido, Laura. *Environmentalism and Economic Justice: Two Chicano Struggles in the Southwest*. Tucson: University of Arizona Press, 1996.

Pursell, Carroll W. *Technology in Postwar America: A History.* New York: Columbia University Press, 2007.

Raffensperger, Carolyn, and Joel A. Tickner. *Protecting Public Health and the Environment: Implementing the Precautionary Principle.* Washington, D.C.: Island Press, 1999.

Rampton, Sheldon and John Stauber, *Trust Us: We're Experts!* New York: Putnam, 2001.

Ray, Sarah Jaquette. *The Ecological Other: Environmental Exclusion in American Culture.* Tucson: University of Arizona Press, 2013.

Revkin, Andrew. *The Burning Season: The Murder of Chico Mendes and the Fight for the Amazon Rain Forest.* Boston: Houghton Mifflin, 1990.

Reynolds, Kristin and Nevin Cohen, *Beyond the Kale: Urban Agriculture and Social Justice Activism in New York City.* Athens: University of Georgia Press, 2016.

Rome, Adam Ward. *The Bulldozer in the Countryside: Suburban Sprawl and the Rise of American Environmentalism.* Cambridge; New York: Cambridge University Press, 2001.

———. *The Genius of Earth Day: How a 1970 Teach-in Unexpectedly Made the First Green Generation.* 1st ed. New York: Hill and Wang, 2013.

Rosenbaum, Walter A. *Environmental Politics and Policy.* 10th ed. Washington, D.C.: CQ Press, 2017.

Roszak, Theodore. *The Making of a Counter Culture; Reflections on the Technocratic Society and Its Youthful Opposition.* Garden City: Doubleday, 1969.

Rothman, Hal. *Saving the Planet: The American Response to the Environment in the Twentieth Century.* Chicago: Ivan R. Dee, 2000.

Rowell, Andrew. *Green Backlash: Global Subversion of the Environmental Movement.* London; New York: Routledge, 1996.

Russell, Edmund. *War and Nature: Fighting Humans and Insects with Chemicals from World War I to Silent Spring.* Cambridge; New York: Cambridge University Press, 2001.

Sale, Kirkpatrick. *The Green Revolution: The American Environmental Movement, 1962–1992.* 1st ed. New York: Hill and Wang, 1993.

Scheffer, Victor B. *The Shaping of Environmentalism in America.* Seattle: University of Washington Press, 1991.

Schumacher, E.F. *Small Is Beautiful; Economics as If People Mattered.* Harper Torchbooks. New York: Harper & Row, 1973.

Sellers, Christopher C. *Crabgrass Crucible: Suburban Nature and the Rise of Environmentalism in Twentieth-Century America.* Chapel Hill: University of North Carolina Press, 2012.

Shabecoff, Philip. *A Fierce Green Fire: The American Environmental Movement.* 1st ed. New York: Hill & Wang, 1993.

Sharp, Gene. *The Politics of Nonviolent Action.* Boston: P. Sargent Publisher, 1973.

Shiva, Vandana. *Stolen Harvest: The Hijacking of the Global Food Supply.* Cambridge; South End Press, 2000.

Sinclair, Upton. *The Jungle.* New York: Doubleday, Page & Company, 1906.

Singer, Peter. *Animal Liberation: A New Ethics for Our Treatment of Animals.* New York: New York Review: Distributed by Random House, 1975.

Sinha, Manisha. *The Slave's Cause: A History of Abolition.* 1st ed. New Haven: Yale University Press, 2016.

Smith, Kimberly K. *African American Environmental Thought: Foundations.* Lawrence: University Press of Kansas, 2007.

———. *Wendell Berry and the Agrarian Tradition: A Common Grace.* Kansas: University Press of Kansas, 2003.

Sowards, Adam. *The Environmental Justice: William O. Douglas and American Conservation.* Corvallis: Oregon State University Press, 2009.

Spears, Ellen Griffith. *Baptized in PCBs: Race, Pollution, and Justice in an All-American Town.* Chapel Hill: University of North Carolina Press, 2014.

Speece, Darren Frederick. *Defending Giants: The Redwood Wars and the Transformation of American Environmental Politics.* Seattle: University of Washington Press, 2017.

Speth, James Gustave. *Red Sky at Morning: America and the Crisis of the Global Environment.* New Haven: Yale University Press, 2004.

Stegner, Wallace Earle. *The Sound of Mountain Water.* Garden City: Doubleday, 1969.

———. *This Is Dinosaur; Echo Park Country and Its Magic Rivers.* New York: Knopf, 1955.

Steinbeck, John. *The Grapes of Wrath.* New York: The Viking Press, 1939.

Steinberg, Theodore. *Down to Earth: Nature's Role in American History.* New York: Oxford University Press, 2002.

Stern, Alexandra. *Eugenic Nation: Faults and Frontiers of Better Breeding in Modern America.* 2nd ed. Oakland: University of California Press, 2016.

Stoll, Mark. *Inherit the Holy Mountain: Religion and the Rise of American Environmentalism.* New York: Oxford University Press, 2015.

Stradling, David. *Smokestacks and Progressives: Environmentalists, Engineers and Air Quality in America, 1881–1951.* Baltimore: Johns Hopkins University Press, 1999.

Stradling, David, and Richard Stradling. *Where the River Burned: Carl Stokes and the Struggle to Save Cleveland.* Ithaca: Cornell University Press, 2015.

Sutter, Paul. *Driven Wild: How the Fight against Automobiles Launched the Modern Wilderness Movement.* Seattle: University of Washington Press, 2002.

Szasz, Andrew. *Ecopopulism: Toxic Waste and the Movement for Environmental Justice. Social Movements, Protest, and Contention.* Minneapolis: University of Minnesota Press, 1994.

Taylor, Bron Raymond. *Dark Green Religion: Nature Spirituality and the Planetary Future.* Berkeley: University of California Press, 2010.

———. *Ecological Resistance Movements: The Global Emergence of Radical and Popular Environmentalism.* Albany: State University of New York Press, 1995.

Taylor, Dorceta E. *The Environment and the People in American Cities, 1600–1900s: Disorder, Inequality, and Social Change.* Durham: Duke University Press, 2009.

———. *The Rise of the American Conservation Movement: Power, Privilege, and Environmental Protection.* Durham: Duke University Press, 2016.

Taylor, Peter J. *Unruly Complexity: Ecology, Interpretation, Engagement.* Chicago: University of Chicago Press, 2005.

Thoreau, Henry David. *Walden, or Life in the Woods.* Boston: Ticknor and Fields, 1954.

Thorson, Robert M. *Walden's Shore: Henry David Thoreau and Nineteenth-Century Science.* Cambridge: Harvard University Press, 2014.

Tokar, Brian. *Earth for Sale: Reclaiming Ecology in the Age of Corporate Greenwash.* Boston: South End Press, 1997.

Turner, James Morton, and Andrew C. Isenberg. *The Republican Reversal: Conservatives and the Environment from Nixon to Trump.* Cambridge: Harvard University Press, 2018.

Turner, Tom, and Bill McKibben. *David Brower: The Making of the Environmental Movement.* Oakland: University of California Press, 2015.

Tyrrell, Ian R. *Crisis of the Wasteful Nation: Empire and Conservation in Theodore Roosevelt's America.* Chicago: The University of Chicago Press, 2015.

Udall, Stewart L. *The Quiet Crisis.* 1st ed. New York: Holt, 1963.

Valenčius, Conevery Bolton. *The Health of the Country: How American Settlers Understood Themselves and Their Land.* 1st ed. New York: Basic Books, 2002.

Vogt, William. *Road to Survival.* New York: W. Sloane Associates, 1948.

Walls, Laura Dassow. *Henry David Thoreau: A Life*. Chicago: The University of Chicago Press, 2017.

Warren, Karen J., ed. *Ecofeminism: Women, Nature and Culture*, Bloomington: Indiana University Press, 1993.

Warren, Louis S. *The Hunter's Game: Poachers and Conservationists in Twentieth-Century America*. New Haven: Yale University Press, 1997.

Weisiger, Marsha L. *Dreaming of Sheep in Navajo Country*. Weyerhaeuser Environmental Books. Seattle: University of Washington Press, 2009.

Wellock, Thomas Raymond. *Critical Masses: Opposition to Nuclear Power in California, 1958–1978*. Madison: The University of Wisconsin Press, 1998.

———. *Preserving the Nation: The Conservation and Environmental Movements, 1870–2000*. Wheeling: Harlan Davidson, Inc., 2007.

Wells, Christopher W. *Environmental Justice in Postwar America: A Documentary Reader*. Seattle: University of Washington Press, 2018.

Weyler, Rex. *Greenpeace: How a Group of Journalists, Ecologists, and Visionaries Changed the World*. Vancouver: Raincoast Books, 2004.

White, Richard. *The Republic for Which It Stands: The United States during Reconstruction and the Gilded Age, 1865–1896*. New York: Oxford University Press, 2017.

Wilkinson, Charles F. *Messages from Frank's Landing: A Story of Salmon, Treaties, and the Indian Way*. Seattle: University of Washington Press, 2000.

Williams, Yohuru R. *Rethinking the Black Freedom Movement*. New York: Routledge, Taylor & Francis Group, 2016.

Wilson, Edward O. *Biophilia*. Cambridge: Harvard University Press, 1984.

Wolcott, Victoria W. *Race, Riots, and Roller Coasters: The Struggle over Segregated Recreation in America*. 1st ed. Philadelphia: University of Pennsylvania Press, 2012.

Wood, Barbara. *E.F. Schumacher: His Life and Thought*. New York: Harper & Row, 1984.

Worster, Donald. *Nature's Economy: A History of Ecological Ideas*. 2nd ed. New York: Cambridge University Press, 1994.

Wulf, Andrea. *Founding Gardeners: The Revolutionary Generation, Nature, and the Shaping of the American Nation*. 1st American ed. New York: Alfred A. Knopf, 2011.

———. *The Invention of Nature: Alexander Von Humboldt's New World*. New York: Alfred A. Knopf, 2015.

Wurster, Charles F. *DDT Wars: Rescuing Our National Bird, Preventing Cancer, and Creating the Environmental Defense Fund*. Oxford; New York: Oxford University Press, 2015.

Zaretsky, Natasha. *Radiation Nation: Three Mile Island and the Political Transformation of the 1970s*. New York: Columbia University Press, 2018.

Zelko, Frank S. *Make It a Green Peace!: The Rise of Countercultural Environmentalism*. New York: Oxford University Press, 2013.

Zimring, Carl A. *Clean and White: A History of Environmental Racism in the United States*. New York: New York University Press, 2015.

Articles and Essays

Alston, Dana. "The Summit: Transforming a Movement." *Race, Poverty, and the Environment* 2, nos. 3–4 (Fall 1991/Winter 1992): 1, 28–29.

Assunção, Lucas. "Turning Its Back to the World? The United States and Climate Change Policy." In *Unilateralism and U.S. Foreign Policy: International Perspectives*, edited by David Malone and Yuen Foong Khong, 297–320. Boulder: Lynne Rienner Publishers, 2003.

Beeman, Randal. "Friends of the Land and the Rise of Environmentalism, 1940–1954." *Journal of Agricultural and Environmental Ethics* 8, no. 1 (1995): 1–16.

Bullard, Robert D. and Beverly H. Wright. "Environmentalism and the Politics of Equity: Emergent Trends in the Black Community." *Mid-American Review of Sociology* 12, no. 2 (Winter 1987): 21–37.

Bunch, Lonnie. "Black and Green: The Forgotten Commitment to Sustainability." In *Living in the Anthropocene: Humanity in the Age of Humans*, edited by John W. Kress and Jeffrey Stine, 83–86. Washington, D.C.: Smithsonian Books, 2017.

Caldwell, Lynton. "Globalizing Environmentalism: Threshold of a New Phase in International Relations." *Society and Natural Resources* 4, no. 3 (1991): 259–72.

Clapp, Jennifer. "The Toxic Waste Trade with Less Industrialized Countries: Economic Linkages and Political Alliances." *Third World Quarterly* 15, no. 3 (September 1994): 505–18.

Conis, Elena. "DDT Disbelievers: Health and the New Economic Poisons in Georgia after World War II." *Southern Spaces*, October 28, 2016, https://southernspaces. org/2016/ddt-disbelievers-health-and-new-economic-poisons-georgia-after-world-war-ii (accessed March 25, 2018).

Connelly, Matthew. "Seeing Beyond the State: The Population Control Movement and the Problem of Sovereignty." *Past and Present* 193 (November 2006): 197–233.

Cronon, William. "Revisiting the Vanishing Frontier: The Legacy of Frederick Jackson Turner." *Western Historical Quarterly*, 18, no. 2 (April 1987): 157–76.

Curtis, Kent. "The Virtue of Thoreau: Biography, Geography, and History in Walden Woods." *Environmental History* 15 (January 2010): 31–53, 33.

DeLoria, Vine. "Review of *The Ecological Indian*, by Shepard Krech." *Worldviews* 4 (2000): 283–93.

Di Chiro, Giovanna. "Nature as Community: The Convergence of Environmental and Social Justice." In *Uncommon Ground: Rethinking the Human Place in Nature*, edited by William Cronon, 298–320. New York: W.W. Norton & Co., 1996.

Dillon, Lindsey, Christopher Sellers, Vivian Underhill, Nicholas Shapiro, Jennifer Liss Ohayon, Marianne Sullivan, Phil Brown, Jill Harrison, Sara Wylie, and the EPA Under Siege Writing Group. "The Environmental Protection Agency in the Early Trump Administration: Prelude to Regulatory Capture." *American Journal of Public Health* 108 no. S2 (May 2018): S89–S94.

Dunlap, Riley E. "Trends in Public Opinion toward Environmental Issues: 1965–1990." *Society and Natural Resources* 4 (1991): 285–313.

Dunlap, Riley E. and Peter J. Jacques, "Climate Change Denial Books and Conservative Think Tanks: Exploring the Connection." *American Behavioral Scientist* 57, no. 6 (2013) 699–731.

Goldstein, Brian D. "'The Search for New Forms': Black Power and the Making of the Postmodern City." *The Journal of American History* 103, no. 2 (September 2016): 375–99.

Gottlieb, Robert. "Beyond NEPA and Earth Day: Reconstructing the Past and Envisioning a Future for Environmentalism." *Environmental History Review* 19, no. 4 (1995): 1–13.

Hare, Nathan. "Black Ecology." *The Black Scholar* 1, no. 6 (April 1970): 2–8.

Hay, Amy M. "Dispelling the 'Bitter Fog': Fighting Chemical Defoliation in the American West." *Endeavour* 36, no. 4 (2012): 174–85.

⸻. "Recipe for Disaster: Motherhood and Citizenship at Love Canal." *Journal of Women's History* 21, no. 1 (Spring 2009): 111–34.

Hayden, Dolores. "What Would a Non-Sexist City Be Like? Speculations on Housing, Urban Design, and Human Work." *Signs* 5, no. 3 (1980): S170–87.

Isaac, Larry. "Movement of Movements: Culture Moves in the Long Civil Rights Struggle." *Social Forces* 87, no. 1 (September 2008): 33–63.

Jacoby, Karl. "Class and Environmental History: Lessons from 'The War in the Adirondacks.'" *Environmental History* 2 (July 1997): 324–42.

Jundt, Thomas. "Dueling Visions for the Postwar World: The UN and UNESCO 1949 Conferences on Resources and Nature, and the Origins of Environmentalism." *The Journal of American History* 101, no. 1 (2014): 44–70.

Kearns, Laurel. "Saving the Creation: Christian Environmentalism in the United States." *Sociology of Religion* 57, no. 1 (Spring 1996): 55–70.

Kinchy, Abby J. "African Americans in the Atomic Age: Postwar Perspectives on Race and the Bomb, 1945–1967." *Technology and Culture* 50, no. 2 (April 2009): 291–315.

Klingle, Matthew. "Spaces of Consumption in Environmental History." *History and Theory, Theme Issue* 42 (December 2003), 94–110.

Kuzmiak, D.T. "The American Environmental Movement." *The Geographical Journal* 157, no. 3 (1991): 265–78.

Manthorne, Jason. "The View from the Cotton: Reconsidering the Southern Tenant Farmer's Union." *Agricultural History* (Winter 2010): 20–45.

Melosi, Martin. "Environmental Justice, Political Agenda Setting, and the Myths of History." *Journal of Policy History* 12, no. 1 (2000): 43–71.

Merchant, Carolyn. "Gender and Environmental History." *The Journal of American History* 76, no. 4 (1990): 1117–21.

———. "Shades of Darkness." *Environmental History* 8, no. 3 (2003): 380–94.

———. "The Theoretical Structure of Ecological Revolutions." *Environmental Review* 11, no. 4 (1987): 265–73.

Mitchell, Robert Cameron, Angela G. Mertig, and Riley E. Dunlap. "Twenty Years of Environmental Mobilization: Trends among National Environmental Organizations." *Society & Natural Resources* 4, no. 3 (1991): 219–34.

Mitman, Gregg. "In Search of Health: Landscape and Disease in American Environmental History." *Environmental History* 10, no. 2 (2005): 184–210.

Nader, Ralph. "The Profits in Pollution." *The Progressive* (April 1970): 19–22.

Nash, Linda. "Furthering the Environmental Turn." *Journal of American History* 100, no. 1 (June 2013): 131–35.

Purdy, Jedediah. "Environmentalism Was Once a Social-Justice Movement." *The Atlantic,* December 7, 2016.

Rector, Josiah. "The Spirit of Black Lake: Full Employment, Civil Rights, and the Forgotten Early History of Environmental Justice." *Modern American History* 1 (2018): 45–66.

Rich, Nathaniel, "Losing Earth: The Decade We Almost Stopped Climate Change." *The New York Times* magazine, August 1, 2018, 1–66.

Rickford, Russell. "'We Can't Grow Food on All This Concrete': The Land Question, Agrarianism, and Black Nationalist Thought in the Late 1960s and 1970s." *The Journal of American History* 103, no. 4 (March 2017): 956–80.

Robertson, Thomas. "'This Is the American Earth': American Empire, the Cold War, and American Environmentalism." *Diplomatic History* 32, no. 4 (September 2008): 561–84.

———. "Total War and the Total Environment: Fairfield Osborn, William Vogt, and the Birth of Global Ecology." *Environmental History* 17, no. 2 (April 2012): 336–64.

Rochette, Annie. "Stop the Rape of the World: An Ecofeminist Critique of Sustainable Development." *University of New Brunswick Law Journal* 51 (2002): 145–74.

Rome, Adam. "'Give Earth a Chance': The Environmental Movement and the Sixties." *The Journal of American History* 90 (September 2003): 527.

_____. "'Political Hermaphrodites': Gender and Environmental Reform in Progressive America." *Environmental History* 11, no. 3 (July 2006): 440–63.

_____. "What Really Matters in History? Environmental Perspectives on Modern America." *Environmental History* 7, no. 2 (April 2002): 303–18.

Rosen, Chris Meisner. "Business Leadership in the Movement to Regulate Industrial Air Pollution in Late Nineteenth- and Early-Twentieth Century America." In *Green Capitalism? Business and the Environment in the Twentieth Century*, edited by Hartmut Berghoff and Adam Rome, 53–76. Philadelphia: University of Pennsylvania Press, 2017.

Russell, Edmund. "Evolutionary History: Prospectus for a New Field." *Environmental History* 8, no. 2 (April 2003): 204–28.

_____. "Lost among the Parts Per Billion: Ecological Protection at the United States Environmental Protection Agency, 1970–1993." *Environmental History* 2, no. 1 (January 1997): 29–51.

Schmidt, Leigh Eric. "From Arbor Day to the Environmental Sabbath: Nature, Liturgy, and American Protestantism." *Harvard Theological Review* 84, no. 3 (July 1991): 299–323.

Schneiberg, Mark, Marissa King, and Thomas Smith. "Social Movements and Organizational Form: Cooperative Alternatives to Corporations in the American Insurance, Dairy, and Grain Industries." *American Sociological Review* 73, no. 4 (August 2008): 635–67.

Sellers, Christopher. "How Republicans Came to Embrace Anti-Environmentalism." *Vox*, June 7, 2017, www.vox.com/2017/4/22/15377964/republicans-environmentalism (accessed June 18, 2018).

Simon, Bryant. "New Men in Body and Soul: The Civilian Conservation Corps and the Transformation of Male Bodies and the Body Politic." In *Seeing Nature through Gender*, edited by Virginia Scharff, 80–102. Lawrence: University Press of Kansas, 2003.

Smithers, Gregory D. "Beyond the 'Ecological Indian': Environmental Politics and Traditional Ecological Knowledge in Modern America." *Environmental History* 20, no. 1 (2015): 83–111.

St. Clair, Jeffrey. "Seattle Diary: It's a Gas, Gas, Gas," *New Left Review* 238 (1999): 81–96.

Steffen, Will, Paul Crutzen, and John McNeill, "The Anthropocene: Are Humans Now Overwhelming the Great Forces of Nature?" *Ambio* 36, no. 8 (2007): 614–21.

Steinberg, Ted. "Can Capitalism Save the Planet? On the Origins of Green Liberalism." *Radical History Review* 107 (Spring 2010): 7–24.

Stewart, Mart A. "If John Muir Had Been an Agrarian: American Environmental History West and South." *Environment and History* 11 (2005): 139–62.

_____. "Slavery and the Origins of African American Environmentalism." In *To Love the Wind and the Rain: African Americans and Environmental History*, edited by Dianne D. Glave and Mark Stoll, 9–20. Pittsburgh: University of Pittsburgh Press, 2006.

Stone, Christopher D. "Should the Trees Have Standing? Toward Legal Rights for Natural Objects." *So. California Law Review* 45 (1972): 450–501.

Sutter, Paul. "The World with Us: The State of American Environmental History." *Journal of American History* 100, no. 1 (June 2013): 94–119.

_____. "When Environmental Traditions Collide: Ramachandra Guha's the Unquiet Woods and U. S. Environmental History." *Environmental History* 14, no. 3 (2009): 543–50.

Taylor, Bron. "Earth and Nature-Based Spirituality (Part I): From Deep Ecology to Radical Environmentalism." *Religion* 31 (2001): 175–93.

Taylor, Dorceta E. "Gender and Racial Diversity in Environmental Organizations: Uneven Accomplishments and Cause for Concern." *Environmental Justice* 8, no. 5 (2015): 165–80.

_____. "The Rise of the Environmental Justice Paradigm: Injustice Framing and the Social Construction of Environmental Discourses." *American Behavioral Scientist* 43, no. 4 (2000): 508–86.

_____. "Women of Color, Environmental Justice, and Ecofeminism." In *Ecofeminism: Women, Nature and Culture*, edited by Karen J. Warren, 38–81. Bloomington: Indiana University Press, 1993.

Turner, Frederick Jackson. "The Significance of the Frontier in American History." *The Frontier in American History*. New York: Henry Holt and Company, 1935, first published 1920.

Turner, James Morton. "'The Specter of Environmentalism': Wilderness, Environmental Politics, and the Evolution of the New Right." *Journal of American History* 96 (June 2009): 123–48.

Uekoetter, Frank. "The End of the Cold War: A Turning Point in Environmental History?" In *Environmental Histories of the Cold War*, edited by John Robert McNeill, Corinna R. Unger, and German Historical Institute, 343–51. Washington, D.C.; New York: German Historical Institute; Cambridge University Press, 2010.

Washington, Sylvia Hood. "Ball of Confusion: Public Health, African Americans, and Earth Day 1970." In *Natural Protest: Essays on the History of American Environmentalism*, edited by Michael Egan and Jeff Crane, 205–21. New York; London: Routledge, 2009.

_____. "Mrs. Block Beautiful: African American Women and the Birth of the Urban Conservation Movement: Chicago, Il., 1917–1954." In *Land and Power: Sustainable Agriculture and African Americans*, edited by Jeffrey L. Jordan, Edward Pennick, Walter A. Hill, and Robert Zabawa, 133–52. Waldorf: Sustainable Agriculture Research and Education Program, 2009.

White, Lynn. "Historical Roots of Our Ecologic Crisis." *Science* 155, no. 3767 (1967): 1203–07.

White, Richard, "American Environmental History: The Development of a New Historical Field." *Pacific Historical Review* 54, no. 3 (August 1985): 297–335.

Young, Terence. "'A Contradiction in Democratic Government': W.J. Trent, Jr., and the Struggle to Desegregate National Park Campgrounds." *Environmental History* 14, no. 4 (October 2009): 651–82.

INDEX

whistleblowers 116, 217
White Plume, Debra 212
white supremacy 9; white nationalism 224; white racial resentment, politics of 208
White, E.B. 65
White, Lynn 96–97
White, Walter 72
Wilderness Act of 1964 89, 90–91, 107, 130, 132, 151
wilderness movement 67–70; support of artists 69; women's activism 69
wilderness preservation: in 1940s and 1950s 55; conservative opposition to 11; displacement of native peoples 9; exclusion of racial minorities 9; Hetch Hetchy 33–34; versus land justice 179–181
Wilderness Society 46, 136–137, 174; ANWR 181; and diversity 174; ITCPN 60–61; membership 84, 89, 135; and population growth 61; Reagan era 134; and wilderness movement 67, 90; *see also* Foreman, Dave; Marshall, Robert; Zahniser, Howard
Williams, Craig 187
Wilson, Edward O. (*Biophilia*) 153
Wise Use movement 11, 184, 208
women's activism 4, 7, 150–151; anti-nuclear movement 149, 151;

anti-toxics campaigns 79–84, 92, 119–121, 141; conservation 31, 33–34, 47, 69; cooperative farming 142; environmentalism 147; environmental justice 112, 189, 215–17; food justice 220; native sovereignty 22, 212, 214; occupational health 40; rural advocacy 98–99; urban reform 25–26, 31, 38–39, 78; *see also* ecofeminism; unacknowledged environmentalism
World Bank 55, 166, 173; environmental impact of projects 167
World Resources Institute 157, 166
World Trade Organization (WTO) 190–192; anti-environmentalism of 190; created 190; Seattle protests *191*, 191–192, 205
World Wildlife Fund 108, 136, 145, 146, 156, 172
WOTUS ("waters of the United States") 226

Yale School of Forestry (formerly Yale Forest School) 63
Yannacone, Victor 91, 100
Yard, Robert Sterling 46, 67
Young, Whitney, Jr. 103, 104

Zahniser, Howard 62, 67, 90, 91
Zero Population Growth (ZPG) 117, 166
Zinke, Ryan 223

Made in the USA
Las Vegas, NV
25 August 2021